Patriotism: The Making and Unmaking of British National Identity

VOLUME III

National Fictions

This is the third of three volumes which explore changing notions of patriotism in British life. Covering aspects from the thirteenth century to the present day, *Patriotism: The Making and Unmaking of British National Identity* is an attempt to come to terms with the power of the national idea through an historically informed critique.

Ideas and images of national character are notoriously chameleon, reflecting the phantasies and phobias of the moment. Yet as imaginative constructs they have persuasive – and enduring – force, being adaptable to almost any social, cultural or political climate.

This volume studies some of the leading figures of national myth, such as Britannia (dating back to the second century AD) and John Bull (a creation of the early eighteenth century). One group of essays looks at the idea of a distinctively national landscape and the ways in which it corresponds to notions of social order. A chapter on the poetry of Edmund Spenser explores metaphorical representations of Britain as a walled garden, and the idea of an enchanted national space is taken up in a series of essays on literature, theatre and cinema. An introductory piece charts some of the startling changes in the image of national character, from the seventeenth-century notion of the English as the most melancholy people of Europe, to the rather more uncertain and conflicting images of today.

See also Volume I: History and Politics, and Volume II: Minorities and Outsiders.

History Workshop Series

General Editor
Raphael Samuel, *Ruskin College, Oxford*

Edited by
Raphael Samuel

Patriotism: The Making and Unmaking of British National Identity

VOLUME III
National Fictions

ROUTLEDGE
London and New York

First published in 1989 by Routledge
11 New Fetter Lane, London EC4P 4EE
29 West 35th Street, New York NY 10001

© 1989 History Workshop Journal

Phototypeset by Input Typesetting Ltd, London
Printed in Great Britain by
The Guernsey Press, Guernsey, Channel Islands

British Library Cataloguing in Publication Data

Samuel, Raphael
    Patriotism: the making and unmaking of
    British national identity.—(History
    workshop series).
    1. Great Britain, Patriotism, to 1987
    I. Title   II. Series
    323.6'5

Library of Congress Cataloging in Publication Data
Also available.

ISBN 0–415–02774–8
ISBN 0–415–02611–3 (pbk)

Contents

Landscape

Literature

Theatre

Cinema

Illustrations

Notes on Contributors

Imruh Bakari is a freelance writer and music critic.

Beatrix Campbell is the author of *Wigan Pier Revisited* and *The Iron Ladies*.

Madge Dresser is Lecturer in Humanities at Bristol Polytechnic.

Jill Franklin (1928–88) was Lecturer in Architectural History and Art History at the University of London, and author of *The Gentleman's Country House and its Plan*.

Geoffrey Hemstedt is Lecturer in English literature at the University of Sussex.

Joany Hichberger is Lecturer in Art History at Manchester Polytechnic.

Alun Howkins is Lecturer in History at the University of Sussex and an editor of *History Workshop Journal*. His *Poor Labouring Men*, a study of the Norfolk farm labourer, is an earlier volume in the 'History Workshop' series.

Louis James is Lecturer in English Literature at the University of Kent, and author of *Fiction for the Working Man* and *Print for the People*.

Nicola Johnson is a curator at the Museum of London.

Preben Kaarsholm is Lecturer in History at Roskilde University, Denmark.

Alison Light is Lecturer in Humanities at Brighton Polytechnic.

Tom Nairn is the author of *The Break Up of Britain* and *The Enchanted Glass, Britain and its Monarchy*.

Benita Parry's publications include *Delusions and Discoveries: Studies on India in the British Imagination* and *Conrad and Imperialism*.

Alex Potts is Lecturer in Art History at Camberwell College of Art, and is an editor of *History Workshop Journal*.

Raphael Samuel is Tutor in History at Ruskin College, Oxford and an editor of *History Workshop Journal*.

Gareth Stedman Jones is Fellow of King's College, Cambridge, author of *Outcast London* and *Languages of Class*, and an editor of *History Workshop Journal*.

Peter Stallybrass is the author (with Allon White) of *The Politics and Poetics of Transgression*.

Jeanine Surel is a researcher attached to the University of Paris.

Ken Worpole is the author of *Dockers and Detectives*, and editor of *The Republic of Letters*.

Introduction: The figures of national myth

RAPHAEL SAMUEL

I National gallery

National character, though it has been a favourite theme of the moralist and the satirist ever since the invention of the printing press – Caxton himself made some contribution to an idealised version of it – has inspired neither critical commentary nor scholarly research. Sociologists, with the maverick exception of Geoffrey Gorer,[1] have left it alone, preferring to concentrate on the niceties of social mobility, or generalities about social class. They are happier at dealing with aggregates than with images, with functional interests rather than fantasy selves. Historians, when dealing with the 'peculiarities of the English' (a recurrent preoccupation), follow suit, making social structure, household formation or, in an older idiom, constitutional progress the leading protagonists in the historical drama. Concerned with nation-building in other spheres, for example, the centralisation of administration or the unification of the national economy, they have shown much less interest in its imaginative components. Childhood fables like the tale of Jack the Giant Killer hardly qualify as subjects for serious research, though the 'Fee Fi Fo Fum' of Jack's terrifying adversary – a catch borrowed, it seems possible, from Shakespeare's *King Lear* – must have been for many a four- and five-year-old the first intimation that they were of English blood. Nor are the toy theatricals discussed elsewhere by Nicola Johnson and used as our chapter motifs in these volumes, likely to be found in the footnotes of learned articles.

Historians do not feel called upon to discuss the caricatures in popular art – not even the crude chap-book woodcuts which served in some sort as the newspaper headlines of the day. Nor do they feel obliged to take into account or even notice the personality types created by the novelist, the playwright, and the poet: the old sea-salt, say, of Smollett's *Roderick Random*, the Village Hampdens of Gray's *Elegy*. The 'age of improvement' can be written about without any central reference to the characters of Dickens, or Hanoverian England without so much as a reference to *Tom Jones*, even when matters of 'country party' ideology are at stake. Only literary scholars seem to have regarded national fictions as a legitimate domain, following the fortunes of the Arthurian legend or the Elizabethan Fool with all the precision which research historians devote to population movements or the Pipe Rolls. Even so, the stage Englishman invented by Oscar Wilde in *The Importance of Being Earnest*, amplified in the West End comedies of Noel Coward and Freddie Lonsdale, and projected on the silver screen by Michael Redgrave and Leslie Howard – boyish, charming, gallant, and ever so slightly mad – awaits a chronicler, as does his lugubrious counterpart the 'Tommy' of Kipling's *Barrack-Room Ballads*.

Historians have also, for the most part, been indifferent to symbolic landscapes, that 'sacred geography'[2] which enters so largely into idealisations of national character, which form the subject of the chapters by Jill Franklin and Alex Potts in this book. Economic historians debate the pros and cons and differential temporalities of enclosure. Agricultural historians engage with the nuts and bolts of 'peasant' farming, and the division between the chalk and the clay. Local historians, following the inspiration of Professor Hoskins, show that there is a history in every hedgerow, an archaeology to every field. They do not feel obliged to address the idea of the garden, whether as a replica of wild nature, or as an enchanted, civilised space; nor yet to monitor those strange mutations in national perception and taste which in the late eighteenth century elevated mountains to the status of the sublime, or which in more recent times have transformed the country cottage from a rural slum into an ideal home. Historians of the agricultural depression of the 1870s and 1880s do not notice one of its more enduring effects, the invention of the 'Home Counties'; nor do their eighteenth-century counterparts, studying drill husbandry and the rotation of crops, feel obliged to consider Herefordshire as the Arcadia of the pastoral myth. With the exception of the Misses Dodds' splendid *Pilgrimage of Grace*, the dialectic of North and South remains to a great extent unstudied, though it has been a fecund source of English characters: a contrast, in one register, between the barbarous and the civilised and, in another, between hardy independence and the effete. At various points in national history it has been a major axis of division: between the religious and the secular at the time of the *Pilgrimage of Grace*; between agriculturists and industrialists in the 1840s, the hey-day of the Anti-Corn Law League; today, perhaps, as a symbolic counter for the division between core and periphery, provinces and the metropolis.

The figures of national myth, with the outstanding exception of Robin Hood,[3] who seems to fascinate Tory and Marxist alike, are assigned to the realm of the folklorist, the subject of 'antiquarian' rather than serious historical research. There are as yet no British studies to match *Marianne au Combat*, Maurice Agulhon's account of France's first lady, the emblem of the Republic,[4] nor the collaborative work which it helped to inspire, *Les Lieux de la Mémoire*, a comprehensive survey of patriotic occasions and emblems, of which four volumes have appeared at time of writing.[5] State symbols such as Britannia and John Bull are taken for granted. St George, the naturalised Greek who had served for some eight centuries as England's patron saint, remains a shadowy figure in the mummers' play, though he is periodically requisitioned by neo-Fascists and the British ultra-Right. Gog, the stone age giant who flanks the Guildhall, still regarded as the 'guardian genius' of London in Dickens's time,[6] seems to have been dropped down the national memory hole, though Jennifer Westwood's *Albion, A Guide to Legendary Britain* (1985) shows us that he is alive and well in the knowledge and affections of the antiquarians. The Pindar of Wakefield, a jest-book hero in early modern times, is now no more than the name of a well known King's Cross pub.

Yet such figures, in the past, exercised an enormous hold on the popular imagination. The legendary kings of Albion, the mythic kingdom of the ancient Britons, were regarded, down to Shakespeare's time, as real life historical personages, providing the nation, as in a family romance, with a heroic ancestry. Ogres and giants, as *The Pilgrim's Progress* reminds us, were a vivid presence in the Christian as well as in the folk imagination.[7] The aristocratic warriors of medieval romance were the subject of alehouse ballads and old wives' tales. The black letter broadsides and chap-books ('a kind of printed folklore'[8]) helped to keep them alive when they were passing out of oral tradition; so did the eighteenth-century theatre of the fairs. For the young Samuel Bamford, a handloom-weaver's son growing up in late eighteenth-century Lancashire, the figures of national myth were the very stuff out of which an idea of the past was formed. His *Early Days* tells us how he came upon them:

And now a wider range was opened to my assiduous quest

after the wonderful. At the corner of Hanging Bridge, near
the Old Church Yard, was a bookshop kept by one Swindells,
a printer. In the spacious windows of this shop . . . were
exhibited numerous songs, ballads, tales, and other
publications, with horrid and awful-looking woodcuts at the
head; which publications, with their cuts, had a strong
command on my attention. Every farthing I could scrape
together, was now spent in purchasing 'Histories of Jack the
Giant Killer', 'Saint George and the Dragon', 'Tom
Hickathrift', 'Jack and the Bean Stalk', 'History of the Seven
Champions', tale of 'Fair Rosamond', 'History of Friar
Bacon', 'Account of the Lancashire Witches' . . . and such like
romances. . . . Of all these tales and ballads I was soon
master, and they formed the subjects of many a long study to
me, and of many a wonder-creating story of my acquaintance
both at the workhouse and elsewhere. For my part I implicitly
believed them all, and when told by my father or others that
they were 'trash' and 'nonsense', and 'could not be true', I . . .
contrasted their probability with that of other wonderous
things which I had read in books that 'it were a sin to
disbelieve'. So I continued reading, and doubting nothing
which I read, until many years after, when a more extended
knowledge with men and books, taught me how better to
discriminate betwixt reason and unreason – truth and
falsehood.[9]

As well as the figures of myth, there are those characters drawn
from life who might, if they were studied, light up hidden passages
in national history. Admiral Vernon, for instance, was the most
popular of naval commanders (if one were to judge by the
frequency with which his name appears on inn signs), a man who
enjoyed a 'hallowed' reputation on the lower deck because he
invented the sailor's ration of 'grog' (i.e. rum and water). The
Marquis of Granby is another, the British commander during the
Seven Years War who, when his wig fell off, led his men into
battle bald-headed. His title to posthumous fame gives us another
unexpected glimpse into what the historian E. P. Thompson has
called 'the moral economy' of eighteenth-century England. 'He
had a warm feeling towards the men under his command and
many of his officers who were disabled were helped by the marquis
to establish themselves as innkeepers. Hence the frequency of
"Marquis of Granby" inns.'[10]
Particularly rewarding for the study of popular consciousness
would be those fallen idols and forgotten heroes who enjoyed a

brief period of celebrity but have now been expelled from the Valhalla of national fame. Enquiry could be made here of those 'theatrical and amatory' figures, no doubt the stars of the day, who (a Royal Statistical Society investigation of 1840 discovered) took up the lion's share of the prints which adorned the homes of the Westminster poor, outnumbering by far (the investigators sadly noted) those representing 'serious' subjects.[11] One might also include the barefist prizefighters celebrated in Staffordshire ornamental ware,[12] or forgotten soldiers like Sergeant MacCaffery, a hero of the ranks, as his ballad testifies, on account of shooting his captain.[13] Among local heroes mention might be made of Mother Shipton, 'Knaresborough's most famous lady', whose words were counted as oracles and whose rhyming prophecies, with later interpellations, were constantly reprinted in chap-books (her predictions were said to include Drake's success with the Armada, Guy Fawkes and the Gunpowder Plot, the Civil War, and the Great Fire of London).[14]

Then there is a whole gallery of Everyman figures (and more occasionally women) who take their cues from the humours of everyday life. Many of them, like the 'country bumpkin', are in the first place comic inventions, seizing on idiosyncracy and caricaturing it to excess. Some have their origins in figures of speech, for example, the 'rough diamond' which Partridge, in his *Slang Dictionary*, dates to 'ca 1750'; some trace their origins to satire, for example, 'namby-pamby', originally a nickname for the poet Ambrose Philips (1674–1749), mocked by writers such as Pope and Carey because of his sentimentality;[15] some to graphic jokes (e.g. 'nosey parker'). 'Lah-di-dah', a derisory term for the posh, comes from the Victorian music hall;[16] and 'Mrs Grundy' from a now forgotten play called *Speed the Plough*.[17] One possible starting point for historical enquiry would be the spoken word as recorded in the slang dictionaries or county glossaries (there is one for the speech of the Derbyshire miners dating from as early as the 1650s). Here one can date the first recorded appearance of such enduring characters as 'Hodge', the farm labourer; follow the fortunes of terms which have migrated from low life to high society: 'the prig', 'the snob'; or monitor, with the aid of 'cant' glossaries, the progress of the 'fly' Londoner. Obsolete terms such as those recorded in J. Reding Ware's *Passing English of the Victorian Era* (1909) could remind us of forgotten, or half-forgotten, characters who once made a great noise in the world. Regressive analysis might be even more rewarding, starting from figures currently in vogue (e.g. the 'yob' as reverse slang for 'boy'), and tracing them back to establish etymological family trees. Geoffrey Pearson's

Hooligan: A History of Respectable Fears shows how such a method could shed old light on what are apparently novel phenomena.

Another set of characters who would surely clamour for inclusion in any national gallery are those carnivalesque figures who exemplify the pleasure of the transgressive. Falstaff, Shakespeare's hugely popular Lord of Misrule, the grimacing counterpoint to honour, justice, and conjugal fidelity, would be an obvious candidate; Sir Toby Belch, defending 'cakes and ale' against their would-be persecutors, another; the fat Wife of Bath, Chaucer's female Lothario, a third. The grotesquely obese John Bull might find himself at home in this company, as a man whose truculence and aggression would be insupportable if it were exercised on anybody else but foreigners; so too would his bibulous second cousin, Uncle Toby, the figure commemorated in a thousand pots and jugs. He appeared on the national stage at about the same time as John Bull and was familiar enough by 1761 to be the subject of a very popular mezzotint and a verse which is possibly the original of 'Little Brown Jug' as belted out in choruses today.[18] Melancholia, once thought of as 'the English malady',[19] has provided a whole line of celebrated dyspeptics, among them Dr Johnson, the best loved character in English letters.[20]

It is interesting that the figures who seem to have lodged themselves most securely in popular affection have frequently been comic or satiric inventions, exemplifying amiable weakness rather than ideal strength. Their behaviour, by conventional standards, is outrageous, their apperance often grotesque. Yet they contrive to insinuate themselves into our affections as loveable old fogies or cards. The grimacing, capering fool would be one example, the monstrous Mr Punch a second, Quilp, the wizard-like figure in *The Old Curiosity Shop*, a possible third. John Bull himself has resemblances to the popular grotesques of the mummers' play and the medieval morality plays. Grossly overweight, choleric in temperament, simple-minded, often put upon, he has nevertheless fared better as an idealised emblem of national being than all the captains and the kings who supposedly symbolise England's glories.

The constitution (or reconstitution) of regional types would repay thought and investigation. Interestingly, they seem to emerge as figures of public myth – in the counties if not in the nation at large – at the very moment when, as historians now argue, new forms of communication such as canals, turnpike roads, and provincial newspapers, were drawing the provinces into a national orbit.[21] Their literary expression, in the form of dialect writing, reaches its apogee in mid-Victorian times, when Britain was the workshop of the world. It flourished above all in the new, or vastly extended, industrial districts: East Lancashire, the West Riding, and Tyneside.[22] The cockney is the best known of these regional types, and is the subject of an illuminating study by Gareth Stedman Jones in the volume on London history which will be published later this year in the 'History Workshop' series. The materials from which the idea of the 'Geordie' might be reconstructed are in some ways richer, coming from insiders rather than outsiders, and recorded in a succession of local 'Garlands'. 'Keep your feet still, Geordie Hinny' (the exasperated complaint of a young man whose dream is interrupted by a fellow lodger) suggests that these songs and poems were written close to the grain of common experience – albeit for the most part, if not exclusively, male experience.

The regional characters are typically happy-go-lucky types. Tim Bobbin, the original of them (the creation of an eighteenth-century Rochdale schoolmaster), is introduced as a grinning figure who delights to exercise himself in outlandish words.[23] Ben Brierley's 'Ab-o'-th'-Yate' is a simple-minded Lancashire lad who contrives to get out of scrapes. John Hartley's Sammywell Grimes is a roving Yorkshireman, chancing his luck by venturing up to London.[24] Bob Cranky, the Newcastle pitman, is described by Robert Colls as a great holidaymaker, making the most of beanos and sprees.[25] The cockney, as represented by Phil May in caricature or Gus Elen on stage, was a cheerful anarchist: a little ragamuffin or street urchin, cheeking authority and unintimidated by the toffs; a married man who did not take his wife too seriously; a bit of a rogue who yet contrived to be straight as a die.

A national gallery, if it were to attempt to reflect popular memory, would need to give as much space to the figures of national myth as to real life historical personalities. Visually, it would take its cue from the catchpenny prints and woodcuts rather than the solemn figures which confront the visitor to the National Portrait Gallery in Trafalgar Square. As effigies and on floats, the figures of national myth have always had an honoured place in pageants and processions; indeed some, like Maid Marian and Peeping Tom, seem to have been explicitly created for that purpose. 'That peculiarly British institution',[26] pantomime, helped to keep them in the public eye when they passed out of the realm of the ballad. They form the stuff of legends and stories, proverbs and jokes. They are stock figures in sentimental painting and comic cards; in charms, mascots, and emblems; in trade signs, labels, and advertisements; at the circus and the fair. They are the paradigmatic

originals which the novel draws on for its characters, and romance
for its plots.

Women – save as beauties – figure less frequently in these
galleries of characters than men. They may personify the abstract
virtues, such as Faith, Hope, and Charity, or represent elements
in national greatness, as Britannia does, or the allegorical lady
personifying Agriculture. But in the transactions of everyday life
they are represented either as an absence, or in the negative stereotype of the 'slattern' the 'slut' and the 'shrew'. There is no Mrs
Hodge, the farm labourer's wife. We know more about Pearly
Kings than Pearly Queens, though the latter seem to be the real
impresarios of Pearly activities. Misogyny, on the other hand, is
very well represented, testifying to the deep strain of anti-feminism
which runs through English national life. It serves as the basis of
a lexicon of abuse, directed not only at women but also at those,
like 'cissies', suspected of being like them. It provides, in *Noah's
Wife*, a famous figure in the medieval miracle plays, the archetypal
shrew: 'the disobedient wife, a disturber of domestic peace and
charity', a gadabout, a gossip.[27] It is inscribed in a whole series of
bad or cruel mothers, faithless or intriguing wives. And it has been
a fecund source of popular anti-heroes. Punch, in his early version,
was a hen-pecked husband, and in his later, more triumphalist,
incarnation, an enthusiastic wife-beater.[28] Andy Capp is the male
rampant, Alf Garnett the father who tries to keep his daughter in
her place.

The influence of negative stereotypes in shaping values – and
establishing ideas of 'normality' – is even more apparent than that
of ideal types. One might think of the ways in which the figure
of the usurer, that 'folk devil' of late medieval and early modern
times, set a limit on commercial sharp practice and acquisitive lust;
of the part played by the figure of Scrooge, the miser, in the
creation of the Victorian Christmas, and the rehabilitation – in
spite of the New Poor Law and political economy – of the idea of
charity and good works. In the field of behaviour one might refer
to the opprobrium visited on the 'upstart', the prejudice directed
at the 'queer', the fierce hostility to the 'nosey parker' (a term
which has been fancifully associated with the ecclesiastical visi-
tations of an Elizabethan archbishop of Canterbury). Children's
lore preserves some of the older terms in aspic while constantly
generating new ones, and the collections made of them by the
Opies give us a glimpse into a seething mass of discriminations.
English Philistinism hardly needs the editorial advocacy of the
Daily Express or *The Sun* when it already has to hand, in the
lexicon of playground abuse, the 'big-head', the 'clever Dick' and

the 'know all'. (The bias of many of these terms is, from a socialist point of view, regrettably conservative, but radicals could take heart from the unpopularity attaching to the 'goody-goody' or the 'tell-tale-tit'.)

II Ideology

National fictions might be considered not as reflections of ideology, whether at second or third remove, but as components in it, an imaginative underpinning, or disguise, for precepts which are the common currency of political debate. It is a matter of some moment, for instance, for the strength of the dissenting tradition in this country, that Gray's *Elegy in a Country Churchyard* celebrates Village Hampdens; that the most pervasive legend in the country, that of Robin Hood, rehearses the joys of a counter-society; and that this country's primordial folk hero, Jack the Giant Killer, was one who took up arms against the over-powerful. The Conservative strain in national life has no doubt received comparable sustenance from the paternalist associations of such benevolent authority figures as Justice Swallow and Lady Bountiful; from the idea of Prince Charming, the patrician young male, as an object of glamour and desire; from the character of the English Rose (hardly someone one could imagine out on the knocker for Labour on a cold wintry night); and more directly from the long-standing Tory association with the altar, the throne and the squire.

One figure who invites attention from anyone concerned with the pre-history of Thatcherism and the more subliminal supports it may enjoy is Dick Whittington, the first historically authenticated yuppie. Along with Jack of Newbury, he is one of the earliest folk heroes of English capitalism. Alan Macfarlane, in *The Origins of English Individualism* (1978), though ransacking the fifteenth-century records for precocious instances of 'enterprise culture', has nothing to say about him; Sylvia Thrupp, whose *The Merchant Class of Medieval London* (1948) remains unsurpassed as an exercise in historical sociology, dismisses him in a footnote. Yet already in *The Libelle of Englische Policye* (1436), a poem on the use of sea-power extolling the merits of economic nationalism, he was being celebrated as the 'chief chosen floure' of Merchandy, a 'Loade sterre' by which England's honour might be redeemed.[29] In the sixteenth century, joined by his legendary cat, he is sentimentalised into the virtuous apprentice, a 'poor country lad', 'born of low degree', but destined for fame and fortune.[30] As an apprentice hero, the guise in which he appears in the chap-books, the 'artisan' plays of Jacobean London, and the theatre of the eighteenth-century fairs, he was possibly one of the originals of Hogarth's illustrations of *Industry* and *Idleness*. Pantomime, where, according to David Mayer, he first appears in the 1780s, established him as a kind of male Cinderella.[31] The nineteenth-century character-building manuals harnessed him to the engine of self-help, while in Samuel Lysons's *The Model Merchant* (1860)[32] he becomes the apotheosis of civic virtues.

> A man in every way in advance of the age in which he lived, and affording a most valuable example to all succeeding generations, whether we consider his perseverance in amassing a fortune, and the right use of it when made; whether we consider his charities, his patriotism, or his loyalty; when we think of the way in which he availed himself of every new discovery for the improvement of his country and his countrymen; whether we consider his unflinching honesty and integrity; whether we look at him as a supporter of the dignity of the crown, or the champion of the rights of the poor.

A more contemporary figure who invites attention, as a talisman of changing attitudes to authority is the Bobby. He occupies today a pinnacle of public esteem, and indeed in the Conservative imagination has replaced the magistrate as the custodian of law and order, and the army and navy as the front line of national defence. Yet in his early days he was the subject of an almost universal obloquy, both as a harbinger of 'French despotism', and as a burden on the rates. 'Justifiable homicide' was the verdict of a coroner's jury in 1833, after a policeman had been stabbed to death in the course of a radical demonstration at Cold Bath Fields. (His alleged murderer was acquitted by a jury at the Old Bailey, and the jury fêted by a river party on the Thames.[33]) Police stations in the provinces were quite often subject to siege.[34] In rural districts the police faced popular conspiracy over the implementation of the poaching laws;[35] and something of the same was true in the towns with the advent, towards the end of the century, of street betting.[36] The music halls took a very cynical view of the police: 'courting cookies on the sly' was the least of their derelictions. According to one favourite conceit, they made a small killing by snaffling watches from drunks:

> And often, too, in their first week
>   They find a chap 'in liquor',
> And it only wants a little cheek
>   To be a master of a 'ticker'.

The middle-class public was by no means always more respect-ful: Offenbach's 'The Gendarme's Duet', with its catchy refrain, 'We run 'em in', was given seventeen encores when it was performed at the Philharmonic Hall, Islington, in 1870. In the early comic postcards (certainly those of Tom Browne, a favourite with Edwardian holidaymakers) the seaside constable is a lecher on the sly, the Peeping Tom of the bathing-machines.

A sea change in attitudes might be hypothesised in 1919, a year of bourgeois panic when there were revolutionary or proto-revolutionary movements in Europe, and a rising tide of industrial unrest at home. The police strike of that year – ruthlessly smashed by the government – was followed by a transformation in conditions of service, tripling rates of pay and elevating the policeman from a despised menial to the ranks of the prosperous and secure.[37] In the general strike of 1926 the policeman emerged as a pillar of social order. At a time of worsening social relations, he served the middle-class public, in some sort, as a surrogate for the 'honest' labourer: dependable, deferential, good-humoured, and keeping essential services going. It is in this guise that he enters children's literature, in the persona of Ernest (the original of Enid Blyton's Mr Plod) the Toytown policeman invented by Sydney Beaman in 1926 and given a national following in 1929 when *Toytown* became a much loved feature of the BBC 'Children's Hour'.[38]

It was in the 1930s, when the domestic peace in Britain was in such striking contrast to the storms sweeping continental Europe, that the character of the 'Bobby' became a matter for patriotic self-congratulation, as reassuring a symbol of national stability as the good-humoured bus conductors or the pigeons in Trafalgar Square.[39] Where Nazi stormtroopers swaggered, the British policeman pursued his measured tread, the very epitome of English understatement and reserve. Where foreign gendarmes, such as those who figure in Hitchcock's 1938 film *The Lady Vanishes*, went about their business with revolvers, the Bobby had nothing more menacing than a whistle. Where his continental counterparts beat up political opponents, the English policeman engaged in a host of kindly duties, shepherding children at the Belisha beacons, helping old ladies across the road, coming to the rescue in an accident. It was above all the passivity of the policeman that was reassuring, 'strength without shouting', 'drill without display'; his very slowness – as represented in popular caricature – showed the superiority of English phlegm.[40]

An altogether more emancipated policeman appears in the post-war years, no longer the deferential servant who knew how to

'Sir' his betters, but rather a kind of idealised representative of
public service. In the very popular radio series *PC 49* (which took
its name from the character of an old-time music-hall song), the
'sarge' is on familiar terms with the man on the beat, and the
police station itself a rough-and-ready democracy. In *Dixon of Dock
Green*, the character created by Ted Willis and played by Jack
Warner in a celebrated television series of the 1950s, he is a kind
of epitome of male working-class decency, a father-figure, wise in
the ways of the world, and also a benefactor on the quiet, ready
to bend the rules when someone is in trouble.[41] He is completely
at one with the East End community which he serves. Not only
is the police station itself one big family, but so are the local people,
with the exception of the occasional 'rotten apple' who gets his
due come-uppance. He reproduces in civilian circumstances the
'carry on' spirit of the blitz. As Ted Willis, a young Communist
by formation, a Unity Theatre actor, and later a Labour peer,
wrote of his creation: 'Ordinary folk often find the strength to
fight through all sorts of trouble and come out smiling.'[42]

The notion of England as (in Disraeli's terms) a 'domestic
country'[43] where the home is 'revered' and the hearth 'sacred', may
owe something to the example of Darby and Joan, the faithful old
couple who first appeared in a ballad of 1735 and were given wide
diffusion by catchpenny prints,[44] – and in more recent times by
Darby and Joan clubs. The late Victorian music hall familiarised
and sentimentalised them into the 'old man' and his 'missus'. Albert
Chevalier gave them a brilliant up-date in 'My Old Dutch', one
of the most effective of Victorian tear-jerkers, and a small blow
against the Poor Law, since he pictured his old couple in the very
shadow of the workhouse gates that were about to separate them
for ever:

> I've got a pal,
>   A reg'lar out an' outer,
> She's a dear good old gal,
> I'll tell yer all about 'er.
> It's many years since fust we met,
> 'Er 'air was then as black as jet,
> It's whiter now, but she don't fret,
>   Not my old gal!
>
> We've been together now for forty years,
>   An' it don't seem a day too much;
> There ain't a lady livin' in the land
>   As I'd 'swop' for my dear old Dutch!

The figure of the good housekeeper is so venerable and appears in such constant use as to make any comment redundant, but if one were searching for the influence of allegorical figures in the making of domestic ideology, one might pause on the term 'family man', a recent coinage but widely current today, a testimony to the progress of the idea of a home-centred society – an outcome, it may be, of the Do-It-Yourself movement of the 1950s, and even more, perhaps, of the package holiday and weekend drive which have given fathers new and more glamorous child-caring roles. An influential figure in earlier times, introduced by Chaucer into English literature and still a favourite of the eighteenth-century chap-books and the theatre of the fair, was Patient Grizzel. Ready with unreasoning submission for every tyrannical command of her despotic husband,[45] she was the very emblem of wifely duty as prescribed by the Christian marriage vows: love, honour, and obedience rolled into one.

Allegorical figures are, of course, an inescapable element in patriotism itself, and indeed, since the very idea of nation belongs to the symbolic order – as an 'imagined' community rather than as an experienced one – it is difficult to see how it can be discussed without them. The discovery (or rediscovery, or invention) of national heroes seems to be a feature of patriotic moments in British history. The 1590s, in the wake of the defeat of the Spanish Armada, are a striking case in point. This period saw the resurrection of Boadicea and her elevation to a national heroine; a determined defence by the antiquaries of the idea of Albion, and, in the hands of the poets and playwrights, a last great flowering of Albion's mythical kings and characters.[46] The civic authorities in London and Plymouth put up statues of Gog and Magog, the ancient British giants.[47] Plays and ballads about Robin Hood and St George were followed by the chap-book appearance of Tom Thumb – allegedly the offspring given by the wizard Merlin to a childless ploughman.[48] There was a powerful revival of Arthurian romance in Spenser's *Faerie Queene*.[49] *King Lear* was very much a part of this imaginative turn, not only in taking its title from the name of a legendary British king, but also in its elemental setting. The well-known words of Edgar in Act III, Scene iv, link it directly with the world of giants:

> Childe Rowland to the darke Tower came,
> His word was still, fie foh and fumme
> I smell the blood of a British man.

More Everyman figures come to the fore in wartime propaganda, sometimes as a form of symbolic reassurance, sometimes as a means of projecting ideal strength. Thus Jack Tar, the jolly sailor, seems to have owed his elevation into a talisman of national strength and the 'freeborn Englishman' incarnate to the naval wars of the eighteenth century. A coinage, it seems, of the late seventeenth or early eighteenth century,[50] he appears in the prints as a more sympathetic and human figure than the grenadier, a type of working-class Bohemian, 'with a dark jacket, shirt, kerchief, and trousers, often barefoot, and usually with a brimmed hat'.[51] The tunes celebrating him are more melodic than the ramrod rhythms of that most wretched of legacies of eighteenth-century militarism, 'The British Grenadiers'. The 'Patriot Party' of the 1750s invoked Jack Tar to champion war with France,[52] and it was at this time that David Garrick wrote one of the most popular of sea-songs, 'Hearts of Oak':[53]

> Come cheer up, my lads, 'tis to glory we steer,
> To add something more to this wonderful year,
> To honour we call you, not press you like slaves,
> For who are so free as the sons of the waves?
>
> CHORUS: Hearts of oak are our ships,
>   Jolly tars are our men,
>   We always are ready,
>   Steady, boys, steady,
>   We'll fight and we'll conquer again and again.
>
> We ne'er see our foes but we wish them to stay
> They never see us but they wish us away,
> If they run, why we follow, and run them ashore,
> And if they won't fight, we cannot do more.

In the First World War the tin-helmeted Tommy occupied the imaginative space of Jack Tar as representative of the nation at arms. But he hardly cut a dashing figure, marooned in the death-dealing world of Nomansland, huddling for protection in mud-filled water-logged holes. Whatever the frantic propaganda of the War Office and the patriotic press, it was the anti-heroic, misanthropic figure of Bruce Bainsfeather's walrus-moustached 'Old Bill' who seems to have come closest to the soldier's true condition, as well as the soldiers' songs which authentically voiced it – in both cases with endurance and survival as the principle of hope. In the Second World War it was the 'carry on' spirit of the civilians which was appropriated by government to represent the nation's fighting spirit: the 'clippies' with their backchat, the firemen, and the WRVS with their cups of tea.

Another whole set of fictions with manifest ideological effects would be those which established an idea of national character by reference to enemies within or without. The negative stereotyping of the Irish is an obvious case in point and it is salutary to be reminded, in L. P. Curtis's *Anglo-Saxons and Celts*, how many eminent Victorians contributed to it. To Thomas Arnold, the public school reformer, the Irish were notorious for idleness and dishonesty; for Charles Kingsley, the Christian Socialist, they were 'human chimpanzees'.[54] That flower of the liberal intelligence, Matthew Arnold, though respecting Celtic literature and praising the Irish for their imaginative powers, had 'the insight of genius' (according to one of his contemporary admirers) to have 'happily hit on the chief weakness of the Celt – his disbelief in the authenticity of fact'.[55] Arnold also believed that the 'nervous exaltation' of the Irish – a feminine weakness by contrast to England's masculine strength – unfitted them for self-government (Arnold was one of the many disenchanted Liberals who in 1886 opposed Home Rule).[56] For the Elizabethans, to follow Professor Quinn's discussion of the subject, the Irish were above all barbarous, the 'wild' Irish whom the plantations were designed to drive from their lairs, naked and dirty as savages.[57] For the Victorians they were a backward people whom the spirit of improvement had passed by, 'distinguished', as Macaulay delicately put it, 'by qualities which tend to make men interesting rather than prosperous'.[58] Incompetent where the English were efficient, lazy where they were industrious, impulsive where the English had learnt self-control, they behaved in the manner of weaklings. They were also, by comparison with the manly independence of the English, slaves to priests and agitators.[59]

France, 'a kind of blackboard on which English character draws its traits in chalk',[60] has been, if anything, even more imaginatively important than Ireland in sustaining, by negative example, British national conceit. In the early nineteenth century it was particularly obnoxious to Tories on account of the French Revolution, but liberals too (Hazlitt, for example, Thackeray and – through the medium of *A Tale of Two Cities* – Dickens) shared in what amounted to a national phobia.[61] Politically, down to 'Palmerston's follies'[62] and the invasion scare of 1859, when the southern ports were put on red alert, France was the national enemy. Behaviourally, it was represented as a moral pit, a place of sexual adventure and infidelity (as in Hardy's *The Woodlanders*), the paradise of atheists, a place of refuge for the bankrupt and the disgraced.

Gallophobia was crucial in the crystallisation of national sentiment in the 1740s – the period of the French wars to which we owe the national anthem and 'Rule Britannia', and also the time when John Bull become a national icon. As Gerald Newman and others have argued, the Gallophobia of this time had a strongly populist undertow, championing plebeian against patrician values and aligning the corruption of things French with the cosmopolitanism of the world of rank and fashion.[63] In the allegory of patriotism, as developed by Hogarth among others, the Frenchman was 'vain, over-civilised . . . pretentious, given to excess in fashion, food and manners'[64] – the very reverse of honest English plainness. He was also accused of being effeminate, talkative where the English were strong and silent, devious where they were blunt. As the caption of a contemporary print has it: 'Ribbands and Lace are the Things without which the *French* cannot live, and tho' they are a People of the least Reflection in the World, are prodigious fond of Looking Glasses'.[65]

III Images

One reason which might be hypothesised for the neglect of national characters is that, whether as subjects or as sources, they transcend the conventional categories of the historian. There is no body of records where they can be systematically studied, no set of vital statistics against which they can be measured, no objective reality to which they can confidently be referred. Geographically, they inhabit a symbolic rather than a territorial space, so that even when we are given a precise location – the Wirral peninsular, say, in the case of *Sir Gawain and the Green Knight* – it may turn out to belong to a past that never was.

The folk heroes are creatures of that fantasy world where repressed wishes are represented as being fulfilled. They do not so much reflect reality as suspend it. They defy, or ignore, the rules of precedence. They overcome seemingly insuperable obstacles, either by good luck or native wit. They scale impossible heights. They slay dragons and take on frightening ogres. They cross class boundaries, exchanging the cottage for the castle with apparently consummate ease. They effect miraculous rescues. They perform wonders and marvels.

The Everyman figures, though ostensibly drawn from life, are composites rather than copies. They are not personages or individuals but types, instantly recognisable by dress and deportment, gesture or speech. In visual representation, they wear their faces like masks. Like the allegorical figures of the medieval morality plays, they exemplify virtue and vice, good or evil. Like the characters in a stage play they always act a part. As Hogarth's famous illustrations of *Industry* and *Idleness* – or Cruickshank's of drink and sobriety – they are often constituted in relations of opposition to demonised (or idolised) others. As in a Dan Leno comic sketch, they carry ordinariness to excess. Often such figures personify class extremes, behaving as born leaders or loyal servants according to their appointed station in life. The values of hierarchy and deference have peopled English literature with ideal types: 'honest' labourers, poor widows, comic cleaners, benevolent masters, wise magistrates, 'true' ladies, perfect gentlemen. In a more radical or Gothic vein, melodrama offers a powerful set of counter-images – cruel parents, bad masters, grasping landlords, lecherous rakes. In place of benevolent authority figures, it gives us incorrigible rebels.

In dealing with the figures of national myth, one is confronted not by realities which become fictions, but rather by fictions which, by dint of their popularity, become realities in their own right. Even when they can be traced back to some historical original (as is the case, it seems, with so unlikely a candidate as Old King Cole, the merry old soul of nursery rhyme)[66] they will have had so much added or subtracted as to be palimpsests which successive generations have inscribed. Thus the idea of 'Bluff King Hal' possibly owes less to the amiable character of the king himself, a wife-killer and a man ready to accuse anyone who crossed his path of treason, than to posthumous assimilation to a whole line of hearty eaters and drinkers – which is precisely as Charles Laughton played him in *The Private Life of Henry VIII*. (On Toby jugs, Reginald Haggar tells us, his face has an uncanny resemblance to Shakespeare's Falstaff.[67]) Boadicea, briefly if vividly referred to by the Roman annalists, disappeared from literature for a thousand years.[68] Geoffrey of Monmouth, whose *Gesta* is a giant assembly of ancestral national myths, had apparently never heard of her. She was resuscitated in the 1590s as part of the revival of British antiquities, but it was not until the reign of Queen Victoria that she was elevated to the status of a national icon. It is in her Victorian guise, as represented in Thorneycroft's statue (featured on the cover of *Patriotism*, Volume I) that we know her today, more of an imperial queen than a tribal chieftain. Our understanding of Alfred the Great also owes a great deal to Victorian times, when he was vigorously promoted as an exemplification of the bourgeois virtues: modest, gentle, and kind, yet a firm ruler; a great warrior who was also a man of peace.[69] Dr Johnson, an admirer of Alfred long before his cult set in, seems, like the writers of Victorian schoolbooks, to have projected the king as a personification of his own ideals. Here is how he saluted Alfred in his 1738 poem, *London*.

A single gaol, in Alfred's golden reign,
Could have the nation's criminals contain.
Fair Justice then, without constraint ador'd
Held high the steady scale, but sheath'd the sword;
No spies were paid, no special juries known:
Blest age! but, ah! how different from our own!

Images such as those discussed in these pages do not belong to the world of empirically verifiable facts. They offer us pictures far clearer than any reality could. In the woodcuts they are little more than silhouettes; on the stage or in toy theatricals they are caricatures. In stories their biography is told as fable. They isolate character traits where the historian would want to contextualise them. They seize on the eccentric and elevate it to the grotesque. As poetic fictions, these images invite literary rather than historical analysis, in terms of the aesthetic conventions they exemplify. Those which began life as graphics, for example, John Bull, need to be discussed in terms of visual rhetoric.

The first instinct of the historian, when confronted with images, is to look for the reality content. Our whole training predisposes us to look for a kernel of literal truth, to eschew metaphor and myth, or to translate them into empircally verifiable terms. Warned against the 'literary' and the 'impressionistic' when dealing with written documentation, we are particularly uneasy when faced with the visual. We may use pictures as cover illustrations, or anecdotally, to lend colour to our texts, but we are poorly equipped to consider them as art objects or to identify what are often contradictory and variant meanings. A common sense rationality also makes us wary of anything which has the taint of the superstitious or the childish, a charge to which the figures of national myth are peculiarly vulnerable.

It may be indicative of this unease that the most influential recent work in the field of popular imagery – and one of the original inspirations behind these volumes on patriotism – is a systematic attempt at what is today called 'deconstruction' and what used to be known as 'debunking'. Hobsbawm and Ranger's collection of essays entitled *The Invention of Tradition* exposes, with wit and learning, 'the modernity of much of what passes for archaic, the manipulated and manufactured character of national ceremony'.[70] Traditions apparently handed down from time immemorial can in fact be shown to have been created for determinate reasons, by identifiable individuals, at a particular point in time: 'All that is solid melts into air.' The highland kilt was invented by a canny lowland tailor; the modern monarchy by far-seeing political strategists. Intentionality and rationality, even in the field of mumbo-jumbo, are restored.

One difficulty here is that the historian typically confronts not newly-minted rituals but the residues of ancient beliefs, whose origins, as with the outlaws of medieval legend, are necessarily a matter of speculation. Provenance, then, even when it can be established, does not explain the imaginative appeal of a symbol, nor account for its subsequent mutations over time. Nor can it help the historian confronted with a resurrection of ancient practices, or a recycling of archetypal imagery. Finally, in its preference for 'brief and dateable' periods, the 'invention of tradition' allows little conceptual space for those more molecular and subterranean processes in which imaginative complexes form.

Folklorists, despised and ignored by the professionally-trained historian (though occasionally raided for evidence) are in many ways better equipped to deal with the figures of national myth and they are also plainly – judging by the amount of work they produce on the subject – fascinated by them. Indifferent to periodisation, they will follow legendary figures over millenia. Comparative in their method, they will ignore the limits of national culture, and look to other countries for analogues and variants of their chosen subject. Theoretically, through the work of Vladimir Propp, they also offer an alternative interpretative framework, one which looks for family likenesses between different figures, and 'tale types' to which the individual narratives can be shown to conform.[71] Images, in short, should be studied in terms of their likeness to others rather than (or as well as) in terms of their correspondence to more mundane phenomena. The affinity between John Bull and Uncle Toby has already been noted, and it is the more interesting in that they enter the public arena at about the same time. Medieval scholars have noted the 'very striking similarity' between the Robin Hood stories and those told of other outlaws, with incidents freely transposed from one cycle of tales to another, and a traffic in imagery between them. There is a similar affinity between Jack the Giant Killer and a series of local heroes credited with dragon-slaying feats, for example Tom Hickathrift of East Anglia, who vied with him for popularity in the eighteenth-century chap-books.[72] More generally he seems to belong to the whole cycle of what the folklorists call 'Jack' tales, in which the young and inexperienced outwit their superiors and perform feats of prodigious strength ('Jack and the Bean Stalk' is the best known example).[73]

To say this is not to deny the value and illumination of more precise historical locations. The theme of the poor boy making good – or the boy from the backstreet becoming a star – may be a tale type in folklore all over the world, and Dick Whittington's cat is found as far afield as the Persian Gulf. But as a major theme in printed literature it emerges at the end of the sixteenth century in broadsides and ballads in the tales of Thomas Deloney, and on the stage in what a literary historian calls 'the apprentice's adventuring play . . . the fantasy of fame and heroism for the ordinary artisan'.[74] Tom Hickathrift, the Fenland giant-slayer, vaguely positioned in Anglo-Saxon times, achieves a local fame and fortune somewhat akin, though in a rural setting, to Dick Whittington's. So too, by making his fortune as a clothier, does Jack of Newbury. Dekker's best known play, *The Shoemaker's Holiday*, appealing directly (writes L. C. Knights) to the 'citizen craftsman', rehearses a narrative almost analogous to that of Dick Whittington: the progress of Simon Eyre, a celebrated London merchant of the fourteenth century, from master craftsman to sheriff and finally to Lord Mayor of London.

One way of approaching these figures, then, would be to see them as a recycling of primordial images. A large number of characters might be grouped together under the generic category of 'holy innocents'. Prose pastorals such as Mary Russell Mitford's 1835 *Our Village*, a three-volume collection of pen portraits allegedly drawn from life, are full of such figures, as is the dialect literature of Lancashire, the West Riding and Tyneside. They are well represented in the nursery rhymes, for example, by Simple Simon, the apparent original of a whole line of street-wise lads. The country bumpkin assumes this character in Restoration comedy and eighteenth-century chap-books, usually as the victim of the 'tricks of the town', more occasionally turning the tables on, and outwitting, his persecutors. One figure worth pausing on would be the Fool, whose progress on the early English stage has been chronicled by Enid Welsford, and whose place in the mummers' play is charted by R. J. E. Tiddy.[75] In *A Midsummer Night's Dream*, Robin Goodfellow's divine simplicity allows him to mock the mighty and beard the higher-ups in their lairs. The clown at the pantomime was traditionally cast in this role and it was of course magnificently resurrected for the silent screen by Charlie Chaplin.

At the other end of the social scale, a generic figure worth pausing on would be the 'old fogey': the Colonel Blimps of the army and navy, drawing up yesterday's battle lines; the Sir Roger de Coverleys of the shires, outdistanced by the metropolis and modernity, but making a whole comedy (or poetry) out of the archaic. As a hero of backwardness, the old fogey has deep roots in the national culture, and it may be symptomatic of his imaginative appeal that when the original Colonel Blimp was translated from caricature to the cinema screen, he emerged as no longer Low's narrow-minded bigot, but in the hands of Michael Powell, as a gallant old buffer, even a romantic dreamer.

Another paradigmatic figure with multiple incarnations is the 'freeborn Englishman'. In the pastoral version of the national myth he is the sturdy yeoman, the jovial blacksmith, the hardy peasant, the peaceful shepherd, the roving young blade, a countryman enjoying the freedom of the open air and living in a state of liberty and independence. In melodrama, he is the honest labourer who stands up to the squire and defends his sister's honour; just like the eponymous hero of *Nicholas Nickleby*. On the music-hall stage he is the free-and-easy cockney, 'doing as you damn well pleasey'. Jack Tar, the common sailor, was cast in this character. In the eighteenth-century prints he bends his knees in a swagger, and wears his hat at a rakish angle. Nautical drama, a phenomenon of the 1790s, associated him with the hornpipe[76] and in the popular theatre of the early nineteenth century he emerges as a proletarian hero, 'always on terms of easy familiarity with his captain, or . . . mutinous'.[77]

The freeborn Englishman has a long lineage, but it was in the eighteenth century, when the 'liberty and rights' of the subject were the dominant idiom of politics, that he came into his own, serving as an ideological fiction for interests and opinions of all kinds. In popular constitutionalism the freeborn Englishman spoke a language of rights;[78] in moral economy he belligerently defended his liberties. Dr Johnson, 'to some degree of excess' (wrote his biographer, Boswell) 'a trueborn Englishman',[79] is perhaps the best remembered, and certainly the best loved representative of this type, taking the principle of opposition into the very marrow of his being. A man of strong opinions, forcefully expressed, he set about his opponents with mournful relish, 'talked for victory' and 'appeared to have pleasure in contradiction'. As a student his main pleasure seems to have been vexing his college tutors.[80] As a writer he poured out his contempt for government. A 'steady and warm Tory' who believed in inequality, he was nevertheless a warm sympathiser with the poor and an ardent supporter of the blacks; on a famous occasion he startled 'some very grave men at Oxford' with the toast 'Here's to the next insurrection of the negroes in the West Indies.'[81] He also had 'great compassion for the miseries and distresses of the Irish nation, particularly the papists; and severely reprobated the barbarous . . . policy of the British government, which, he said, was the most detestable form of persecution.'

Boswell on another occasion describes him as 'bursting forth with a generous indignation' to say 'The Irish are in a most unnatural state; for we see there the minority prevailing over the majority.'[82]

Ideologically these figures have multiple significations, being subject to rival or contradictory interpretations. They are also quite chameleon-like, being adopted now in a radical sense, now in a conservative one, and changing their meaning over time. John Bull, as Hugh Cunningham and Jeanine Surel show in these volumes, was originally an opposition figure, representing an oppressed people at the mercy of arbitrary government. It is only in Disraelian times that he goes over to the Conservative camp. 'The freeborn Englishman' is an even more ambiguous figure. He traces one line of ancestry to the 'free' Anglo-Saxons, and the 'peasant commonwealths' which allegedly flourished before the imposition of the Norman yoke. But in another version, descending from Magna Carta and finding its most complete expression in the eighteenth-century constitution, he is an aristocratic figure, defending his immunities and privileges against the encroachments of central government and the crown. The gentleman, too, until recently a hegemonic character ideal, has been through many mutations in the course of a long career. Originally the title attached to a warrior class (Chaucer's 'gentil parfit' knight), but it came to be associated in later years with the parson and the squire, and later still – towards the close of the nineteenth century – with the idea of public service. Under the influence of the Victorian public school, and on the Victorian model of Hellenism, it changed gradually from a status to a character, an ineffable quality attaching neither exactly to birth nor to breeding, yet taking its cue from notions of hereditary descent.

The cross-class appeal of many of these characters makes it hazardous to assign them to a specific group, and the attempt to do so, as in the famous debate on whether Robin Hood was a peasant or an aristocratic hero, has always seemed to the present writer forced. The idea of the 'born gentleman' has at least as much currency among working-class people as it does among higher-ups; so too has an almost feudal contempt for the 'upstart': the sergeant major of soldiers' songs, the foreman or overseer of factory jokes. One of the features of the chap-books – to go back to character ideals in earlier times – is their fascination with the marvellous, and in particular the magical translation from low to high estate. Another – distressing to anyone of egalitarian sympathies and beliefs – is the glamour accorded to the well-born. If there is an unofficial ideology in the ballads of tradition or the chap-books which carried them to the alehouse and cottage, it is not peasant protest but rather aristocratic romanticism, one in which a warrior class occupies a pinnacle of esteem.

Notes

1 Geoffrey Gorer, *Exploring English Character*, London, 1955.
2 Patrick Wright, *On Living in an Old Country*, London, 1985, p. 119.
3 Maurice Keen, *The Outlaws of Medieval Legend*, rev. edn, London, 1977; ed. Rodney Hilton, *Peasants, Knights and Heretics*, London, 1976; J. C. Holt, *Robin Hood*, London, 1982.
4 Translated as *Marianne into Battle*, Cambridge, 1981.
5 Pierre Nora, *Les Lieux de la mémoire*, 4 vols, Paris 1984–.
6 Charles Dickens, *Nicholas Nickleby*, ch. XI.
7 Christopher Hill, *A Turbulent, Seditious, and Factious People*, Oxford, 1988. See pp. 28–38 and pp. 197 seq. for some of the sources.
8 Leslie Sheppard, *The History of Street Literature*, Newton Abbot, 1973, p. 26.
9 Samuel Bamford, *Early Days*, London, 1849, pp. 90–1.
10 A. W. Coysh, *Historic English Inns*, Newton Abbot, 1972, p. 52.
11 'Report on the state of the working classes in the parishes of St Margaret and St John, Westminster', *Journal of the Royal Statistical Society*, III, 1840, pp. 20–1.
12 Reginald G. Haggar, *Staffordshire China Ornaments*, London, 1955.
13 A. E. Green, 'MacCafferey: a study in the variation and function of a ballad', *Language and Lore*, 3–5, 1970–1.
14 'Mother Shipton – the rhyming prophetess', *The Lady*, 11 October 1988; also the *Dictionary of National Biography* has an entry on her.
15 Martin Manser, *A Dictionary of Eponyms*, London, 1988, p. 204.
16 A. Barrere and C. G. Leland, *A Dictionary of Slang, Jargon and Cant*, n.p., 1890, vol. II, p. 7.
17 Reginald Nettel, *Seven Centuries of Popular Song*, London, 1956, p. 195.
18 Vic Scholer, *British Toby Jugs*, London, 1986, p. 3.
19 G. Cheyne, *The English Malady*, London, 1733. For a helpful recent discussion of this theme, see Derek Jarrett, *England in the Age of Hogarth*, Paladin, 1976.
20 Among radio and television 'characters' exemplifying this trait, one might mention Mona Lott, the misanthropic charlady of the war-time comedy show *ITMA* ('It's being so cheerful as keeps me going'); Tony Hancock, the comedian (who killed himself), and Gilbert Harding, the dyspeptic compere.
21 Linda Colley, 'Whose nation? Class and national consciousness in Britain, 1750–1830', *Past and Present*, 113, November 1986.
22 Martha Vicinus, *The Industrial Muse*, London, 1974; Robert Colls, *The Collier's Rant*, London, 1977; *Allan's Tyneside Songs*, Newcastle-upon-Tyne, 1891.
23 *The Complete Works of Tim Bobbin*, Manchester, 1862.
24 Vicinus, *op. cit.*, pp. 198, 202.
25 Colls, *op. cit*, pp. 34–6

26 A. E. Wilson, *Christmas Pantomime*, London, 1934, p. 17.

27 G. R. Owst, *Literature and Pulpit in Medieval England*, Cambridge, 1933, p. 492; T. W. Craik, 'Violence in the English miracle plays', in Neville Denny (ed.), *Medieval Drama*, London, 1973; Glynne Wickham, *Early English Stages*, London, 1963, vol. I, p. 152.

28 George Speaight, *The History of the English Puppet Theatre*, London, 1955.

29 *The Libelle of Englische Policye*, Oxford, 1926.

30 F. J. Harvey Darnton, *Children's Books in England*, Cambridge, 1960.

31 David Mayer, *Harlequin Observed*, London, 1969.

32 Rev. Samuel Lysons, *The Model Merchant of the Middle Ages exemplified in . . . Dick Whittington,* London, 1860.

33 Gavin Thurston, *The Clerkenwell Riot*, London, 1967.

34 For some Lancashire examples, see *Preston Pilot*, 2, 30 May 1840, 6, 25 July 1840; *Blackburn Gazette*, 8 July 1840; James Carr, *Annals and Stories of Colne and Neighbourhood*, Manchester, 1878, pp. 228–32; Lancs. R. O., QEV 181/4 for a village siege of 1864 at Lees, near Oldham. For this early period generally, see Robert Storch, 'A plague of blue locusts', *International Review of Social History*, XX, 1975. For an overview, see Clive Emsley, *Policing and its Context, 1750–1870*, London, 1983.

35 Raphael Samuel, 'Quarry thoughts', in R. Samuel (ed.), *Village Life and Labour*, London, 1975.

36 Ross McKibbin, 'Working-class gambling in Britain, 1880–1939', *Past and Present*, 82, February 1979; Raphael Samuel, *East End Underworld*, London, 1981.

37 G. W. Reynolds, *The Night the Police Went on Strike*, London, 1968; A. V. Selwood, *Police Strike, 1919*, London, 1978, for the strike and its immediate aftermath.

38 S. G. Hulme Beaman, *Tales of Toytown*, Oxford, 1928. Humphrey Carpenter and Mari Prichard, *The Oxford Companion to Children's Literature*, Oxford, 1984, p. 539; Sheila Ray, *The Blyton Phenomenon*, London, 1982; Bob Mullan, *Enid Blyton, A Biography*, London, 1985, for the evolution of her version of Toytown, and the storms it later ran into.

39 George Orwell, *Homage to Catalonia*, Penguin, 1966, pp. 220–1.

40 Alan Ivimey, *Robert of London*, London, 1939.

41 For details, T. E. B. Clarke, *This is Where I Came In*, London, 1974, pp. 121–3, 187; Charles Barr, *Ealing Studios*, Newton Abbot, 1977, pp. 81–95; Ted Willis, *The Blue Lamp,* London, 1950.

42 *My Life by George Dixon*, London, 1960.

43 Benjamin Disraeli, *Selected Speeches*, ed. T. E. Kebbel, London, 1882, vol. II, p. 494.

44 *Brewer's Dictionary of Phrase and Fable*; for visual examples, see *The Catchpenny Prints*, New York, 1960.

45 Helen Bosanquet, *The Family*, London, 1906, p. 268. Peter Burke describes Patient Grizzel as one of the two heroines who took the place

of saints in Protestant northern Europe. Peter Burke, *Popular Culture in Early Modern Europe*, London, 1978, p. 164.

46 Thomas Kendrick, *British Antiquity*, London, 1950; F. J. Levy, *Tudor Historical Thought*, San Marino, Calif., 1967.

47 Jennifer Westward, *Albion, A Guide to Legendary Britain*, London, 1981; F. W. Fairhold, *Gog and Magog, The Giants in Guildhall*, London, 1859.

48 Margaret Spufford, *Small Books and Pleasant Histories*, Cambridge, 1985, p. 59.

49 R. F. Brinkesley, *The Arthurian Legend in the Seventeenth Century*, Baltimore, Md., 1932.

50 Eric Partridge, *A Dictionary of Slang*, 8th edn, London, 1984, p. 609.

51 Herbert M. Atherton, *Political Prints in the Age of Hogarth*, Oxford, 1974, pp. 178–9.

52 *Ibid.*, pp. 178–9, 189, 254–5.

53 Richard Baker and Anthony Miall, *Everyman's Book of Sea-Songs*, London, 1982, pp. 29–30.

54 L. P. Curtis, *Anglo-Saxons and Celts*, Bridgeport, Conn., 1968, pp. 43, 84. For some criticism, see Sheridan Gilley, 'English attitudes to the Irish' in Colin Holmes (ed.), *Immigrants and Minorities in British Society*, London, 1972.

55 Thomas Nicholas, *The Pedigree of the English People*, 2nd edn, London, 1868, pp. 525–6, quoting an article by Arnold in *The Cornhill Magazine*.

56 Curtis, *op. cit.*, pp. 44–5, 61.

57 David Quinn, *The Elizabethans and the Irish*, Ithaca, NY, 1966, pp. 24–8, 68–9, 76.

58 Curtis, *op. cit.*, pp. 36–7.

59 James Platt, *Political Economy*, London, 1882, pp. 36–7.

60 Ralph Waldo Emerson, *English Traits*, London, 1966, p. 94.

61 Christopher Campos, *The View of France from Arnold to Bloomsbury*, Oxford, 1965, pp. 74–7; H. W. Massingham, *The Englishman Abroad*, London, 1962, pp. 28–9, 80–1.

62 These fortresses still stand in Portsmouth harbour as monuments to a nation-wide panic.

63 Gerald Newman, *The Rise of English Nationalism, A Cultural History, 1740–1830*, London, 1987.

64 Atherton, *op. cit.*, p. 85.

65 *Ibid.*, p. 88.

66 Charles Knightly, *Folk Heroes of Britain*, London, 1982, pp. 56–93.

67 Reginald G. Haggar, *Staffordshire China Ornaments*, London, 1955, p. 38; *English Country Pottery*, London, 1950, p. 116.

68 Donald R. Dudley and Graham Webster, *The Rebellion of Boudicca*, London, 1962, pp. 113–30.

69 Valerie Chancellor, *History for their Masters: Opinion in the English History Textbook, 1800–1914*, Bath, 1970, pp. 70–1. The story of the burnt cakes is an Elizabethan interpellation.

70 Eric Hobsbawm and Terence Ranger (eds), *The Invention of Tradition*, Cambridge, 1983, p. 1.

71 Vladimir Propp, *The Morphology of the Folk Tale*, London, 1968.

72 For Tom Hickathrift, see Margaret Spufford, *op. cit.*, pp. 247–9; Enid Porter, *East Anglian Folklore*, London, 1976, pp. 94–101.

73 Funk and Wagnall, *Standard Dictionary of Folklore*, London, 1972.

74 L. C. Knights, *Drama and Society in the Age of Johnson*, London, 1937; Martin Butler, *Theatre and Crisis, 1632–1642*, Cambridge, 1984; Andrew Gurr, *Playgoing in Shakespeare's London*, Cambridge, 1987.

75 R. J. E. Tiddy, *The Mummers' Play*, Oxford, 1923; Enid Welsford, *The Fool*, London, 1935.

76 See Frank Rohill's excellent chapter on 'The British Tar as proletarian hero' in *World of Melodrama*, Pennsylvania, 1967. See also Derek Forbes, 'Water drama', in David Bradby, Louis James, and Bernard Sharratt (eds), *Performance and Politics in Popular Drama*, Cambridge, 1980; Louis James, 'Was Jerrold's Black Ey'd Susan more popular than Wordsworth's Lucy?' in *ibid*.

77 Gilbert Abbot à Beckett, *Quizziology of the British Drama*, London, 1846, p. 7. I am grateful to Louis James for this reference.

78 For popular constitutionalism, see J. A. W. Gunn, *Beyond Liberty and Property*, McGill, 1983; John Brewer, *Party Ideology and Popular Politics at the Accession of George III*, Cambridge, 1981.

79 Boswell's *Life of Johnson*, Everyman, I, p. 577.

80 *Ibid.*, I, p. 35

81 *Ibid.*, II, pp. 146, 161.

82 *Ibid.*, I, pp. 389, 483–4.

National gallery

1
John Bull

JEANNINE SUREL

[Translated by Kathy Hodgkin]

I

When we think of John Bull, we pick out from the jumble of popular and national mythologies a pot-bellied man in immaculate boots, carrying sometimes a riding-crop, sometimes a club, neither of which detracts in the slightest from his peaceable air. This simple soul, this easy-going, Pickwickian character, sure of his tranquil strength, is in reality a Victorian John Bull; its diffusion in the second half of the nineteenth century was ensured by *Punch* magazine, which appeared for the first time in 1841; and it significantly altered those earlier models which are the subject of this chapter.

Caricature, as a branch of popular iconography, may serve as a means of expression for antagonistic groups, in the same moment and on the same themes, and may draw on opposing ideologies. It can help to sustain traditional values, or introduce subversive ideas – including the simplest and most subversive idea of all, that criticism of the established order and its representatives *is* possible. None the less, in the period 1789–1815 that principally concerns us here – for reasons arising out of the very nature of political life – it would be too schematic to reduce satirical imagery to two categories, one expressing a conservative ideology, the other an anti-establishment view. While there was at this time a ministerialist group and an 'opposition', it is impossible to use the notion of 'party' (in the sense which this word gradually acquired during the nineteenth century) to define and to contrast them. Nor was the personalisation of politics (to which caricature bears witness, and which it to some extent reinforced) the same as that which can be identified later on. It portrayed real-life political personalities, easily recognised and identifiable, and was in no way related to the idealisation of leader figures, a process which was to develop as public opinion itself came to count for more.

Between 1790 and 1816 caricature was the business of many people, and the livelihood of some. The names of a few cartoonists reappear regularly at the foot of the engravings. James Gillray (1757–1815), Isaac Cruickshank (1756?-1811?), Thomas Rowlandson (1756–1827), James Sayer(s) (1748–1823), Robert Newton (1777–98), are usually both the artists and the engravers of their own work. Newton even became briefly his own shopkeeper, setting up in the Strand. Other artists gave their drawings to an artisan-engraver, or simply furnished him with a sketch or an idea, such as J. M. Woodward, who often worked with Thomas Rowlandson. Finally there were those about whom little is known, such as W. C. Ansell, or J. Cawse (1779–1862); and the anonymous caricatures, or those signed with an unidentified pseudonym. In this study, the examples cited will be mainly drawn from the work of Gillray, because of the high quality of his caricatures. But Gillray is no more than the most representative, the most fascinating perhaps, of the many artists illustrating English political life at this time; his subjects, although treated with particular skill, are the same as those attempted by many others, perhaps with a lesser talent, a slower pencil, or a blunter chisel.

It is very difficult to identify the political affiliations of the cartoonists, or to use such identifications to provide the elements of a systematic classification of the images produced. There were undoubtedly some, like James Sayers, who were favourable to the ministerial group, that is to say, to the particular statesman taken as representative of this group; and others who were 'opposition' cartoonists, criticising the political stance of the dominant party. But where can one put an artist like James Gillray, whose services were literally purchased, and who none the less produced cartoons ridiculing Pitt? The part played by an individual, or individualist, apolitical reaction to a politics perceived merely as the battleground of rival ambitions cannot be neglected. Pitt and Fox, Dundas and Sheridan, were sent up side by side; all political adversaries for the moment, but in reality identical with regard to their ultimate objectives (gaining power), and indifferent to the fortunes of the nation and of its incarnation, John Bull, half-duped and eternally the victim.

It would be more or less true to say that the John Bull character was born out of caricature; at least it cannot be denied that here he found his personified reality, if not his definitive form. It was in truth a paradoxical reality. Struck from hot iron in the heart of the European crisis, the iconic character representing the nation

1 'The Tree of LIBERTY – with the Devil tempting John Bull'.
Cartoon by James Gillray, 1798. (Mansell Collection)

was necessarily the bearer of nationalist propaganda; at the same time, as offspring of the cartoonists' pens, he became the mouthpiece for certain demands, and had the function of criticising those institutions whose defence he nevertheless assured. A national myth incarnated in a satirical image, John Bull inevitably possessed contradictory virtues.

II

John Bull was not born in a day, under a cartoonist's pencil or an engraver's chisel. He was a product gradually elaborated over two centuries, out of disparate elements: a symbolic animal (the bull, and sometimes the mastiff) which was added to the bestiary of the heraldic tradition (unicorns, lions); a work of literature, *The History of John Bull* (1712), by the satirist John Arbuthnot, which humanised this symbolic representation; a graphic tradition, for a certain type of popular Englishman was appearing during the eighteenth century in pictures and engravings, and although he had not yet been awarded the title 'John Bull', the situations in which he found himself and the roles which he played connected him with the John Bull of the end of the century.

It is not my intention to investigate the motives leading to the selection of the bull as a national symbol. It may be observed that when he first appeared in the satirical engravings of the seventeenth century, the bull manifested vitality and mobility, in contrast to the lion and the unicorn; the significance of these heraldic beasts was indissolubly linked to a determinate and unchanging function, and a sacred one, which would explain their relatively limited use in caricature. The symbolic image of the bull (or the English bulldog) was to lose out to the human character John Bull, which became increasingly conspicuous towards the end of the century. Between 1800 and 1810 John Bull appeared in more than 400 caricatures, and only four times as an animal; this metamorphosis of beast into man owed a great deal to Arbuthnot's literary character, which was in fact created for particular ends.

At the time Arbuthnot was writing, there was a problem in justifying to public opinion the pacific foreign policy of the Tories, who had come to power in 1710. Although the country was on the whole favourable to peace, the diplomatic manoeuvres of the government, its secret discussions with France, and Britain's abandonment of its traditional system of alliances, needed some explanation. This was the task that Arbuthnot set himself when he wrote *The History of John Bull*, a sort of political fable whose characters are allegorical, and whose events refer to contemporary political, economic and religious problems. In the story, John Bull is presented as a small proprietor and tradesman, a double sociological characterisation which immediately indicates the proposed audience of this work of propaganda. Arbuthnot draws the following psychological portrait of John Bull:

> *Bull*, in the main, was an honest plain-dealing Fellow, Cholerick, Bold, and of a very unconstant Temper, he dreaded not old *Lewis*[1] either at Backsword, single Faulcion or Cudgel-play; but then he was very apt to quarrel with his best Friends, especially when they pretended to govern him: If you flattered him, you might lead him like a Child. *John*'s Temper depended very much upon the Air; his Spirits rose and fell with the Weather-glass. *John* was quick, and understood his business very well, but no Man alive was more careless, in looking into his Accounts, or more cheated by Partners, Apprentices and Servants: This was occasioned by his being a Boon-companion, loving his Bottle and his Diversion; for to say Truth, no Man kept a better House than *John*, nor spent his money more generously. By plain and fair dealing, *John* had acquired some Plumbs.[2]

The physical attributes of the hero are sketched in later, in a few rapid touches, as though the character traits given at the opening were sufficent in themselves to flesh out his personality. We learn only that '*John* look'd ruddy and plump, with a pair of cheeks like a Trumpeter'.[3] The character which the cartoonists were to construct, in their own language, would largely reflect this very stereotypical personality with which Arbuthnot had already endowed his John Bull.

One of the earliest representations of this type of Englishman – corpulent, peaceable, although of legendary strength, and a man of the people – is to be found in William Hogarth's engraving *Beer Street*. There are two versions of this engraving. The first one (to extract only what is of interest here) depicts a fat, placid butcher, raising his overflowing tankard to the prosperity of his country, and brandishing a haunch of beef; in the second version the meat has been replaced by a wretched French traveller, whom the butcher holds at arm's length, luggage and all, with as firm a grip. In both cases, this London butcher, portrayed as a gallophobic cockney, unites in himself enough national myths to seem a sort of pre-publication version of John Bull. One might even say that Hogarth's butcher bears a closer resemblance to the John Bull of the last few years of the eighteenth century than the character who appeared under that name in 1779, joined for the first time to a picture, in two engravings. The two are very similar; one is simply a more elaborate version of the other (although in the second he is called not John Bull but Jack English). The author, probably Gillray, presents two sharply contrasting figures: sitting with their backs to one another, they cast furious glances over their shoulders. One wears high boots and a scarf round his neck. His club rests between his legs, he holds a pot of beer; it is the solid countryman John Bull. The other is a Frenchman, a skinny, powdered, beribboned courtier. A thin greyhound can be seen beneath his chair, while beneath that of the Englishman, of course, is a bulldog. Every detail has symbolic weight, and the important thing is to emphasise the differences, the contrasts, rather than to hint at the nuances. These two engravings, although interesting in that they offer the first 'named' appearance of John Bull in English iconography, possess only a few of the characteristics of Hogarth's butcher, and the future outline of the national hero can be no more than guessed at.

In fact, the shape in which John Bull appears in caricatures from the 1780s onwards owes most to the old – and tenacious – myth of a well-fed, prosperous English race, gorged on beef and good beer. The process by which this myth took root and flourished served both to contradict the contemporary reality – a sad trail of economic crises and hunger riots (1795, rising food prices, riots in Birmingham; 1800, riots in London) – and also to draw an advantageous contrast between the English race and those inferior sorts of nationality, Scottish, Irish and above all French, poor heretics in rags and tatters, barefoot or dragging the wooden clogs of servitude, for ever eating snails and raw onions. Thus the unique image of England and the English came to predominate, that of a people bursting with rich food, a pot-bellied, gout-ridden horde. The watercolours of Rowlandson fixed their silhouettes in elaborate flowing lines with no hint of angularity, rounded to the point of bloatedness. Thus the character of John Bull as the incarnation of the country established itself in cartoon form.

The reasons for the humanisation of this national symbol are diverse. In terms of formal artistic development, the evolution of John Bull follows that of the genre of satirical engraving. So long as the caricaturist preferred to use a symbolic or allegorical language, John Bull appeared as an animal; as political figures and celebrities came to be represented through the use of exaggerated characteristics which rendered them immediately and perfectly recognisable, John Bull, a character with no particular identity, took on a human form, or rather human forms. The same process of humanisation can be seen in the case of Charles James Fox, for instance, in 1757 the foxcub son of an old reynard,[4] but to whom James Gillray from 1782 on gave the features that were to pass into history.[5]

At the same time the John Bull character was becoming a sort of stand-in for the heraldic, or mythological, representations of the English nation. As we have seen, he quite rapidly ousted the British bull. From the 1790s on he appears more and more often with Britannia, an English Minerva, whose shield was emblazoned with the Union Jack. The goddess existed; Rowlandson met her, a vigorous girl with bare breasts who brandished in the air those two traitors to the nation, Fox and Sheridan, accused of sympathy with the Parisian rebels. Gillray found her clinging to a tree, while Thomas Paine, one foot planted in the lady's behind, pulled with all his might at the laces of the too tight corset (French, and constitutional) into which he wished to force her.[6] These are specific situations, in which decorum is absent. And the examples might be multiplied. This propensity on the part of the cartoonists to depict Britannia in petticoats, or alternatively as a robust gossip, in no way prevented John Bull from gaining ground; he did not supplant Britannia, but at least he found himself her equal.

What hypotheses might be advanced to explain his presence?

The English cartoonists perhaps wanted to oppose to the mythological goddesses brought into play by the French Revolution (Liberty, Reason) a common man, a being of flesh and blood, and a male one at that. During the brief period when English public opinion seemed sympathetic to the events in France, Gillray published (August 1789) a cartoon representing 'The Goddess of Liberty on the ruins of the Bastille'. This indicates that the English public was aware of the symbolic language used by the revolutionaries. Might John Bull, that simple soul, have been the English reply to Liberty with the attributes of a goddess, who in Great Britain after 1791–2 became synonymous with a bloody anarchy? France was undergoing a cultural transformation of huge scope, designed to instil into the popular consciousness a patriotic republican ideology which drew its inspiration from the Ancient World. Answering one mythology with another, England opposed to this model the heritage of the 'glorious revolution' of 1688, and John Bull as the beneficiary of this.

John Bull's success was perhaps due to a certain disquiet, as if the traditional symbols of national unity avowed themselves insufficient to preserve that unity, in times troubled as much by internal social tensions as by the general situation of Europe; as though abstractions could only serve as collective points of reference so long as the consensus was assured and the state all-powerful. While a symbolic image could bring about the arbitrary fusion of all social groupings into some sort of national identity, John Bull, an imaginary character, could represent a variety of categories from the social hierarchy, if not all categories. The arrival of John Bull in satirical drawings signified the recognition of a social diversity which the unitary and nationalist symbolic system completely failed to take into account.

And as a logical and complementary step, the recognition of this diversity in the heart of British society made it the more imperative to find a common denominator for the multiple fractions of which it was composed. The historical situation very naturally enabled hatred of the French Revolution, then of Bonaparte, then of the Emperor, to play this role of common denominator, although this self-definition through opposition was itself a long-standing tradition; the French aristocrat and dandy had been the subject of John Bull's threats and sarcasms since his first appearance in 1779. It was an ancient antagonism which, dressed to suit the taste of the day, was to renew national unity and reconcile the diverse social forces of the country.

III

John Bull's gallophobia was a constant attribute of the character, whatever the guise in which he appeared; but the utilisation of John Bull in cartoons became more widespread from the 1790s on. That is to say that recourse to this character was accelerated by a climate of crisis which was shortly to develop into international conflict. A few figures will give a measure of this acceleration. Before 1789 – from 1784 to 1789, for example – some fifteen or so caricatures devoted to John Bull can be found. Between 1789 and 1800 more than 100 were to appear (sometimes representing him as an animal – about twenty instances of this). This figure was to triple between 1801 and 1810, with a record of seventy-one caricatures in the year 1803 alone.[7]

It is noticeable, however, that although John Bull was continually present, the heroic use of the character was a function of specific situations, and remained fairly limited. It might be to celebrate an English victory, a rare satisfaction in difficult times. In *John Bull taking a Luncheon*,[8] an ogre-like John Bull is devouring the French ships which the chiefs of the British admiralty are serving up to him. With the same purpose of warding off danger (the risk of invasion, the reopening of hostilities) the enemy French army is ridiculed by a suggestive use of geography. In *A new map of England and France, the French invasion, or John Bull bombarding the bumboats*, a John Bull whose body is represented by the map of Great Britain, and whose profile is that of George III, drops his excrement onto the coast of France and the French fleet. The French 'republicans', chased away by the bold English sailors beneath the amused gaze of John Bull, are mocked in *High fun for John Bull, or the Republicans put to their last shift* (November 1798)[9]; there are attempts to exalt national courage by presenting John Bull easily triumphing over his adversaries – *Buonaparte forty-eight hours after landing* (July 1803), or *John Bull offering Little Boney fair play* (August 1803).[10] In this last cartoon James Gillray gives John Bull the appearance of the 'gallant sailor' celebrated in popular songs, who had little in common with the miserable victims of the press gang or with the crews who mutinied at Spithead and the Nore in 1797. Here caricature takes on the qualities of an exorcism, intended to dissipate anxieties in the face of external peril.

However, apart from these brief accesses of patriotism, John Bull expresses fundamentally and more or less continually a desire for peace, which is presented as corresponding to the aspirations of the majority of the King's subjects. In the period 1790–1800 John Bull shows an occasional tendency to swagger, but when danger threatens he is more likely to yield his place to another popular character with whom, around 1780, he was sometimes confounded – the gallant English sailor Jack Tar, or Jack English (although Gillray's Jack English in the cartoon mentioned earlier was not a sailor), who was then as valuable a national symbol as John Bull. Nelson's victories, and the battle of Trafalgar, consolidated this characterisation of the sailor, a symbol of English nautical power and defender of the realm, to whom the caricaturist G. M. Woodward gave a visual identity. This sailor became in some sense John Bull's protector, for the two prototypes represented different values and assumed distinct roles, one finding himself charged with the security of the other, who showed little inclination to play soldiers. (It may be noted in passing that while the sailor was a popular favourite, the soldier, on the contrary – and in particular the army command - was almost always portrayed as absurd and incompetent.) For all this, the heroic British tar was a character brought out only in exceptional circumstances, linked to international events: the civilian (and the anti-hero) John Bull rather than the sailor incarnated the nation.

Examples of John Bull's pacifism are plentiful. In a cartoon of 1790, John Bull looks suspiciously at the coronet inscribed with the word 'Glory' which Pitt is attempting to put on his head; in another, dating from December 1792, Pitt drags a soldier John Bull along by the ear, thinking he sees the enemy on the horizon and ready to do battle. It might reasonably be thought that the function of these engravings was primarily satirical, mocking the English lack of enthusiasm for war. But this would be to limit their significance, for these cartoons were also intended to bring to the attention of those responsible for the country the voice of those they governed, who wished for peace. Such an expression of pacifism seems surprising, given the historical circumstances in which the details of the national prototype were modelled and refined; all the more so, considering that before 1790 John Bull appeared to exhibit more aggression, or at least a certain potential combativeness. An investigation of the motives for this pacifism (other than those which could be of any country and any time) brings us to the question of John Bull's social allegiances. Did he represent 'English public opinion' at large, or a fraction of that opinion?

From a study of the innumerable caricatures appearing between 1790 and 1815, the following observations may be made.

1 It need be only briefly mentioned that George III in a handful of cases plays the part of John Bull,[11] and that John Bull very occasionally appears as an incarnation of the state.
2 In the majority of cases the prototype is related essentially to two social groups:
    John Bull is a peasant, a tenant farmer, or even a cottager, rather than a large proprietor or landlord;
    John Bull is a city-dweller, a 'cit', an artisan or shopkeeper in the capital.

Thus he is related to Arbuthnot's John Bull, but can none the less be distingushed from him in that numerically he is more often urban than rural, and close to the urban petty bourgeoisie. His character is more 'popular' than the John Bull of the early eighteenth century. Arbuthnot's John Bull wanted to be treated as a gentleman; in the cartoons of the 1790s he asks only not to be exploited.

It is my contention that John Bull, the national stereotype, was deeply rooted in the economic realities of the nation whose symbol he became; and that this fact enables us more fully to understand the messages he bears.

A cartoon in four episodes by James Gillray admirably summarises the fate of the peasant seduced by visions of military glory. *John Bull's Progress* (1793) depicts in the first frame a cottager peacefully installed at his hearth, a pot of beer in his hand, his family around him. After this highly idealised version of rural England we see John Bull enlisting, despite the tears of his wife and children. A few months, a few years later, wife and children are obliged to take all their possessions to the pawnbrokers, notably the tools with which they earn their livings (spinning wheel, agricultural implements). Epilogue: an unrecognisable cripple returns to a home, now afflicted with the direst poverty. The disruption of a particular type of rural economy by the mechanics of war is thus explained in a few images.[12] It is a valid representation, in this particular case, but also restricted to a single section of rural society, failing to take into account the 'positive' aspects of the war for another category of farmers and landowners; inflation in the price of corn brought them considerable benefits, which were shortly to be consolidated by the Corn Laws.

In the case of John Bull the townsman, the plea for peace rests on an argument different in form, but essentially the same. It is John Bull the 'cit' who is the victim of the budgetary and fiscal constraints imposed by the succession of ministers at the head of the state. Pitt, Addington and Fox all play here the same negative part; that is to say, their tactics are similar, although their political strategies seem different or even opposite. Among the measures denounced are the issue of paper money in 1797 in *Bank Notes – Paper Money, ah, poor John Bull* (1 March 1797) and the creation of a sinking fund to wipe out the national debt in *The national parachute, or John Bull conducted to plenty and emancipation* (10 July 1802) and *John Bull and the sinking fund* (29 February 1807). But above all, it is John Bull who carries the weight of taxation necessary to finance the war. He sees himself overwhelmed by taxes,[13] which appear to him as arbitrary and vexatious impositions (taxes on windows, on felt hats, etc.), and threatened by what he perceives as an encroachment on the fundamental rights of the English citizen – income tax (introduced in 1798). In *John Bull at his studies, attended by his guardian angel* (13 March 1799), William Pitt as the 'guardian angel' leans attentively over a perplexed John Bull, who vainly attempts to make sense of the new fiscal regulations imposed on him.

Another complaint against the war was the hardship caused to British industry and trade; not economic activity in general, on a national scale, but the artisanal industries, the small traders, in short the system of production and exchange in forms which were, if not 'archaic' (for at that time the 'new' features of Britain's economic future were only beginning to take shape), at least traditional. Thus between about 1790 and 1815 various elements were starting to mix and to combine.

1 A protest of a long-standing nature against the indirect excise

tax, which had been going on throughout the eighteenth century. In April 1790, unusually, John Bull appears in animal form, snorting from his nostrils the fateful, and inseparable, words 'Liberty and no excise' (*John Bull baited by the dogs of excise*, 9 April 1790). This demand was to be exacerbated after 1793 by the war; and a fiscal innovation, the income tax, was to be included in it.

2 An economic argument. War is a hindrance to production and trade. (An argument which, by a dialectical effect – production and exchange are the best guarantees of peace – found its theoretical expression in the theses of economic liberalism formulated by Adam Smith.)

This theme of the exploitation of the common people by their leaders was a constant presence in the caricatures of the time, in spite of the variations and upheavals in international affairs which seemed rather to demand an appeal to the loyalty and the heroism of His Majesty's subjects. But protests against taxation, made heavier by some specific historical situation, are both by nature less immediate, and no doubt more disturbing, for the government; a simple return to peace will not necessarily eliminate them. Refusal of taxation took on a fundamental significance, in that it could be used as a political argument by those who, since about 1769, had been campaigning for parliamentary reform – that is, for an extension of the suffrage. This campaign, which gained momentum from the events in France, led to defensive reactions on the part of the British government (especially between 1793 and 1798) which were a measure of its importance, and of the extent to which it frightened those in power.

If one seeks in this political critique of the taxation system a contemporary echo of the John Bull of the 1790s, a theory, certain aspects of which (if not the more radical conclusions) were adopted by the reformers, it may be found in the works of Thomas Paine. In Chapter V of *The Rights of Man* (Ways and means of improving the condition of Europe), Paine declared:

If commerce were permitted to act to the universal extent it is capable, it would extirpate the system of war . . . The invention of commerce . . . is the greatest approach towards universal civilization, that has yet been made by any means not immediately flowing from moral principle.[14]

He explained, with statistics, how a state of peace made it possible considerably to diminish the burden of taxation; an alliance between France, Great Britain and the United States of America would bring about a policy of reciprocal disarmament ('Ship for ship on each side'). Pursuing his exposition, Paine denounced internal mismanagement as equally responsible with the war for the fiscal oppression of the English people.

There is a second analogy between the critique formulated by Paine and that explicitly advanced in satirical imagery. Both Paine and the cartoonists had by the end of the century begun to attack the cost to the nation of the monarchy. The national budget, Paine asserted, should be rebalanced, pruned of superfluous expenditure, and in particular of the 'million pounds sterling' destined to keep 'a family of foreigners.' One might almost be looking at Gillray's caricature *Monstrous crows at a coalition feast* (29 May 1787), where 'coalition' indicates that the royal family is for once in agreement, in drawing from a great cauldron spoonfuls of gold pieces, the lifeblood of John Bull; or, at the later one, dealing with connivance between the political milieu and the court – *John Bull ground down* – in which John Bull is literally put through the mill by Pitt so as to pay off the debts of the Prince of Wales. Thus we see a rejection of taxation, expressed both in text and image, whether destined to finance the war (or even other allied states, since Britain acted as the banker of the coalition – *Blind man's buff, or too many for John Bull*, 12 June 1795), or to pay for the expenditure of the King and his family. In popular iconography, the Prince of Wales figures as a prodigal son, George III more as an old miser; but extravagant spending or petty parsimoniousness had, for John Bull the taxpayer, identical effects.

Finally, a point linked also to the demand for a reform in parliamentary representation – a mark of radical opinion since the time of John Wilkes – there was the refusal to continue with the upkeep of statesmen enjoying their privileges and sinecures, and of rulers who were mercenary and corrupt. Contrasting American democracy with the British system, Paine wrote in his *Letter to Dundas* (6 June 1792) that in America the money earned by working men was kept by them for their own use, and for the education of their children; they did not have to give it up in the form of taxes to subsidise the requirements of an extravagant court, and of innumerable placemen and pensioners. This letter, 12,000 copies of which were reprinted by the Society for Constitutional Information, was Paine's response to Dundas, the home secretary, who had just put through Parliament a bill censoring 'seditious' texts – a measure aimed directly at *The Rights of Man*. Thus John Bull's major causes of dissatisfaction, as they were put forward in caricatures, were also to be found in a text whose author in 1792 was wanted by the English courts and forced to emigrate to escape imprisonment.

It would be tempting to conclude, adding up all these different observations and accumulating the examples, that the national prototype was the bearer of a message tainted with radicalism. John Bull's adversaries, whether as a city or a countryman, are less the French *sans-culottes* or Little Boney than his own leaders, the politicians of whatever persuasion nourished by the parliamentary system, the parasites secreted by the monarchy. Such a conclusion, moreover, would not be at odds with John Bull's 'social origins'. His affinities with the world of the small traders and artisans, with the urban London environment, have already been noted. It was from amongst these groups that members were recruited to the London Corresponding Society (founded 1792) and the Society for Constitutional Information (founded 1780, very active in London and Sheffield in 1790 and 1794) and, later, to the Society of Spencean Philanthropists (1812) and to the Hampden Clubs. In the same milieu the reformers, seeking a cleansing of the parliamentary system and an extension of the franchise, found their audience and their support; and the term 'reformer' was soon to become equivalent in English courts of law to 'revolutionary', 'enemy of the nation'. There was, then, a convergence between demands arising from the complaints specific to a certain social category, and the terms of an opposition whose objectives were clearly political. It is not my intention here to consider whether this opposition actually wished to call into question the entire English system of government; but it is certain that in the international context of the time, those in power saw it as a symptom of a dangerous popular movement which might at any moment spill over into insurrection. The word 'revolution', acceptable so long as it referred to the Glorious Revolution of 1688 (a Revolution Society was founded in 1788 to celebrate the centenary of these events), by 1790 had taken on a very different emotional charge. Had not the secret commission set up by the House of Lords to investigate subversive tendencies in reformist societies discovered, in 1793, the existence of a 'conspiracy', whose leaders planned to arm their troops with pikes supplied by supporters in Sheffield?[15]

None the less, to see John Bull as the mouthpiece of a radical opposition would lead to an unsatisfactory and a partial interpretation. The character did not in fact present only a single face. He appears in a cartoon already mentioned (*John Bull bother'd*, 1792) subjected to two contradictory influences, which make him a man divided. In his right pocket is a book with the clearly legible title *The Rights of Man*; in his left, a copy of *A Pennyworth of Truth*, a loyalist and anti-revolutionary tract. On one side of his hat he sports the revolutionary tricolour, on the other a cockade with the inscription, 'God Save the King.' This image deserves close attention. It summarises the historical situation; it signifies that anything can happen in a kingdom whose administrators are busy searching for the enemy in the distance, while in the very heart of the country popular opinion does not follow them or, worse, hesitates between remaining faithful to the regime and perhaps rejecting it entirely. What, in the end, would be John Bull's choice, and how could his decision be influenced? Was there still time to lead him back to the fold by assuring him of his loyalty?

I turn now to the cartoons in which John Bull becomes the advocate of English political traditions – specifically those defended (after 1792) by the Association for Preserving Liberty and Property against the Levellers and republicans. This organisation was presided over by John Reeves, man of law by profession and man of order by nature, and was better known under the name of the Crown and Anchor Society. Its title clearly proclaims its philosophy and its aims. It financed various nationalist propaganda enterprises, and bought the services of several engravers and cartoonists. James Gillray indirectly satirises the scanty philosophy of the Association when, in *French Liberty, English Slavery*, he contrasts a thin ragged revolutionary in a red bonnet, devouring a few raw onions, with an enormous John Bull seated in front of a haunch of roast beef and a foaming pot of beer, with a carafe of hock to top it up. French liberty, it is clear, doesn't fill the belly. But an image like this, ridiculing the discourse favourable to the French revolutionaries and those who attempt to spread the word in England, conceals a strong dose of irony directed at the gluttonous and gouty oaf who represents happiness to the English.[16] Gillray's adoption of this position did not prevent him from turning out to order, a few months later, two cartoons contrasting English peace with French anarchy. One must live.

The keyword in the loyalist engravings was the idea of liberty – an authentic English liberty, as opposed to the fraudulent liberty of the French '*citoyens*'. In thus claiming ownership of this concept, popular English imagery created a manichaean universe in which the word 'liberty' was never used to describe what the other side thought it was defending, except in derision. The events in France demanded a vigorous statement in response. Before 1789 the subjects of the French kings always appeared as poor heretics, miserable slaves in those wooden clogs which were the symbols of their servitude. After 1789 it was imperative to demonstrate that the change of regime brought with it destitution and disorder, and in no way implied access to liberty – that liberty in which the English rejoiced by political tradition as a result of the victories of 1688, as Edmund Burke had just reminded them (*Reflections on the Revolution in France*, 1790). Nationalist propaganda designed to preserve social order in Britain organised itself around this theme. The caricature, in which the smallholder and the city artisan spoke turn by turn through John Bull, asserted the existence of a rural and urban petty bourgeoisie capable of having its own opinions, and perhaps even reservations. It was indispensable to offer these groups ideological nourishment, to remind them of certain traditionally established values; and the caricature was charged with the dissemination of these values.

The campaign which opened around 1792 undoubtedly looks like the response of the defenders of order confronted with potential danger, the threat of internal subversion. But national sentiment, even amongst those who complained of the intrigues of those in power, remained dormant. John Bull possessed a double face because the social groupings he represented were not homogeneous; their ideology was not necessarily coherent, and their reactions varied according to the conjuncture – that is, according to how serious the danger to England's coasts appeared. A propaganda message, the message of the loyalist caricatures, only had a chance of being noticed because it answered some need, some desire to be called on to participate. Two techniques were used: the creation of an 'anti-model', a foil to John Bull, whence the multitude of caricatures directed at the French revolutionaries or at the men of the Empire (soldiers, the 'Corsican ogre', etc.); and conservative propaganda, intended to persuade John Bull of the excellence of his institutions and the necessity of preserving them. Thus the 'Farmer John Bull', faithful to his 'Master George', refuses to listen to the demon who tries to corrupt him (*Alecto and his train at the gate of Pandemonium, or the recruiting sergeant enlisting John Bull into the revolution service*, 4 July 1791); the devil in person may take a hand, as in the *The tree of liberty with the devil tempting John Bull* (23 May 1798). All proposed reform is equated with revolutionary initiatives which would put John Bull and his kingdom in peril. In a fairly elaborate engraving which appeared in 1805, it may be noted that the Pope and the dissenters are alike treated as the enemies of England; John Bull forbids them entry to a church inscribed 'King, Church, The Constitution' (*John Bull's turnpike gate*, 15 May 1805). This recalls the cry of the Gordon rioters of June 1780, who demonstrated against freedom of Catholic worship. There were close and recognised links between the dissenting Protestant groups, who in 1787 demanded the abolition of the Test and Corporations Acts (discriminatory laws forbidding nonconformists access to certain offices, and limiting their rights as British citizens), and the reformers. The same men – Dr Price[17] and Dr Priestley, dissenting ministers – demanded in 1790 the abolition of the Test Act and the reform of Parliament; both requests were rejected by a House increasingly uneasy at recent developments in France. Members of the opposition too were treated at times as enemies of the nation and of its institutions. In 1794 James Sayers attacked the peace overtures proposed by the opposition (Lansdowne, Stanhope, Grafton) in a cartoon showing Stanhope as an executioner preparing to decapitate the bull John Bull, while Grafton delivers the Magna Carta over to the butcher. The slide from defence of liberty and its symbols to an absoolute insistence on loyalty amongst those who are its guardians was easily accomplished. It is thus possible to see in John Bull, during the period in which he took shape, the playing out of a rivalry between two contradictory tendencies. This rivalry bears witness to the dissatisfaction of a section of public opinion with regard to political power, its representatives and their acts; and, simultaneously, to the will to spread nationalist and loyalist propaganda at the point where this dissatisfaction was becoming manifest, among the urban and rural common people – and not without success.

While the provenance of the ideological campaigns around the theme of 'Church and King' may be readily identified, it is more difficult to attribute to some reforming group or any other organisation of the flood of caricatures showing John Bull complaining about his rulers, the measures for which they are responsible, the situations in which they have involved the country. This type of caricature expresses a demand which it is possible to localise in social terms, and which, as I have emphasised, converges with a set of political objectives, defined by those who in 1792 declared their refusal 'to be considered either of a ministerial or opposition party (names of which we are tired, having been so often deceived by both)'.[18] But the convergence established here in no way implies that these caricatures were produced by the reformist movements so disturbing at that time to the English government, and it would be a mistake to reduce them to the level of anti-governmental propaganda, disseminated with the aim of encouraging these shifts in public opinion. John Bull's 'radicalism' is not so much a clearly formulated political message as the reaction of a fraction of the social body, in a particular historical situation, to the practices of the interchangeable actors of institutional political life.

IV

The content of the John Bull character, its contradictory aspects (both 'malcontent' and 'loyalist') included, expressed an ideology specific to one socioeconomic group. Two other points, to do with, on the one hand, the process by which the engravings were produced, and, on the other, with their nature as commercial objects, point to a particular social location for this national stereotype.

To attribute political positions to the authors of the caricatures, or, similarly, to reduce their function to that of paid propagandists of one political coterie or another, is (as I have already observed) a hazardous matter. Undoubtedly, politicians occasionally tried to purchase the services of a satirical artist, and obtained complete or partial satisfaction. (Thus Gillray moderated, though he did not stop, his attacks on political personalities such as Pitt and Sheridan, and on members of the royal family, following the orders of Canning, who had promised him a pension – and who gave him one.) There is, however, a difference in kind between the mental process which satirises an identifiable celebrity (and the more identifiable because caricatured), and that which is dealing with a stereotype, the 'real' representative of a general category of individuals. The authors of the caricatures must have felt some affinity with this anonymous and yet distinctive character. Artisans, engravers established on their own account or working to order, printsellers, cartoonists, all were part of that 'popular' London which was also a source of political dissent. John Bull's complaint was not strange or indifferent to them. They certainly heard it; they probably took it up and repeated it. In one of Gillray's cartoons, *John Bull and his dog Faithful*, published on 20 April 1796, a ragged, mutilated, blind John Bull is insiduously drawn towards the abyss by his dog Pitt, while the dog Sheridan ferociously attacks his wooden leg. Draper Hill rightly draws attention to the remarkable resemblance between John Bull's face and that of the artist himself (see his self-portrait, done around 1795, in the National Portrait Gallery)[19] It would be difficult to take the process of identification with the national stereotype any further.

Secondly, at that time in England there was a highly developed market for cartoons which was limited not by censorship, but only by the restrictions on raw materials imposed because of the war in 1793 (since wood was required for the building of ships, paper pulp became a superfluous luxury and excessive consumption was punishable by fine). Buying cartoons, or hiring an album of caricatures for the evening, was not only the pastime of court families or of politicians, but also of a more popular public, the artisans and small traders of the capital, and of those hotbeds of radicalism, Westminster and the City. John Bull was the mirror, a distorting one of course, of the public he addressed, customers to whom it was important to offer a merchandise that would reflect their preoccupations and which summarised through example, in terse and forceful language, the reasons for their discontent. The essence of these reasons is to be found in the petition presented by the Common Council of the City of London to the Prince Regent in 1812, who had by then reigned in the place of his demented father for over a year. The representatives of the City regretted that this transfer of power had not led to a cleansing of the political system. They observed:

> We have continued to witness the same system of profligacy
> in the expenditure of the public money; the same system of
> governing by undue influence and corruption; the same system
> of delusion in regard to the circulating medium and finance
> of the country; the same system of arbitrary and grievous
> assessment and collection of taxes . . . ; the same system of
> introducing into the heart of the country foreign troops; the
> same system of persecuting the press . . . and finally, the
> same system of coercive restrictions on the freedom of
> commerce, by which many of our merchants and
> manufacturers have been involved in ruin.[20]

In another language, readable by and visible to anyone, the John Bull character repeated this over and over again in the years between 1790 and 1815.

It may seem surprising that a public should so readily identify itself with this lump of flesh, lacking in attraction as in malice. Should we evoke here a hypothetical 'national psychology', anti-intellectual, proud of its bluntness? Or rather ask whether this problem of identification with a 'model' is not in fact that of a later period, and of a different social group, more demanding with regard to the appearance of its own image? John Bull was later to become a respectable gentleman farmer, sufficiently comfortable financially for identification to seem desirable, yet near enough for it also to be plausible. This elevation in the social hierarchy during the course of the nineteenth century indicates that a different class in its turn claimed the national myth as the representative of its own values, the mouthpiece of its ideology.

At the turning of the eighteenth and nineteenth centuries, John Bull belonged primarily to the urban petty bourgeoisie. As an invention, he is in fact more a townsman than a countryman, and

2 'STAMPING IT OUT. A painful necessity both for John Bull and for the Afghan Scorpion.'

in this latter role he seems more closely related to the village rustic as the townsman imagines him than to the real English agricultural worker. He may be socially defined by an examination of his constant attributes at any given period; his outlines can also be delineated by excluding everything which he is not – all those who he is not, and who, perhaps, do not recognise themselves in him. If John Bull complains of the income tax, it is because he finds himself hit by it, and therefore enjoys a standard of living which places him above what would a century later be called the 'poverty line'. George Cruickshank, at the time when the Corn Laws were voted in, created a disturbing, half-starved John Bull, ready to emigrate to escape destitution.[21] This was an exceptional case; such a character has no future as the prototype of a nation. Should one conclude that when the revolt of the most impoverished creates its own mythical characters, they generally remain invisible? There is no popular traditional image of Captain Swing, no General Lud implanted in any folk memory. They are faceless heroes.

Popular iconography, since it is part of the shifting patterns of society, contains no unchanging archetypes. One may find constant factors, deriving from aspects of the myth (John Bull is well-nourished, etc.); but a 'national' image is primarily an image projected by a social category within that nation. The character of John Bull, in the form in which he was known between the beginnings of the French Revolution and the end of the Napoleonic Wars, possesses attributes which make him the representative of a particular group, and it is reasonable to suppose that he addresses himself above all to those from amongst whom he came. This might lead us to believe that the 'national stereotype' is effective only in so far as it expresses a unitary ideology which the social reality denies. The ability of social group at a given moment to impose its image indicates that at this point the group possesses a certain coherence, that it is becoming aware of its economic vitality, its political weight. By tracing the evolution of a national stereotype, then, it may be possible to follow the ebb and flow of the diverse classes which compose the social tissue of the nation, and their changing self-perceptions.

Notes

1 The French king, Louis XIV.
2 John Arbuthnot, *The History of John Bull*, Clarendon Press, Oxford, 1976, p. 9. (Translator's note: The author uses C. Bruneteau's bilingual edition – Aubier, Paris, 1976 – and adds 'For a complete and detailed analysis of this work, Bruneteau's introduction . . . is indispensable'.)

3 John Arbuthnot, *op. cit.*, pp. 49–50

4 *The Sturdy Beggar*, British Museum Print Room.

5 *Gloria Mundi*, British Museum Print Room.

6 *Fashion before Ease*, 2 January 1793, British Museum Print Room.

7 M. D. George, *The British Museum Catalogue of Political and Personal Satires*, British Museum London, 1938, 1942, 1947, vols VI, VII, VIII.

8 An allusion to the naval victory at Aboukir, called by the English the Battle of the Nile.

9 See note 8.

10 These five caricatures are all by Gillray, British Museum Print Room.

11 *A new map of England and France*, already mentioned, or *Antisaccharites, or John Bill and his family leaving off the use of sugar* (Gillray, 27 March 1790). George III appeared as John Bull some ten times between 1789 and 1810.

12 Isaac Cruickshank treats the theme in an identical way: *He would be a soldier, or the history of John Bull's warlike expedition* (1 July 1793).

13 Besides the works by Gillray already mentioned, there are numerous satirical engravings on the subject of taxation. For example on 24 November 1797 Pitt proposed to Parliament a considerable rise in indirect taxation (it was to be almost trebled). Between the date of his speech and mid-January 1798, out of a total of fifteen caricatures produced, this measure was attacked more or less explicitly in ten (M. D. George, *The British Museum Catalogue of Political and Personal Satires*).

14 Thomas Paine, *The Rights of Man*, Penguin, Harmondsworth, 1969, pp. 234–5.

15 In 1795 Parliament passed two laws (the Combination Acts) forbidding 'seditious' publications and public meetings. Around this time the government was taking a whole series of repressive measures (arrests, trials, etc.) to control the population.

16 Another engraving, identical in technique and intention, published in 1793 shows a Bible on the mantelpiece of the 'miserable Englishman', and pinned to the wall are the words of the song 'O the Roast Beef of Old England' (*French Happiness, English Misery*, 3 January 1793).

17 On the forenoon of the fourth of November last, Doctor Richard Price, a Nonconforming minister of eminence, preached at the Dissenting meeting-house of the Old Jewry, to his club or society, a very extraordinary miscellaneous sermon, in which there are some good moral and religious sentiments, and not ill expressed, mixed up with a sort of porridge of various political opinions and reflections; but the Revolution in France is the grand ingredient in the caldron. (Edmund Burke, *Reflections on the Revolution in France*, Penguin, Harmondsworth, 1973, p. 93).

18 Society for Constitutional Information, 14 March 1792; quoted by S. Maccoby, *The English Radical Tradition*, London, 1966, p. 56.

19 Draper Hill, *Mr Gillray, the Caricaturist*, Phaidon, London, 1965, p. 149.

20 New Annual Register, 28 April 1810; quoted by S. Maccoby, *The English Radical Tradition*, London, 1966, p. 75.
21 George Cruickshank, 1792–1878, the son of Isaac Cruickshank, who was the author of many caricatures representing John Bull.

3   A FANCY PORTRAIT
John Bull in his new walking dress

2
Britannia

MADGE DRESSER

The earliest sculptural representations of Britannia were excavated in 1980 in Aphrodesias in Turkey. There, a series of commemorative reliefs dating from the first century AD celebrated the Roman conquest of Britain by Claudius. Britannia, her name probably derived from the name of one of the native Celtic tribes, denotes the genius or local spirit of the land. There had long been a convention in Greek art to represent cities and provinces as idealised female figures. By Hellenistic times, subject nations were sometimes also modelled on actual male and female captives.[1] The Britannia of Aphrodesias seem to belong to the first category.

In one of the reliefs[2] Britannia appears heroically naked save for a military cloak and a Phrygian hat. The Phrygian hat, originally a sign of a liberated slave, was conventionally the symbol of free status. However, Britannia's impending subjugation is denoted by the fact that she is leaning against the Emperor Claudius, who seems to be about to carry her off. In the relief reproduced in Figure 3,[3] Claudius appears helmeted and naked with a 'cruel expression on his face'. He is manifestly in the act of overpowering Britannia, who is here explicitly represented as an Amazon, in a short tunic with one breast bared. I suspect this allusion to the battle between Hercules (Claudius) and Hippolyte the Amazon Queen, itself an allegory about the rule of men over women, may have been inspired by contemporary accounts about Britain being ruled by women. William Camden, the Elizabethan antiquarian maintained that 'learned men think Aristotle spoke of the Briton when he writeth that "certain war like nations beyond the Celtes were subject to the government of women" '.[4] Camden adds that a number of Romans including Tacitus believed it was 'usual . . . with the Britons . . . to make warre under the conduct of women; neither mattereth it whether(sic) sex beare rule over them'.[5] This

4   Claudius overpowering Britannia (the
'Aphrodesias relief').

interpretation of the Amazon motif seems even more likely when
we consider that Boadicea's exploits against the Romans must have
been fresh in the minds of those commissioning the sculptures at
Aphrodesias.

A figure[6] excavated at Dumfriesshire and dating from *c.* 210 AD,
picturing the highly syncretistic deity 'Brigantia' was probably a
local fertility goddess, yet she bears many of the features associated
with the Britannia figure found on Romano-British coins from the
reign of Hadrian and Antoninus Pius, and seems to be a prototype
of the Britannia goddess whose cult was followed in Britain.[7]
Brigantia (the name of a large Celtic tribe) bears the wings of
victory, wears Minerva's aegis and holds her shield and spear. Her
head is encircled by a turreted crown (probably representing the
city of York). The turreted crown underlines the resemblances
between Brigantia, Britannia (of the coins minted in 210–11 AD

and the figure Roma. Jocelyn Toynbee observed that the Dea Roma also descended from 'a fusion of the Pallas and the Amazon types'.[8] There are also resemblances between Roman representations of Italia and Britannia in certain coins. The turreted crown and the half moon which appears on Britannia's shield in one of these early coins[9] link Britannia to the moon goddess Cybele. This Phrygian goddess commanded an orgiastic cult which itself is associated with that of the Great Mother cults of Asia Minor.[10] There are hints in the historical record of a possible continuity linking the worship of Cybele with that of the Britannia cult and with the later veneration of St Brigit, the Virgin Mary and Elizabeth I. Could this be what Robert Graves had in mind when he explained the 'extraordinary hold' Elizabeth had over her subjects' affections in terms of their 'unconscious hankering' for the old moon goddess cult?[11]

Be that as it may, Britannia herself seems to have disappeared after the fall of Rome. She does not re-emerge until after the Reformation. In the interim she was probably reabsorbed into the myriad array of Celtic, Roman and Anglo-Saxon goddesses, many of whom were themselves incorporated into early English Christianity. Indeed, most of modern Britannia's attributes seem to have been anticipated by a variety of pagan and Christian figures. Before Britannia's return, it was, for example, the Anglian goddess Herth (Earth) and, later, Fortuna who presided over the national fate. The connection between Mother Nature, Earth, Fortune and Britannia are later evidenced in eighteenth-century cartoons which on occasion show the national muse with the wheel of fortune.[12]

Britannia's moral qualities appear to stem directly from the seven virtues, faith, hope, charity, justice, prudence, temperance and fortitude. These female personifications, along with Lady Fortune's wheel (itself associated with the wheel of the zodiac), adorned the interiors of a number of medieval English churches and were familiar figures of religious lore.[13]

Britannia's more martial qualities remind us not only of Athene, but of the Virgin Mother, whose powers as a calmer of the seas and protector of the righteous in battle were well honoured in England after the Crusades.[14] But there was no call for Britannia herself to exist until there was conceived a politically united entity for her to represent.

In a cosmos suffused with moral purpose, symbolism in the form of emblems, personifications and myth was profoundly necessary.[15] It was central to the medieval culture and continued to be so into the early modern period in Britain. The Tudors, for example, were symbolically asserting their political authority when they claimed Brute, the nephew of the fabled Aeneas, as their putative ancestor. They were confirming this authority when they filled their coronation processions with children personifying nature, grace and fortune, and when they identified Queen Mary with Athena, the virgin goddess of wisdom, rectitude and virtue.[16]

It was under Mary, incidentally, that a Catholic prototype of Britannia, 'Anglia', makes an appearance on a medal struck by Giovani Covino in 1554.[17] Based on a Roman theme, 'Anglia Resurges' (in contemporary dress) is shown kneeling at the feet of Pope Julius III with Cardinal Pole and the King of France (?) looking on. This intermingling of religious and national themes was to become a commonplace of English national symbolism after the break with Rome.

The ceremonies and celebrations of Elizabeth's reign were similarly shot through with allegorical meaning. They were typical of a world of which it could still be said that 'nothing had a single meaning and nothing lacked significance'.[18] The outburst of 'intense patriotic pride' characteristic of the Elizabethan age [19] found symbolic expression in the chivalric cult around the queen. Influenced by the 'rediscovery' of classical culture, Tudor poets and playwrights compared their monarch to Cybele, Isis, Pandora and, most interestingly for our present purposes, Astraea.

The importance of the symbol of Elizabeth as Astraea has been deftly drawn by Frances Yates, who explains that Astraea (whose cult, by the way, had a following in Roman Britain) was a Roman goddess identified with fertility and justice.[20] Legend had it that Astraea had once reigned on Earth during a golden age, but fled when human misrule and corruption prevailed, to take her place amongst the stars as the sign of Virgo. She would, however, some day return to earth, when a strong imperial monarchy, head of both church and state, reasserted itself. Only then, could a new worldwide golden age ensue.[21]

This story's theme of messianic redemption had long led Christian commentators to identify the fertile yet virgin Astraea with the Mother of Christ.[22] Its advocacy of imperial rule had a particular appeal for Reformation England which was enjoying its own golden age of prosperity and colonial expansion under its own virgin queen. In these ways, the identification of Elizabeth with Astraea 'touched tremendous spiritual and historical issues'.[23] It confirmed an English patriotism, a dislike of the Papacy, a loyalty to the monarch and a sense that the destiny of the world rode on the shirt-tails of English predominance.

Even after Elizabeth, allegory continued to perform an important political function. The 'significante signes' employed in court masques, royal processions and civic pageants were closely modelled on the (largely Italian) emblem books which had been circulating widely in England since the late sixteenth century.[24] A study of the 'hieroglyphics' thus employed suggest that shifts in political ideology may have been reflected in political imagery. For example, is it not significant that Britannia, who makes her reappearance when James I first assumed the somewhat wishful title of King of Great Britain, becomes increasingly supplanted by the image of Pallas Athene (Minerva)? Why did this happen? And why, at about the same time, did the image of Astraea fade into relative insignificance? Was Astraea too closely associated in the popular consciousness with the virgin queen to be successfully exploited by James?[25] Or was it also that Astraea may have been identified with proponents of an occult mysticism whose supposed tendencies toward witchcraft and political partisanship were soon to earn them the disfavour of the king?

It is in the first decade of James's reign that Britannia is most frequently invoked as a symbol of national unity. The earliest extant portrayal of Britannia since Roman times, the frontispiece to the 1610 English edition of William Camden's chorographical work *Britannia*,[26] features a relatively unimpressive Britannia compared to the evocative drawings of Neptune and Ceres below her. The larger figures symbolised the union of ocean and earth, so important to an island nation. But Britannia had a significant function here, as the incarnation of a common British identity. This bareheaded Britannia, with her ensign, short tunic and spiked shield, is clearly derived from certain Romano–British coins which Camden himself had studied and which presented a specifically 'British' Britannia rather than a standardised replica of Pallas Athene.[27]

Nor is there much of Athena in the wild-haired Britannia pictured in England's first emblem book, published by Henry Peacham in 1612.[28] The verse accompanying this oddly emblematic figure suggests Britannia is shown as she was 'Drawen in Old Antiquities'. Possibly this alludes to the Roman coin thought to commemorate the defeat of an unsuccessful Brigantian uprising of 155 AD. Unlike the more imperial Britannias of other Roman coins, this particular one had been designed to convey an air of 'dejection and defeat'.[29]

It is the Britannia accompanying Michael Drayton's poem *Poly-Olbion* published in 1612[30] which is the most remarkably distinctive of these early symbols. Drayton's emblem is a resplendent and queenly figure who holds a sceptre of rule in one hand and a cornucopia in the other. She resembles the figure of *Fides Publica* (public happiness), a conflation of the emblems of peace and plenty.[31] Her robe 'of white taffaty, [is] limm'd with the mappe of England'.[32] Her breast is bared, Amazon style, reminding us of the Aphrodesias relief (Figure 3). Her pearls represent virginity, despite the fact that Brute, Caesar, Hengist and William I, shown dwarfed beside her, are described in the accompanying verse as her chosen, if insistent, lovers. This seeming contradiction is explained by the fact that her virginity is here associated, as it would have been in pre-Christian times, with autonomy rather than chastity.[33] This is a puissant female figure who strongly recalls the majesty of a *Magna Mater*.[34] But the most striking point about this Britannia is that it is nearly identical both in pose and surrounding attributes to the picture of Astraea in the 1605 edition of Pierre Matthieu's *L'Histoire de la France*.[35]

Britannia is seldom invoked as the national genius under the early Stuarts after this first flurry of early portrayals. Instead the symbolic incarnation of the nation becomes increasingly bound up with the authority of the King himself, and as such Pallas Athene/Minerva rather than Astraea or Britannia becomes the favoured goddess.

Athene was used in the popular emblem books of the day as the basis of a variety of emblems symbolising aspects of statecraft and governance.[36] Representing wisdom and defensive war, the virgin Athene was also the goddess of weaving and numeracy, two activities which made her particularly suitable for an emerging commercial nation. If Astraea dominated the 'New World Arch' of James's coronation procession,[37] it was Pallas Athene which James's queen chose to portray in a Hampton Court masque shortly before.[38] This masque, in which the goddesses were amended to embody political virtues befitting the occasion, demoted Astraea into a not very important representative of justice.

A later court masque by Ben Jonson of 1615 plainly established the superior status which Pallas was to enjoy over Astraea (and her sister figure 'the Golden Age') in Jacobean iconography. Jove is clearly the divinely-endowed James. Minerva is here the instrument of James's wisdom. This distinctly patriarchal association between Pallas and kingly authority was purposefully made. Pallas, who sprang, fully armèd and grown from Jove's forehead, was allied in classical myth with the male rather than the female gods of Mount Olympus.

It is not surprising that one influential contemporary in James's court envisaged the proposed union between England and Scotland (Wales is rarely referred to) as a fair and beautiful goddess called Pallas 'because having one only parent, she resideth in Jupiters braine, even in the chiefe seate of his wisedome'.[39] How much more appealing Pallas must have been to James with his hatred of witches and his insistence of the divine right of kings than the visionary ambitions of the occult Astraea.

Britannia does appear in a 1628 Lord Mayor's Show by Thomas Dekker. It is only in this civic pageant that we still get a feel of Drayton's mother goddess. 'Majestically attirde, fitting to her Greatnesse', she occupies the dominant seat in 'her watch tower', the pillars of which represent the houses of York and Lancaster, 'once divided, but now Joyned into One Glorious Building, to Support this Royal Kingdom'. Her addresses to the Lord Mayor are exhortatory and described by the figure herself as 'a Mother's Counsel'.[40] Readers will have noticed that Britannia here is an emblem of English unity. This ambiguity is to remain a feature of the Britannia figure. Sometimes she represents Britain, sometimes England alone.

Britannia's affinity with the Virgin Mary is historically and iconographically complex. We have seen that Mary has had symbolic associations with Astraea. A nursing Mary had also been transmuted into a personification of the Catholic Church, one which itself resembled pagan and gnostic representations of Mother Nature (Ceres), and Divine Wisdom (Sophia) respectively. Elizabeth was similarly characterised as 'the lactating mother of the church',[41] and as late as the 1740s Britannia was portrayed in one print as a nursing mother.[42]

In Catholic symbolism, a ship had long been a metaphor for the church. A mid-seventeenth-century print shows a female in a ship representing the Anglican Church whose resemblance to the Catholic Church is undeniable and whose pagan connections are evidenced by symbols which formerly belonged to moon and fertility goddesses.[43] Like the Virgin Mary, Britannia is the intermediary between God and man, a function also performed by the female world soul of the neo-Platonists and popularised in Francis Quarles' best-selling emblem book of the late seventeenth century.[44] The garden precinct and the rose, both symbols which had been used in connection with England, were also Mary's symbols.[45]

Britannia as Mary Dolorosa can be seen in the engraving of 1682 featured in Figure 4. Here she is closely identified with the Established Church and linked to the eye of Providence. Defenceless (Astraea's sword of Justice is now firmly in the hands of the male Almighty), this demurely downcast lady is about to be importuned by a Janus-headed creature – half Jesuit, half Puritan. Britannia here represents right religion about to be martyred 'by her own viperous brood'.

In one print of 1684 the hydra of religious heresy threatens, not

5 'Britania', 1682 (British Museum).

Mary, as was traditional, but a decidedly Minervan Britannia. This Britannia is unarmed, for it is Charles II who, significantly, receives the sword of justice from heaven and who tramples the hydra. [46]

Britannia still retained this religious dimension after the Glorious Revolution of 1688. An engraving produced the following year represents 'Britania' in possession of her religion and liberty under the protection of William of Orange. She is shown trampling on a Catholic mitre and other papist symbols. [47]

But despite such Protestant sentiments, the influence of the Virgin lingered on in political imagery. In one print published on the occasion of the Lisbon earthquake in 1756, Britannia replaces the Madonna. Called 'The Acceptable Fast: Or, Britannia's Maternal Call to Her Children to Deep Humiliation, Repentance and Amendment in Heart and Life,' [48] it is among the first of an increasing number of drawings which by mid-century had begun to feature Britannia. [49] Here, her links with the Virgin Mary and the *Magna Mater* are evidenced by her pose. [50] Arising from the globe from which she has just risen, her arms are outstretched in a Madonna-like supplication toward the slightly smaller figures representing her nation. She appeals to them for unity and morality. This is an interesting document of the embryonic class tensions generated by economic growth, for on Britannia's right are the upper classes and, on her left, mingled together, are the middling ranks and the labouring poor. Britannia, with an almost ostentatious impartiality, tells magistrates to be fairer, lawyers to be less greedy, and ladies less frivolous. The poor are enjoined merely to be virtuous. Britannia, then, had become an acceptably Protestant version of the Virgin Mary. And just as respectable Englishwomen became the little madonnas of the familial hearth, Britannia had come to represent the conscience of the nation.

Commercialisation and colonialisation intensified the exploitation of a desacralised mother earth. These developments seem to have affected the imagery of the nation-as-female, especially in British political caricature. Whilst there is still a continuing tradition of referring to Britannia as a dignified mother, there is also by the mid-eighteenth century the tendency to portray her as innocent virtue outraged. 'Again and again', Herbert Atherton tells us in his study of *Political Caricature in the Age of Hogarth*, Britannia is shown 'naked and disgraced'. These portrayals, usually in protest against some political abuse, are characterised by what Atherton discerns as 'chivalry conjoined with patriotism'. [51] But it is a debased sort of chivalry compared with that accorded to Astraea. Britannia is variously dismembered, buggered, ridden and even flogged naked with 'a Scottish Thistle'. [52] There is a salacious prurience about the expressions of indignation her unjust punishments excite, and there is the clear implication that the lady nation, like one's lady wife or one's private property, should be enjoyed only by those who legally own her. Atherton does note the 'vital and masculine tone' and elsewhere the 'cavalier' attitude that informs some of these prints where patriotism and personal honour seem conflated.[53] I agree that the origins of this chivalry are aristocratic. They are allied to warnings against the dangers of an effeminising luxury. As such, they are part and parcel of what Kenny calls 'the country house ethos'. The honour with which patriotism is identified is a specifically *male* defined honour[54] based on the mastery and ownership of nature and woman. This becomes all the more apparent when we contrast the sentimentalisation of Britannia's plight to the openly lascivious treatment of non-European nations in these caricatures. Such nations are almost always personified as naked and available females, bearing the trappings of nature's produce. The difference between the portrayals mirror the double standard of sexual conduct 'at home' and abroad.

The chivalry which persists is not wholly cynical, and still has some links with an older organic world view where the earth's resources were to be 'husbanded' with respect. But such respect goes not to mother nature now but to one's nation alone. Furthermore, the legacy of chivalry in the hermetic-cabalistic tradition was always double-edged, coming as it did from a world in which the masculine and female spheres were 'separate but equal'. The eighteenth-century heir of this tradition was freemasonry. It evolved its lodges and ceremonials at the same time as women were consigned to a dependent domestic sphere, and there is a misogynist ethos about many of the rules and rituals of English freemasonry. Margaret Jacob has shown that whilst freemasonry in Holland interpreted the egalitarian principle and notions of chivalry in a manner which allowed for the equal status of women as freemasons, its English counterpart 'clearly advocated equality for men (other than bondsmen) within the lodges, glorified domesticity and sexual fidelity, yet at the same time betrayed resentment and discomfort on the question of rights and abilities'. Thus whilst mason's wives at one lodge were presented with a pair of gloves on their husband's initiation, they were barred from membership along with 'irreligious libertines' and other reprobate males. One lodge's rules baldly stated 'no women, no eunuchs.' Ceremonials reputedly involved the baring of the breast to prove one was not a female. The imagery and attitudes of freemasonry in Britain influenced the political discourse not only of Jacobites and Hanoverian royalists but of pantheistic radicals as well.[56]

'The Parricide', published in 1776, is an example of the more sensationally misogynist treatment of Britannia discussed above. In this print[57] America is represented by the Indian woman, who, untypically for this period, is fully clothed. She approaches her mother Britannia with murderous intent. A tomahawk in one hand, a knife in the other, she tramples Britannia's shield, urged on by the radical Wilkes. Behind the treacherous America is the hag of revolution, with flaming torches held high over her Medusa-like head. This is a very old emblem, probably deriving from the orgiastic cults of the Magna Mater in Greece and Asia Minor. In 'The Parricide' the terrible aspect of female-identified nature is identified with revolution and distinguished from the patriarchal order symbolised by the Minerva/Britannia figure. We seem to be looking at the two opposing aspects of the *Magna Mater*, a dichotomy which appears again and again in political caricature and which suggests a connection between female chastity and political order. Certainly the shrew betokens anarchy and violent revolution in France as well as England after 1789 and whatever its origins had tremendous psychological power, playing as it did on fear not only of murder but possibly of castration as well.[58] The heroine of 'The Parricide' is Britannia. Her plight is designed to arouse more than righteous indignation in what would be its largely male as well as anti-revolutionary audience. Britannia is held fast by members of the opposition (who style themselves 'patriots'). Her girdle (symbol of virginity) is missing, her legs are open, her torso is naked, and her face looks out to the audience with a passivity John Berger has found is characteristic of female nudes intended for male patrons of the arts.

It is revealing that a pro-American print, 'The Able Doctor, or America Swallowing the Bitter Draught', (1774) protesting against the tax on tea, used a similar approach. A half-naked America is held down as her buxom mother (Britannia) weeps helplessly. The hapless 'patient' is force-fed tea, and, whilst the doctor politicians restrain her, the Earl of Sandwich peers up her skirts. The misogyny here is drawn from eighteenth-century attitudes toward nature and is interestingly couched in terms of contemporary medical practice. The point I should like to emphasise is that although it is true, as Hugh Cunningham has pointed out, that patriotism could be invoked on behalf of radicalism, such patriotic radicalism shared certain attitudes about women and nature with its political enemies.[59]

A less passive Britannia, in a martial guise, was depicted grappling with a female France and hurling thunderbolts on two commemorative medals of the early eighteenth century.[60] But more conventionally, this 'Minervan' Britannia was utilised in the glorification of the war hero. Her portrayal on the ceiling of the Great Hall at Blenheim Palace, commemorating Marlborough's celebrated victory against the French, is perhaps the most famous example of this theme. Painted by Sir James Thornhill in 1716, it shows an armoured and helmeted Britannia surveying the battle plans which the kneeling Duke has had presented before her. In her left hand is a laurel wreath which she is shortly to bestow upon him. (There is probably an intention here to associate Britannia with that 'combination magistrate and Great Mother', Queen Anne, but the identification with the sickly Queen, who lost all seventeen of her children, does not seem to have proved very popular.)[61]

The Royal Norfolk Regiment which had fought under Marlborough at Blenheim later adopted Britannia as its emblem during the Napoleonic Wars.[62] But, not surprisingly, Britannia tended generally to be associated with naval power. Nelson's death was an extremely popular theme in the broadsides, paintings and commemorative pottery of the early nineteenth century, and Britannia is almost invariably shown with him. Nelson's apotheosis followed the classical tradition in which great heroes gained a sort of immortality which placed them midway between gods and men.[63] In the memorials to Nelson, Britannia played a role which sometimes recalled that of the *Mater Dolorosa* ('Behold the portrait of my darling son . . . Britannia weeps!'),[64] and sometimes the Athene/Mary figure who ensured victory to the righteous ('Thy name, (my son) shall be recorded in the page of History, on tablets of the brightest gold').[65]

As the weeping Mary, Britannia, like the women of that period, could express the emotions which men were expected to suppress. Britannia weeps at the death of war heroes and royals, but John Bull seems to cry only when he has to pay too much tax. In one broadside commemorating Nelson's death, Britannia with trident in hand walks on water:

> O'er Nelson's tomb with silent grief oppress'd
> Britannia mourn'd her hero now at rest
> But thou bright laurels ne'er shall fade with Years
> Whose leaves are water'd by a nation's tears

The poem ends with a cheer for 'England, home and beauty' which underlines the connection between patriotic sentiment, domesticity and a proprietorial attitude toward the loveliness of both the English landscape and its female inhabitants.[66]

In a painting on glass from the collections of the Nelson museum

Britannia brings her hero home to shore accompanied by Fame
and Peace(?) in an aquatic chariot. The scene contains elements
which remind us both of Mary at the cross and the myth of the
Valkyries.

Although the masonic influence on political imagery was broadly
patriarchal and at times explicitly misogynist, this was not the only
legacy of the old hermetic tradition. There was still a popular
undercurrent of reverence for a living mother earth. This reverence
was based on what J. F. C. Harrison has called a 'simple unintellec-
tual type of neo-Platonism' which continued to inform folk culture
even after industrialisation.[67] This neo-Platonism was closely
connected with some of the radical millenarian sects of the late
eighteenth and early nineteenth centuries. The female messianism
of Smith, Southcott and the St Simonians, along with the feminism
of many Owenites, formed the less well-known legacy of the
occult tradition. These cults were grounded in a belief in a gendered
and organic cosmos in which the feminine as well as the masculine
principle was to be accorded due respect. The thrust of scientific
rationalism had not fully penetrated the millenarian mentality.
There, Dekker's mother goddess rather than Bacon's Athene felt
more at home. So perhaps it was no mere fluke that at least
one feminist correspondent to an Owenite journal signed herself
'Astraea'.[68]

However, this radical sectarian tradition was like a subterranean
river which surfaced briefly only to go underground again. The
dominant patriarchal imagery featured far more prominently by
the nineteenth century on behalf of both reactionary and
progressive political causes.

The symbolism of patriotic reaction is fully exploited in Cruickshank's well-known cartoon of 1819 (Figure 5).[69] The title,
'DEATH or LIBERTY! or Britannia & the Virtues of the Constitution in danger of Violation from the grt. Political Libertine, Radical
Reform!' just about says it all. Political radicalism and sexual licence
are conflated at every opportunity; see the note by Britannia's feet
which reads 'Radical Libery – i.e. To Take Liberties'. This idea
dates back to at least the Civil War.

In this print death replaces the hag of revolution, though a
broadside of 1804 shows that the connection between women,
witchcraft and death had already been established:

> Of the maxims of France let us ever beware
> Her Liberty's – chains and her Friendship a snare
> Her boasted Equality, is but a Breath
> Her fraternal Embraces – the Dagger of Death[70]

6 'DEATH or LIBERTY! or Britannia & the *Virtues* of the *Constitution* in danger of *Violation* from the grt. Political Libertine, *Radical Reform*', by G. Humphrey, 1819.

Death's private parts consist of an hourglass (the emblem of mortality) and a deadly shaft which again combine to confirm the ancient Chrisitian equation of sex and death. There are snakes (a negative female symbol in traditional iconography, if not in Freudian symbolism) stealing out from under Liberty's pole. Behind death, various chained and demonised personifications of sin take shelter under the cloak (literally) of radical reform. Behind them, a conflagration rages and casts the left side of the print (the side of Reform) into darkness.[71] On the side of light is Britannia. She has slipped from the rock of religion and is being overpowered by the monster whose embraces (he is grabbing at her bosom and running his bony fingers through her hair) are clearly more than fraternal. Her shield still protects her virtue, but only just. She carries the sword of 'laws' (note, not justice) which doubles as an emanation from a kingly crown in heaven. This is an almost Burkean allusion to the mystical function of law and establishes Britannia once more as an intermediary figure between the patriarchal *logos* and the realm of human affairs.

The pages of *Punch*, founded in 1841, are full of cartoons of Britannia, at least as far as up to the First World War. Although *Punch*'s accomplished cartoonists were clearly acquainted with classical symbolism, the Britannias they drew often owed as much to their individual preoccupations and preconceptions as to the emblematic conventions of the Western tradition. Britannia is usually prettified or made slightly ludicrous in the incidental cartoons which abound in *Punch*. In the full-page drawings she tends to fall into one of four categories: the vulnerable virgin courted and/or threatened by the powers of the day; the compassionate weeping madonna who mourns national tragedies and cares for the helpless; 'She Who Must Be Obeyed', the slightly ridiculous but rather formidable nanny figure, whose commanding power, alas, endures to this day; and the war-like Athena who is the most conventionally emblematic and stylised of the four types, but who now exhorts[72] rather than participates directly in battle.

Of course Queen Victoria is closely identified with Britannia as the courted virgin and later as the formidable dowager. But, as I hope will be clear from the previous discussion, most of these motifs have a longer pedigree, deriving from the sometimes awesome and sometimes passive nature goddess, from Pallas Athene and from the Virgin Mary. The foolish virgin first seems to become a common theme in the late eighteenth century, as in the famous print of 'Fashion Before Ease' which shows a boorish Tom Paine trying to lace up a discomfited Britannia.[73] This spoof, based on a French fashion print of the day, shows that commercial influences were having their impact on political imagery by this time.

Another figure sometimes conflated with Britannia is that of Mrs John Bull, the symbol of the good English housewife, frugal, modest and hospitable. She is a nostalgic figure who embodies the domestic virtues of a pre-industrial England and who we first meet, as the second Mrs Bull, in Arbuthnot's satire. In 'A Plain Question' of 1852 by Tenniel, Britannia was demoted to the role of John Bull's ward.[74] Domesticated to the point of dependency, the former patroness of weaving and the trades and arts is now confined to knitting. Her helmet and spear are put neatly aside, her shield is hung over the mantlepiece. Her hair (a standard symbol of sexuality) is modestly plaited and Britannia looks decidedly repressed. Her hesitant suitor is 'Disraeli, whose Jewish origins, ridiculed elsewhere in *Punch*, cast doubt on the honourableness of his (political) intentions. John Bull, dog at his heel, is pugnaciously determined to ensure this upstart does not trifle with his charge's reputation.

By the early twentieth century, Britannia, like the respectable and decidedly upper-middle-class ladies she has come to represent (Mrs Bull is definitely a bit more downmarket), will be doing her own courting. There is a particularly telling cartoon of 1912 for example, in which Britannia, very much the 'new woman', disdains a rather philistine King Coal for a younger and more gracious Lord Petroleo.[75] 'Retribution', a deeply racist caricature which appeared in *Judy* in 1879, shows Britannia in another kind of independence which was to be frequent in the half-century leading up to the war of 1914–18, that of Britannia as the nation armed (see Figure 4).

Britannia, then, has had a varied career. From her very beginnings as a Romano-British deity she has been a syncretistic construct which linked Amazonian fertility goddesses with patriarchal assertions of imperial power. The relation between her seventeenth-century persona and the pagan survivals of medieval Christendom are doubtless convoluted and await further research. There is also the vexed but important question of the connection between the cosmological status of (mother) nature and the political and social status of actual women in the ruling and popular culture of seventeenth-century England.

The identification of Britannia with Minerva appears to co-exist with an older conception of a Britannia, more directly derived from a mother earth figure. Britannia's religious significance both links her with and distinguishes her from the Catholic Church, and much of Britannia's power as a symbol has its origins in her

7 'Retribution': Britannia and Cetewayo as seen by *Judy*, 1879 (Mary Evans Picture Library).

identification with the Virgin Mary. As Frances Yates noted about Astraea, there is an ambiguity about Britannia which appeals to both the Protestant and the Catholic, the occultist and the Jesuit, and, I would add, to the royalist and the radical.

By the late eighteenth century, as traditional symbolism became increasingly subject to the personal interpretive whims of individual artists and writers, Britannia became more directly a vehicle for portraying contemporary attitudes towards women and gender roles. The chivalric current fed into both a Ruskinesque exaltation of woman as conscience and virtue and an openly misogynist contempt.

So what of it? The examination of national symbols may be satisfying for the academic historian, but what practical insights can it afford? Well, for one thing it is important that people are aware that the symbols used in posters, cartoons, advertisements, pageantry and slogans have had a long and, to a surprising extent, continuous history.

But, it will be argued, surely people today neither know nor care about the obscure origins of political imagery. Yet this century has borne witness to the power of the political symbol. and its ability to convey a multiplicity of meanings at many levels. It is difficult to judge just how much of a symbol's historically-evolved meaning is imbibed today, but something must still stick, and their half-remembered meanings still affect patriotic sentiment.

In any case, there remains the symbol's inherent logic and psychological force. There is something about symbols, especially visual ones, which reach the parts rational explanation cannot reach. Moreover, if we establish that implicit in patriotic symbols are certain statements about gender relations which transcend 'conservatism' or 'radicalism' as it has been conventionally defined, then the Left had best take heed. For if we put 'a requisition order on patriotism'[76] without questioning its implications for sexual equality, we may get less than we bargained for.

Notes

This article is an abridged version of a paper presented to the History Workshop Conference early in 1984. Since then Marina Warner's *Monuments and Maidens, the Allegory of the Female Form* (London, 1985), has been published. Her work contains a brief consideration of the Britannia symbol and addresses some of the same source material considered here. However, despite the overlap, there are differences of emphasis and interpretation between our two studies.

My thanks go to Ellen Malos, Diana Grant, Myna Trustram and Pam Gerrish Nunn of the Bristol Women's History Group; to my colleagues

Steward Mossman, Glyn Stone and Andrew Lambert and to my post-graduate students at Bristol Polytechnic; to those who attended my session at the History Workshop Conference on Patriotism, especially Olivia Harris and Peter Stallybrass; and finally to Carolyn Merchant, Raphael Samuel, Wilfred Summerbell and Helen Dresser.

1 J. M. C. Toynbee, *The Hadrianic School, A Chapter in the History of Greek Art*, Cambridge, 1934, pp. 6–10.

2 B. Sewell, 'A great city lives again', *The Sunday Times Magazine*, 15 Jan. 1984, pp. 30ff. In the frieze of Claudius and Britannia pictured in the article and discussed in my text, Britannia is carrying a large axe by her side. Thanks to Diana Grant for this clipping.

3 This photograph is taken from the archeological journal *Britannia*, XIII, 1982, frontispiece, cf. pp. 279–90. I am grateful to Professor Kenan T. Erim who heads the Aphrodesias excavation and to Professor J. J. Wilkes and Patricia Grant of the Society for the Promotion of Roman Studies for permission to reproduce this photograph.

4 William Camden, *Britain or a Chorographical Description of the Most Flourishing Kingdomes, England, Scotland and Ireland*, London, 1610, p. 31.

5 *Ibid*.

6 See J. M. C. Toynbee, *Art in Roman Britain*, London, 1962, plate 77 and p. 157.

7 J. M. C. Toynbee, *The Hadrianic School, A Chapter in the Hisotry of Greek Art*, Cambridge, 1934, pp. 57–63; for worship of Britannia, see *The Gentleman's Magazine*, X, April, 1740, p. 139.

8 Toynbee, *op. cit.*, pp. 10–11, 137.

9 Toynbee, *op. cit.*, p. 63n. The 1789 edition of William Camden's *Britain or a Chorographical Description of the Most Flourishing Kingdomes, England, Scotland and Ireland*, London, plate LXX facing p. 65.

10 Toynbee, *op. cit.*, pp. 68 and 128. The Amazons were also linked to the moon goddess, cf. R. Graves, *The Greek Myths*, Baltimore, Md., 1955, vol. I, p. 355.

11 R. Graves, *White Goddess, A Historical Grammar of Poetic Myth*, London, pp. 406–8; F. Bowen 'The cult of St Brigit', *Studia Celtica*, 8–9, 1973, pp. 33–47. Whereas Graves asserts Brigit was originally a mother goddess with a triple aspect (mother, virgin, hag), Bowen describes her as a fertility goddess associated in some British localities with the hearth.

12 See, for example, F. J. Stephen and M. D. George, *Catalogue of Prints and Drawings in the British Museum: Division I, Political and Personal Satire*, London, 1878–1954, 11 vols, no. 2582 and H. Atherton. *Political Caricature in the Age of Hogarth*, Oxford, 1974, plate 121.

13 C. E. Keyser, 'The mural paintings at Kempley Church Gloucester-shire', *Archeological Journal*, XXXLV, 1877, pp. 271–4 cf. *Archeological Journal*, II, 1846, p. 89; XLV, 1888, pp. 112, 419–21; Jean Seznec, *The Survival of the Pagan Gods*, Princeton, 1972, esp. pp. 37–56, 84–92; Keith Thomas, *Religion and the Decline of Magic*, London, 1971, pp.

54–5; Marina Warner, *Alone of All Her Sex, the Myth and Cult of the Virgin Mary*, London, 1976, pp. 256–7.

14 Warner, *op. cit.*, pp. 240–1, 261, 267; for Mary's association with Pallas Athene/Minerva, pp. 107, 304. See also R. Wittkower, 'The transformation of Minerva in Renaissance imagery', *Journal of the Warburgh and Courtauld Institutes*, II, 1938–9, pp. 194ff, esp. 199.

15 Rosemary Freeman, *English Emblem Books*, London, 1948, pp. 19–22; Cf. Seznec, *The Survival of the Pagan Gods*, Princeton, 1972, for his discussion of euhermerism, pp. 11–26, 32–6.

16 Sydney Anglo, *Spectacle, Pageantry and Early Tudor Policy*, Oxford, 1969, pp. 284–6, 320; cf. Frances Yates, *Astraea, The Imperial Theme in the Sixteenth Century*, London, 1975, p. 50. Cf. also, E. Hobsbawm and T. Ranger, *The Invention of Tradition*, Cambridge, 1983.

17 British Museum, Dept of Coins and Medals, *Medallic Illustrations of the History of Great Britain and Ireland*, Lawrence, Mass., 1979, plate LV, no. 13.

18 Rosemary Freeman, *English Emblem Books*, London, 1948, p. 1.

19 Hans Kohn, 'The genesis and character of English nationalism', *Journal of the History of Ideas*, I. 1940, p. 71.

20 Frances Yates, *Astraea, The Imperial Theme in the Sixteenth Century*, London, 1975, pp. 29, 87; J. M. C. Toynbee, *The Hadrianic School, A Chapter in the History of Greek Art*, Cambridge, 1934, p. 63, cites a coin of Commodus (c. 185 AD) which features 'not a real Britannia', but a *Fides Publica* (public happiness) emblem which held a cornucopia in one hand and the *specifera* (ear of corn) in the other. As the *specifera* denoted Virgo, one is led to wonder if this figure alludes to the Virgo cult in Britain.

21 J. M. C. Toynbee, *The Hadrianic School, A Chapter in the History of Greek Art*, Cambridge, 1934, p. 63.

22 *Ibid.*

23 Frances Yates, *Astraea, The Imperial Theme in the Sixteenth Century*, London, 1975, p. 87.

24 Rosemary Freeman, *English Emblem Books*, London, 1948, esp. pp. 95–7; Allardyce Nicoll, *Stuart Masques and the Renaissance Stage*, New York, 1937, pp. 154–5. D. J. Gordon, 'The imagery of Ben Jonson's *The Masque of Blacknesse and the Masque of Beautie*', *Journal of the Warburgh and Courtauld Institute*, VI, 1943, pp. 122ff.; A. H. Gilbert, *The Symbolic Persons in the Masques of Ben Jonson*, Durham, North Carolina, 1948. For later period cf. P. J. Korshin, 'Figural change and the survival of tradition', in *Studies in Change and Revolution: Aspects of English Intellectual History 1640–1800*, London, 1972, pp. 99–117.

25 Graham Parry, *The Golden Age Restored, The Culture of the Stuart Court, 1603–1642*, Manchester, 1981, p. 20.

26 William Camden, *Britain or a Chorological Description of the Most Flourishing Kingdomes, England, Scotland and Ireland*, London, 1610.

27 J. M. C. Toynbee, *The Hadrianic School, A Chapter in the History of Greek Art*, Cambridge, 1934, plate XI, nos 23 and 24, and pp. 58–9.

28 Henry Peacham, *Minerva Britanna*, London, 1612.

29 J. M. C. Toynbee, *The Hadrianic School, A Chapter in the History of Greek Art*, Cambridge, 1934, plate XI, nos 26 and 27, p. 59.

30 Michael Drayton, *Poly Olbion*, London, 1612.

31 This figure ('not a real Britannia') found on Romano-British coins issued by Comodus later appears as plenty or public happiness in early modern emblembooks. Cf. J. M. C. Toynbee, *The Hadrianic School, A Chapter in the History of Greek Art*, Cambridge, 1934, p. 63 and H. Green, *The Mirrour of Majestie*, London, 1869, p. 25. Cf. note 18.

32 The description of Britannia's robe is actually taken from the description of 'peace' in Middleton's London Lord Mayor's Show of 1613 which may possibly have been inspired by Drayton's frontispiece. Cf. D. W. Bergeron, *English Civic Pageantry 1558–1642*, London, 1971, p. 173.

33 The pearls also associate her with the moon, cf. Marina Warner, *Alone of All Her Sex, The Myth and Cult of the Virgin Mary*, London, 1976, p. 48; Frances Yates, *Astraea, The Imperial Theme in the Sixteenth Century*, London, 1975, pp. 33, 86–7, 218; and also Esther Harding, *Women's Mysteries*, London, 1982, pp. 103–4.

34 Frances Yates, *Astraea, The Imperial Theme in the Sixteenth Century*, London, 1975, p. 33 refers to Astraea as 'tinged with oriental moon ecstasies', a reference to the link with the *Magna Mater* cult of the near East of which J. M. C. Toynbee wrote in her *Hadrianic School, A Chapter in the History of Greek Art*, Cambridge, 1934, p. 128. See Esther Harding, *Women's Mysteries*, London, 1982, pp. 138, 141–2.

35 Frances Yates, *Astraea, The Imperial Theme in the Sixteenth Century*, London, 1975, plate 42c, pp. 66–8. Astraea was used by Charles V of France to glorify imperial rule. This may help to account for the more sedate and Ceres-like personifications of the French Republic described by Maurice Agulhon, *Marianne Into Battle: Republican Imagery and Symbolism in France, 1789–1880*, Paris, 1979, p. 82.

36 Cf. Cesare Ripa, *Iconologia*, London, 1709, pp. 64–5, 80–1 and plates 258 and 271a. This is the English translation of an extremely influential book first published in an Italian illustrated edition in 1613. As Herbert Atherton has pointed out, there is a picture of a 'Minervan' Britannia as the emblem of *Potesta* in Ripa's English edition: H. Atherton, *Political Caricature in the Age of Hogarth*, Oxford, 1974, p. 92.

37 D. M. Bergeron, *English Civic Pageantry 1558–1642*, London, 1971, p. 84; Graham Parry, *The Golden Age Restored, The Culture of the Stuart Court, 1603–1642*, Manchester, 1981, p. 15.

38 John Nicols, *Progresses and Processions of James I*, London, 1828, vol. I, p. 310.

39 Quoted in D. J. Gordon's '*Hymenaei*: Ben Jonson's Masque of Union', *Journal of the Warburgh and Courtauld Institutes*, VII-VIII, 1945, p. 127.

40 D. M. Bergeron, *English Civic Pageantry 1558–1642*, London, 1971, pp. 173 and 93.

41 Cf. for example E. Neuman, *The Great Mother, An Analysis of the Archetype*, Princeton, 1972, plates 174 and 175; I. Illich, *Gender*, London, 1983, pp. 154n., 160n.; E. Spenser, *The Faerie Queene*,

London, 1912, vol. II, canto 11, v. 6. Cf. the nursing republic by Daumier in Maurice Agulhon, *Marianne Into Battle: Republican Imagery and Symbolism in France, 1789–1880*, Paris, 1979, p. 83.

42 F. G. Stephens and M. D. George, *Catalogue of Prints and Drawings in the British Museum: Division 1, Political and Personal Satires*, London, 1878–1954, 11 vols, no. 3,043.

43 F. G. Stephens and M. D. George, *op. cit.*, no. 674. Elizabeth I is shown in a shop in the title page to J. Dee's *Memorial* of 1577, cited in Frances Yates, *Astraea, The Imperial Theme in the Sixteenth Century*, London, 1975, plate 7b. Cf. Maurice Agulhon, *Marianne Into Battle: Repubican Imagery and Symbolism in France, 1789–1880*, Paris, 1979, pp. 81–6.

44 Francis Quarles, *Emblems Divine and Moral*, London, 1866, Book 5, p. 202. Cf. Rosemary Freeman, *English Emblem Books*, London, 1948, pp. 117, 179.

45 Marina Warner, *Alone of All Her Sex, the Myth and Cult of The Virgin Mary*, London, 1976, plate 46, p. 307. Rosemany Freeman, *English Emblem Books*, London, 1948, p. 179.

46 F. G. Stephens and M. D. George, *Catalogue of Prints and Drawings in the British Museum: Division I, Political and Personal Satires*, London, 1878–1954, 11 vols, no. 1,130. Britannia here is draped with what looks like a cloak 'limn'd with the map of England', and does have a spear, but no sword.

47 British Museum, Department of Coins and Medals, *Medallic Illustrations of the History of Great Britain and Ireland*, Lawrence, Mass., plate LXVIII, no. 6.

48 F. G. Stephens and M. D. George, *Catalogue of Prints and Drawings in the British Museum: Division I, Political and Personal Satire*, London, 1878–1954, 11 vols, no. 3,341.

49 H. Atherton, *Political Caricature in the Age of Hogarth*, Oxford, 1974, p. 92.

50 Marina Warner, *Alone of All Her Sex, the Myth and Cult of the Virgin Mary*, London, 1976, plate VIII facing p. 197. This *Magna Mater* is a good deal larger relative to the surrounding figures than the Britannia in the print discussed.

51 H. Atherton, *Political Caricature in the Age of Hogarth*, Oxford, 1974, pp. 90–7.

52 Cf. F. G. Stephens and M. D. George, *Catalogue of Prints and Drawings in the British Museum: Division I, Political and Personal Satire*, London, 1878–1954, 11 vols, nos. 3,548, 4,877, 5,987; M. D. George, *English Political Caricature*, Oxford, 1959, vol. I, plates 40, 41, 61, and vol. II, plate 5. Cf. also H. Atherton, *Political Caricature in the Age of Hogarth*, Oxford, 1974, plate 113 especially. Atherton is perhaps unwittingly ironic when he refers to Britannia as the guardian of a 'rampant patriotism' since according to the *Oxford English Dictionary* the now obsolete definition of rampant was 'lewd and vicious'.

53 Atherton, *op. cit.*, pp. 169, 267.

54 'The idealized image of a woman's eternal traits and qualities is a

medium through which to express or produce the solidarity and unity of male groups. They need a female to symbolize what they are fighting or a woman whose defilement and dishonour they can avenge' (Marie Louise Janssen-Jurreit, *Sexism, The Male Monopoly in History and Thought*, London, 1982, pp. 35–6).

55 M. C. Jacob, *The Radical Enlightenment, Pantheists, Freemasons and Republicans*, London, 1981, pp. 208–9.

56 M. C. Jacob, *op. cit.*, pp. 10, 32, 38.

57 F. G. Stephens and M. D. George, *Catalogue of Prints and Drawings in the British Museum, Division I, Political and Personal Satire*, London, 1878–1954, 11 vols, no. 5,334. Cf. M. D. George, *English Political Caricature*, Oxford, 1959, vol. I, plate 47, pp. 152–3.

58 F. G. Stephens and M. D. George, *Catalogue of Prints and Drawings in the British Museum: Division I, Political and Personal Satire*, London, 1878–1954, 11 vols, no. 8,284. Cf. M. D. George, *British Political Caricatures*, vol. II, plate I, p. 1.

59 Hugh Cunningham, 'The language of patriotism 1750–1914', *History Workshop Journal*, 12, Autumn, 1981, pp. 13–21.

60 British Museum, Department of Coins and Medals, *Medallic Illustrations of the History of Great Britain and Ireland*, Lawrence, Mass., plates CXXVI 13/14, CLXXX 10. This goes against Atherton's contention that Britannia in her martial guise was not shown fighting in the eighteenth century because it was not in accord with her femininity or her status as a goddess. Cf. H. Atherton, *Political Caricature in the Age of Hogarth*, Oxford, 1974, p. 97. I would argue that her passivity and the passivity of female mortals and goddesses is historically specific.

61 The Blenheim Estates Office, *Blenheim Palace*, Oxford, 1982, p. 14 for photo of Thornhill's ceiling. For more on representations of Queen Anne, cf. Virginia Kenny, *The Country-House Ethos in English Literature 1688–1750: Themes of Personal Retreat and National Expansion*, Sussex, 1984, pp. 70–4.

62 T. Carew, *The Royal Norfolk Regiment*, London, 1967, pp. 9ff.

63 Cf. 'The Apotheosis of Nelson' by Benjamin West in the National Maritime Museum, reproduced in the *Journal of the Warburgh and Courtauld Institutes*, II, 1938–9, p. 21d; J. and J. May, *Commemorative Pottery 1780–1900*, London, 1972.

64 A. Lane, *Porcelain Figures of the Eighteenth Century*, London, 1961, has some fine weeping Madonnas. I am grateful to Andrew Hemes, Museums Officer of Monmouth District Council, for the postcard of a wonderful Gillray etching on 'The Death of Admiral Lord Nelson' (1805) from the collection of the Nelson Museum, Monmouth, which shows Nelson leaning against a weeping and helmetless Britannia. For the source of the quotation cited in the text, cf. 'Britannia's Address to the People of England on the Death of Lord Nelson', nd, *Miss Banks Collection of Broadsides and Ballads*, British Museum, LR 301 h6.

65 F. G. Stevens and M. D. George, *Catalogue of Prints and Drawings in the British Museum: Division I, Political and Personal Satire*, London,

1878–1954, 11 vols, no. 10,439 and M. D. George, *British Political Caricature*, vol. II, plate 32 and p. 84.

66 Baring Sabine Gould, *Broadside Ballads*, British Museum LR271 a2, p. 64.

67 J. F. C. Harrison, *The Second Coming: Popular Millenarianism 1780–1850*, London, 1979, pp. 39–41. For earlier sectarian connections, cf. C. Hill, 'Science and magic in seventeenth century England', in R. Samuel and G. S. Jones (eds), *Culture, Ideology and Politics*, London, 1982, pp. 176–94.

68 B. Taylor, *Evex and the New Jerusalem*, London, 1983, esp. pp. 167–71 and 220. M. Agulhon, *Marianne Into Battle: Republican Imagery and Symbolism in France, 1789–1880*, Paris, 1979, pp. 55–8, 114–15.

69 F. G. Stephens and M. D. George, *Catalogue of Prints and Drawings in the British Museum: Division I, Political and Personal Satire*, London, 1878–1954, 11 vols, no. 13,279. Cf. M. D. George, *British Political Caricature*, vol. II, plate 72 and pp. 183–4.

70 'The Royal Captain and Volunteer Crew of the Good Ship Britannia', *Miss Banks Collection of Broadsides and Ballads*, British Museum, LR 301 h6.

71 For the neo-Platonic symbolism of the notion of light and darkness, cf. D. J. Gordon, 'The imagery of Ben Jonson's *The Masque of Blacknesse and the Masque of Beautie*', *Journal of the Warburgh and Courtauld Institute*, VI, 1943, pp. 122ff, esp. pp. 124–7, where twelve aethiopian nymphs seek to lose their blackness in the temperate and refining sun of Britannia. Light is associated here with moral enlightenment and this association is rooted in ancient Greek religion according to G. Lloyd, 'Right and left in Greek philosophy', in R. Needham (ed.), *Right and Left*, Chicago, 1966, pp. 180–1n. Lloyd states that light, virtue, right-handedness and masculinity were all associated with the Olympian as opposed to the Titan earth-related deities (who included Metis). See also J. L. Jordanova's relevant analysis of Mozart's *The Magic Flute* in which light (patriarchy and culture) struggles against darkness (matriarchy and nature), in her essay 'Natural facts: a historical perspective on science and sexuality', in C. MacCormack and M. Strathern (eds), *Nature, Culture and Gender*, Cambridge, 1980, pp. 59–60.

72 F. G. Stevens and M. D. George, *Catalogue of Prints and Drawings in the British Museum: Division I, Political and Personal Satire*, London, 1878–1954, 11 vols, no. 9,284. Pat is not so benignly portrayed in the pages of *Punch*.

73 F. G. Stephens and M. D. George, *op. cit.*, no. 8,287, dated 1793. Note that Britannia is daintily clinging to an English oak instead of a bedstead and that Paine is wearing the Phrygian cap. His over-familiarity with the national muse again appealed to the chivalrous sentiments of the intended (male) audience.

74 *Punch*, 1852, p. 129.

75 *Punch*, 10 April, 1912, p. 263.

76 E. Hobsbawn, 'A requisition order on patriotism', *The Guardian*, 24 Dec. 1982.

3
Old soldiers

JOANY HICHBERGER

Other essays in this book will have demonstrated that there were many coexisting constructions of national character in patriotic iconography. The aim here will be to show how a special form of visual representation, academic painting, as one of a network of forms, helped to construct an image of 'patriotism' in relation to the old soldier. The quality of 'patriotism' in a serving soldier was defined in terms of discipline and loyalty – to the regiment, to the army and to the monarch. In simplest terms, military patriotism was manifested in support for the *status quo*. It is in relation to this concept of patriotism that representations of the ex-soldier, the veteran, will be considered. It will be argued that, far from being neutral 'stock characters' in genre paintings, ex-soldiers in early nineteenth-century Britain were potent symbols of the potential violence of the mob, and that their political ambiguity, as former soldiers in the recent wars and as uncontrolled fighting men, precluded their representation in academic art. In the period from the end of the Waterloo campaign in 1815 until the decade of the Crimean War, the 1850s, the only representations of veterans were in the form of physical cripples, or, more typically, in the guise of Chelsea Pensioners, a group whose political allegiance and 'patriotism' was believed to be beyond dispute.[1]

From the 1850s the 'common soldier', and by extension the veteran, was rehabilitated in ruling-class mythology. The Crimean War was crucial in this change in perception. The problem of the veteran as a threat to political stability was succeeded by concern about the social deprivation he represented. In the 1850s representations of non-Chelsea veterans began to appear regularly at the Royal Academy exhibition, for the first time since the 1800s.[2] The veteran was portrayed as a symbol of the 'deserving poor', worthy because of his 'patriotic' military service.

In 1815, at the close of the Waterloo campaign, thousands of British soldiers were shipped back to their homeland and disbanded. Only a fraction of these veterans, the maimed or severely diseased, were entitled to a pension from the state, and all veterans were expected to return to their families and friends for care.[3] However, the dislocation caused by years of military service and the stigma attached to joining the army meant that few veterans were able to blend back into their pre-service lives. A large majority of the returning veterans were unable to find work. Unemployment had been an important factor in their initial enlistment and their position as older men, unskilled and unhealthy, was even worse.[4]

The presence of this large rootless group of trained fighting men who converged on the cities was a source of anxiety to members of the ruling class. It was feared that they would form robber-gangs to attack property. C. J. Napier recounts that, in 1815, weapons for the defence of houses exchanged hands at inflated prices, in anticipation of the influx of ex-soldiers.[5] This civilian fear was merely an extension of their distrust of serving soldiers, the crucial difference being that serving soldiers were controlled by a severe system of discipline and punishments, while the veterans were without any such controls but still retained their knowledge of weapons and fighting.

The flood of veterans was also perceived as a threat by the government. It was feared that they might constitute a new and dangerously effective element in social unrest. A large number of discharged soldiers and sailors were present at a radical meeting at Spa Fields in December 1816, at which speakers called for revol-ution.[6] It was feared that radical veterans would enlist the support of their friends who were still serving in the ranks and lead the army into mutiny.[7] Since the government was unable to control the activities of discharged soldiers, it reacted by reinforcing existing laws to prevent the subversion of the army.[8]

A Select Parliamentary Commission on Mendicancy was set up to investigate the large numbers of ex-servicemen and others begging on the streets of London. The report, published in May 1816, did not offer any solutions to the mass destitution, concen-trating instead on the criminal actions of a few Chelsea out-pensioners. Almost no remark was made of the much larger majority of veterans who received nothing from the state, after a small sum on discharge. The tone of the Report was reproachful of the 'ungrateful' Chelsea out-pensioners and, by implication, of those mendicants who had no cause to feel gratitude. This approach was to be typical of ruling class commentators until the 1850s, who dwelt on the privileged minority at Chelsea, to the exclusion of all others.[9]

The Royal Military Hospital at Chelsea had been founded in 1681, by order of Charles II, reputedly at the instigation of Nell Gwynn. Despite the efforts of nineteenth-century historians to discredit it, the story of how her warm cockney heart had been moved by the plight of the old soldiers remained popular.[10] After two centuries, Chelsea remained the only support for ex-soldiers on mainland Britain.[11] A small number of wounded or sick veterans were paid a small half-yearly pension through Chelsea, although they lived outside the institution. The group who dominated public perceptions of Chelsea were the picturesquely-clad in-pensioners.[12] These old men were provided with board and lodgings as well as a very small pension. The Hospital was administered by a board of governors chosen by the government. Disquiet about the political and social activities of veterans never extended to the pensioners at Chelsea. Out-pensioners were used as special constables in controlling riots and meetings, and this enhanced the image of the in-pensioners at Chelsea.[13] The principal appeal of Chelsea, however, was that it provided 'evidence' of the state's munificent treatment of its deserving servants. Inmates of Chelsea were carefully screened, not on the basis of need, but to ensure that only soldiers with blameless military and personal records were admitted.[14]

In the first three decades after Waterloo, Chelsea Hospital was a popular venue for tourists. The chaplain in the late 1830s, G. R. Gleig, wrote a guide to the Hospital in which the inmates were described in terms of living exhibits. Gleig particularly recommended visiting on Wednesday or Friday, when the visitor might be fortunate enough to witness the touching and picturesque ceremony of burial.[15] The ruling class's appropriation of Chelsea was taken for granted, with a sentry posted at the gate to ensure that only persons of rank were admitted to watch the pensioners at work and prayer.

David Wilkie's painting 'Chelsea Pensioners receiving the London Gazette Extraordinary of Thursday June 22nd 1815 announcing the Battle of Waterloo' was exhibited at the Royal Academy of 1822 and was greeted with enthusiasm, needing to be protected by a rail from the clamouring visitors.[16] Much interest had been aroused by the picture before its execution. The Duke of Wellington, commander of the Allied Army at Waterloo and the leader of London society, had commissioned a 'Chelsea scene' from Wilkie, an already celebrated and fashionable artist.[17]

Wilkie's fulfilment of the commission was innovatory, although the subject of revellers, celebrating a military victory outside an inn, was not new. His departure lay in taking a genre scene of everyday life, and marrying it to an event of historical and national importance, elevating a form that was lowly-esteemed in academic terms to the intellectually revered level of history painting.[18] Wilkie's success was dependent on his audience's acceptance of Chelsea pensioners as a group whose patriotism was beyond question. The title of the painting did not explicitly state the way the pensioners received the news of Waterloo, but Wilkie's choice of Chelsea veterans as receptors banished any possible ambiguity, since the Chelsea institution was believed to be completely integrated with the ruling-class's view of the state's interest. The responses to Waterloo and the defeat of Napoleon were by no means universal joy and celebration; by 1822 Wellington's military and political enemies were beginning to suggest that Waterloo had been overestimated as a battle and the defeat of Napoleon was perceived by radicals as the crushing of the spirit of liberty in France.[19] Wilkie's painting represented a well-known group of working-class men, responding in a desirable way to the victory. The position of this group in ruling-class mythology established their response as the 'normal' response of the worthy poor, thus placing negative responses to Waterloo into the category of the abnormal or delinquent.

A close analysis of the painting reveals that the title is a misrepresentation of the subject.[20] Only seven of the sixty-odd figures are old enough or infirm enough to have been attached to Chelsea Hospital. Wilkie's letters and journals reveal that this evasion of age and disease was dictated by his patron. When asked to choose between two sketches for the picture, Wellington selected one showing young figures and only as a concession accepted that a few suitably old veterans should be included. 'He wished that the piper might be put in, also the man with the wooden leg; but he objected to the man with the opthalmia.'[21] This raises an interesting side issue as the pictorial acceptability of certain categories of disability in academic art. Wooden legs are not uncommon in nineteenth century representations of veterans, whereas blindness, facial scarring and other forms of disability are never shown.[22] A wooden leg seems to have been an acceptable symbol for the physical dangers of war, without having a shocking impact upon the sensibilities of the Academy audience. Wellington was evidently unwilling for any grim reminders of the consequences of war to obtrude into a picture celebrating his victory. The initial effect of the painting is of tremendous vigour and vitality, created by the rhythmic use of red and white. Although the central group of figures does contain several elderly Chelsea pensioners, any sense of frailty is dispelled by the flanking groups. On the left, a group of Highland soldiers toast the victory, and on the other side are several pretty young women and a young soldier lifting his baby in the air in celebration of the news. It is interesting that by no means all the faces register delight. This is not because Wilkie wished to infer that Waterloo was not universally acknowledged as a triumph, but because he intended a sophisticated exercise in showing news percolating across the picture from the left side of the canvas to the right.

One of the most popular aspects of the picture was the wealth of 'historical' information provided about the figures. Wilkie exhibited the picture with a 200 word catalogue entry, describing the military career of each pensioner, implying by his use of this biographical technique that they were 'real' people, depicted during a 'real' event. As well as reinforcing the documentary sense of the picture, the biographies were vital in establishing the pensioners as an expert audience. The pensioners are described as survivors from historically distant but celebrated episodes of military history; 'a Glengarry Highlander who served with General Graham at Barossa . . . a survivor of the Seven Years War, who was at the taking of Quebec with General Wolfe . . . a black, one of the band of the 1st regiment of Footguards', etc.[23] The applause of such veterans might be seen as important for two reasons; that they were 'ideal' and at the same time 'typical' representatives of the poor; and that they constituted a group uniquely able to judge the merits of Wellington's victory.

In the late eighteenth and early nineteenth century, the old soldier had been a potent symbol of the 'deserving poor' who were neglected by an ungrateful nation. In this period representations of mendicant veterans were often shown as recipients of private charity, from the hands of responsible and Christian members of the ruling class. Such representations vanished from the walls of the Royal Academy in the post Waterloo period, when only depictions of tended veterans appeared – as Chelsea pensioners. It has been argued that an important factor in this change in representation was the anxiety created by the vast numbers of mendicant veterans after the Napoleonic Wars.

Chelsea pensioners continued to be numerically dominant as representations of veterans in academic art until the decade of the Crimean War.[24] After the Crimean War, 1854–6, the dominant ruling-class view of the 'common soldier', in the ranks, underwent a remarkable transformation. As has been shown by Edward M. Spiers, a number of factors contributed to this important change.[25]

It is evident that, after the severe losses sustained by the British Army during the winter of 1854-5, media attention focused on the men in the ranks rather than their generals and high-ranking officers.[26] This change in interest was partly motivated by the emergent upper-middle-class desire to show how the war had been mismanaged by the incompetent aristocrats who commanded the army. The Crimean War was described as having only been won by the extraordinary 'patriotism' and courage of the 'common soldiers'.

Representations of respectable, domestic, patriotic soldiers and veterans began to appear with increasing regularity at the Royal Academy in the post-Crimean era. In ruling-class mythology the veteran of the Crimea became an unthreatening patriot. Most representations of veterans located them within domestic settings, surrounded with several generations of their family, living out a prosperous and contented old age.[27] Despite the emergence of these alternative forms for the representation of 'safe' veterans, Chelsea pensioners remained popular subjects for painters.

Hubert von Herkomer's painting 'The Last Muster – Sunday at the Royal Hospital, Chelsea' (Royal Academy 1875) seems at first remarkably close in spirit to Wilkie's picture exhibited fifty years earlier.[28] The theme of patriotism is, however, articulated through desirable social behaviour rather than through an overt display of nationalistic fervour. Herkomer was following the lead of such writers as Gleig in celebrating the Hospital's moral influence on the inmates, manifested in their deportment at prayer.

> Let me, however, recommend to such as are desirous of seeing this part of the hospital [the Chapel] to advantage, to pay their first visit on a Sunday morning, during the performance of divine worship. The benches are then crowded with old soldiers whose grave but not austere countenances, lighted up from time to time by a display of deep devotional feeling . . . present to the eye of the painter subjects too inviting to be over-looked. How decent, how much more than decent is the deportment of these worn-out warriors: how humble their attitude in prayer; how keen and animated their attention.[29]

Gleig makes an equation between this religious observance and the moral character of soldiers in general, in his view much maligned.

In a letter to American relatives, Herkomer expressed pleasure at the sight of the Chelsea veterans in chapel being 'reclaimed' spiritually and morally by religious fear. 'It is a grand sight to see these venerable old warriors under the influence of divine service. They have been loose, (most of their lives) and now coming near

8   'The Last Muster' by Hubert von Herkomer, 1875 (Merseyside County Art Galleries).

their end a certain fear comes over them and they listen eagerly to the Gospel.'[30] To Herkomer, in common with his ruling-class audience, the sight of working-class men at prayer implied not only spiritual salvation but the absorption of desirable moral lessons. The Chelsea pensioners are therefore again used as arche-types of the poor, in accepting social control in the form of religion.

The subject of Herkomer's picture is not merely the poor at prayer; it is observing the poor at prayer. The ruling-class audience is not only implied by the presence of the viewer but by the row of ruling-class civilians and officers in the background. One critic referred to the notion of 'reclamation' by suggesting that the man on the far left could be read as a 'hard case'. 'In front of the principal group is a big-headed, argumentative-looking trooper, whose long upper lip bespeaks an obstinate disposition, while his bright eyes show his intelligence. He sits with his hands on the head of a stick, and listens, not without approval, to what is recited before him.'[31] Chelsea, in this picture, is depicted as a place not only of sanctuary for aged 'heroes' but also of moral reclamation. The view that soldiers were ripe for religious education and salvation was to be found in many contemporary ruling-class inter-ventions in soldier's welfare.[32] The narrative line of 'plot' of the picture is humorously described in the title. The foreground veteran has been called to a heavenly 'last muster', died during Sunday service. Only one of the Academy critics failed to interpret and appreciate Herkomer's meaning.[33]

Herkomer's picture, like Wilkie's, was highly popular when it was exhibited at the Royal Academy. All critics commented upon the 'realism' of all the figures – a 'close-up' technique which demanded that each man's face be 'read' and conclusions drawn about his character. The scale of the figures was nearly life size, more usually reserved for portraiture or history painting. By treating the subject in this way, Herkomer gave the veterans liter-ally stature and heroic quality. This handling of what was more usually a genre subject in a noble idealised way was not unique to Herkomer. Frank Holl and Luke Fildes were, during the 1870s, painting themes of urban poverty in this manner.[34] All three pain-ters worked for the illustrated weekly newspaper *The Graphic* and sometimes transferred subjects from their magazine illustrations into oil paintings for the Royal Academy. One consequence of this borrowing from another medium was that Herkomer's 'Last Muster' had an unpremeditated look in its composition. The painter reinforced this sense of instantaneity by cutting off some of the figures in an accidental-looking manner, reminiscent of photography.

The critic of *The Academy* did not regard the painting as in any sense an idealisation of the pensioners, believing that its 'realism' lay in its simple uncomplicated subject and closely observed details:

'a subject of actual life (common in itself yet far from common in its pictorial externals) . . . invested by resolute unswerving realism'.[35] Another critic stated that its lack of pictorial conventions 'proved' that it was factual. 'As we own to the influence of such a work, boasting none of the graces of intricate design or cunningly schemed harmonies of colour, we are made to feel that a fact, reverently and gravely rendered, has always its rightful place in art'. The effect of this implied 'realism' was to reinforce ruling-class mythologies of the Chelsea pensioner into the realms of 'fact'.

Thomas Faed's 'From Hand to Mouth' (exhibited 1880) was based on the recognition that there were veterans, like Faed's hero, who were forced on to the streets, either to starve or support themselves by playing music for pennies.[36] The picture was painted during a climate of debate in the press about the high level of unemployment among ex-soldiers. Five years later, in default of any state intervention, a group of former army officers founded the National Association for the Employment of Ex-soldiers.[37] It had been anticipated by the military and government authorities that the problem of veteran unemployment would disappear with the introduction of short-service terms in 1870 since the average age of 'veterans' would be only twenty-six and they would be easily assimilated back into civilian occupations.[38] An important factor in post-1870 veteran unemployment was that such men were required after discharge from the regular army, to serve in the army reserve. Reservists were paid a small retaining fee, which was sometimes deducted from their wages on the rationale that the employer as a taxpayer had already contributed to the reservists' income. Such ex-servicemen as found work were always at a disadvantage during contractions in the job market, since employers disliked employees who could be called away to train or go on manoeuvres. Such prejudice was condemned by some sympathetic ruling-class commentators as 'unpatriotic'.[39] Others, including the leading military spokesman General Sir Garnet Wolseley, claimed that veteran beggars who attributed their unemployment to the reserve were idle frauds who probably 'would not want work if it were found for them'.[40] Even without the complication of reserve service, ex-soldiers were at a disadvantage in the job market. Unemployment was a significant factor in causing men to enlist initially, and recruits were usually from the unskilled sector. After army service their situation was worsened by their older age, ill-health, and the stigma which still attached to the army in the working-classes.[42]

Faed showed himself to be aware of such views as Wolseley's by subtitling his veteran 'He was one of the few who would not beg'.[42] This device established his veteran as a member of the class

9 'From Hand to Mouth' by Thomas Faed, 1880.

of the 'worthy poor' rather than as a professional beggar, making the old man a legitimate target for 'pity'. 'Pity' as a response to a social group can be seen as a mechanism for defusing the power of that group. Instead of arousing fear, a group which is pitied can be dealt with in terms of charity and concern, without requiring any modifications of existing social structures. It is as part of the formation of ruling-class pity for the veterans that this picture may be considered. The narrative line of the painting was concerned with an itinerant veteran in a grocer's shop who finds himself unable to pay for his purchases. An element of doubt rested on the response of the two other adult protagonists, the shopkeeper and his wealthy female customer. The diverse nature of the critical responses to the picture suggest that there were ambiguities in the way the subject was presented. The large scale of the painting in relation to a subject more traditionally associated with small pictures was remarked upon: 'It is, perhaps, not desirable that subjects such as his [Faed's] should be treated in a nobler fashion'.[43] The critic from the *Athenaeum* went on to suggest that the subject, and Faed's technique, would have been better displayed on a canvas one-eighth the size. As with the Herkomer picture, the effect of enlarging the figures was to bring them into a genre which merited serious consideration. Faed's painting was accorded important status at the Royal Academy, and was hung in 'the place of honour'.[44] It received extensive and favourable reviews in the art press. Like the painters known as the 'social realists', Holl, Fildes and Herkomer, Faed was always successful at the RA with his 'social problem' pictures.[45] This is not the place in which to consider anything other than the bare outlines of 'realist' painting in nineteenth century Britain, but it must be asserted that such pictures were not received by the ruling class as an attack upon their social structures, nor were they 'designed to help the cause of social reform'.[46]

The picture revolved around the interaction of, and contrasts between, the three main adult figures; the elderly veteran-musician; the middle-aged shopkeeper; and the young 'lady'. The lady is described by critics variously as showing 'pity' and 'compassion' and her charitable intervention on the musician's behalf was predicted by one critic.[47] The 'fat grocer' was seen by critics as being 'suspicious' of the old man, as 'hard and plethoric' and of 'no disposition to bate a penny'.[48] The musician was described in interesting terms which combine an interpretation of his character as 'worthy' with an insistence on his helplessness – 'mingled independence and long-enduring suffering' and 'confused yet honest'.[49] The confrontation between the shopkeeper, as a prosperous member of the working class, and the destitute musician was seen by critics to be resolved by the intervention of the representative of the ruling class. Interestingly, in terms of contemporary constructions of gender and age, she was the least powerful person of the three, but her rank and wealth had the effect of reversing the positions.

The characters of the lady and the musician were 'read' by all contemporary critics as admirable and that of the grocer, by all but one critic, as unsympathetic.[50] This understanding of the picture is to some extent, supported by a close analysis of the role played by the children in establishing the character of their parent. The musician's two children are touchingly idealised; his little girl fallen asleep with exhaustion on a corn-sack and the boy is fresh-faced and beautiful like a Murillo child. The lady's child runs to her for comfort, frightened of the performing monkey. But the grocer's two grown-up daughters look pale, unhappy and overworked – perhaps demonstrating that their father's avarice, that forces them to overwork, will be shown in his treatment of the poor musician. It is noteworthy that, in all the descriptions of the picture, no mention is made of the scene on the far right. In a backroom a crowd of elderly men are playing games and reading, enjoying a retirement denied to the old musician-veteran.

Faed's motive in painting this picture was to arouse sympathy for the type of poor veteran he depicted. It would not be possible to state that he intended to stir his audience to change laws or even to donate money to veteran charities, since his work was not reviewed in such terms by his contemporaries, but was rather discussed in apolitical, personal terms. The old man is stated to have been 'compelled to practise music on the streets' but the process and circumstances which caused this reduction are not discussed. Even such reviews as *The Times'* which locate the musician specifically as a 'ragged old soldier reduced to the tramp' do not pass any comment on the wider social problem implied.[51] It would be wrong, therefore, to see this painting as in some way constituting a protest against prevailing social conditions. The terms of its reception suggest that it was part of a discourse for 'understanding' the problem of the poor. Part of this depended on the idealisation of the ruling class as providing a solution to social problems from private charity, rather than collective legislation, and also as being aware of social deprivation among the worthy poor. Faed's painting reinforced this sense of the ruling class as compassionate and charitable. Faed's representation of the itinerant musician-veteran drew upon and disseminated a reassuring image of a dislocated and potentially alarming social group. His veteran was idealised in terms of his humility and implied domesticity, placing him in the social category of the poor whose 'condition' could and should be ameliorated by the caring society.

Notes

1 This point about physical disability is discussed below, note 22.
2 'Ruling class' is used throughout as a shorthand term for that section of the aristocracy and upper-classes who constituted the ruling class in terms of economic power and governmental control. This class overlapped to a considerable extent with the 'buying audience' of the Royal Academy. The ruling class of 1880 was different in composition from that of 1815, but this broadening of the powerbase was matched by a larger audience for the Royal Academy. The RA cannot be deemed to be state controlled in the overt way that the *Salon* was in France, but powerful controls operated through the Academy and were crucial in determining the quality and content of paintings exhibited at the prestigious annual summer exhibition.
3 A. R. Skelley, *The Victorian Army at Home*, 1977, p. 52.
4 G. Stedman Jones, *Outcast London*, 1971, p. 79.
5 C. J. Napier, *Remarks on Military Law*, 1837, p. 73.
6 E. P. Thompson, *The Making of the English Working Class*, 1977, p. 693.
7 One section of the meeting marched on the Tower of London, and urged the soldiers there to mutiny and hand over the armoury. This incident did not lead to a revolution but demonstrated clearly the dangers of radicals 'subverting' soldiers and veterans.
8 The death penalty was enforced for attempting to subvert any serving members of the Forces. Thompson, *op. cit.*, p. 527.
9 In-pensioners and out-pensioners at Chelsea never amounted to more than half the estimated 50,000 veterans in the post-Waterloo period. This over-generous estimate from Anon., *An Historical and Descriptive Account of the Royal Military Hospital at Chelsea*, 1805, p. 68.
10 G. R. Gleig, *Chelsea Hospital and its Traditions*, 1839, p. 23.
11 Kilmainham Hospital in Dublin was the sister institution to Chelsea.
12 Out-pensioners outnumbered inmates by 160 to 1, according to figures published in the 1885 official handbook. Anon., *Handbook for Visitors to Chelsea Hospital*, 1885, p. 15.
13 F. C. Mather, *Public Order in the Age of the Chartists*, 1959, p. 151.
14 Anon., *Handbook for Visitors to Chelsea Hospital*, 1885, p. 15.
15 G. A. Gleig, *Chelsea Hospital and its Traditions*, 1839, p. 334.
16 Arts Council of Great Britain, *Great Victorian Pictures*, 1978, p. 7.
17 Allan Cunningham's *Life of Sir David Wilkie*, 3 vols, 1843, is the most exhaustive biography of the painter.
18 T. S. R. Boase, *The Oxford History of English Art, 1800–70*, vol. 10, 1959, p. 195.
19 Museum of London, *Paintings, Politics and Porter*, 1984, p. 27.
20 Wellington Museum, Aspley House, London, 36/1/2/ x 60/1/2/ ins.

21 Allan Cunningham, *Life of Sir David Wilkie*, 1843, vol. II, p. 18.
22 Many early nineteenth century representations of veterans show them as either decrepit or disabled. The effect of this was to minimise any sense of physical threat from the veterans and to make them into recognisably suitable cases for pity.
23 Royal Academy, *Summer Exhibition*, 1822.
24 Statistics on RA exhibits are far from accurate since many pictures are lost and now known only from their titles, but, of nine veteran pictures exhibited 1815–54, only one does not show him as either ill, disabled or as a Chelsea pensioner.
25 E. Spiers, *The Army and Society*, 1980, pp. 97–117 *passim.*
26 There were many instances of ruling class intervention into military affairs in the areas of health, food, accommodation, family life and sexual conduct. A. R. Shelley, *The Victorian Army at Home*, 1977, p. 17.
27 J. Saxon-Mills, *Life and Letters of Sir Hubert Herkomer, CVO,RA*, 1923; an interesting but patchy biography of the painter.
28 Lady Lever Gallery, Port Sunlight, 82 x 61 ins.
29 G. R. Gleig, *Chelsea Hospital and its Tradition*, 1839, p. 334.
30 J. Saxon-Mills, *Life and Letters of Sir Hubert Herkomer, CVO, RA*, 1923, p. 87.
31 *The Athenaeum*, no. 2484, 5 June 1875, p. 755.
32 See note 26.
33 *The Academy*, 22 May 1875, p. 538.
34 L. Nochlin, *Realism*, 1971.
35 *The Academy*, 22 May 1875, p. 538.
36 M. McKerrow, *The Faeds*, 1982, has a short biography of the painter.
37 E. Spiers, *The Army and Society*, 1980, p. 27.
38 A. R. Skelley, *The Victorian Army at Home*, 1977, pp. 204–28 has an excellent discussion on this point.
39 E. J. Hardy, 'Time-expired men', *Good Words*, 1891, p. 765.
40 G. J. Wolseley, 'The army', in T. H. Ward (ed.), *The Reign of Queen Victoria*, 1887, p. 213.
41 G. Stedman Jones, *Outcast London*, 1971, p. 79.
42 Royal Academy, *Summer Exhibition 1880*, p. 16.
43 *The Athenaeum*, no. 2,742, 15 May 1880, p. 637.
44 *Art Journal*, 1880, p. 186.
45 M. McKerrow, *The Faeds*, 1982, p. 102.
46 New South Wales Art Gallery, *The Victorian Social Conscience*, 1976, p. 8.
47 *The Times*, 6 May 1880, p. 10.
48 *Illustrated London News*, 1 May 1880, p. 435.
49 *The Times*, 6 May 1880, p. 10.
50 *The Athenaeum*, no. 2,742, 15 May 1880, p. 637.
51 *The Times*, 6 May 1880, p. 10.

4
Pearly kings and queens

RAPHAEL SAMUEL and
GARETH STEDMAN JONES

Pearlies are often held to symbolise the spirit of London – good humoured, free-and-easy and enjoying a bit of a spree. Like the Beefeaters in the Tower, they demonstrate our love of pageantry and tradition. They link us, if only vicariously, to the London of Bartholomew Fair and Bankside, to the cockney characters in Dickens, to the costers of Mayhew and Phil May. Certainly, the 600 or more people who fill St Martin-in-the-Fields for the annual Pearly Festival are given every encouragement to believe that they are participating in a great cockney occasion, while the camera-clicking tourists, gazing at the spectacle with incredulity, seem to believe that they are witnesing the performance of some ancient British rite – a plebeian equivalent to the Trooping of the Colour or the Changing of the Guard.

Yet the Festival at St Martin-in-the-Fields only came into being in the early 1960s, and owes its origins not so much to 'tradition' as to the initiative of the Rev. Austin Williams, seeking out new functions for the church in an underpopulated parish (the folk club in the crypt is another of his initiatives). It is true that for many years there used to be pearly services at St Mary Magdalene, Southwark, a church which was destroyed in the Blitz, but a ceremony in Trafalgar Square can hardly be linked to it. The communicants are drawn not from the neighbourhood but from as far afield as Portsmouth, Stevenage and Croydon, and they drive to church not in donkey and cart – the traditional coster carriage – but by motor car. The pearly queens wear ostrich-feathered hats, very much in the manner of the 1890s; but their dresses are cut to modern length, and their gifts of fruit and vegetables are carried in cellophane wrappers. Numbers of the kings come in collar-and-tie rather than in a 'kingsman' (the costers' coloured scarf) or the choker; lapels sport such un-traditional badges as 'Holiday Inns of South Africa'.

Pearlies are generally thought of as synonymous with costers and their traditions as in some sense coterminous. Thus the Museum of London (normally scrupulous in its historical reconstructions) clothes its waxwork Victorian coster in a pearly dress, as though it were a tribal costume. Pearl Binder (*The Pearlies*) while admitting that 'the pearlies did not burst upon the London scene until the 1880s, asserts that 'their advent had been prepared by many centuries of coster tradition'. The costers' 'adoration for royalty', she says, goes back to medieval times. In a more populist version, the coster pearly kingdoms are derived from that age-old figure in folk custom, the Lord of Misrule.

The real story is interestingly different. Pearlies were an invention of late-Victorian London. Their connection with the inherited customs of costers is at best speculative, while their subsequent relationship to popular culture has been as much a matter of life imitating art as of art imitating life. The bare facts are these. The first Londoner to adorn himself in a pearly costume was not a coster, but a roadsweeper, Henry Croft of Somers Town, St Pancras. In 1880 or 1886 – stories differ – he sewed pearl buttons all over his jacket, trousers and waistcoat to help in fund-raising for a local charity (the Temperance Hospital, Hampstead Road). There was no traditional connection between costers and pearl buttons: indeed according to one version, Croft's idea was a plebeian imitation of an upper-class vogue. What is certainly apocryphal is the idea that, inspired by his example, costers started imitating his dress (Binder suggests that some 200 factories were set up to cope with the demand for pearl buttons). It may not be true, as a writer claimed in 1902 (*Living London*, vol. 1, p. 77) that the real coster 'never dreams of sporting such buttons', but the notion that it entered everyday dress is absurd, if only on grounds of weight.

However bogus the lineage, the pearly king undoubtedly drew on pre-existing elements in street art. As a living advertisement, attracting the attention of passers by, he can be likened to the sandwichboardmen who paraded the streets in liveried uniform, or the barkers employed by tradesmen and market stallholders to attract customers. As a money-taker he is second cousin to the street entertainers, buskers and showmen. As a grotesque, he has obvious affinities to such carnivalesque figures as the Jack-in-the-Green (paraded about the London streets on May Day, the chimney-sweeps' festival), the clowns on the fairground or circus parade, or the comic figures who accompanied the floats on such occasions as Guy Fawkes Day and Fairlop Friday. The pearly costume was made up by precisely that process of *bricolage* or totting which was so fundamental to survival in the homes and trades of the poor. Buttons themselves played a conspicuous role in the street games of children (in poorer neighbourhoods buttons served as a surrogate currency) and it does not seem fanciful to suggest a family resemblance between pearly dress and the 'grottoes' (wayside begging shrines, made up of oyster shells and pebbles) which children in the poorer London streets put up to coax coppers from the passerby. The idea of a local 'king', too, was a familiar one, particularly in outcast groups. (The gypsies are an obvious case in point, and the whole question of Romany influence on the pearlies is one which might merit a work of family reconstitution.)

But however indigenous some of the elements of pearlydom may appear, the context which gave rise to it was anything but folklore. Unlike the kings of the gypsies or the underworld, the pearlies occupied a strictly subaltern role, collecting for institutionally-promoted charities. They were rewarded for their pains not by power but by clerical and philanthropic patronage. Unlike such 'flash' forms of proletarian dress as that of the teddy boys and punks – or indeed of the mid-Victorian London coster – the pearly costume, so far from provoking class anxiety, was associated from the start with deference and respectability. Henry Croft, 'the original pearly king', was according to his obituarists, a paragon of sober virtue, eschewing smoking, drinking and playing cards, and devoting his energies to philanthropy and Christian mission.

The advent of the pearlies coincided with a populist turn on the part of the hospital authorities. 'Sensational' methods of fundraising were inititated and Hospital Saturday and Hospital Sunday emerged as red-letter days in the local calendar, the occasion for colourful street processions and the parading of carnival floats. In Bethnal Green, where such processions were supported by the numerous local benefit clubs as well as by the lodges of the national friendly societies, Hospital Saturday demonstrations in the 1880s would stretch to half a mile or more in length. It was for such an occasion that Henry Croft invented his pearly suit, and numbers of the early 'kings' (Pearl Binder tells us) emerged from the provident and benefit societies which were the mainstay of the hospital processions. In the early days the pearlies took their place alongside the comic policemen, cowboys and indians, Robin Hoods and Maid Marians who adorned the carnival floats. Support for the local hospitals was the pearlies' very title to existence and charitable fund-raising has remained the rationale of their activity down to the present day.

The hospital processions and carnivals of the 1880s were the products of – or response to – a remarkable and virtually uncharted turnabout in working-class opinion. Up to the 1870s, when there was a steep fall in mortality rates, hospitals had been an object of loathing and fear. Fever patients were sympathetically concealed in times of epidemic, for fear that they would be forciby hospitalised, while during the cholera of 1832 there had actually been riots against the hospitals. In the 1830s there were frequent rumours that hospitals were using poor people's bodies as 'subjects' for anatomical demonstrations, and long after the decline of the Burking panic there was a very general belief that hospital was a place to which people were sent to die. Some time during the last quarter of the century there was a gravitational shift in popular opinion, and hospitals began to be regarded not as enemy institutions but as a source of comfort and help. The friendly societies, who previously had devoted a large share of their savings to paying out funeral benefits, began to devote a larger proportion of their expenditure to the provision of medical care. In poor parts of London, such as Bethnal Green, hospital tickets began to be used as a lever of political patronage and there was a large expansion of local 'benefit' clubs providing insurance for the sick. The appearance of the pearlies, and their participation in hospital carnivals, was thus symbolic of a newly-formed cross-class alliance and the opening of a new chapter in social medicine.

Pearlies were also adopted, and indeed promoted, by official religion, though the precise dating of the association is unclear. Just as the hospitals were establishing a new place in the popular calendar, so there is evidence of the Church attempting the same. From the 1860s evangelical missions were taking an active part in costermongering affairs, providing the costers with stables for their donkeys (in an effort to force the pace of sanitary improvements), and promoting donkey shows as a way of fostering kindness towards animals. On a larger scale they promoted an annual donkey festival at the Crystal Palace, and both here and in the local shows the pearly kings, by the 1900s, were being given pride of place. In another sphere, high Church clergy in the slum parishes were initiating a policy of aggressive open-air witness and of colourful street processions, e.g. on Good Fridays, strikingly similar to the hospital-rags, though with spiritual rather than carnivalesque motifs. It is in contexts such as these that one should see the incorporation of the pearly phenomenon within the ritual of the established Church. The dating awaits investigation, but by the 1900s the pattern was clear. The Church officiated at the 'coronation' of the pearly kings and queens; it presided at pearly christenings, at pearly weddings and at pearly funerals. Thus, by the 1900s, pearlies were not only philanthropic: they were also henceforth Anglican.

A third major social change which coincided with the appearance of the pearlies, and may explain the phenomenon, was the dramatic rise in the social reputation of the costers. In the literature of early and mid-Victorian times they constantly appear as the 'dangerous classes', a hidden menace, to both the domestic and the social order. In the 1890s they are celebrated as lovable types. Phil May was largely responsible for this revolution in graphic art, but it was probably Albert Chevalier, the self-styled coster serenader, who projected it on to the widest stage, and at the same time made the coster dressed in pearly buttons an epitome of the cockney. Chevalier was both a music hall singer and a 'drawing-room entertainer'. Born and bred in Forsyte's Bayswater, he straddled the world of Mayfair and Belgravia, where he gave private concerts, and that of the working-class audience who thronged the halls. His coster songs – 'My Old Dutch' is the best remembered – were simultaneously reassuring to the rich and profoundly flattering to the poor, suggesting that beneath the coster's 'flash' exterior there beat a heart of gold. In Chevalier's songs and sketches – interestingly devised in the first place for the drawing-rooms rather than for the music-hall stage – the coster came to stand for the virtues of cheerful domesticity and acceptance of a caste-like social hierarchy in which rich and poor both occupied an accepted place. It was Chevalier, the salon impersonator of the plebs, rather than the proletarian Croft, who defined the pearly stereotype and secured at least its limited acceptance as a cockney self-image. Chevalier's intention was cheerfully adopted by Fred Tinsley, himself an ex-music hall performer, who, as a coster, founded the first of the pearly associations in 1902.

It doesn't seem fanciful to suggest that in some way 'Old Dutch' and other sentimental cockney songs helped to precipitate a transformation in the pearly king, from a carnivalesque male clown to a much more domesticated *paterfamilias*. Certainly, by the 1900s there were not only pearly kings but also pearly queens and pearly princesses. Here indeed is one of the most radical departures from such 'folk' figures as the Mock Mayor or Jack-in-the-Green – the carnival king or lord of misrule elected for a single day. The pearlies were organised as family groups; the families intermarried; succession to the titles became hereditary; and it is this dynastic

10 John and Rose Marriott en route to America when they were King and Queen of Finsbury.

character of the pearlies which partly accounts for the tenacity with which they have maintained themselves in the public eye.

Whatever the different elements in the mix, there is no doubt about the potency of the pearly stereotype. By 1911 London was divided up into twenty-eight pearly 'kingdoms'. At Henry Croft's funeral in 1930 (he died in St Pancras workhouse), his bier was accompanied to the grave by 500 pearlies and a crowd numbered in thousands.

The pearly phenomenon has outlived its original conditions of existence, and seems to flourish today by dint of its very archaism. The hospitals for which the pearlies made their collections have long since been taken over by the NHS; the families from which they were drawn have been dispersed by post-war housing and redevelopment; the boroughs from which they took their name have been submerged in wider bureaucratic conglomerates. Yet pearlies flourish and in recent years it seems that their number has increased. Only fourteen attended the harvest festival in 1973: in 1981 there were some forty or fifty of them, including such new-fangled creations as 'The Original Pearly Queen of the London Borough of Redbridge' and a pearly king of the new town of Stevenage, chosen by the council in 1977 'because of all the Londoners who have come down here'. Hotels invite the pearlies to represent England to foreign visitors; firms send them abroad to advertise British goods; newly-formed charities (eg. Holiday Homes for the Blind) call them in to preside at garden parties. In their newest incarnation, pearlies have come to stand for the world that we have lost, a gorblimey London of 'knees up Mother Brown', where times were rough but the spirit of the people indomitable.

The pearlies seem to represent a clear case of manufactured, or invented, tradition, a product of the fantasy world of the carnival float – or, in latter-day times, the tourist – rather than of the workaday struggle for survival. Talking to the pearlies, however, dispels such hard antinomies. They certainly sound more cockney than the generality of present day Londoners, and some boast a mastery of Romany or rhyming slang. Their titles, by whatever circuitous routes they have been arrived at, are genuinely bound up with family tradition; their lives, however much they may diverge from the public stereotype, do suggest a continuing association with street art. George Hitchin, Pearly King of the City of London, is an example. Now in his seventies he stands at Petticoat Lane every Sunday morning, as he has done since the early 1970s, collecting for charity. His first job was as a news-stand boy at Dalston Junction; later he had a flower stall at London Fields and then a fruit stall in Ridley Road. In the course of an adventurous life he has opened four local restaurants (among them an eel-and-pie shop in Blackstock Road), and run a number of mobile canteens, including the night coffee-stand which stands outside the church in Spitalfields Market. At one stage in his career he was a professional boxer; he now takes on engagements as a comedian round the clubs. Dick Montague in his eighties, the Pearly King of Stevenage, may owe his title to the initiative of the town council, but he claims a descent from five generations of showmen. As a boy he used to stand beside his father's barrow in Kilburn High Road ('We used to have a giggle . . . When the police pulled us up for obstruction we used to step across the road and they wouldn't touch us – we was in Willesden'). Later he had a stall at the fair, and he remained a street trader into his sixties. His grand-daughter, Dawn Harman, also bears an artificial title. But she has her own reasons for asserting pearly princessdom and (albeit in a new-town exile) a defiant London pride. 'When I was at junior school a teacher told me that I'd never get a job because of the way I talked – because of being a cockney. Well I just told her I couldn't help it. I've got a job, so she's wrong.'

5
Britain's royal romance

TOM NAIRN

Monarchy is far from dead, either in Britain or outside it. R. F. Tapsell's encyclopedia of monarchy (*Monarchs, Rulers, Dynasties and Kingdoms of the World*, 1983) lists twenty-six surviving specimens. Some of these are in small countries like Tonga, Bhutan and Bahrain; but the list also contains Japan, Spain and Malaysia. And the 'United Kingdom' monarch remains titular head of many Commonwealth nations, bringing the number of royal states to well over thirty.

Mr Tapsell's survey does not try to cover the growing penumbra of quasi-monarchy, either – that is, nations where individual rulers like Mrs Ghandi and Rajiv Ghandi in India and Kim II Soung in North Korea have built up informal family rule with at least some attributes of old-fashioned dynasty. Once straightforward dictatorship is taken into account – 'temporary' or lifetime absolute rulers put in place by armies or political parties – the picture becomes plainer, if darker. At least superficially, the political globe remains all too similar to the days of pre-1789, when royal power was a rule with few and partial exceptions.

His Highness was most meticulous about financial matters.
Any expenditure, anywhere in the Empire, of more than ten
dollars required his personal approval . . . To repair a
minister's car – the Emperor's approval is needed. To replace
a leaking pipe in the city – the Emperor's approval is needed.
To buy sheets for a hotel - the Emperor's must approve it.
How you should admire, my friend, the diligent thrift of His
August Majesty, who spent most of his royal time checking
accounts, listening to cost estimates, rejecting proposals, and
brooding over human greed, cunning and meddling . . .

Thanks to that system of accountability, the King of Kings had everyone in his hand, and everyone knew it.

This picture of living absolutism was not drawn in the middle ages: it shows life in the Ethiopian court in the 1970s. *The Emperor* (1983), Ryszard Kapuściński's great hallucinatory account of Haile Selassie's last days, was based on the testimony of the last pillow-and purse-bearers, and even of that unfortunate ('His Distinguished Majesty's cuckoo') whose official task consisted in bowing before the King of Kings at appropriate moments of the day or night.

Backwardness?

An easy answer lies in Ethiopian (or other) 'backwardness', imagined as the fossil-like persistence of social anachronism. If most nation-state governments were republican democracies this might have some justification. As things actually are, it smells of complacency – indeed, of a special kind of complacency which (I will argue later) has chronically enfeebled British understanding of our own monarchical state.

Kapuściński shows how the Emperor's regime was by no means entirely given over to fossilised routine. As the Romanovs, the Hapsburgs and Hohenzollern had done up to 1914, the Solomonic monarchy strove above all to 'modernise' – the sole condition being, naturally, that such reform had to proceed wholly from above, a work of pure imperial wisdom. Had it not been for the famine of 1973–4 the work might be proceeding still. More widely, no serious imputation of backwardness can be made against the Scandanavian kingdoms, and not much against the Netherlands, Belgium or Luxembourg, while in Spain a reconstituted throne has so far used its authority to defend parliamentary rule from new attempts at military autocracy.

But the situation is significantly different as regards the British crown. There are two obvious aspects to this. First, the degree of its ideological power; no other contemporary monarch enjoys anything like the adulation which constantly laps about Queen Elizabeth and her family. She is not mildly but intensely popular, and there is a touchy, obsessive element in this popularity which surfaces the instant any criticisms are made. The throne exerts little direct political influence, so such a taboo is both odd and interesting. Second, British monarchy reigns over a country where 'backwardness' does have a relatively precise meaning, one that figures with monotonous prominence in all official and party rhetoric – the supposed 'decline' of Her Majesty's realm from the world-dominance to mediocrity and economic failure.

  Reconsideration of this old problem is now greatly aided by an important revision of the 'backwardness' theme itself. In *The Persistence of the Old Regime* (1981) Arno J. Mayer argues that the liberal and left wing writers responsible for our dominant overview of modern history were invariably over-optimistic. They tended to assume that the definitive triumph of the bourgeoisie must be just around the corner, if not already achieved – at any date from 1789 up to the middle of this century. In reality, as Mayer demonstrates brilliantly in every area, the European 'old regimes' did much more than survive until 1914: they found new life from imperialism and the expansion of the state, twisted modernisation into the service of the aristocracy, and fostered new cults of monarchy and blood or 'breeding'. It was their very success which made war inevitable – not as too many theorists have believed then and since, some inherent tendency of capitalism itself.

  Where are we in history? This is the grand question so ably confronted in Mayer's revision of Marxism. His answer is that now (as in 1848) it is a great deal sooner than we have tended to think. As regards monarchy – and perhaps the UK one especially – this insight makes its 'survival' less amazing. No peculiar foolishness or strain of atavism need be imputed to the British peoples. In a world generally more backward than the Enlightenment's progeny have been willing to admit, the bizarre intensity of Britain's royalty-cult should be seen as less surprising. Rather than outrage, some calm curiosity about the special features of British development is called for.

Strange Silence

Such curiosity about the crown has been singularly lacking. This absence of serious reflection on a phenomenon of obvious importance to the national psyche is surely itself significant, above all when set beside the Matterhorn of royal junk churned out every year by British presses. Yet in this century no subject has been so ignored by the left. The socialist intelligentsia can boast of only two general works on the modern monarchy. Unfortunately both were by the same author, Kingsley Martin. More humiliatingly still, the second (*The Crown and the Establishment*, 1962) was little more than an updating of the first (*The Magic of Monarchy*, 1936), and both rested on the same desperate argument: nothing much wrong with monarchy, really, if only it could be made more sensible and ordinary, and less tied up with the establishment. In

1936 the editor of the *New Statesman's* confidence in British progress made him foresee a quick advance to Scandanavian levels of reasonableness. By the 1960s however, even his faith had worn rather thin. He felt compelled to tell the Windsors they had better snap out of it on pain of becoming irremediable 'symbols of the past and not part of the new England that waits to be born'.

While radical thinkers have been paralysed by the Medusan Head of royal popularity, conservatives have felt little need to explain something so obviously congenial to their instincts. It is only in the field of constitutional lore that much continuous attention has been paid to monarchy; and there it is quite inescapable, since what we dwell under is of course no mere 'constitutional monarchy' but a truly monarchical constitution which (as Samuel Finer put it in his *Comparative Government*, 1970) 'preserves not only mediaeval forms but the mediaeval essence' of sapient and secretive guidance from above. Yet any search for a broader or non-legalistic reading of the crown's significance in this area ends in frustration; Worse than frustration perhaps, because it is a sad fact that Walter Bagehot's complacent commentary of 1867 remains the main reference-point. *The English Constitution*'s feebly cynical remarks on the 'theatrical show' of monarchy bamboozling the lower orders into accepting authority have been worn away by force of re-quotation.

There is an element of truism in this view, which may help to explain its permanence. And it also suits the professors and journalists who comment on such questions to affect a Bagehot-like knowingness. No matter how profound their reverence for the institutions may be (usually bottomless), so much absurdity is only digestible with a dose of irreverence. More seriously, the famous 'Dorsetshire peasant' (that 'miserable creature' who 'knows scarcely anything of Parliament' and thinks the Queen makes the laws) never existed outside Bagehot's pages. And, within ten years, under Disraeli's captaincy, Queen Victoria's crown had been swollen into the mighty totem it remains a century later – a fetish, one must add, most exalted by those solid middle classes Bagehot thought above such silliness.

Class or nation?

Like virtually all such commentators, Bagehot perceived the monarchy primarily in relation to social class. Conservatives have remained grateful for such a useful symbol capable of stretching over class frontiers and winning the hearts of the poor. When the latter became the working class their representatives often denounced this imposture. In every identifiable aspect Britain's chief family embodies the traditional aristocratic establishment; how dare it presume to be the emblem of a toiling majority whose life (perhaps the commonest anti-royal complaint) it knows nothing about'? This, along with unnecessary cost, is the burden of such republicanism as exists in Windsor Britain (William Hamilton's *My Queen and I*, 1975, is the best known example of its plaintive voice.)

However, as soon as uttered, such protests are frozen by the Medusa's gaze. The mass of devoted subjects knows perfectly well that the Queen and her entourage belong to the topmost social crust, and have a fair notion of 'how much it all costs'. Alas, such knowledge has no effect whatever on royal popularity. All it does – in other words, all that republicanism achieves – is a certain amount of 'tut-tutting' and occasional shameful debates about whether the public gets value for money out of its monarch. As long as republicans cannot manage a dignified public campaign they ought to reckon the silence generally forced on them a blessing; it is preferable to such performances (and far less counter-productive).

As we noticed, theoretical silence has been in any case the rule on the left. When the gilded panoply of royal archaism is set in this way against a stratified and adoring civil society, no reasonable explanation is possible (other than a 'Dorsetshire peasant' one, too discouraging for most radicals to entertain consciously). Much easier then to turn aside from the puzzle and, like almost every critic or serious commentator over the past century, to say that really the monarchy doesn't matter. Bagehot's bourgeois intellectuals mostly ended up nursing this alibi; since the sensible middle class had got control of affairs, it could afford an anachronistic (and peasant-fooling) social headpiece. Later, socialist thinkers were to repress their republican instincts, with the same forced complacency; too bad working folk didn't want to be rid of kings and queens, but no need to lose votes through principled fuss when – after all – Her Majesty's Labour Party had been awarded control of affairs without it.

But this cramp comes, it is time to insist, from a characteristically mistaken perspective on royalty. The distinctive British emphasis on class and social tradition is the very thing which renders Britain's royal infatuation incomprehensible, for both the genesis of the contemporary monarchy and its apparently unstoppable popularity are quite clearly phenomena of *national* rather than merely social significance. They are elements in a drama of unresolved national identity. This is not to imply that (as its own ideology proclaims) royalty actually is above and indifferent to class conflict. But it is a fact that all classes have an inevitable stake in the nation and overall national culture, however defined. In England-Britain that definition has, since the defeat of chartism (and the virtual elimination of republicanism), been overwhelmingly – and on the whole successfully – archaic, traditionalist, politically deferential and royal.

Conservative-national identity

Of course, British self-definition has for most of the same period also been liberal. Indeed the once omnipotent Whig ideology of history decreed that, despite empire and Eton, this was the central theme. Rational progress was the *leitmotif*, the 'backwardness' merely a respectful (and in its way sustaining) counterpoint. Amid the wreckage of the 1980s, one minor blessing to count must surely be the fatal looking blight now afflicting this belief-system. Internally, Mrs Thatcher has gnawed most of its main root away. Externally, the European political world, that once gave rough plausibility to our conceit – during the long era when old regimes persisted, or festered into counter-revolution – has turned since the 1950s into a community putting it to shame. We can begin to see more clearly how Whig (or more precisely, Whig-Labour) interpretations of the national essence consistently inverted the truth by pretending that tradition inevitably served progress.

We are at last beginning to grasp something of how the twentieth century's dominant traditionalism was constructed. For example, an outstanding essay by David Cannadine, 'The context, performance and meaning of ritual: the British monarchy and the "invention of tradition", 1820–1977'. (in *The Invention of Tradition*, edited by Hobsbawm and Ranger, Cambridge, 1983) shows how much of our 1,000 year old grandeur was hastily contrived towards the end of Queen Victoria's reign. Before then, the rude and incompetent ceremonials of our *parvenu* dynasties had been the laughing-stock of courtly Europe.

The change was of course an insular chapter in Mayer's general counter-revolution; here too the old regime discovered a wonderful new elixir in its mounting battle for empire and against the menace of socialism. However, certain insular conditions made a crucial difference to the result. While not a democratic republic, Britain's state and constitution remained different from (and in advance of) the more authentically *anciens régimes* of continental Europe. It remained what 1688 had made it – a capitalist (but non-industrial) oligarchy, a transitional polity which had endured into permanence thanks to naval power and colonial assets. The assorted simulacra of democracy this regime had rigged up between the 1830s and the 1880s did not (and still do not) amount to the genuine article. They were conserving and concessionary, both in spirit and lasting effect. But, though tested to near-destruction in the years 1910–14, they afforded none the less a basis, allowing our counter-revolution to remain relatively mild.

Then, when the real coelocanths of central and eastern Europe disintegrated into the dragons' teeth of post-1911, Britain's sham-old royal state not only survived but drew fresh nourishment from both great wars. How was this possible? A most stimulating new approach to the whole problem has been made possible by the historian Linda Colley in her article 'The apotheosis of George III: loyalty, royalty and the British nation, 1760–1820' (in *Past and Present*, no.102, February, 1984). (It is no coincidence that both this and *The Invention of Tradition* have come out of the *Past and Present* stable.)

It may seem a long way from George III to questions of twentieth-century survival, but one should remember that our subject is a system which exhibits (even if its own self-esteem has somewhat exaggerated the trait) notoriously long *durées* of development. Ms Colley's thesis is that George III's reign – and particularly the years around the jubilee of 1809 – showed the nascent structure of an effective Anglo-British nationalism. Germinated in the self-doubting decade after the loss of the American colonies, it grew to more distinct self-affirmation in the long battle against France. So strong and so conservative was this new populist tide that even the wholly unpromising figure of the ageing and disturbed George could be elevated to national sainthood – Britain's answer to Napoleon. In its name radical patriotism (the kind Dr Johnson had associated with scoundrels) was finally squashed into the margins.

There is of course a major irony at work here, as Ms Colley does not fail to underline. This epoch of triumphant conservatism, when our old regime first proved its powers of persistence and forged the nation we have had to live in ever since, has been in recent times publicised above all as that of the semi-revolutionary 'making of the English working class.' A poetic celebration of the moral superiority of the vanquished has consistently drawn attention away from the victorious state, and so from the architecture of national hegemony.

After George's 'apotheosis' there were to be many decades in which that hegemony remained far less stable than the usual Whig labour retrospect pretends. Monarchy traversed moments of even deeper unpopularity than it had known in the eighteenth century. However, a template had been cast and tested which, when circumstances once more demanded, could easily be revived. As we know, these conditions were realised from the 1870s onwards. After its mid-century supremacy, the state was again menaced by powerful foreign empires and mined from within by the political rise of new urban masses. And this time these threats were more serious, and permanent, One aspect of the ruling order's mobilis-ation against them was to be an equally intense and permanent exaltation of the crown, that enduring apotheosis which has, with only the minor hiccup of Edward VIII, taken up our century of decline.

The empire was certainly important in getting the machinery going again, but it is a great merit of Colley's study that she stresses the underlying national element more. The royal hypnosis is a variety of nationalism not of imperialism. Were this not so, it would be incomprehensible how the crown's symbolic passion has managed to outlive so well the disappearance of political empire. As the latter has dwindled, the familial talisman of our community identity has loomed ever larger.

Mistaken identity?

Like the Hanoverian original, that identity has been largely justified and consolidated by success in war. Defeat would have consigned it to the same graveyard as the other old regimes. From Trafalgar to Port Stanley, each new victory has in fact contributed to forming an Anglo-British *gemeinschaft* in Tönnies' sense – a pre-modern 'community', familial in instinct and outlook. Orwell's famous description was 'a family with the wrong members in control'; it did not occur to him that the 'family' part might in the end be a greater threat than the wrong members, since Labour's dream of the family with the right members in control happens to be unrealisable. A British socialist nation may be conceivable, but not a British socialist 'family' in this distinctive archaically-weighted sense.

Just how has the feat been accomplished? How essential is the monarchy to its ideological mechanism? On this plane of analysis a great deal remains obscure. The apparent simplicity of Britain's sentimental fixation on Royalty dissolves under analysis into a weird thicket of questions. It is heartening, though, that the That-cher years have seen a great increase in concern with such prob-lems. The 1984 History Workshop was devoted to the theme of patriotism for example, 'Ideology and myth in the making of English national identity'. The three volumes of papers drawn from this conference, of which this volume is one, will surely encourage a still more determined radical onslaught on these issues, till now often despised as secondary or eccentric.

Some interesting suggestions have come forth from these and other recent discussions. The class fixation of conventional English thought encouraged critics to see monarchy as an endorsement of hierarchy. Yet ostensibly (and for the most part sincerely) the modern royal families have denied the charge, as they have rejected any association with racism. The point is, surely, that their primal and determining ideological link is with the state rather than directly with civil society. They are totems of Westminster, of the political traditions that have always made up the main substance of Anglo-British nationalism. Only secondarily and indirectly do they underwrite social privilege; for of course, the constitution of which they are a talisman has always been an instrument of élite governance and self-preservation. In a people's monarchy royal support for the archaic social fabric can only be covert; if such support is also strong, this is because of its indirectness.

Why is such a prominent talisman needed at all, if the old ideal fire-power of Black Rod and the law remains so devastating? Because without it the constitution delivering this force would be meaningless; it would have to be revised in written contemporary form, meeting the norms of western Europe. Today, the basis could not fail to be the contrary of Finer's 'mediaeval essence' – that is, popular sovereignty as distinct from mere rights and liberties permitted from on high. Our old regime is one where, in Dicey's ineffably pompous but exact phrase. 'the prerogatives of the crown have become the privileges of the people', via a parliamentary system guiding the sacred authority downwards in safe dosages, at moments least likely to destabilise. The resultant state-order bears at many points a disconcertingly close if specious resemblance to democracy. But, while the Brito-Falklands ethos decrees the eternal superiority of this steam-driven apparatus to the flashy novelties on show in the EEC or the UN, those worried about entering the third millenium AD with the House of Lords and 'first-past-the post' should reflect more on the spirit of such processes.

This is surely what monarchy is really about. 'What is of real importance is the spread of a real Republican spirit among the people,' remarked Joseph Chamberlain during his abortive flirtation with anti-monarchy over a century ago. The risk of a crownless Britain is simply the risk of such a spirit emerging to find open voice in the state, rather than the systemic bafflement which our peculiar civil élitism requires for survival. In its day (incidentally) Joe Chamberlain's Birmingham seemed a spiritual threat of just this kind, but wasn't Ken Livingstone's London smothered in essentially the same way?

As for national identity, a conceptual mistake parallel to that enshrouded in the Whig notion of history has almost always been made. It was expressed with classic vigour in Hans Kohn's influential *Nationalism: its Meaning and History* nearly thirty years ago. 'The first full manifestation of modern nationalism', he observed 'occurred in 17th century England' through the revolution and civil war. These created the consciousness of being a 'new Israel', the chosen people of Protestantism. But of course (as Kohn's own argument unwittingly shows) the one thing this could not be was a full manifestation of nationalism in any developmental sense. The earliness of absolutism's end here, the religious matrix, and the élite's successful repression of democracy, all restrained national identity, just as they did the new state-form. Both were to remain permanently transitional; compromises between the old and new ages, originally uneasy yet assuming permanence (and then the semblance of antiquity) in the stabilised polity of later eighteenth-century England.

A genuine popular democratic national identity could, after that, only be forged by further revolution (or counter-revolution) or else, by some overwhelming battle against an invader – by a 'liberation struggle'. The great boast of the Whig-Labour system is to have saved Britain forever from the former; Great Britain's imperial position and insular geography saved her from the latter. True, during the Second World War a truculently democratic spirit did get about in both the military and domestic fronts, giving some hint of what was missing. But as we know, it was the identity analysed in Linda Colley's article which proved stronger. By the time of the coronation in 1953, the old regime was back in charge, secure in the knowledge there would never be another 'people's war' and that the modest bolt of people's government had been shot by Mr Attlee and Sir Stafford Cripps.

'Ordinariness'

As we saw the crown is essential to the theory and (ultimately) to the practice of the old constitution. It is no less essential on the more psychic plane of Britain's identity. On both levels its magic works powerfully against hasty and ill-conceived change (a category which includes all democratic presumption from below).

In the terrain of nationalist ideology Britain's royal symbolism has a specifically fetishistic character. Fetishism attributes the essence of a desired whole to some part or fragment, which is then worshipped (in a way seemingly irrational to outsiders) as an embodiment of the totality. The whole woman (or, in our analogy, the whole nation's reality) is, because of early trauma, feared as well as desired. The substitution of a fetish maintains sexuality (nationality) and keeps its reality at a safe distance, exorcising all its potentially disturbing features. Moreover, such a personality structure is self-perpetuating, in the sense that under threat the fetish is automatically intensified – the greater its incomparable glamour becomes, the more unthinkable its loss (unconsciously identified with castration, effacement of national manhood).

It is surely of some significance that in his study of *Fetishism* (1927) Freud was driven to precisely the analogy under discussion here. Referring to the fear of unbearable loss which the fetish keeps at bay, he adds: 'In later life a grown man may perhaps experience a similar panic when the cry goes up that Throne and Altar are in danger, and similar illogical consequences will ensue.' Again looking at 'later life', when the fetishistic way of life is stably established, he points out with a touch of ironic humour that now

> the fetishist feels that he enjoys yet another advantage from his
> substitute for a genital. The meaning of the fetish is not
> known to other people, so the fetish is not withheld from him:
> it is easily accessible and he can readily obtain the sexual
> satisfaction attached to it. What other men have to woo and
> make exertions for can be had by the fetishist with no trouble
> at all.

Conservation of the fetish requires considerable ideal effort, from individual or community. The British nation-state happens to be especially well-furnished with the means for this; since the spread of general literacy it has enjoyed a uniquely pervasive national press and then an even more influential broadcasting media. But other and deeper cultural currents work to keep the royal regime afloat and ship-shape.

As imperial symbolism has waned from the 1920s onwards, it has been gradually replaced by more domestic icons in tune with the shrunken lineaments of 'this small country of ours'. The psychology of fetishism is intrinsically male-oriented; but in this epoch it has been both disguised and extended by ever more familial imagery. A 'royal family' is a more potent sacral object than a king or queen because of its supplementary appeal to the universal kinship ties for which women feel responsible. Emblematically blessed in this way, women's burden (and oppression) is at the same time awarded a second dimension; analogy with the warming larger family of national community, with a British cohesiveness at once stifling and comforting – the very essence of traditionalism.

As well as the family there is an even broader alteration in the climate of contemporary royal ideology, without which it could not hope to attain its actual intensity. Ever since Geroge V (who took the measure of British socialism early on) remarked to Ramsay MacDonald while dismissing the first Labour government, 'You have found me an ordinary man, haven't you?' the onslaught of 'They're just like us' has been unceasing. Each reign has, in the language of sycophancy, brought the throne closer to the people. If pomp and pageantry were creations of Victoria and Edward VII, the 'public relations' of ordinariness have been the boast of the present monarch.

The converse of 'They're just like us' is of course that, despite unpromising appearances, 'We're just like them' still the royal folk of new Israel. It cannot be banal coincidence that Elizabeth II's thirty year reign has witnessed a general transformation of British literary culture precisely in the direction of a cult of ordinariness. Donald Davie has commented on Philip Larkin's power 'to give England an image of itself'; an image, surely, of what must be called transcendent ordinariness, of a national realm whose very drabness and decline radiate still an incomparable poetic glamour. The canonisation and vast popularity of such a culturally untranslatable figure as John Betjeman is an even more obvious signpost. 'The movement' was a typically low-key defence of the same realm, the family bungalow splendid in its very seediness. From anger (at those 'wrong members' again) to belching celebrations of insular-family values, still (once the family row is over) better than anyone else's a generation of conventional novels and plays has articulated to perfection, the spiritual climate of intensified royalism.

Ordinariness is certainly not the sole wider credo offering some support to royal traditionalism. I underline it here only because it has failed to get due attention from critics. There are also of course older, more exposed staples like English empiricism and the nature-romanticism exuded by so much music and civil culture. After swallowing his anger, the typical régime intellectual will undoubtedly migrate to rural parts, and console himself with Vaughan Williams and reflections on the awfulness of foreign theorising. It is, surely, the interaction among these various elements that makes up the overall ideology of Windsor Britain; much more discussion of their articulation is needed than I can attempt here.

Republican problems

Returning to the salient aspects of British monarchy mentioned earlier – popularity, taboo, and the puzzling relation to 'backwardness' – we can now see how the nationalist framework begins at least to explain them. The genuine love for the crown is only that of people for their nation – a standard feature of modern nation-state existence. But its over-popularity betrays a neurotic or displaced character, defended by an intense taboo against criticism. Analysis of this in turn leads towards the historically deformed structure of post-revolutionary English nationality, cramped permanently under the powerful (and internationally successful) ego-system of the old élite.

The 'backwardness' sanctified in regal hysteria is not, therefore, the banal one bemoaned by ministers and economic pundits (though naturally this has aggravated the situation since the 1950s). It is rooted in the nature of the state and the patrician class-order which prevailed long before British industry entered on its current road to ruin (prevailed indeed while the industrial revolution itself was made, and determined its political outcome). These have in a variety of ways suppressed democratic and egalitarian nationalism (while making the required concessions and obeisances, above all during wars). Though always (in the sense demanded by our metaphor) 'pathological', all deformation was for long both justified and concealed by the different and graver backwardness prevalent in Europe – the long catastrophe of counter-revolution and war. Only from the middle of this century onwards did its character become an irrefutable and mounting burden, to be eased by ever more frantic absorption in the main national fetish.

Consider, for instance, the utterly typical English attitude towards nationalism, which has (to the baffled fury of Scots, Welsh and Irish alike) surfaced so often since the mid 1970s. This consists in indicating, at first with polite astonishment, then (when peripheral fanaticism persists in its demands) somewhat brusquely, that the English are above that sort of thing (mixed-up Scotch grandmothers, etc.). The vein of truth here is of course that the English are not above but below 'that sort of thing'. They have not yet got there. Empire, crown, establishment and Labour party have prevented them forging a modern democratic national identity, and this obstruction itself has become a revered proof of superior civilisation and tolerance (the Hapsburg régime too went in for this kind of thing but fortunately did not command the resources needed to make it stick).

The pre-nationalist aspect of the royal cult does give it extra utility in a multinational entity like the UK. It is doubtful if this has had much importance in sustaining it, however; Anglo-metro-politan dominance is so great and (outside Ireland) has been so easily attained that it must be considered a problem of the heart-land. It is England's living and malignant archaism which consti-tutes the principal vast barrier to the advance of the republican spirit. The trouble is that (to end with a paradox) republicanism in this sense has so little to do with the monarchy as such: it has to do with what the Monarchy 'stands for'. A serious republicanism, demanding the return of England's republican spirit, entails little less than that political and social revolution which the English Parliamentary Left has solemnly and repeatedly renounced throughout its modern history.

Now, while little has altered in this general perspective, it is interesting that there has been a small but perceptible change in the general climate of affairs monarchical. Some have been mere rumours (like Her Majesty's displeasure over the invasion of Grenada); but there have also been facts like her handshake with Ken Livingstone over the Thames Flood Barrier, some intelligent journalistic concern with the question in the *New Statesman*, *Marxism Today*, and *Time & Tide*, and the attack by Mrs Thatcher's super-ego, Enoch Powell, on the Queen for paying too much attention to her Commonwealth subjects. The interesting thing is that (like the political resurrection of the Church of England) these stirrings should have occurred after the Battle of Port Stanley and the subsequent war-election; in other words, since it has been beyond reasonable doubt that Mrs Thatcher's counter-revolution is here to stay and that many vital features of the old establishment are being shaken out of their time-honoured grooves from the right.

No doubt the prime minister's role as an alternative quasi-regal idol in the national pantheon may also be important here. But what counts, surely, is that once again we are seeing the counter-revolution beginning to achieve, in its own crooked and damning fashion, those very things which the forces of radicalism and revol-ution had previously failed to carry through. The egalitarian populism renounced by Professor Hobsbawm's 'responsible' left has reappeared in caricatural form in the right's radical-capitalist ideology. After a century of suffocation at establishment hands, the resentful quest for a national identity engineered from below enjoys a revenge as a house-owning and Telecom-share-buying 'democracy'. The élite hands themselves, so well inured to domi-nating the left, are having their knuckles smashed by rabid upstarts from the lower ranks of the right. Too long baffled and deprecated, a people's urge to get rid of caste domination has soured into a manipulated general hatred of 'the state'. Betrayed for equally long by its protagonists, socialism has fallen face-first into the fantasy of a life-giving and classless capitalism.

The British old régime's counter-revolution was, as we noticed, a mild one. But the very conditions favouring this have also made it last an interminably long time – that gradual reassertion and hardening of traditional order which always counter-pointed (and actually dominated)the more publicised 'gradualness' of reform and progress. Under Mrs Thatcher the process has begun to lose patience and shed the vestment of consensus. However ominous this turns out to be, there is no denying it has shaken the old order up and let in some air. That is presumably what has put monarchy back into critical consciousness. Another few years of the counter-revolution, in short, and the conditions may yet exist for a serious British republicanism (though that will depend on the Left's doing more than at present to catch up with the Right).

Music

6
Greensleeves and the idea of national music

ALUN HOWKINS

> The art of music, above all other arts, is the expression of the soul of the nation.
>
> Ralph Vaughan Williams

From at least the end of the eighteenth century a connection was made by theorists and composers of classical and art musics between music and nationality. It was argued that the 'sounds' of music could literally express the soul, and that the soul had a national character. This national idea of music reached its high point during the nineteenth and early twentieth centuries, when music became an integral part of national movements. The work of Grieg, for instance, was closely linked with the attempt to establish a Norwegian cultural identity as part of the struggle for independence from Sweden. Similarly the work of Bartok in Hungary asserted an Hungarian as opposed to an Austro/Germanic identity.

Examples of this kind could be multiplied. But while there is a clear connection between an emergent nation, or national liberation movement, and the need to establish a distinct culture, it is less clear that other movements towards a national music fit in with this model.[1] For instance the great Russian musical revival of the mid-nineteenth century was certainly not linked to any new geographical nation; rather, it was linked to a notion of Slavism within Russia as a new national identity. This was also the case in England.

The stimuli for this search for a new national identity are complex, and a full discussion of them is outside the scope of this short essay.[2] However the key factors were the economic problems experienced by industrial capital, imperialist expansion into Africa, and perceptions of an urban, and occasionally racial, crisis 'at home'.[3] The parameters of this new national identity are gradually being sketched out. Gareth Stedman Jones has written about the music hall and the new Londoners, as well as about the crisis in middle-class ideology when confronted with the problems of the inner city.[4] John Burrow has pointed to the refashioning of English history under the influence of Froude and Seeley,[5] while David Cannadine, Bernard Cohn and Eric Hobsbawm have provided accounts of the production of a range of legitimating rituals, ceremonies and traditions for the new order.[6]

This search for a national identity had an important cultural dimension. In the same way that social and political writers saw England dominated by foreign ideas and values, so artists saw English culture 'swamped' by foreign values and ideas. In this, music had a central role. If, as many composers of élite music believed, music was the 'the expression of the soul of the nation', then that soul was in a sorry state. As Cecil Sharp, the folk song collector, put it:

> Since the death of Purcell . . . the educated classes have patronized the music of the foreigner to the exclusion of that of the Englishman. Foreign vocalists, singing in a foreign tongue, have for two centuries monopolized the operatic stage; while English concert platforms have, during the same period, been exclusively occupied by alien singers and instrumentalists, singing and playing compositions of European writers.[7]

At one level this was certainly right. There were no English élite composers of any real note during the nineteenth century. As Peter Pirie says, 'the sum total of our musical achievement in the Victorian era was meagre, reactionary and undistinguished'.[8] But it was more than that; what was composed was dominated by Mendelsshon, then by Brahms and then by Wagner. Any performer who sought any sort of fashion adopted a foreign name, German if an instrumentalist, Italian if a vocalist. In popular music the German bands became increasingly the only point of contact with semi-serious music for two generations of English people. Even in 1910, when Vaughan Williams was on his way to being an established composer and the 'English musical renaissance' was an established fact, he wrote to Harold Child, the librettist of *Hugh the Drover*, 'I see *hardly any* (sic) chance of an opera by an English composer ever being produced, at all events in *our* (sic) lifetime.'[9]

Sharp, Vaughan Williams and others brought to this situation a crusading zeal to create an English music based on two different but related traditions. The first was that of a past English musical

greatness, when 'we proved ourselves capable of holding our own
side by side with the foremost of the musical nations of Europe'.[10]
This meant returning in essence to before 'the time of Charles I
[when] music in England began to languish'.[11] The second route
lay through folk song. 'We have a literature of folk song of our
own, which affords incontrovertible evidence that, as a nation, we
possess a natural and inherent musical faculty of no mean order.'[12]
These two traditions sought out roots for an English music in a
'natural' society – pre-industrial England and the countryside –
where, in a sense, 'Tudor' England still lived. As Vaughan
Williams wrote, 'I am like a psychical researcher who has actually
seen a ghost', the ghost being old English music preserved,
unknowingly, by the 'more primitive people of England.'[13] Folk
song and pre-modern music were not only linked by their apparently shared social situation but by their modality – the scales in
which they were performed. The 'modes' are the 'old' scales,
abandoned by élite music in the sixteenth century and finally over-
taken by the dominance of the major scale in the eighteenth and
nineteenth centuries.[14] The discovery that many country singers
sang modally provided another link between the survivals of the
late nineteenth century and the late medieval/early modern period.

The twin pillars of pre-modern, and especially Tudor and Stuart,
music and folk song were the basis of the English musical renaissance. True, there were other influences, especially through Elgar,
but these, in the medium term at least, seem to have contributed
little to the actual flowering of composition. Indeed most recent
work on Elgar stresses his continental aspects, as against his Englishness which contemporaries saw. For example, Peter Pirie wrote
in 1980 that Elgar was 'a European figure who is English almost
by default'.[15] Similarly both Stanford and Parry, although associated with both the folk-song movement and the revival of Elizabethan and Stuart music, were Europeans steeped in nineteenth-
century continental composition whose Englishness appeared only
rarely.

We can see the importance of these influences and indicate more
precisely the ideology which grew out of them by looking at the
work of Ivor Gurney (1890–1937). Gurney was born in Gloucester,
the son of a tailor. Through the choir of the Cathedral and the
support of patrons he went to the Royal College of Music and
studied under Stanford. In 1914 he volunteered and served as a
private in the 2/5th Gloucester Regiment. In 1918 he was invalided
out of the army suffering from a non-specified mental condition.
He returned to music, but only briefly. In 1922 he was committed
to an asylum and he died, still incarcerated, in 1937.[16]

Gurney is one of the most interesting artists of his generation, both as a poet and a composer, though little of his music is available on record. In his music in particular we see the force and impact of Englishness on the prewar generation. It is as a song writer that Gurney excels, and it is in the eleven songs, or rather settings, from the period immediately before the war that we can see his ideas most clearly. Five of the eleven form what Gurney regarded as a cycle and which he called the 'Elizas'. All are settings of 'Elizabethan' pieces, two by Shakespeare, one by Nashe and two by Fletcher. In setting them Gurney clearly identifies Englishness not only with the lyrics but also identifies his music with that of the Elizabethans. In a letter to his friend Will Harvey in 1912 he wrote:

> I have done 5 of the most delightful and beautiful songs you ever cast your beaming eyes upon. They are all Elizabethan – the words – and blister my kidneys . . . if the music is not as English, as joyful, as tender as any lyric of all the noble host.[17]

'as English, as joyful' could almost serve as a sermon text for those aspects of the movement which rejected Brahms and Mendelssohn.

But it was not only the Elizabethans. The remaining six songs include not only settings of Hardy, Bridges and Masefield – all, especially the latter, associated with the ruralist movement of the early twentieth century – but also, more significantly, settings of two folk ballads, 'The Twa Corbies' and 'Edward'.[18] Like Vaughan Williams, Gurney saw the ballads and songs of the rural poor as a vital part of his heritage, of his national music. In 1915 he wrote from his regiment, then in Essex, of a fellow private in the Gloucesters, who

> has been a morris dancer and whose fathers and grandfathers, uncles and other relations know all the folk songs imaginable. High Germanie, High Barbary. Chock full of an immense tolerance and good humour and easy to get on with . . . So strong in himself, set fast on strong foundations . . . He whistled 'Constant Billy' which I had never heard before.[19]

What we see in Gurney is an identification of the country with the real England ('strong and steadfast') and a kind of conflation of Elizabethanism into this identification. A more obvious example of this conflation, from outside the world of music, is the Tudor style in domestic architecture, in which half timbering and thatching (both regionally specific forms) come to be identified with a kind of rural organicism as a symbol of England ('There'll always be an England,/ While there's a country lane/As long as there's a cottage small/Beside a field of grain').

Musically we can see this conflation very precisely in one of the best known works of the English musical renaissance – Vaughan Williams' 'Fantasia on Greensleeves'. This short piece of music is worth looking at in some detail as it brings together several different aspects of the music of the period and many of the ideas of the English musical renaissance in its earliest phase.

The tune/song called 'Greensleeves' was first registered at Stationers' Hall in 1580 but, as in many such cases, it is possible that it had a prior existence within the oral tradition. Indeed, popular belief still attributes it to Henry VIII, written, the story goes, as a love song to Anne Boleyn. By the end of the sixteenth century it was established as one of the repertoire of tunes used frequently for popular ballads and even religious songs. It is mentioned in Shakespeare, and in Beaumont and Fletcher who instructed that it be used in their play *The Loyal Subject*. The tune also appears in Dowland's lute manuscripts, as well as in transcripts of virginal music from the late sixteenth and early seventeenth century.[20]

From the seventeenth century the tune continued a lively existence in the oral tradition, both in its dance form (it is the tune used by Headington Quarry Morris for 'Bacca Pipes Jig') and as song, ironically often with obscene words. It also had an active political life. The Royalist song book *A Collection of Loyal Songs written against the Rump Parliament* contains fourteen songs written to the tune and, as Chappell says, it took the form of a Royalists 'party tune' in the revolutionary period. In the eighteenth century the tune was used in eleven ballad operas according to Simpson, including the *Beggars Opera*.[21] In many of these operas, as in a version in the late seventeenth century collection *Pills to Purge Melancholy*, the words deliberately reverse the accepted royalist musical/political double meaning. (Another and clearer example of this widespread practice is singing 'God save Good Thomas Paine' to the tune of 'God save the King.')

Although many oral versions of the tune continued well into the twentieth century, the tune was fixed when Chappell printed a late sixteenth-century version from William Ballet's manuscript lute book in his *Popular Music of the Olden Time* in 1859. This version gave not only the tune but the words which are now popularly linked with the tune ('Alas my love you do me wrong' etc.). It seems likely that it was from this version that Vaughan Williams derived the theme which provides the basis of the first and third parts of the 'Fantasia'.

However the second/middle part of the 'Fantasia' comes from a quite different source. The tune which forms the basis of this section is 'Lovely Joan', a traditional tune linked to a song about a young woman who uses her sexuality to hoodwink and rob a would-be seducer. The song was collected by Vaughan Williams in Norfolk in 1908.

The two tunes were brought together in 1912 for a production of *The Merry Wives of Windsor* at Stratford-on-Avon by Sir Frank Benson. The basis of their use were two references in the *Wives* to the tune 'Greensleeves', while the theme of 'Lovely Joan' fitted well with the plot of the play. Vaughan Williams also used the tune 'Greensleeves' as the entry music 'for the Queen and her suite' in *Richard II* in the same year. In 1929 he returned to the tune, using it in his opera about Falstaff, *Sir John in Love*.[22]

Through all this the stature of 'Greensleeves' grew. It was used in Alexander Korda's film on Henry VIII (though not I think Vaughan Williams' version) and thereafter became obligatory background music for anything vaguely 'Elizabethan'. In my own childhood it figured regularly on 'Family Favourites' and even in 'Children's Favourites'. By the 1950s it had assumed the role of an alternative national anthem. Only the first part was usually played, and its opening phrase, followed by the lyrical string section, suggested to me, and millions of others in those wireless-dominated days, the rolling open downlands of southern England. Reinforcing this, the tune was used time and again in the 1960s and 1970s for television advertising. 'Greensleeves' had come to represent England and Englishness.

What Vaughan Williams does in the 'Fantasia' is to bring together the two separate elements of the English musical renaissance in one piece of music – the folk song and the Tudor. But, more than that, they are brought together in a specific cultural context which gave the piece a 'special meaning'.

Firstly, the 'originals', the tunes that form the basis of the 'Fantasia', are 'old' – 'Greensleeves' because, as Vaughan Williams knew, it has been in print since 1580 and 'Lovely Joan' because it is modal. Even 'Greensleeves', although it is in a minor key, has elements of modality in its feel and, indeed, some of the traditional versions are modal. Thus the tunes were pre-industrial, situated in the period of English musical greatness and untouched by the 'contamination' of the nineteenth-century cosmopolitanism. This was especially true of 'Greensleeves', which came from the period of the Elizabethan empire, a period frequently looked back on by the new nationalists and others in the 1890s as a model of English power. Additionally, 'Lovely Joan' was a folk song, the product of natural and national spirit. As Sharp wrote, 'the natural musical idiom of a nation will . . . be found in its purest and most unadulterated form in folk music'.[23]

Secondly, the specific origins of the 'fantasia' lie, as already noted, in Benson's pre-First World War productions of Shakespeare at Stratford. The re-evaluation of Shakespeare and the minor Elizabethan and Jacobean playwrights and poets is a matter of another essay, but was closely linked with the emergence of English nationalism. Whether it was Rupert Brooke and the others who founded the Marlowe Society at Cambridge to act the plays of Shakespeare's period in a 'correct' way, or the architect Lutyens recreating Bradford-on-Avon at the Paris International Exhibition, the 'Tudor' became a symbol as well as a guiding principle of Englishness. Along with the rural, in reality the southern English, the mock Tudor passed into English popular mythology as defining characteristics of national identity. Yet we should be cautious. Vaughan Williams was a socialist, as was Sharp, before the First World War at least; even that most patriotic figure, Rupert Brooke, was a member of the Fabian Society.[24] The Englishness created by the musical renaissance had, and has, strong progressive overtones. Folk music for instance is not only a national inheritance, it is also specifically the music of the 'common people'. Even in their arranged form, folk tunes often drew the scorn of sections of the musical élite, while the Englishness of the early twentieth century was often associated with an idealisation of sections of working people.[25]

It was, and is, more the use and association of such tunes and songs which have given them their particular meanings. A good example is Parry's 'Jerusalem'. Along with 'Greensleeves', this probably has a better claim to being a national anthem than the tedious eighteenth-century dirge 'God Save the Queen'. 'Jerusalem' was written in 1916 and first performed in March that year at the Queen's Hall.[26] It was written for an organisation called 'Fight for Right', whose aims, it had been stated a month earlier, were

> so to brace the spirit of the nation that the people of Great Britain, knowing that they are fighting for the best interests of humanity, may refuse any temptation, however insidious, to conclude a premature peace, and may accept with cheerfulness all the sacrifices necessary to bring the war to a successful conclusion.[27]

At the first performance Robert Bridges, then Poet Laureate

pointed out that the object of the meeting and the motto of

the 'Fight for Right' movement had been perfectly expressed by William Blake, who 100 years ago at the time of the Napoleonic Wars wrote,

> I will not cease from mental strife,
> Nor shall my sword sleep in my hand,
> 'Till we have built Jerusalem
> In England's green and pleasant land.

These words, he said, he had asked his friend, Sir Herbert Parry, to set to music for performance at that meeting.[28]

The song was performed by a choir of 300 under the conductor Sir Walford Davies. Within a few months the song had achieved enormous popularity and when in 1924 the entry on Parry was written in *A Dictionary of Modern Music* 'Jerusalem' was singled out as 'a new National Anthem, which has already taken deep root in Britain'.[29] In that same year it assured itself a permanent place in a particular part of Englishness when it was first sung at the Women's Institute annual meeting, this time arranged by Sir Walford Davies.[30]

Yet again it is not that simple. As well as being adopted by the WI, the song, more in keeping with its words as well as with Blake's intention, was sung from the 1930s by the Women's sections of the Coop. It was included in the song book of the Woodcraft Folk.[31] And the song was also sung outside Transport House as the results came in during the 1945 General Election.

'Jerusalem' is not obviously a direct product of the Englishness of the English musical renaissance, yet indirectly it is part of it. Parry was a Victorian but he also taught Vaughan Williams. More importantly, he was one of the first vice-presidents of the Folk-Song Society and delivered its inaugural address. Although his ideas on folk song were very different from those of Vaughan Williams or Sharp, he encouraged its collection and dissemination. Above all, Parry's evolutionary notion of song placed folk song at an earlier stage in the development of music - but one nearer to the soul of the people.

To end I want to return to the the 'Fantasia'. 'The Fantasia on Greensleeves' is not only Vaughan Williams' best-known piece of music: it is probably the best-known piece of 'classical' music of the twentieth century. This popularity is a testimony to the success of the English musical renaissance. It seems to me, as it did to Vaughan Williams, the height of foolishness to argue that music is some kind of mystic international language. One only has to stop and think of the use made of, say, Borodin, or Wagner or even Ravel (the skaters Torville and Dean) to create a mood of exoticism or militarism or simply strangeness. On the other hand Vaughan Williams, or Butterworth, or even Britten, make us feel at ease, at home, above all perhaps safe. This is partly because of visual or other images associated with them over the years, but it is also at least as much to do with a musical idiom which has become familiar.

This in turn is obviously not only to do with music. Many papers in this volume, as well as work done elsewhere, point to the creation of a new and very specific kind of nationalism in England in the last years of the nineteenth century and the first years of this century – and music was a part of that. The composers who wrote that music both responded to the new nationalism and helped form it into Englishness. What in the end though is most striking is the lack of aggressive or imperialist nationalism in the music. Apart from Parry's setting of 'Jerusalem', which is nationalist in this sense as much by association as by style or content, the only notable nationalist music of the period was that of Elgar. What is surprising perhaps is that Elgar rejected Englishness as an ideal, in music at least, and stands much more in the tradition of the continental great romantics – there is more Mahler in his music than in 'Lovely Joan'.

Notes

1 For an excellent discussion of the relationship between culture and nationality see F. S. L. Lyons, *Culture and Anarchy in Ireland 1890–1939*, Oxford, 1981.

2 For a fuller discussion of these topics see Alun Howkins, 'The discovery of rural England', in R. Colls and P. Dodds (eds), *Englishness: Politics and Culture 1880–1920*, London, 1986.

3 See Rudyard Kipling's poem 'The Islanders' (1902) for a succinct expression of these ideas.

4 Gareth Stedman Jones, 'Working-class and working class politics in London, 1870–1900: notes on the remaking of a working class', *Journal of Social History*, 7, 4, Summer, 1974; and his *Outcast London*, Oxford, 1971.

5 John Burrow, *A Liberal Descent*, Cambridge, 1981, esp. Chapters 9 and 10.

6 All these articles are in E. Hobsbawm and T. Ranger (eds), *The Invention of Tradition*, Cambridge, 1983.

7 Cecil Sharp, *English Folk Song: Some Conclusions*, London, 1965 edition, p. 163.

8 Peter J. Pirie, *The English Musical Renaissance*, London, 1980, p. 22.

9 Quoted in Ursula Vaughan Williams, *R. V. W. A Biography of Ralph Vaughan Williams*, Oxford, 1964, p. 402; see also Vic Gammon, 'Folk

song collecting in Sussex and Surrey, 1834–1924', *History Workshop Journal*, no. 10, esp. pp. 75–9.

10 Cecil Sharp, *op. cit.*, p. 169.

11 *Ibid.*, p. 168.

12 *Ibid.*

13 Ursula Vaughan Williams, *op. cit.*, p. 100.

14 See Vic Gammon, 'Folk song collecting in Sussex and Surrey', *op. cit.*, n. 10.

15 Peter J. Pirie, *The English Musical Renaissance*, London, 1980, p. 50.

16 There is now an excellent life of Gurney, Michael Hurd, *The Ordeal of Ivor Gurney*, Oxford, 1984.

17 Quoted in Hurd, *op. cit.* p. 37.

18 Hurd, *op. cit.*, pp. 37ff.

19 R. K. R. Thornton, *Ivor Gurney War Letters*, London, 1984, p. 38

20 See William Chappell, *The Ballad Literature and Popular Music of the Olden Time* (1859), New York, 1965, vol I., pp. 227ff.

21 Information from Vic Gammon.

22 Ursula Vaughan Williams, *op. cit.*, pp. 103–4, 174–5.

23 Cecil Sharp, *op. cit.*, p. 165.

24 Christopher Hassall, *Rupert Brooke, A Biography*, London, 1964, p. 157. See also Norman and Jeanne MacKenzie, *The First Fabians*, London, 1979, esp. pp. 367–70.

25 Alun Howkins, 'The discovery of rural England', *op. cit.*

26 A. Eaglefield-Hall (ed.), *A Dictionary of Modern Music*, London, 1924, p. 374.

27 *The Times*, 2 March 1916, p. 5.

28 *The Times*, 29 March 1916, p. 11.

29 A. Eaglefield-Hall (ed.), *op. cit.*, p. 374.

30 Inez Jenkins, *The History of the Women's Institute Movement of England and Wales*, Oxford, 1953, p. 123.

31 Personal communication from Vic Gammon.

7

Calypso and reggae

IMRUH BAKARI

It is in itself a fact of great significance that within the realms of historical and cultural study there is now a recognition of calypso and reggae as being part of the 'black music' tradition. Soon perhaps the same recognition might be afforded to the various music styles from the African continent which are increasingly being heard in Britain. Until now – since the late 1970s at least – black music as a cultural force in Britain referred mainly to jazz, blues, R & B – Afro-American forms which have shaped British pop music since the mid to late 1950s. To consider the phenomenon of calypso and reggae in British society is to accept that the cultural influences of Caribbean people have profoundly affected British life, and that these influences will play a major role in the forseeable future.

What I will attempt to do quite briefly is to take a candid look at the British national character as shaped by and developed as part of what is known as 'pop culture'. It will also be important to look at the development of both calypso and reggae as definitive cultural expressions of the Caribbean people and to note the ways in which British society has responded to both - the music and the people.

Cold ground was my bed last night, rock stone was my pillow

Music may be the universal language, but no musician has yet been able to produce music that is free of cultural and/or political values. Black musicians have traditionally not tried to deny or disguise this fact. Their music has been used as a platform for the overt propagation or communication of political ideas and ideals, as well as other things. In recent times, nowhere has this been more evident than in the music generally known as reggae. However, in spite of much of the rhetoric being alienating to the 'pop' audience, the music has become a major influence in contemporary music. This has happened with limited help from the media – radio, television or the music press. More recently, this general indifference seemed to do a somersault and, culminating around the death of Bob Marley in 1981, many versions, unauthorised and otherwise, have appeared. The music and Marley himself reached cult status and in the eyes of the media 'johncrow', subsequently died to make way for another fad, trend, fashion.

Looking back to 1975, the magazine *Black Music* had been in existence for two years. At that time it was the only publication in Britain making any attempt to reflect the various forms of black music on their own terms. The September issue was a Wailers Special. Just for the record, it is worth noting that this issue contained features on Sunny Ade – Juju Giant, Funkees - Afro funk, a feature on blue-eye soul, Isaac Hayes, Johnny Mathis and the Impressions. Do you remember that time in September? The Wailers feature was headed 'Dread in a Babylon', words by erstwhile reggae music's pioneer journalist Carl Gayle and pictures by Dennis Morris. This feature marked a memorable and historic event in British life. It is in a way the pivot of all that has happened in British pop music since that time. 'From the Trench Town ghetto to the concert halls of the World . . . the rebel music of The Wailers has finally arrived' wrote Gayle. In his characteristic graphic style he described the scene many encountered at the band's London concert.

> The Lyceum had never been like it was on that Thursday night. Never had I known it so crowded, so hot, so clammy, so atmospheric. I walked up the first street. Nothing but Dread and their sweet tobacco scent. I walked up the second street. People seated at my feet, more white than black, like it was a pop festival. Big blondes with 38–inch busts, pretty little girls still in their teens, hard working Dreads with beer in their guts, everybody in their tightest blue jeans.

It was the first personal encounter 'uptown' (London, Britain) had had with 'downtown' (Brixton, Afro-caribbeans). For the first time Natty Dread and his Queen met with Harry and Jane Hippy, and each claimed equal rights to the territory. 'Never before had I seen a London West Indian audience let themselves go to the extent they did on Friday, or the night before. Never before such a torrent of emotional demonstration. Black and White surrendering to the sound of Kingston Jamaica', Carl Gayle wrote.

Prior to this pop music see-sawed between the soul music of Stax and Tamla Motown on one hand and post-Hendrix rock on the other. The Caribbean community was much talked about in political circles, but for the most part remained unrecognised. The dynamic music culture being nurtured in the various clubs, shebeens, blues dances and record shops to be found wherever Caribbean people had settled, remained an unknown, and at the same time feared, reality.

When these two 'posses' met at the Lyceum, though sharing the common musical experience, their individual intentions were quite different. In 1973 the pop audience had become aware of Bob Marley and the Wailers with the release of the album 'Catch A Fire' followed by 'Natty Dread' in 1974. Complementing this, the film *The Harder They Come* (1973) depicting the urban Jamaican experience and forcefully portraying the environment that gave birth to reggae music, had become a cinema hit and had gained cult status. For the Caribbean youth at the time all that was portrayed in the music and the film was a manifestation of his/her nurtured self-image being thrust uncompromisingly into the mainstream of British consciousness. For the pop fan or ex-hippy the longing for an experience of the pathos of violence, politics and religious dogma which came with the music was an urgent desire.

> The music media realised quickly that Bob, with his uncompromising lifestyle and cultural roots, his hairstyle and his religion, was very attractive for the rock music public. And they've lapped it up. Island Records have always had that progressive/cult image and Marley fitted in neatly. (Gayle)

At the same time Marley's significance for the black community was underlined by Gayle, who saw the situation in the context of the current Rastafarian rhetoric which saw Natty not only as 'taking over' but also as the one who had the key to the future of humanity:

> He alone brings us out of ourselves. He's bigger than he was last year, better. There's a whole new audience so we got to cheer louder so that everyone will understand that Natty Dread is ours. A selfish kind of thinking, one of real pride that says something, like, you may love him too, but he belongs to us. Natty Dread, the only music figure able to bring down the house on both sides of the colour line with so much wild enthusiasm.

That year, 1975, was an extremely important year for the black community in Britain. With hindsight, it marked the beginning of an era which culminated in the burning of British cities in 1981. A convenient reference point can be located in October 1974 on the night of the 11/12.

> Hundreds of young blacks are dancing to the sounds of SUFFERER at the Carib Club in Cricklewood, North London. In the South, scores of others are returning home on the Northern Line after a night out at the Caxton Hall Club . . . 22 young blacks, who set out on that evening to boogie, found themselves at the Old Bailey a year later answering charges of affray, assault on police and offensive weapons etc. Twelve of them were charged after a night of police terror at the Carib Club – the Cricklewood Twelve. And ten were charged after a tube train carrying them from the Caxton hall was ambushed by London Transport Detectives – the Stockwell Ten.[1]

These incidents, particularly the Cricklewood/Carib Club 'riot', were brought to the living rooms of the British public by the media, with all the terror and menace it could muster. Never before had such a high profile been given to the 'volatile' black community that threatened to 'swamp' the British Isles. What was ignored by the media was the fact that, to the black community, incidents like these had long become a regular occurrence. Confrontations with the police were, even at that time, something different generations could exchange stories about. The Carib Club incident was a little different, it seemed to heighten the mood to the status of Custer's last stand.

It is no surprise that this incident (like the Stockwell Ten) was related to music, the night club, the blues dance, the sound system. For almost twenty years Caribbean people in Britain had sustained their own music. Musicians made records, records were imported, mainly from Jamaica, sound systems played them and record shops sold them: Radio One, etc., 'Top of the Pops'. and the music press generally ignored them. The blues dance and sound system were central to the black community's life. Both had long become the target for police attack and harrassment.

It was reported that the police arrived at the Carib Club chasing a suspect who had abandoned a stolen car. The chase continued into the club, where hundreds of black youth were dancing to the music of Sufferer Hi Fi. An affray ensued. Reinforcements – riot shields and dogs – were brought into action. It is alleged that in the melee, Dennis Bovell, then of London reggae band Matumbi, and now famed record producer and leader of the Dub Band, who was also at the time a DJ for Sufferer, put on the turntable the popular record 'Beat Down Babylon' which was said to encourage the fighting. His charges included one of incitement.

In 1975 Horace Ove's feature film *Pressure* was shown at the London Film Festival. The Spaghetti House Siege occurred. The Notting Hill Carnival came of age, when half a million people converged on Notting Hill to dance to calypso rhythms. The organisers were elated, the police taken by surprise, the British public were asked to be enraged. That November on Bonfire Night in Chapeltown, Leeds, black youths fought a pitched battle with the police. *The Yorkshire Post* (12 November 1975) attempted to explain 'how the calypso people have got out of tune'.

Roots – a brief encounter

It is impossible to discuss calypso and reggae seriously, as well as other aspects of the cultural (and political) experience of the African diaspora, without beginning with the European slave trade and the transportation of millions of Africans to the Caribbean and the Americas. No other people in history have had such a devastating experience of bondage, genocide and enforced labour. It must be understood that any manifestation of culture emanating from these people is nothing less than an assertion of political will, and an act of defiance and survival. Unlike other manifestations of African culture in slave and colonial society – language, family and religious practice for example – relatively little reconstruction was necessary in the realm of music; so much so that, today, music is the most advanced art form in the African diaspora.

However, as folk forms are developed to classical dimensions, what happens to a particular music, how it is perceived, received and nurtured, is determined by the same social and political forces which determine every aspect of daily life. The options are clear; dead caricature or dynamic expression. It is within these two opposite poles that calypso and reggae have had to exist in Britain and, significantly, in the Caribbean.

But firstly, let us focus on the relationship between Britain and the people who created and defined the musics, calypso and reggae. At its base is the 'civilising mission' and the 'empire'. It is ironic that the British empire is something which most Britons have had no real perception of, but which provided all the benefits and privileges which have become accepted as virtues of 'the British way of life'. These virtues and the assumed state of affluence, well-being and liberty, and the chauvinism that went with it, continues to determine the responses of Britons to those who could be said to be of the colonies – born in Britain or not. Today, racism is the operative word. The idea of civilised society was founded on this, inherent in which is the belief in a desirable and exclusive state of superior ethics and culture which instructs the inferiority and subordination of everything else.

Inherent in these attitudes is the right to appropriate any production or creation of the inferior and subordinate without due recognition or enumeration. The luxury of contributing to or adopting from the universal human experience as and when required is not afforded to those designated inferior or subordinate. This, Caribbean playwright Caz Phillips was to discover when he was rudely stopped in his tracks by a critic who wrote of one of his plays: 'Mr Phillips has pillaged the whiteman's theatre knowledgely for a powerful rangy, tragic play which is ironically, about a black man's roots.'[2] The colonial *modus operandi* has been and is still dominant in present-day Britain and seeks to determine the response to and status of calypso and reggae as well as any cultural or political expression by the black community now settled here.

Working for the Yankee dollar

Calypso and reggae, each in their own right, represent two distinct areas of social and cultural/political development in the Caribbean. It is not accidental that each is identified with territories at either end of the archipelago – Trinidad and Jamaica. It is also no accident that reggae has a religious affiliation, and calypso is distinctly secular. Trinidad has long been regarded as the metropolis of the eastern Caribbean. Since the end of slavery there has been a marked population flow of Afro-Caribbeans to the 'urban' and, later, industrial areas of Trinidad. On the island itself, African plantation slave labour was replaced by Indian indentured labour.

By the sixteenth century, Trinidad was regarded as a 'much neglected outpost of the Spanish Empire in decline'.[3] As such, it became a refuge for the French plantocracy from other islands, fleeing the repercussions of the French revolution. With them they brought as many slaves as they could afford. Though Spanish law remained in force for a considerable time, the language of communication became French *patois*. The British conquest of the island in 1797 had little effect on the language or the immigration flow – in fact it was encouraged to meet the labour needs of the British. Today, the population is made up of various racial groups, as well as many Afro-Caribbeans who, even in more recent times, have immigrated from other islands in the eastern Caribbean. It is in Trinidad that the first characteristically urban communities began to develop in the English-speaking Caribbean. These communities gave rise to both carnival and calypso in their most developed form.

'The term "calypso" came after the fact of calypso and seems to be either an attempt at refinement or a corruption on the part of the population, struggling at the turn of the century [the 20th] with a fading French patois.'[4] It is generally agreed that the correct terminology is *kaiso*. Originally sung in an (or a mixture of) African language, French *patois* became the *lingua franca* of the early songs:

> the earliest version developed during gayap, a form of organised communal work that does in fact have African parallels. After the day's work was done, the work song leader, according to Quevado (Atilla the Hun – a legendary calypsonian, politician, and calypso historian – a pioneer of modern calypso whose heyday was the 1930s and 40s) would improvise praise songs for their own team and songs of derision about others.[5]

It is claimed that the calypso began to be sung in English around 1870. Later, into the twentieth century, the inability to sing in English was to become a target for derision. However, by this time calypso and the celebration of carnival had won many battles against the colonial authorities and established themselves as distinct art forms and cultural activity. Both were closely associated with the working class and '*lumpen*' urbanities. By the late nineteenth century calypso was considered 'very much a music of the Port of Spain underworld, and many of the singers and subjects of the songs, like many of the people responsible for the blues, were pimps, prostitutes and obeahmen'.[6]

Both calypso and carnival aroused the displeasure of firstly the French plantocracy and later the British colonial authorities. Carnival in particular had been shed of its French pomp and exclusivity and transformed into a raucous African celebration. Mask and drums were introduced. As a result the pursuit of the business of calypso and carnival became a political act which led to confrontation and riot.

> In 1858 and 1859 Governor Keate, a most inept administrator, decided to stamp out forcibly the people's carnival. He failed. The police were routed and troops had to be called to disperse the masqueraders . . . all these incidents took place in Port of Spain. In 1871 and 1872 it was San Fernando's turn to oppose suppression of the carnival in the Southern capital of the island. Revellers fought with police and were later convicted

of rioting. Nine years later occurred the historic canboulay riots in Port of Spain, which matched the redoubtable Captain Baker of the police force with some of the best stick fighters in the land. The report of the Commissioner dispatched by the Secretary of State to investigate this latest disturbance resulted in a ban of the skin drum (1883) and the presence of war ships in the harbour each carnival thereafter.[7]

The banning of the skin drum led directly to the invention of the steel pan and the steel band later into the twentieth century.

The golden age of calypso is set as 1927–46. In this time the legendary names like Atilla The Hun, Lord Invader, The Lion, Lord Executioner and The Caresser established the roots of the modern calypso and popularised the form worldwide. This ran parallel to significant political developments in the Caribbean which led to the mobilisation of the working class and peasantry, and the birth of the trade union movement.

By the 1930s calypso singers were going to New York to record popular songs. Amongst these was Lord Invader, who as well as singing about how he got lost on the New York subway, sang about the 'esteem' of the Yankee dollar and the notorious 'Rum and Coca Cola'. Both of these songs were in fact barbed political statements on the American military presence in Trinidad and Tobago at the time. 'Rum and Coca Cola' in particular gained wide international popularity. Due to misrepresentation and disregard for its social context by those who pursued its exploitation, this song helped to establish a trivial and condescending attitude towards calypso outside the Caribbean.

However, calypso developed as a vibrant art form reflecting and commenting on contemporary life, both locally and internationally. The musical influences were Afro-Caribbean, Latin American and big band jazz.

> World War I had taken Trinidadians and Tobagonians abroad as volunteers. Returned home, these veterans became the leaders for reform movements in areas of labour, home rule, politics and popular education . . . businessmen and politicians alike began to really exploit calypso as a means of advertisement and propaganda. By 1935 'syndicates' of composers were formed for the presentation of calypsoes and the tent era was well in progress.[8]

It is important to note that the 1930s also saw the birth of 'West Indian literature'. Centred around two magazines *Trinidad* and *The Beacon*, the prime movers, among them C. L. R. James, Albert

Gomes, Mendes and de Boissiere, 'formulated the basic postulates for an indigenous West Indian literature'.[9]

All this cultural and political activity was interrupted by the Second World War, during which time, with the availability of the oil drum in Trinidad, the steel band was born. In 1946, so the story goes, a certain Spree Simon (considered the inventor of the steel band) brought a steel pan out in public. He played to an audience which included the governor. After his rendition of 'a classical, a spiritual and the National Anthem', he got a standing ovation. This set a stamp of approval of sorts on the steel band. It was accepted not for what it was – an ingenious invention by a working class (maybe *lumpen*) Trinidadian – but because it had been proved to be capable of playing 'respectable' music.

By 1956 calypso and carnival had become a significant element in the new political awareness which brought nationalist leaders like the late Dr Eric Williams to power. The greatest exponent of the art of calypso, the Mighty Sparrow, emerged at that time. He became one of the innovators of the modern calypso and in his work to the present day he has expressed more consistently than any other person the changing reality and perception of the Caribbean. Until the late 1970s, preceding a wave of major political and cultural upheavals in Trinidad and the wider Caribbean region, the calypso form remained unchanged. With the emergence of a new generation of calypsonian, including many from other eastern Caribbean islands, calypso has evolved to soca. The music now has a new urgency and vitality which is more in tune with the international urban experience. As such it is the first serious challenge to the long established international image of calypso – the straw hatted, guitar strumming, grinning singer spouting improvised nonsense lyrics. This was the image which Caribbean people arriving in Britain in the 1950s were being asked to live up to. At that time, to the British public, calypso was just another variation of the 'exotic' Latin American rhythms (generally called Afro-Cuban) which had become popular in the 1930s and 1940s.

Calypso cannot be fully understood outside the context of carnival and steel band music. No exponent of the art has ever gained any reputable acclaim independent of this annual ritual which is at the hub of Trinidad and eastern Caribbean culture. By its very nature, carnival is a wholly secular activity. The religious preoccupations of these islands remain apart, and often aloft, yet each in many ways cultivates the other.

The origins of carnival date back to pre-Christian Europe.

Since the first masquerade . . . carnival has exhibited certain recognizable features wherever it has taken root and flourished. Clearly originating in the worship of a nature diety – whether the Egyptian Isis, the Greek Dionysus, the Roman Saturn, or some other is immaterial – carnival proceedings have included street processions, costuming and masking, music making, energetic dancing, singing of satiric or laudatory songs, jesting, mummery, feasting and general revelry.[10]

The Catholic church later adopted this as a pre-Lenten festival, no doubt because it served as a means of fulfilling the needs of the ritual obsessions of their faith symbolised in 'sin', 'guilt' and 'repentence.' During the pre-Lenten period devotees are expected to exorcise themselves from sin and evil through a ritual death, in preparation for the fasting and penance of Lent, Carnival served that purpose.

In Trinidad, carnival has developed its own characteristics. The influence of the African population ensured this particular evolution. The distinctly secular nature of the festival has also remained intact. Catholicism is not the dominant religion in all the eastern Caribbean islands; neither is carnival necessarily a pre-Lenten festival. It is however, the major annual cultural event in all of the islands.

Calypso developed as part of carnival and is essentially an 'irreverent' music. When religion is brought into the form whether by way of musical influence or lyrical content (both of which are rare) there is no escape from the music's definitive qualities of satire and candid cynicism. 'Soca Baptist' recorded in 1980 by Blue Boy illustrates this accurately. In this song there is no political allegory. Instead the singer mischievously observes the similarities between a prayer meeting and a carnival band of revellers. Of course, in true 'kaiso' tradition, it gave rise to much controversy that year.

With the development of the Notting Hill carnival in London, for the first time it is now possible to recognise the emergence of a calypso tradition in Britain. It has equally provided the framework for a new popularity and awareness of the music. This has not escaped the attention of the commercial world.

The name most prominent in this new 'soca' explosion is that of Arrow. He is from Monserrat and has established himself as one of the best of the generation of calypso singers who emerged in the late 1970s. They brought a new vitality and the new name, 'soca', to the music. As in Jamaican music with ska, rock steady, and reggae, so too there is calypso and soca. It is not a contrivance of soul and calypso: put simply the new sound has emerged due to a restructuring of the music around its rhythmic and percussive elements.

If we look briefly at Arrow we see him sweeping the Caribbean in 1981 with 'Soca Rumba'. By 1983 he became known to the pop world in Britain with 'Hot, Hot, Hot'. For those familiar with the music it is mediocre though infectious. Full of anxiety, a major record company got involved in selling the record (but not promoting the artist). A few months later, the record having been released three times, there was frustration and disinterest.

Calypsonians do not re-release old (last year's) music. The functionality of the art form militates against this practice. According to the Mighty Sparrow,

> In addition to the regular routine difficulties that all artists must face, as calypsonians its in my opinion, a little bit more difficult because you have to be able to come up with at least one LP each year in order to stay competitive. A lot of other entertainers all over the world, when they come up with an LP, especially a good LP, it can run maybe two, three years, but not the calypsonian.[11]

The Mighty Sparrow should know. He has been doing it since 1956. His acclaim for his contribution to Caribbean culture, which has bestowed upon him the title of Calypso King of the World, would have been impossible if he had disregarded the cultural relevance of calypso and the context that gives it legitimacy.

Like death, carnival it is said, serves as the great equaliser in Trinidad and the eastern Caribbean. Temporary though it may be, this festival of absolute abandon is a social safety valve and political barometer which finds vocal expression in calypso/soca. Nothing like this exists in Jamaican society, where class and race are usually (but not necessarily) synonymous, and the stark reality of contrasting wealth and poverty is reinforced as a daily preoccupation. For the dispossessed and the alienated, the predicament and its possible solutions assume apocalyptic proportions which find expression in Biblical allegory.

Man in the hills

Jamaica developed in relative isolation to the rest of the English-speaking Caribbean. In the post-slavery years the majority of people in Jamaica remained in rural communities and the situation continued up to the 1940s. When emigration did take place it was to Latin America and the neighbouring Spanish territories. 'In the late 19th Century thousands of Jamaicans left for Panama to help dig the canal, and for Cost Rica to build the railroad . . . Jamaican labour was [also] recruited by Costa Rica to work the banana estates, and in 1918 Jamaicans left to cut cane and perform domestic services in Cuba'.[12] In these territories they undoubtedly met with other English-speaking Caribbeans, but they most definitely vastly outnumbered them. Later, in the twentieth century the same thing was to happen in North America and Britain. What had developed in Jamaica was an extremely self-sufficient and almost exclusive peasant society/community. The island as a whole had seen constant British rule from 1655 to independence in 1962, and as such many structures and influences became entrenched and remain significant even to the present day.

By the late seventeenth century maroon communities – slaves who had fought for and won their liberty – were being set up with a kind of autonomy in certain areas on the island. In 1831 the Sam Sharpe rebellion, and in 1865 the Morant Bay rebellion led by Paul Bogle, were major insurrections by Afro-Jamaicans. Importantly, these established the tradition of religious philosophy as an instigator for political action – both Bogle and Sharpe were men of the church. Of course, the roots of this tradition go back to the function of the observance of African religious practices common to all slave communities. However, in the case particularly of Paul Bogle, the British colonial establishment was threatened in a way that had never been experienced before.

It is not surprising that the Morant Bay Rebellion happened in a period of Jamaican history when the free churches were on the upsurge, a period referred to as Revivalism (or The Great Revival) . . . especially since the coming of the Baptist under George Liele, a Black man, had created for the black masses a socially mobile and expressive vehicle of their discontent and grievances . . . When George Liele established his Ethiopian Baptist Church, identification was total. Membership of the Baptist Church exceeded that of every other denomination put together. It was a reflection of what the people thought and an expression of their needs and aspirations.[13]

In the twentieth century Marcus Garvey and the Rastafarians after him were to play the same role, not only for Jamaicans but for the entire African world.

In the 1940s, Jamaican society was transformed rapidly from one that was predominantly rural to an urban one which was highly conscious of the outside world. Out of this experience has come the modern Jamaican music known as 'reggae'. In the years after World War II the established popular music was mento and dance band music, which was jazz and Latin orientated. Mento, though possessing many parallels and similarities to calypso, was distinctly a rural music. The dance bands, comprising many formally-trained musicians, entertained the relatively small 'middle-class' town dwellers. Also existing in the towns was a small '*lumpen*' population whose music can be traced back to the slave-plantations labour process. The Burru music of this community was to be the major influence in the evolution of Rastafarian music, which later helped shape reggae music.

> The Burru men of earlier time were regarded by the rest of the community even in their own social strata as ne'er-do-wells and criminals . . . In Kingston the Burru drums were used for secular dances on holidays but they also had a special function. It was the custom of the slum dwellers in the early '30s to welcome discharged prisoners back to their communities by Burru drums and dances on the night of their return.[14]

The Rastafarians eventually adopted the Burru drum ensemble – bass drum, fundeh and repeater – as the focus of their music and chanting. The leading exponent of this music was Count Ossie who was to lead the famed Mystic Revelations of Rastafari, a community of musicians whose regular Nyabingi/Groundation sessions nurtured many of the early pioneers of reggae – Rico Rodriques, Don Drummond, Tommy McCook amongst them. In addition, there was radio, which brought to the population the attractive music of Afro-America – R & B – and the sound systems which responded to popular demand and made this music very much a part of daily life.

> In effect, sound system men are the owners of mobile discotheques. Armed with powerful amplifiers and heavy wooden bass-laden speakers, they have been waging war with each other in the underworld of grass roots Jamaican music ever since the Fabulous Fifties, the days when American rhythm and blues was the music of the time and of the ghetto. They thrive on competition and popularity. By tradition, sound system men title themselves after the various tiers of the British Aristocracy as a show of power and prestige. Each system is never without its ardent followers. They become popular by playing what another system cannot play, and by introducing fast jive talking deejays who can win applause with his skill, and pull the crowds. And they stay popular by

making their own sounds when the rarest records are no longer rare.[15]

All these elements came together to produce reggae and the Jamaican music industry. The ability to make records and sell them presented the Afro-Jamaican with a unique opportunity to exert an unprecedented degree of influence/power. In the distinctly racially-stratified Jamaican society the political possibilities were potentially subversive. In many cases, for the first time, the working class and peasantry had a direct and uninhibited contact with the outside world. The financial possibilities also presented an accessible means of earning a living. Both these elements contribute directly to making reggae the international success which it has become. This was also the focus of the film *The Harder They Come.*

> Jamaican music embodies the historical experience of the Jamaican masses – it reflects, and in reflecting, reveals the contemporary situation of the nation. He who feels it knows it, the saying goes, and it is the sufferer from the urban ghettoes, the 'creation rebel' who has 'travelled up that old rough road' to find his bread, who really has the say as to what is happening down in Jamaica way today.[16]

The development of reggae coincided with the experience of Jamaica becoming an independent nation in 1962 and its quest for national development. As Jamaican musicians fused their influences into the first distinctive sounds, ska emerged, then rock steady, followed by reggae – the name now used generally to describe Jamaican music.

The music became a powerful cultural and political force, to be used by musicians, entrepreneurs and politicians to whatever end they desired. Although the Rastafarian influence has always been a part of reggae music, it was not until the 1970s, with political tribal warfare at its height in Jamaica and the 'rebels' and 'rude boys' of the 1960s reaching maturity, that Rasta philosophy and rhetoric became the dominant feature/message in the music. The career of Bob Marley and the Wailers epitomises this development.

By some (not so) strange coincidence the experience of Caribbean people in Britain found common expression in the music of Jamaica. Up until the mid-1970s the music was virtually confined to the homes and the venues of leisure operated by the black communities in the various British cities. The sound system was introduced here in the 1950s, almost at the same time as it was developed in Jamaica. Over the years, both the sound system and the music have become symbols of resistance and cultural assertion for Britain's black community. It seems quite accurate to state that from the early 1960s until about 1981, when major uprisings by mainly black youths swept British cities, the main musical expression of the Caribbean community was Jamaican music – reggae. Suffice to say that since 1981 music taste and appreciation have become more diverse. In general, various forms of black music produced in Britain have established their own presence, and reggae music has played a major role in this development.

How has it been possible for reggae music to make such an impact in Britain? How could the evocation of the 'destruction of Babylon' emanating from the ghetto yards in West Kingston ring true in London? The clues are not difficult to identify.

Deductions can be made from the fact that migration from the rural to the urban areas in Jamaica took place almost at the same time as Caribbean migration to Britain. The urban experience, though materially different, was essentially the same. In fact, the colony or neo-colony had in essence been recreated in Britain. 'There are no guns/Gas or napalm/To be seen/Only black youths/Who have aged/Like cold steel/Left in the sun/And others who find/Slender relief from hunger/Along the path where/Their souls are fed/To the incinerators/Of mass production.'[17] Napalm has not, as yet, reached Jamaica either, but the guns have long been present and active. As the youths (Bob Marley and the Wailers among them) confronted the farce of independence, much like those who had made the 'journey to an illusion', their music which had become the national expression of Jamaica began to express their discontent, as well as their joys and aspirations. Its universality was as widespread as the imperial presence.   ·

Calypso, limited by its umbilical relation to carnival, was unable to extend its influence in this way. It is my view that it was the social relevance of reggae much more than the numerical strength of Jamaicans in Britain which ensured its popularity here and in the rest of the world, including the entire Caribbean. In Jamaica there is nothing like the carnival/Catholic dichotomy found in Trinidad. In Jamaica, in what was predominantly a stable peasant society, religion asumed the form of a lived experience rather than a Sunday divergence. This remained the focus of life as the plantocracy for years (centuries) remained indifferent.

When the English came, the Church of England followed, but they paid no attention to the African population. One hundred and sixty-one years after England took over Jamaica and established the slave trade, no attempt had been made to christianize the slaves. All this time the slaves continued to serve their African deities. It was not until 1816 that the Jamaica House of Assembly passed an act to 'consider the state of religion among the slaves, and to carefully investigate the means of diffusing the light of genuine christianity among them'. The act was not heeded.[18]

Apart from the Church of England clergy being considered a debauched and decadent lot, the plantocracy did not regard the slaves as being human enough to merit Christian teaching. As with the rest of the Caribbean the church/state identification was total. It was the nonconformist churches – Methodist, Moravian, Baptist – who took it upon themselves to christianise the early slave and peasant communities. Using examples of early christians in their defiance of Roman authority to illustrate their sermons, they championed the abolitionist cause. Their rhetorical style has remained central to Jamaican political oratory and, significantly, the melodies of many of their songs have found their way into contemporary Jamaican music.

However, as the nonconformist churches established their own orthodoxy, so they began to lose favour with the recent converts. It is clear that African religious practices were never totally erased and more significantly 'the slaves' ready conversion to christianity in some areas probably had less to do with religiousity per se than with social and material expectations'.[19] The expectations remained unfulfilled. The Great Revival of 1860–1 filled the void. This was a religious movement spearheaded by congregational ministers from the USA which swept the island and firmly established christianity as a part of the Jamaican social and political fabric.

> The Great Revival allowed the African religious dynamic – long repressed – to assert itself in a christian guise and capture what might have been a missionary victory. Since then Christianity has been a handmaiden to a revitalized African movement known as Revival Religion.[20]

Out of this milieu came Paul Bogle and the Morant Bay rebellion. Later, in the 1920s, Marcus Garvey proclaimed 'One God, One Aim, One Destiny' as the motto of his Universal Negro Improvement Association (UNIA). In 1930 the coronation of Hailie Selassie I as Emperor of Ethiopia was for many a political/religious fulfilment. It concretised fundamental beliefs and aspirations, and marked the beginning of the Rastafarian movement, the legitimacy of which was to be reinforced by Ethiopian resistance to the Italian invasion of Ethiopia in 1935.

In the 1960s religious allegory rapidly became a significant part

of popular music. Songs like 'Beat Down Babylon' were banned
by the ruling Jamaica Labour Party (JLP), then led by Hugh Shearer
(the song was also popular in Britain at the time). Later, during
the 1972 elections in Jamaica, Michael Manley as leader of the
People's National Party (PNP) utilised Rastafarian rhetoric to help
him gain popular support and subsequently win the election. He
assumed the persona of Joshua with the 'rod of correction'. By
1979 the JLP, now led by Edward Seaga, was able, with the overt
assistance of external forces, to engineer the defeat of Manley.
'Deliverance' (from communism) was his watchword.

Over the years Rastafarian rhetoric has become a familiar part
of reggae music. It may express itself in the restrained poetry of
Bob Marley's 'Redemption song' or in the apocalyptic lyrics of
Big Youth evoking 'Fire fi di Pope/Di Pope of Rome'. It may find
poignant meaning in London, New York or Lagos, but its relation
to the Jamaican sociopolitical experience cannot be denied.

Inglan is the place

In 1949 West Indian immigration to Britain more or less began
with the arrival of the *Empire Windrush*. Caribbean workers, having
supported the fight for freedom and liberty during the war years,
now arrived to join the many ex-servicemen who had decided to
stay in Britain rather than face the depressing Caribbean condition.
Along with their 'cardboard' luggage, the newly-arrived immigrants also brought with them their relatively sophisticated musical
taste and the culture that went with it. This was most visibly
expressed in terms of dress and dance, a way of walking and indeed
a way of talking.

Those who had been here since the war had already introduced
much of this to Britain, only to find themselves the target of
hostility and physical attack. Dance halls quite frequently became
theatres of confrontation. By the time the immigrant workers
began to arrive, the small Caribbean community in Britain were
already importing records – calypso, R & B and jazz – to meet
their own needs. This small community was made up of mainly
young 'middle-class' men, full of optimism and worldly ideas.
British society, however, nurtured a quite different and opposite
view of them. In 1950 the West Indian cricket team made a
triumphant tour of England which was celebrated by the calypsonian Lord Beginner in his song, 'Cricket lovely cricket'. The
lyrics and the musical arrangements are a clear illustration of the
calypso art form at that time. The singer relates a witty narrative
about England's defeat, backed by a well-arranged piece of music

featuring a jazzy clarinet. However, it was the novelty of West Indians demonstrating their passion for cricket, contrived by the line 'Those little pals of mine/Ramadin and Valentine', which caught the imagination of the British public.

Not long after, a young calypsonian, Lord Kitchener, arrived on one of the many passenger boats bringing immigrants to the various British ports. A newsreel camera crew, given the task of explaining to the British public something about the kind of people steadily flowing into the country, aproached Lord Kitchener. 'I hear you sing calypso', they said (or something like that). Having given a positive answer, Kitchener was asked to sing a calypso. The newsreel crew was to record a historic impromptu performance of the calypsonian's unaccompanied rendition of 'England is the place for me.' This image, complete with the missing palm tree, was established in the minds of the British public, and was to be exploited and reinforced by British entertainers like Lance Percival.

During the 1950s however, Caribbean people, by virtue of the records they were listening to, and the music some of them were playing, began to influence the emerging British music culture. At that time in Britain the rebel instincts of university students in places like Oxford and Cambridge were claiming blues and jazz, particularly the newly-evolved sound, bebop, as their exclusive possession. The disillusioned working class moved towards R & B and what became known as rock & roll. Young musicians listened to everything that was foreign. This included Latin American music, calypso and West African highlife. A lot of this music could be heard in West End night spots, being played by musicians from these places.

At that time British society was being told that it had 'never had it so good'. A new age of affluence was upon them. Something called 'subculture' began to be defined.

In the early fifties, Savile Row attempted a revival in Edwardian men's fashion. In Savile Row it failed, but quickly succeeded in Hammersmith Palais. Like the hipsters' zoot suit it became, for the English teenagers, the first uniform which distinguished the group from their floppy-trousered fathers. The shield dropped a little further. Teddy suits with their frock-coats, fancy waistcoats, moleskin collars and drainpipe trousers, and for the girls, hobble skirts, black seam nylons and coolie hats, were the first public showing in England, at any rate, of radical social divergence on the part of young people. No Teddy Boy at the time was sufficiently articulate to say what his deepest responses knew, that the established world was the emanation of gigantic falsehood and he wanted out.[21]

This was to mark the beginning of youth culture with its intrinsic rebellious character, into which black music and culture was to be incorporated and used as a battering ram against the establishment.

The Teds were sparked into violence by any and every occasion. It became a means of celebration and signature. The smashed lamp standard or the lacerated train compartment was no gesture of anger against the local government or society at large. They were simply a means of saying 'Tom, Dick or Harry was here'.[22]

This culture of mindless violence was totally contrary to the sensibilities and attitudes of Caribbean people. The musical culture, in particular, which they brought to England was a creative assertion, a highly sophisticated response to the colonial condition. It embodied the base elements of a national culture. However, within the context of Britain, Caribbean culture/music has become identified with youth culture and discussed in terms of deviancy and facile rebellion. In this way an accessible device was provided for the disregard of the black community, even in those instances when elements within the youth culture – teddy boys, skinheads, punks or the neo-Fascist rank and file – chose to use black people as the object of their sadistic rage.

By the end of the 1950s the Caribbean community had experienced much of this, culminating in the Notting Hill riots of 1958. By that time the black clubs that were being opened, the weekend dances that were being organised, the christenings, the weddings, the house parties and the sound systems had all become the focus of the black community. This community was to play the role of sustaining the music and providing the base from which it was to influence British music and pop culture in the coming years.

Feel it in the one drop

The obvious effect of Jamaican/reggae music on British society can quite accurately be assessed by looking at the years 1975 to the present. Here can be clearly seen the impact of the Marley era and popularisation of Rastafarian culture. Within this we witness the emergence of the two tone ska revival which followed the punk movement. The Specials, The Beat, Selecter, Madness, and more recently, UB40, who have progressed to reviving rock steady hits, are synonymous with this trend. It was also the period in which a new generation of black musicians began to define and expand the music on their own terms. Among them rank Aswad, Steel Pulse, Misty in Roots, Dennis Bovell and Matumbi.

This generation of Caribbean musician differed from their predecessors in the sense that they had either been born in Britain or had spent most of their lives here. The music they were playing was not separate from, but a continuation and development of, the reggae music which they had grown up with in Notting Hill, Brixton or Handsworth. That they were about to influence British pop culture significantly was evidence to the fact that Britain could no longer resist the presence of the black community or its music.

A recognition of the influence of Caribbean music/musicians on British pop (music in general – developments in jazz are worth noting, Joe Harriott for example) has been slow, to say the least. In reality, the disregard engendered towards the black community as a whole has been well entrenched in the media and in public responses to the music. Few radio deejays – literally one or two – ventured to play the music, and the situation, particularly in terms of national broadcasting, has changed very little to this day. This remains a point of contention and frustration to many reggae musicians, who now find greater acceptance in other European countries, or even further afield.

> Reggae music has been trying to establish itself for a long time and as soon as an English person or someone of a different nationality do it outside of black people here, it gets a hundred percent coverage, prestige, is like taking away the music from us . . . you find out that they want the music but not the artist. That has been going on in reggae for a long time.[23]

This effort (unconscious maybe) to separate the music from its cultural/political environment has long been the preoccupation of the music industry and the media. One method of doing this is illustrated by the media response to the two tone movement. In this case a fad, or at best a genre, of reggae music was being raised to the status of being a definitive music in its own right. However, there was nothing innovative or definitive about two tone. Bands made up of black and white youths (that was not new either) were remaking ska hits of the 1950s and early 1960s. It was soon revealed for what it was, a transient fashion, popular only in Britain. Within the tradition of British youth culture it was a 'knees-up Mother Brown with coconuts' which lacked a dynamic motivation. The music industry and media, along with a recent school of sociocultural thought, have also (with some justification) tried to reduce the phenomenon of Rastafari to the level of youth culture and deviancy. In the process reggae and Rastafari have been confused as being one and the same.

> Rasta is a force, a historical force. It began as an anti-colonist movement in the Thirties and acquired other dimensions over the years. The youth in Britain are drawn towards Rastafarianism through reggae music because Rasta is the most powerful force in Jamaica right now and it permeates all reggae music. So for the youth of Britain it's a kind of cult, something they can identify with.[24]

Of course, for many black youths in Britain (some whites too) Rastafari was a cult. Others discovered its cultural and political essence.

> To see the Rastafari world view as limited to some religious proclivity . . . is to ignore the vitality of the culture in Jamaica, in the Eastern Caribbean and, now, in the metropolitan cities where children of black immigrants are alienated from the servile culture of consumption. Rastafari culture remains an indelible link between the resistance of the Maroons, the Pan-Africanist appeal of Marcus Garvey, the materialist and historical analysis of Walter Rodney and the defiance of reggae.[25]

Bob Marley emerged at a time when the music industry and the media considered Rastafarianism to be exploitable. Had he lived, Marley would no doubt have been able to sustain his career beyond this phase. However, with Rasta no longer media currency, many of the major companies lost interest in reggae music, thus giving rise to the myth that the music died with Bob Marley. This was never the case in the black community, neither was it the case that black people were 'shedding their Caribbean mores' as one journalist put it. Just as the islands from which they come have changed, so too have the people and their descendants living in British and North American cities changed in response to their new environments. They have done so within the context of their own historical experience.

An important development in reggae music has been the lovers rock genre. In effect it is a British version of the rock steady era and its preoccupation is with melodic love songs. In Britain however, unlike Jamaica, it has been an area where female vocalists have gained prominence. Lovers rock in itself is the creation of Lloyd Coxone, Dennis Bovell and Dennis Harris, all of whom have a long involvement with reggae music in Britain. Coxone is a sound system operator turned record producer; Bovell is a musician, formerly of Matumbi and presently leading the Dub Band. He had also been involved with sound systems (as shown in the Carib Club incident) and is now one of the most sought after recording engineers and producers. Denis Harris is a promoter and record producer.

Lovers Rock was the record label (like Blue Beat in the 1950s) from which the music took its name. The label was created by Dennis Harris in response to the youth talent he was discovering. The first lovers rock record came out in 1977, 'I'm in love with a Dreadlocks' by Brown Sugar, an all-girl trio, but the genre as a British-produced music had emerged three years earlier with Louisa Mark's 'Caught you in a lie', produced by Lloyd Coxone, and the Matumbi hits 'After tonight' and 'The man in me'.

Parallel to this development came groups like Aswad and Steel Pulse, who established a more political music tradition based on the experience of black youths in the British inner cities.

Dub encounter

Taken at face value it can be argued that all the developments in British reggae do not amount to much when viewed against the British scene in totality. If national chart successes and media presence were considered in isolation, this argument could go a long way. It is a fact that reggae artists enjoy much greater respect and national acclaim in other European countries, and in Japan for example, than they do in Britain. To understand the significant influence which reggae has had on British pop culture is to recognise how the recording industry has been transformed since the mid-1970s. The main changes are reflected in the new aesthetics of record production, and in this the Dub music genre has made a major impact.

Throughout its history in Britain 'reggae' music has always had a white following who, while they may have sometimes overlooked the lyrical preoccupations, were always interested in the music as an art form. For this group, along with the dedicated sound system followers and blues dance-goers, reggae music reached unprecedented heights in the dub genre. In fact, dub became the most precise and powerful musical expression of the black British inner city experience. Today there is a proliferation of deejays and dub poets who have emerged, influenced by the Jamaican innovators. Reggae music is probably the only music in which recording engineers reach 'star' status. In fact, dub music is entirely their creation.

Dub music is the engineer's creative response to the possibilities of various technological advances and recording techniques. In many instances the recording equipment would be pushed to its limits or 'misused' to achieve the desired effect. It is in the sound system tradition of 'making their own sounds when the rarest records are no longer rare', as Carl Gayle put it. Dub is a 'surrealist' music which has all the elements of call and response and collective improvisation, only in this case the engineer 'plays' all the instruments/voices. The music is reorganised around the bass and drum for maximum dramatic effect. The dancer/listener is entrapped in a milieu of musical extremities. At opposite poles are the high treble and the deep bass. As instrumental passages are mixed in and out, melodic lines are unexpectedly dropped in and out, echo, reverb and other electronic distortions wash over bass and drum rhythms – at its best, a highly cathartic and unpredictable musical adventure is contrived. 'It's the psychedelic music I expected to hear in the '60s and didn't', writes Luke Ehrlich in *Reggae International*. Behind this music are the new familiar names like King Tubby, Lee Perry, Scientist, Prince Jammy, to name a few. In Britain the frontiers of this music have been extended by Dennis Bovell (who, for what its worth, comes from Barbados). His albums with Matumbi under the name of the 4th Street Orchestra remain definitive. More recently his work with Linton Kwesi Johnson, and his own Dub Band, particularly on the album 'Making history', has most definitely established him as a major force in British music. And the influence of dub can be seen in the work of contemporary pop/rock groups – Culture Club, Thompson Twins, etc. Here the emphasis of rock has shifted from the 'aesthetics of the scream' to a focus of rhythm centred on the bass and drum. This has been influenced by the work of people like the Barrett Brothers of the Wailers, and Sly Dunbar and Robbie Shakespeare.

Today British pop culture reflects the influence of many Third World cultures. Contemporary music from the African continent is gaining widespread acceptance. The same can be said for calypso/soca. The music scene is more vibrant that it has ever been. There is, from the USA, electro-funk, rappin' and scratch music, all bearing some cross-cultural influences of reggae. Reggae has long become 'a familiar part of the language of popular music, a vocabulary to be utilized and drawn upon as much as any other structural device'.[26] At the same time in Britain, more than at any time in its history, the black community is locked in an intense cultural/political battle for its future.

Notes

1 *Race Today*, November, 1975.
2 *Artrage*, Autumn, 1983.
3 Errol Hill, *The Trinidad Carnival*, 1972.
4 Keith Warner, *The Trinidad Calypso*, 1982.
5 John Storm Roberts, *Black Music of Two Worlds*, 1972.
6 *Ibid.*
7 Errol Hill, *The Trinidad Carnival*, 1972.
8 J. D. Elder, *From Congo Drum To Steelband*, 1978.
9 Reinhard W. Sanders (ed.), *From Trinidad*, 1978.
10 Errol Hill, *The Trinidad Carnival*, 1972.
11 Mighty Sparrow, Interview with Alex Pascal, Radio London, 31 May 1984.
12 George Beckford and Michael Witter, *Small Garden . . . Bitter Weed*, 1980.
13 Sebastian Clarke, *Jah Music*, 1980.
14 Verena Reckord, 'Rastafarian music: an introductory study', *Jamaican Journal*.
15 Carl Gayle, 'Marcus Garvey meets the rockers uptown', *Black Music Magazine*, February, 1976.
16 Linton Kwesi Johnson, 'Jamaican rebel music', *Race and Class*, XVII, 4, 1976.
17 Imruh Bakari, *Sounds and Echoes*, 1980.
18 Leonard E. Barrett, *The Rastafarians*, 1977.
19 Marian B. McLeod, 'Rev. Thomas P. Callender and the Jamaican Church', in O. R. Dathorne (ed.), *The Afro World – Adventures in Ideas*, 1984.
20 Leonard E. Barrett, *The Rastafarians*, 1977.
21 Jeff Nuttall, *Bomb Culture*, 1968.
22 *Ibid.*
23 Interview with David Hinds of Steel Pulse, February, 1984.
24 Chris May interview with Linton Kwesi Johnson, *Black Music and Jazz Review*, October, 1978.
25 Horace Campbell, 'Rastafari: culture of resistance', *Race and Class*, XXII, summer, 1980.
26 Lenny Kaye, 'White reggae', in Stephen Davis and Peter Simon, *Reggae International*, 1982.

Landscape

8
Village school
or blackboard
jungle?

KEN WORPOLE

I

I was brought up in Leytonstone, East London, and Southend, Essex, both essentially urban environments. But at school our pictures of real life were entirely rural. At primary school the frieze which went round the wall of my first classroom portrayed the months of the year, all set against a highly formulaic rural background – the ducks skidding across the frozen pond in January, a ruddy-faced farmer hand-broadcasting the seed in March, lambs leaping in April, harvesting in August in the fields, blustery winds shaking the leaves from the trees in the forest in November, and so on.

The world, we were lead to believe, was really a large farmyard, where hens clucked, donkeys hee-hawed, cows moo-ed, sheep baa-ed and pigs grunted. We all made the noises daily in unison and then sang 'Old MacDonald had a farm'. In the spring the teachers would bring in sticky buds and they would be put in jars so that we could watch them flowering. They also always brought in frog-spawn which was put in a tank so that we could watch the eggs hatch out into tadpoles and then, by metamorphosis, turn into tiny frogs, at which point they generally seemed to die off or disappear, and then the tank was cleaned out to wait for the next year's cycle. This was all certainly better than 'desk-work'- sums and reciting of tables – but it also brought its own perplexities. One was that every primary school teacher I ever had always seemed to have a limitless supply of horse-chestnut twigs, bluebells, frog-spawn, hawthorn, and other exemplary products of 'nature' which seemed to be for them available on tap. Thus, I gathered at an early age, teachers always seemed to live somewhere else, in this place called 'nature', which was supposed to be 'all around us'. The women teachers brought in home-made jams which we were all allowed to taste, made from fruit picked in their own gardens. (Now, of course, *I* myself live in one of those houses.)

But 'nature', I also gathered, was not wholly beneficent and fecund. There was (the poster is etched in my mind to this day) the 'Colorado beetle'. In every school corridor I ever walked down or hung around in, in every classroom that I ever stepped foot in, up until the age of eleven, there was that ominous poster pinned up: 'Look out for the Colorado beetle!' Underneath a large coloured illustration of this seemingly innocuous ladybird-type beetle, was a text of the most fervid – and nationalist – paranoia. The Colorado beetle, I gathered, was the enemy without, threatening to become the enemy within. John Buchan or Guy Thorne would have been hard put to summon up the contaminatory fear which these Ministry of Agriculture posters enjoined on our innocent minds. Were we to see one of these terrible brute creations, it was our immediate duty to put it in a matchbox and either take it to the nearest police station or send it to an address in Lincolnshire. Finding one of these seemed tantamount to performing an act of patriotism comparable to that of the child in Holland who had put his or her finger in the hole of the dyke wall and saved the nation. Britain was in danger of being eaten entire, leaf by leaf.

Yet out in the playground, three times a day, for the boys at least, the talk was of Stanley Matthews, Journey Into Space, racing car drivers, Turf cigarette cards, marbles and five-stones, all of which seemed somehow mean-spirited and 'common' compared to that richer, hallowed and sacred spirit of 'nature' which the teachers so constantly evoked. For, because the hymns sung every morning in assembly were so often about rural life, I grew quite naturally to associate spirituality with rural life; the life that I found myself in was somehow a reduced version of all it could possibly be. God made the country, man made the town! We townies were already lost souls, cast out of the garden for ever. But we could still write about it, and did.

This ruralism goes back to the earliest days of state education, and it was particularly associated with the teaching of English. H. C. Dent, an elementary school student who later became editor of *The Times Educational Supplement*, remembered his schooling thus:

> I was a pre-adolescent pupil in an elementary school in 1904. Like millions more, I intoned my way monotonously (and uncomprehendingly) through the multiplication tables; I was bored to nausea by the one and only 'Reader' we were allowed

each year – which had to serve the dual function of giving us practice in the mechanics of reading aloud (why aloud!) and of being our introduction to English life and letters. I wrote, endlessly, in 'copybooks' morally elevating maxims – 'A stitch in time saves nine', 'Too many cooks spoil the broth' – *but I never composed, much less wrote, in class a single original sentence* . . . I memorized the names of the capes, bays, county towns, mountains and rivers, literally all round Britain. And once each week I painted blobs (we called them flowers), and wove wet reeds into work baskets: the school's sole concession to 'activity'.[1]

Many of the strands which make up the rural idiom come together in this one passage: the learning of folk-sayings and proverbs and their explication (a practice that was still a compulsory part of the English language GCE syllabus until the 1960s); the assumption that the student's own experiences were not a subject matter for writing ('writing from experience' or 'personal writing' only got on the 'agenda' similarly in the 1960s); and the painting and crafts practices which were part of the rustic idiom also. Look at any of the photographs of classroom settings in this period and you will usually come across one set-piece of the painting lesson; fifty children sitting in fifty desks with fifty daffodils in jars in front of them. The poet James Kirkup remembered his South Shields school days with loathing: 'On the walls hung religious pictures, maps of the Empire, photographs from *Child Education*, a large calendar and the alphabet. On the window-sills were bulb vases of dark green glass, and a saucer or two with carrot-tops growing in them.'[2]

The hymns that children sang every day were, of course, completely rural in imagery and pre-industrial in sensibility: 'We plough the fields and scatter/The good seed on the land', 'There sheep may safely graze', 'All things bright and beautiful', 'The rich man in his castle/The poor man at his gate'. There are simply no hymns which acknowledge the urban experience. Likewise, the proverbs and sayings that were taught were largely pastoral in origin: 'Might as well be hanged for a sheep as a lamb', 'Casting pearls before swine' (most teachers wallowed in the crude ironics of explaining this to their captive subjects), 'What is sauce for the goose is sauce for the gander', 'It's no good locking the stable door after the horse has bolted', and so on.

II

The Newbolt Report of 1921, a fundamental document for the teaching of English in school, had some very specific things to say about the experience which children brought with them into the schools. The great difficulty of teachers in elementary schools 'in many districts is that they have to fight against the powerful influence of evil habits of speech contracted in home and street. The teacher's struggle is thus not with ignorance but with *a perverted power*'.[3] Once again this 'perverted' experience is given an urban inflection in the evocation of the baleful influence of the 'street' which, from the sixteenth century onwards, is given the associations of criminality and promiscuous social relationships. Thus we have had the dubious cultures of 'street literature', 'street-walkers', 'street arabs', and 'the streets' being associated with all that is unregulated and volatile; though the great working-class writer of the 1930s, Jack Common, called his collection of essays on culture, assertively, *The Freedom of the Streets*. But in general, the streets have not earned themselves an honourable place in the language of available cultural spaces, except within popular youth culture, where 'street credibility' is *de rigueur* today.

For the Newbolt committee, and for George Sampson, whose seminal *English for the English* was published four years later, 'English is not really a subject at all. It is a condition of existence.'[4] Thus it became clear that, at least from 1921 onwards, the role of the subject English in schools was not simply that of a set of technical skills that had to be acquired – reading, writing, listening (but not speaking) – but constituted the main conduit through which key cultural values were to be channelled from one generation to the next. And from one class to another, too, for as Sampson had also written in 1925, 'Deny to working-class children any common share in the immaterial, and presently they will grow into the men who demand with menaces a communism of the material.'

These precepts were nowhere more influential than in the shape of children's writing. In the one or two extant collections of children's poetry written in the 1930s, *First Fruits* edited by Norman Morris and published by Oxford University Press in 1939 ('the first full-scale anthology of children's writing presented in its own right' according to David Shayer[6]) and an anthology published by the Tottenham Education Department in 1936, the poetry is full of 'haths' and 'doths', of Reynard the Fox, and of bucolic, red-faced huntsmen quaffing ale outside ye olde innes, and clouds of daffodils, of office workers dreaming of escape to the countryside.

In a very interesting study by B. Whitton in 1974, the writer noted perceptively how:

> There is plenty of urban longing for the pastoral, but it is of pastures which have come from books, not experience, which are longed for. Almost all the writers are distanced from their subject matter by a river of received literature. There is no sense of 'being where the action is' which is so apparent in the modern selections.[7]

'Being where the action is' in fact meant lived experience. And that, in Tottenham, meant urban London.

The themes of the Newbolt Report were powerfully developed in the 1930s by the writers associated with *Scrutiny* magazine and its most influential editor, F. R. Leavis. Though taking the criticism of literature as its platform, it had from the start a pedagogical side. whose biases have been excellently discussed by Francis Mulhern in a chapter of his book *The Moment of Scrutiny*. *Culture and Environment* by Leavis and Denys Thompson, first published in 1932, combines an educational programme with a systematic attack on mass culture. The introduction to that book located the key cultural problem – urban society.

> Many teachers of English who have become interested in the possibilities of training taste and sensibility must have been troubled by accompanying doubts. What effect can such training have against the multitudinous counter-influences – films, newspapers, advertising – indeed, *the whole world outside the classroom*? Yet the very conditions that make literary education look so desperate are those which make it more important than ever before; for in a world of this kind – and a world that changes rapidly – it is on literary tradition that the office of maintaining continuity must rest.

> But literary education, we must not forget, is to a great extent a substitute. What we have lost is the organic community with the living culture it embodied. Folk-songs, folk-dances, Cotswold cottages and handicraft products are signs and expressions of something more: an art of life, a way of living, ordered and patterned, involving social arts, codes of intercourse and a responsive adjustment growing out of immemorial experience, to the *natural environment* and the rhythm of the year. That is why it is difficult to take revivals seriously. It is not merely that life, from having been predominantly rural and agricultural, has become urban and industrial. When life was rooted in the soil town life was not

what it is now. Instead of the community, urban or rural, we have, almost universally, suburbanism. We dwell where we find it convenient or where we can, pay our rates and taxes if we have to, and live in agglomerations united only by contiguity, the system of transport and the supply of gas, water and electricity. (my italics)[8]

There are many things to note about this peroration. Firstly, that the classroom and 'the whole world outside' are bound to be antagonistic. Secondly, the 'natural environment' is, ontologically, a rural environment (even though people have been living in cities as far back almost as the invention of writing). And, thirdly, that there is nowhere in the account any understanding of that unquenchable human agency that, whatever the material environment, manages to create active forms of social relationships and reciprocal patterns of living. Apart from the distinct dislike of all things urban, the other major targets were the new forms of popular mass culture which had emerged in the early part of the century, notably the cinema and the wireless. They endorsed the analysis made in Q. D. Leavis' *Fiction and The Reading Public* (1932) which asserted that 'attending the cinema, like listening to the gramophone or wireless, is a passive and social amusement, whereas, since reading aloud in the family circle is no longer practised, fiction is a solitary pleasure, and the public to-day prefers communal to private pastimes'.[9]

Ironically, then, whilst inveighing against that loss of community assumed to be a feature of urban life, they also disliked the new forms of popular culture because of their 'communal' forms of participation – listening together, going to the cinema in groups, and often dancing to gramophone records. In fact, the cinema, wireless and gramophone opened up whole new worlds to hitherto isolated and culturally restricted individuals and groups – the worlds of international film, dance band music, jazz, classical records, radio drama, worlds in which there may have been large amounts of fairly banal material but in which there were also phenomenal new cultural excitements and possibilities. Not everything that goes on outside a window is interesting and worth looking for, but windows are always preferable to walls.

Against the twin demons of urbanism and mass popular culture, F. R. Leavis and Denys Thompson offered a revival of the notion of 'the organic community'. This they themselves had derived from the writings of George Sturt, notably *Change in the Village* (1912) and *The Wheelwright's Shop* (1923). The 'organic community' was that of the 'coherent and self-explanatory village life' of nineteenth-century rural England, wedded inextricably to the seasons and the diurnal life of primary production. There was – and is – clearly much that was wholly enviable about the world which Sturt described. It was a world in which lived experience and learned skills were awarded a much higher value than that of formal education or 'book-learning'. It was a world in which the division of labour was permanently visible for all to see; in which, though labour was paid, it was not simply reducible to 'wage labour'. It was also a world in which popular language was still closely bound up with the language of folk-lore and emanated from a pre-literate sensibility. But for every thriving Cotswold village there were probably hundreds of other kinds of rural environment: the flat windswept potato fields of the East Anglian Fens, described in Mary Chamberlain's *Fenwomen*; the worlds of dawn-to-dusk work in the West Riding described by Fred Kitchen in his aptly-titled *Brother to the Ox*; the bleak Herefordshire fields described in the opening chapter of Walter Brierley's *These Poor Hands* which made him leave to work in the South Wales coalfields; or the potato-picking gangs in Scotland described in Patrick McGill's *Children of the Dead-End*; environments and conditions of existence from which tens of thousands fled each year into the cities or by emigration to the colonies. It is also salutary to remember the kinds of rural scenes which Thomas Hardy evoked in the hiring fairs in *Tess of the D'Urbervilles* or the early years of crow-scaring which led Jude to become a stone-mason and make his way to Oxford to try to find a different and better way of life. The 'organic community' was only one version of the pastoral: there were many others.

In *Scrutiny* in this period, Denys Thompson and Frank Chapman were advocating the use of the publications of the Council for the Preservation of Rural England in the classroom, and mixed the general call for an 'anti-industrial anti-commercial' educational curriculum with one which was also commendably anti-jingoist and anti-war.[10] The *Scrutiny* position was also strongly against conventional examination forms and scathing about 'intelligence tests' and other quasi-scientific ways of monitoring educational achievement. There was nothing piecemeal about the *Scrutiny* programme for educational reform: it was radical in the very proper sense of that word – to the roots.

In time those teachers and educationalists associated with *Scrutiny* decided to set up a journal specifically to take its message to the schools. The date of this intervention is quite significant – Christmas 1939. This was when the first edition of *English in Schools* was published, edited by Denys Thompson and bringing together a cluster of English teachers, either in the universities or grammar schools, who would remain loyal to the common programme for many years after; people such as G. D. Klingopolus, James Reeves, Boris Ford, and Thompson himself. To start a new journal in the first months of what was obviously going to be a major war was presumably precipitated by the idea that some central values had to be protected. *English in Schools* was a cadre journal, going underground, as it were, during a period of enormous social and civic upheaval, hoping to emerge after the war as an organised movement. In this they were highly successful, for after the war the Leavisite position dominated English teaching for nearly thirty years.

An editorial in one of the early editions of the journal (Christmas 1940) opened up a new line of attack against urban values. It took issue with the then prevalent notions of 'citizenship' and 'civics' which were becoming part of the language of the national war effort:

> The new stress of 'community' in official reports and recommendations, has been confidently interpreted by educational publishers and others as a boom in 'Citizenship' and 'Civics'. Such instructions can be useful, but compared with the kind of community which an English master tries to evoke, 'Civics' is a minor and superficial subject.

The attack on 'civics' and 'citizenship' rejoined some of *Scrutiny*'s classic themes – the contempt for mass society above all. But though radical in feeling, it was one to which Labour – the inheritor of wartime notions of equality and fair shares – was vulnerable. Moreover, the causes with which Labourism was associated in the postwar years – mass housing, state welfare and health programmes, even talk (though premature) of 'multi-lateral schools' with possibly 2,000 or more pupils - were very much associated with that urban existence whose influence *Scrutiny* deplored. 'Equality of opportunity', Labour's other great watchword, was also not one with which *Scrutiny* sympathised. Geoffrey Bantock, 'the dominant educational voice of the post-war *Scrutiny*'[11] took up arms against it in a series of articles and books. In the *Scrutiny* of spring 1948, Bantock published his essay on 'Some cultural implications of freedom in education', a savage attack on the collectivist programmes of the postwar Labour government, particularly criticising plans for providing further educational opportunities for working-class children. In Bantock's view, education was essentially a stabilising process which should reproduce inherited social and economic relationships. He characterised the more progressive educationalists (including some of his fellow-Leavisites writing for *English in Schools*) as arguing for reforms so that 'the mediocre must have their chance', and particularly attacked the two key concepts of the new child-centred pedagogy, the educational concepts of 'freedom' and 'self-expression'.

Bantock's educational programme, for which he was still arguing in the 1970s, was a binary system of education with a 'folk' curriculum for 'the less able', involving a more talk-based education with an emphasis on practical subjects and crafts.[12] In arguing thus he was simply maintaining a tradition that went back well into the nineteenth century in which, fearful of the more aggressive economic demands of the working class, the schools inspectorate in the 1860s were busy thinking of a curriculum in which, as Richard Johnson has written, 'Certain aspects of working class culture too were not to be condemned outright, commonly the more folksy, Merrie-England aspects: Cornish Parish Feasts, some forms of singing, some sports'.[13]

Underpinning this kind of thinking was the assumption that the working class as 'the folk' posed a much less serious threat to the established order than did the working class as an urban proletariat. It has to be admitted, though, that there were important strengths to the argument, notably in the acknowledgment given to the self-defining qualities of customary experience. The radical conservative tradition exemplified by Bantock did at least recognise that people themselves had their own sources of knowledge, and as such it has some affinities with a major line of cultural and educational criticism on the left, as for example Raymond Williams' discussion of the relationship between 'customary' and 'educated' experience, or what E. P. Thompson in his Mansbridge lecture at Leeds in 1968 simply described as 'the necessary dialectic of education and experience'. Hardy and Wordsworth are, respectively, the significant embodiers of this distinction for Williams and Thompson, both, notably, assuming that it was essentially a rural experience and customary tradition which state education had failed to respond to.

English in Schools discontinued publication and in 1949 a successor was launched, again edited by Denys Thompson, called *The Use of English*, a journal which survives to this day. *The Use of English* carried on advocating the folk idiom as the only hope against the ravaging winds of popular culture or Bloomsbury urbane introspection and decorativeness. In a rallying call in the journal in 1953 (vol.IV, no.4), the poet James Reeves suggested a return to the use of folk songs and ballads made by the people and exemplifying the eternal human values. Denys Thompson himself edited many anthologies of poetry for use in schools, anthologies which contained many translations from folk cultures throughout the world. Waley's translations from the Chinese were widely admired and used in schools. This was all very fine, accessible poetry, profoundly humanistic, and honourably internationalist in its intentions, yet it has to be said that the exclusive concern with this folk tradition was a way of side-stepping the lived realities of the situation in which the readers found themselves.

In the 1950s in particular, though the movement went on well into the 1960s, there is a very clear sense that in the development of progressive ideas in the teaching of English, the countryside surrounds the towns. In Wiltshire, under the influence of Dora Pym, the 11–plus examination was radically changed from 1947 onwards, in that it gave, for the first time anywhere in Britain, an opportunity for the candidate to choose a 'free writing' option in the examination; that is to say, an opportunity to write imaginatively rather than produce *The Times* fourth leader type of essay on 'The motor car is a great asset to civilisation' and other similar titles. Dora Pym made a very great impact on all Wiltshire schools with her passionate espousal of 'free writing'. Margaret Langdon's *Let the Children Write* (1961) was based on her experience in a village school, and was another key text for its time. Sybil Marshall's *An Experiment in Education* (1963) came out of her extraordinary teaching work in a Cambridgeshire village school, as did, of course, David Holbrook's angry and passionate *English for the Rejected* (1965) and *The Secret Places* (1964). Brian Jackson's polemic against exams is called *Report From a Country School* (1965), which was also written from Cambridgeshire. Underpinning all these marvellous and free-spirited texts, though, was a strong attachment to the cause of nineteenth-century romanticism, which itself was predicated on a belief in the innate wisdom of the rural poor. In this period many began to unsheathe bright swords to defend the educational rights of the rural working class, yet one has a strong feeling that the children of the cities had already been given up for lost, their spirit broken amidst the smoke and grime of the noisy town and dusty city.

Laurie Lee's *Cider with Rosie* was published in 1959 and brought fresh hope to the cause of ruralism. It rapidly became a set text in schools throughout Britain and once again young people everywhere were invited to reflect on the world that had been lost and the values that had gone with it. The book was consciously pre-Lapsarian in intention, the chapter on the narrator's first sexual involvement being called 'First bite of the apple'. Yet this was also the year which saw the publication of Colin MacInnes' *Absolute*

Beginners, a novel about young people at large in a cosmopolitan city of pubs, clubs, coffee bars, dance halls. A cultural battle began in earnest in this period between ruralism and urban popular culture which was fought quite intensely from the mid-1950s onwards, and rapidly affected what was happening to English studies in schools.

III

We can focus these idioms in one way by looking at one particular year, 1956, and two books about schools which were published then to intense popular interest; one was *Village School* by Miss Read (a pseudonym), the other *Blackboard Jungle* by Evan Hunter. One was British and the other American. *Village School* is a detailed account of a year in the life of a rural school written by its head-teacher. The account of school life is closely connected with the pattern of the seasons. The book is divided into three sections: Christmas Term, Spring Term and Summer Term. It is thoroughly absorbing and embodies all that is best in that very English tradition of detailed observation of daily life, particularly rural life, which is very much there in Gilbert White's *Selborne*, the Reverend Kilvert's *Diary*, in Fred Archer's Vale of Evesham books and more recently in the James Herriot books about life as a veterinary surgeon in the Yorkshire Dales. The pattern of life goes on unbroken; the new children coming across the playground on the first day of the autumn term do so as their own parents did some twenty-five years earlier; and 'Miss Read' taught them all. In *Village School*, the school is the world and the world is the school. It is actually a very moving and evocative book. And it is not sentimental. Yet it cannot avoid imposing a pattern on life which for the people living in the village was probably never there for most of the time. Such was the great popular success of *Village School* that it was followed by further accounts of village life in *Village Diary* (1957), *Storm in the Village* (1958), *Thrush Green* (1959) and several other books. *Village School* was a set textbook in many teachers' training colleges from then on. This was an educational utopia to which all teaching aspired – the oneness of the school with the life around it.

Nothing like this could be said of Evan Hunter's *Blackboard Jungle*, which as a book was greatly helped to fame by the film of the same name which had a soundtrack which included songs by Bill Haley and the Comets. (This is symbolically very important because one of the major themes of rock music – 'the sound of the city' as it is aptly called in Charlie Gillett's history – is a very deeply-rooted antagonism to school. The songs are too numerous to mention; from Chuck Berry to the Pink Floyd, school is the great Moloch of all dreams and aspirations.) *Blackboard Jungle* was the first great popular portrait of the urban school[14] as it actually sometimes was – a battleground of antagonistic values and cultures which seemed to be totally irreconcilable. Although the portrait was of an American school in urban downtown Manhattan, much of the picture was clearly recognisable in Britain; teenagers who simply didn't want to be in school, knew what kinds of jobs and careers lay open to them, and who lived for the out-of-school world of the cinema, coffee bars, street life and the dream-like world of popular culture.

John Dixon, one of the most influential advocates of progressive English teaching from the mid-1960s, remembered when London teachers first began to come together to re-think the English curriculum:

> We did develop the idea of kids talking over experience when the *Universities and Left Review* started up their Carlisle Street centre (where they had the Partisan coffee bar and the library we used to use). That must have been about 1958 or 1959. What happened was that Stuart Hall was teaching in Vauxhall at the time, supply, and a group of us knew him, and we started up a teachers' discussion group.[15]

He remembered also that it was 'fantastic looking back at that period how few novels were even based in the city, in the working class. It really was a trememdous gap'. He remembered that they were enthusiastic about the work of Marjorie Hourd and David Holbrook, but wanted to go beyond it, to adopt these developments and put them into an urban context:

> in 1961 David Holbrook was giving talks about his Cambridge school class of so-called backward children who had written all these poems. But I think that by that time, partly through Harold Rosen's influence in LATE (London Association for the Teaching of English), we were thinking very much about the urban context, about working class kids having the need to talk about their experience *and having some sense of authority about that experience*. I think we had got that explicit in the early 1960s if not the late 1950s.[16]

Significantly the materials which were used in the beginning to talk about city life with city children in English lessons were not literary – there wasn't the writing available – but were in fact visual. Dixon remembered how important Roger Mayne's photographs of London were in that period for evoking a sense of the city, as well as the early documentary films of the 'free cinema' movement which produced such films as *We are the Lambeth Boys* and others depicting working-class youth culture.

The Leavisites fought back. David Holbrook in an excoriating review of *The Popular Arts* by Stuart Hall and Paddy Whannel in *The Use of English* in the spring of 1966, once again evoked the folk idiom as the one true standard of cultural seriousness against which any attempt to empathise with any form of popular culture was bound to fail. Hall and Whannel argued for discrimination *within* the genres of popular culture, but to no avail: 'I see no value in such "discriminations",' argued Holbrook; 'if we are to have muck, let's have outright, sheer muck, rather than muck that pretends, by snobbery or irony, to be superior.' Thus were the novels of Raymond Chandler, the films of John Ford, the Beatles' songs and everything else touched by commercialism swept aside completely. Holbrook's polemic ended with that old demon of the rural idiom, the urban 'mob'. Evoking a recent visit to Italy, he recalled that,

> In the peasant households one was still met with an ancient, proud courtesy: in the town markets there was a rich working-class vitality. *On the main roads* one returned to the loutishness, and, in the gathering places, to the offensive meaninglessness, the reduction of life, of the transistor, the demonstrative sex-cults, of the raucous mob. (my italics)[17]

This kind of polemic was already too late; 1966 was the year which saw the famous DES circular 10/65 enjoining local authorities to submit schemes for comprehensive education, and this in turn forced many education authorities, and teachers, to face up to the realities of a multi-racial and multi-cultural society. Education, belatedly, discovered the city.

But what has this to do with patriotism and the English national identity? A lot, I believe. For it seems to me that in England, and in many other countries also, patriotism is green. That is to say it is quite frequently evoked by appeals to the image of a still and timeless countryside which is thought to compose the quintessential England. The windswept moors and downs, the chalk streams, the wooded dales, the lakes and heaths, the Cotswold villages and small Suffolk hamlets, where the sturdy English yeomanry still abide and where Arthurian knights sleep beneath the hills – this, we have been told so often, is the real England.

This was certainly the case, I found, when I looked at the popular literature of the Second World War in *Dockers and Detectives* (1983), where so often the England which was evoked as the country being fought for and defended against fascism was one of oak-beamed pubs, punting on the Cam, and the image of cool summer evenings in country lanes or on velvet smooth lawns. The literature evoked the rural; it was largely the films which reminded people that there were cities to be defended. And the rural idiom in English pedagogy was a party to the power of that patriotic idyll.

The role which films have played in this mythologising process has been the subject of an excellent recent study by Jeffrey Richards and Anthony Aldgate[18] on both 'ruralist' and 'urban realist' themes in the British cinema. (In one sharp insight they point out how in the iconography of English values on film, St Paul's Cathedral has become the symbol of the metropolitan tradition, whereas Canterbury Cathedral has served as the quintessential symbol of the rural idyll.) In a long and persuasive essay on the film *A Canterbury Tale*, made as wartime propaganda as a way of exhorting people to remember the Britain (or was it England?) that was being fought for, the authors describe at length the context in which the film was scripted, cast and made, as part of a conscious attempt both to improve Anglo-American relations (there is an American sergeant in the film as a main character whose function is to be convinced of deeper values than that which he espouses when he first arrives in Britain) and to affirm national unity. The press release for *A Canterbury Tale*, which was released in 1944, stated that 'A Canterbury Tale is a new story about Britain, her unchanging beauty and traditions, and of the Old Pilgrims and the new.' The production company for the film was called 'The Archers', reminding us of another pervasive creation of popular culture in the radio series of that name which promoted the Britain-is-a-working-farm metaphor to a very large postwar audience. The very family name of Archer is of course steeped in the mythology of Agincourt and the English longbow and that famous shower of arrows which is the major spectacle of Oliver's wartime film of *Henry V* and which same image concludes (quite consciously I understand) that seminal postwar poem of Englishness, Philip Larkin's *The Whitsun Weddings*.

IV

This essay may be thought of as being cruelly unfair to the great dedication and industry of the teachers associated with *Scrutiny* and its educational journals. It is not intended to be. Neither is it intended as a clever metropolitan dismissal of the great liberating themes of the nineteenth-century romantic movement and its espousal of the democratic notions of popular 'customary' knowledge and good sense – themes which remained quite profoundly influential in the beliefs and practices of teacher-training colleges right through to the present. (I was once told by an elderly lecturer at one such teacher-training college that right up to the 1950s in many colleges a close reading and study of Wordsworth's *The Prelude* was a compulsory part of the curriculum for all would-be teachers.)

Yet there is no doubt in my mind, also, that one of the unintended effects of this powerful ideological movement – and neither individuals nor movements can be fully aware in advance of what the unintended consequences will be of whatever they do - was the major diminution of the value of the urban experience, and a refusal to acknowledge that life in the cities also offered possibilities for human self-consciousness and popular self-dignity. In *The Country and the City* Raymond Williams noted that 'even after the society was predominantly urban, its literature, for a generation, was still predominantly rural'.[19] With regard to education the time-lag was even more startling, since it amounted to nearly a hundred years - that is to say, from the advent of compulsory state education in 1870 right up to the 1960s. In all that time the dominant idyll in English pedagogy was that of the village school. The blackboard jungle was at least as near as being the reality for the majority of children in Britain.

Notes

1 H. C. Dent, *1870–1970: Century of Growth in English Education*, London, 1970, pp. 69–70.
2 James Kirkup, *The Only Child*, London, 1977, p. 125.
3 Cited in Stephen Humphries, *Hooligans or Rebels?*, London, 1981, p. 54.
4 Francis Mulhern, *The Moment of Scrutiny*, London, 1979, p. 102.
5 Margaret Mathieson, *The Preachers of Culture*, London, 1975, p. 75.
6 David Shayer, *The Teaching of English in Schools 1900–1970*, London, 1972, p. 122.
7 B. Whitton, *An Enquiry into Some Aspects of the Development of Children's Poetry*, London, 1974.
8 F. R. Leavis and Denys Thompson, *Culture and Environment*, London, 1960, pp. 1–2.
9 *Ibid.*, p. 102.
10 Francis Mulhern, *The Moment of Scrutiny*, London, 1979, p. 101.
11 *Ibid.*.
12 G. Bantock, 'Towards a theory of popular education', in R. Harper (ed.), *The Curriculum: Context, Design and Development*, London, 1971.

13 Richard Johnson, 'Education policy and social control in early Victorian England', *Past and Present*, 49, 1970.

14 Though in Britain Edward Blishen's *Roaring Boys* (1955) and Michael Croft's *Spare the Rod* had cleared the ground.

15 From a private interview with John Dixon in 1982.

16 *Ibid*.

17 David Holbrook, *The Use of English*, vol. 17, no. 3, spring, 1966, p. 199.

18 Jeffrey Richards and Anthony Aldgate, *Best of British: Cinema and Society 1930–1970*, Oxford, 1983.

19 Raymond Williams, *The Country and the City*, London, 1975, p. 10.

9

The liberty of the park

JILL FRANKLIN

It is generally accepted that the eighteenth-century landscape garden is one of England's outstanding artistic inventions, acknowledged both here and on the continent as a major contribution to European civilisation.[1] Right from the start it was significant not only for its aesthetic qualities but for its association with liberty, usually referred to as English liberty, which was favourably contrasted with French autocracy.[2] And, just as English liberty found expression in the landscape garden, so did French autocracy in the regimented gardens typified by those at Versailles.[3]

The first authoritative history of the English landscape garden was written by Horace Walpole in or before 1770,[4] and though recent research has changed some of his emphasis and attributions, the canonical version up to Capability Brown is still much as he formulated it. It is not surprising that, Walpole being the son of his father and himself at the heart of the world of Whig taste and politics, the liberty of the park turns out to wear a Whiggish air. In Whig eyes, liberty and property were virtually coterminous: 'Britain is the only kingdom and Britons the only people who can truly say, we have a property in what we enjoy', or as Lord Hardwicke put it in 1757, 'Our men of property are our only freemen.'[5] Perhaps the liberty of the park should be restricted in the same way.

According to Walpole, the landscape garden had its prophet in Milton, who, in the days of his blindness, had a vision of Eden; his description of it was 'a warmer and more just picture of the present style than Claud Lorrain could have painted from Hagley or Stourhead'. Walpole quoted a passage evoking each of these famous landscape gardens from *Lycidas* and *Paradise Lost* respectively.[6] The relevance of Milton for Walpole's theme is that in the

eighteenth century his fame rested quite as much on his champion-
ship of freedom as on his poetry. From the 1690s he was being
claimed as the forerunner of the Glorious Revolution, from which
all the present liberties flowed.[7] There was a strong implication
that the liberty of the landscape garden grew from the same roots.
Milton's prophetic vision began to be realised, the history
continues, with 'the capital stroke, the leading stage to all that
followed', possibly he thought, Charles Bridgeman's, which was
'the destruction of walls for boundaries and the invention of fossés
– an attempt then deemed so astonishing that the common people
called them Ha!Has!' Once the walls were down, levelling,
mowing and rolling followed, then William Kent 'appeared' and
in a famous phrase 'leaped the fence and saw all nature was a
garden'.[8] But if all nature was a garden, then the abrupt transition
and traditional contrast between ordered garden within and wilderness beyond must be done away with so that nature's garden could
be exploited to best advantage. 'Why may not a whole estate be
thrown into a kind of garden?' asked Addison.[9] From now on the
key theme, endlessly repeated in verse and prose, was that gardens
must be laid out in accordance with nature.

> O study nature and with thought profound
> Previous to laying out your ground
> O mark her beauties as they striking rise
> Bid all her adventitious charms surprize[10]

And so on. Of course, nature for Kent's generation was not the
same as for Walpole's, and different again for Payne Knight's or
Repton's. But through all the changes in the perception of nature
she remained more or less synonymous with freedom, and the aim
of the landscape gardener was always that the freedom of nature
should be realised in the garden.[11] Repton summed up the general
opinion when he said that it was an essential feature of the landscape garden that it 'should give an appearance of extent and
freedom' and he also declared that '[modern taste] has thrown
down the ancient palisade and lofty walls because it is aware that
liberty is the true portal of happiness'.[12] Even the deer and cattle
were part of the picture: 'The animals fed in such a park appear
free from confinement, at liberty to collect their food from the
rich herbage of the valley, and to range uncontrolled to the drier
soil of the hills.'[13]

Given that the landscape garden was intended to express nature
and freedom, it is startling that someone as sensitive to the beauties
of the countryside as John Constable should have written in 1822
in reference to the magnificent landscape of Fonthill Abbey, 'a

gentleman's park is my aversion, it is not beauty because it is not nature'.[14] The century between Kent's leap and Constable's aversion takes in the creation of all the greatest landscape parks, so Constable was evidently looking in a different direction from the rest and a different nature met his eye.

A clue to Constable's reaction may lie in the appearance of the landscape outside the park, which had changed greatly in the previous century. Across England generally, the countryside could be divided, from an agriculturalist's point of view, into three categories, not counting parks and gardens. First, even by the early eighteenth century, much of the country had already been enclosed into hedged fields. Second, a large area of central England from the East Riding down to Dorset, but excluding the south east, was still cultivated on the old communal two- or three-field system. In 1750 this accounted for between 44 per cent and 55 per cent of the land in eight counties.[15] Third, large tracts of the most infertile and unpromising land remained uncultivated. These areas were referred to as 'the waste' or even 'desert'.[16] Village commons were normally included in the category of waste and though, in law, virtually all waste land was owned by the lord of the manor,[17] a variety of rights of common often came into conflict with rights of ownership. The gentry were apt to think of the inhabitants of the waste as particularly lawless and dangerous.[18]

The countryside was thus much more varied than it is now. The formal gardens were small compared to the landscape park and early paintings of houses in their grounds and above all the engravings of Kip and others published in the early eighteenth century give a vivid impression of the look of the countryside, even when they overstress the importance of the great houses and their gardens.[19] The bird's-eye view presents a panoramic spread, but is able to show detail more naturalistically than a map can. In the engravings of the county of Kent, which had long been enclosed, the mosaic of small fields with their luxuriant hedgerow timber is drawn in detail, the pattern of ploughed field, grass meadow, cornfield or haycocks being rendered with a verve that occasionally suggests Van Gogh's pen-and-ink landscapes. The large square fields usually associated with later Parliamentary enclosure are sometimes depicted, as at Shobdon, Herefordshire, and, more rarely, the old open fields, as at Exton, Rutland,[20] but most views show the land surrounding the park as only partly under cultivation and, in some cases, not cultivated at all, the contrast between the rough vegetation of the waste and the formal order of the garden being strongly emphasised.

Comparably informative views for the age of Capability Brown are notably scarce, for just when landscape gardening was coming widely into fashion, bird's-eye panoramas went out. Even for house portraits, the viewpoint usually drops to eye level after about 1750 and those wealthy country-house patrons whose taste ran to landscape painting had no wish for detailed naturalistic renderings of the English countryside. The minority who enjoyed realism bought seventeenth-century Dutch paintings, but most collectors preferred ideal Italian landscapes.

The extent to which Italian landscape painting directly influenced the design of the English landscape garden is a matter of dispute,[21] but there is no doubt that the same idealising taste was at work in collecting and landscaping. Isaac Ware's analysis of the aims of gardening applies with perfect aptness to contemporary taste in pictures. They were:

> to collect the beauties of nature, to separate them from those
> rude views in which her blemishes are seen; to dispose them
> in the most pleasing order and create an universal harmony
> among them . . . everything pleasing is thrown open,
> everything disgustful is shut out.[22]

A bird's-eye panorama can play down rude views, but cannot easily omit them entirely, whereas an eye-level Claude landscape or Brown park selects what can be seen, guides the viewer or visitor by means of repoussoirs or planting, eliminating the disgustful, while apparently preserving the freedom of nature.

Separating the beauties was becoming all the more urgent since men of taste were aware that nature outside the park was not entirely the garden Kent had seen and that the disgustful was on the increase. In other words Parliamentary enclosure was under way. Although possibly as much as 75 per cent of the countryside had already been enclosed (though not necessarily hedged) by 1750, Parliamentary enclosure, which by 1914 accounted for another 20 per cent of the land, was very heavily concentrated into the period 1755–1815, about 80 per cent of all enclosure bills being passed in these sixty years. Within this period there were two major phases: the first, 1755–80, 37 per cent of the total, which as it happened coincided almost exactly with Capability Brown's working life, (he lived 1716–83); the second, 1793–1815 (42 per cent), coincided with Humphrey Repton's (1752–1818).[23]

Parliamentary enclosure took place almost entirely in the open-field area of central England where most of Brown's and Repton's work was done, so that by the time Repton died a great number of parks were surrounded by enclosure landscape.[24] For financial reasons, enclosure and emparking (usually enlarging an existing park) were often associated. Woodlands apart, parks produced far less income – perhaps half – than farms and it was always hoped that if enclosure took place, its extra revenues would offset the expense of the park.[25] The many seats where emparking and enclosure of neighbouring tracts took place within a short time of each other include Stowe and Hartwell, two Brown parks – Blenheim and Sandbeck – and two where Repton worked, Althorp and Woburn.[26]

In consequence, the landscapes inside and outside the park, far from blending imperceptibly, as the Kentian revolution assumed, were once again in marked contrast to each other. What is more, the appearance of the commissioners' fields was deeply distasteful to contemporary sensibility. The mid-eighteenth century preferred natural forms to be free-flowing, asymmetric and above all, curved – witness Hogarth's Line of Beauty – and as to landscape:

> Yon stream that wanders down the dale,
> The spiral wood, the winding vale . . .
> all combine
> To recommend the waving line[27]

The corollary, naturally, was shudders of dislike at straight lines and right angles: 'Let no strait lines your slopes deform'; 'there is nothing more disgusting to the eye than walks when stiff and formal'; and Althorp park 'is planted in strait lines and no taste'.[28]

So when it came to the enclosure landscape, Gilpin wrote that 'the marks of the spade and the plough, the hedge and the ditch; together with all the formalities of hedgerow trees and square divisions of property are disgusting to a high degree'.[29] At Oatlands Lord Lincoln chose to spoil a splendid view with his planting, in order to exclude the sight of the enclosure fields and farming activity.[30] Payne Knight thought hedges offensive when

> marked with lines of shredded elms, seen from great heights
> in what are called bird's eye view; or spread along the sides
> of mountains, where they give the inclosures the appearances
> of square divisions cut on the surface, than which nothing
> can be more harsh, meagre and unpleasant[31]

and according to Repton, 'the shape and colour of cornfields and the straight of fences, are totally at variance with all ideas of picturesque beauty'.[32] So in the garden, 'Nature and Fancy demand that every step of Rule be quite eraz'd and 'Line and Rule are forever dropped'.[33] The word 'Rule', powerfully ambiguous and frequently used in this context, initially referred to the old formal gardens, but by 1770 was being applied to the enclosure landscape.

Unsightly it might be, yet obviously the most efficient, economical and profitable scheme for enclosing was to lay out large square fields with the hedges running as directly as possible. 'In rural economy, straight lines and right angles are first principles which can seldom be deviated from with propriety', wrote William Marshall.[34] Gilpin summed up the position with admirable clarity:

> moral and picturesque ideas do not always coincide. In a moral light, cultivation, in all its parts, is pleasing: the hedge and the furrow; the waving corn field and the ripened sheaf. But all these, the picturesque eye, in quest of scenes of grandeur, and beauty, looks at with disgust.[35]

The enclosure landscape of line and rule is the domain of moral life and, he says, of the 'laborious mechanic':

> Poor yet industrious, modest, quiet, neat . . .
> I praise ye much, ye meek and patient pair,
> For ye are worthy; chusing rather far
> A dry but independent crust, hard earn'd[36]

Praiseworthy Cowper's old couple may be, but they are hardly expressive of propertied liberty and so they have no place in the picturesque domain of the park, where the

> arts of industry are rejected and even idleness, if I may so speak, adds dignity to a character. Thus the lazy cowherd resting on his pole or the peasant lolling on a rock may be allowed . . . but the characters most suited to these scenes of grandeur are . . . figures in long, folding draperies; gypsies; banditti.[37]

Given such an attitude, it is clear why country house patrons did not want realistic paintings of the working countryside and not surprising that in Stubbs's famous paintings of haymaking and harvesting, the laborious mechanics, dressed in snowy linen, adopt the graceful and seemingly effortless poses of dancers in a Frederick Ashton ballet.[38]

Obviously, if the mechanic at work was an eyesore to be banished, the park was hardly the place for his village either. Many early manor houses once formed part of a tight-knit complex with the village and the church, but eighteenth-century taste now found such proximity intolerable. In addition, emparking brought many further-off villages within the boundaries for the first time. The village church sometimes proved immovable and was left stranded in the park, isolated as at Harewood and Exton, or remodelled or rebuilt as an eyecatcher or adornment as at Wimpole, Gunton, Ayot St Lawrence and Great Packington.[39] The villagers and their village were easily removed by their landlord, so that a surprising number of parks contain a deserted village, though it may have left no visible traces.[40]

> Where then, ah where, shall poverty reside
> To 'scape the pressure of contiguous pride?

asked Goldsmith.[41] In some cases no provision seems to have been made. Henderskelfe vanished when Castle Howard was built, its main street becoming the path from the house to the Temple of the Winds and an early example of the serpentine line in the grounds. A settlement planned for the villagers at Welburn was never built and the community apparently just dispersed itself.[42] In many parks, however, a new village was built, usually just outside the gates, and many of the earliest examples form stiff lines of houses, as at Houghton, Nuneham Courtenay and Harewood. Later the layout was occasionally picturesque, as at Milton Abbas, but still, of course, neat, orderly and controlled.

And so, by the early nineteenth century, the landscapes have changed place. Line and Rule, squares and parallels, banished from the garden, are displaced on to the agricultural scene outside the park, where they are reproduced on a larger scale in the commissioners' fields, and the free wild garden of nature has been recreated inside the fence. You may not agree with Constable that 'a gentleman's park is not beauty', but it is no wonder he found it unnatural.

So the place where park liberty met agriculture and industriousness deserves another look. In theory the boundaries had vanished but even the revolutionary ha-ha was not quite what it seemed. For those on the inside, the fences had certainly sunk, but they still presented a formidable barrier in the other direction. An illustration of Bridgeman's ha-ha at Stowe shows ferocious spikes sticking out horizontally into the hollowed trench.[43] At the end of the century a drawing by John Plaw gives equally ferocious diagonal and vertical variants of the same device.[44] Alternatively a thick row of thorns could be planted out of sight in the trench, with 'prickly boughs impenetrable',[45] However once the formal garden had been opened up, the principal use of the ha-ha was to conceal divisions within the park, not to mark the boundary between the park and outside, where something more emphatic was needed. A unifying ring fence was an asset and this too was normally unseen from inside, being masked by trees, while presenting a powerful, defensive barrier to the outside world.

Sir John Vanbrugh, who was perfectly in tune with the ideas and feelings of early Whig landowners, was the first to see the

11   'Gypsies cooking on an open fire' by Thomas
Rowlandson (Yale Center for British Art). The gypsies are
beside a stout boundary fence, probably a park pale.

charm of a 'castle air' for the eighteenth century.[46] At Castle
Howard he built 'Fortifications' in the 1720s, big castle walls punctuated by immense bastions round the more conspicuous stretches
of the park perimeter. Various friends – a duke and three lords –
were 'all vastly surprised and taken with the walls and their towers,
which they talk much of' and he concludes, 'I always thought we
were sure of that card'. As to a plan not to have a gateway opposite
the front door, 'My Lord Cobham [of Stowe] is mightily for this
Expedient'. He had seen it done in Germany with 'admirable good
effect, the plain wall in the Front looking with a bolder air of
Defence than if there had been a gate through it'.[47]

12 The park-keeper's lodge at Cobham Hall, designed by Humphrey Repton, who also landscaped the park (c. 1813–31). The lodge is a fantasy Tudor castle and the stream seems to represent its moat. From Humphrey Repton, 'Fragments . . .', 1816, reprinted 1982, Fragment XXX.

The ring fence was not only solid and strong, it could also be extremely expensive. The wall at Blenheim, erected 1727–9, was 7 foot high, 9 miles long and cost £1,196 per mile. In the 1760s Brown proposed putting castellations along its entire length, which would no doubt have given an even bolder air of defence.[48] Where iron railings were preferred they often had the same air, for realistic spearheads on the spikes were a favourite design throughout the landscaping period, and by Regency times the spears even had iron tassels.[49]

Inside the park wall, ornamental buildings often formed an essential element of the landscape design; originally their meaning was as important as their visual effect and was often intended to convey quite complex ideas or concepts. Whig Liberty was one of these. At Stowe a statue of Public Liberty stood in the middle niche of the Temple of Concord and Victory. Figures in the Temple of British Worthies, designed by Kent c.1735, included Milton and Hampden; the three monarchs honoured were Queen Elizabeth as champion of Protestant religion, William III as champion of 1688 and King Alfred, who, according to the inscription, 'guarded Liberty and was the founder of the English Constitution'; in addition Liberty had its own temple not far off, designed by James Gibbs and begun in 1741, which was surrounded by Saxon deities of the age of Alfred:

> Gods of a nation, valiant, wise and free,
> Who conquered to establish Liberty

explained Lord Cobham's nephew.[50] At Stourhead, Alfred the Great's Tower, planned in 1762 and built 1766–72, was making the same point, the inscription there calling him, 'The Father of his People, the Founder of the English Monarchy and Liberty'.[51] In 1801 Henry Holland was asked to design a miniature Temple of Liberty for the sculpture gallery at Woburn. It was for busts of the fifth duke's political heroes, the most notable being Charles James Fox. Flaxman designed the pediment sculpture of Liberty.[52]

In the eighteenth century Alfred was regularly viewed as the first English guardian of liberty, along with his Saxons, and his age was favourably contrasted with the 'grievous yoke' of Norman rule, when our constitution was 'full of radical inconveniences'.[53] In addition, the Saxons were frequently equated with the Goths: 'in all ages of the Saxon monarchy there was no distinction of Goths from Saxons' as Batty Langley put it.[54] As a result the Goths could join Alfred and the Saxons as co-founders of our liberty and our 'noble and ancient Gothic constitution' – meaning early Saxon – was referred to with pride.[55] From an architect's point of view, the identity of Goth and Saxon was very handy, which is no doubt why Batty Langley dwells on it. He supposed that genuine Saxon architecture had all been destroyed by the Danes, but he and other architects felt that Alfred, the Saxons and Liberty could all be fittingly represented in Gothic style, as they were in the temple at Stowe. Gothic style was all the more appropriate since it was also connected with the period of Magna Carta, when it was held that freedom once more returned to the constitution.[56]

Gothic also happened to be the castle style. In the *Beauties Of Stow* (sic) of 1753, the author, in admiring the Temple of Liberty, observed, 'This is a Kind of Castle',[57] and so too was Alfred's Tower at Stourhead. Thus temples of liberty and feudal castles, far from being contrasted, could look very like one another, which Whig landowners, as well as their architects, perhaps found handy.

In any event, castles, whether complete or built as ruins, were immensely popular from Vanbrugh's time on. Sham castles have been described as a prime example of 'the element of make-believe which has often been central to English architecture'.[58] But though sham castles are plainly not military structures, they are not necessarily make-believe in the sense of pretending or playing a game, any more than Temples of Liberty or Concord. It is far more likely that they are to be taken in the same spirit as the Roman portico on the landowner's mansion, the Roman armour he wore on his tomb statue, or the trophies of plasterwork arms on his hall walls, all of which are a reminder of his very real power. A mediaeval castle symbolised territorial might and building a sham one in the grounds was perhaps the equivalent of providing a pedigree in stone for its modern descendant, the Palladian mansion. At Doddington Hall, Cheshire, 'an ivy-mantled tower, built, as supposed, in Edward the Third's time . . . has statues of the Black Prince . . . and his four esquires . . . from one of whom Sir Thomas Broughton [the owner] is lineally descended and whose ample possessions he now enjoys'.[59] Lucky Sir Thomas. But a man of much newer descent was equally free to build himself an ivy-mantled tower. Again the word commonly used to describe the site of a hill-top mansion is perhaps more appropriate to a general reporting on battle terrain, for it is said to 'command' - 'extensive views', delightful prospects', and so on.[60]

Thus, Gothic castles can simultaneously conjure up English liberty and the rights of landed power. The Whig connotation is made explicit in a castle-Gothic tower at Richmond, Yorkshire, built in 1746, for it celebrated, and was named for, Culloden.[61] And it must be more than coincidence that the first important castle ruin was built in 1747–8 at Hagley, one of the gardens foreseen by Milton. Designed by Sanderson Miller, it was praised by Horace Walpole, who did not generally care for Miller's work, as having 'the true rust of the Barons' Wars' about it.[62] This well-known expression may hold a nuance beyond aesthetic appreciation, for the outcome of the Barons' Wars was the establishment of Parliament. Similarly, Miller's next ruin, designed 1749–51 though not built till 1772, could well be more than a patron's picturesque fancy. The patron was Lord Chancellor Hardwicke, who bought Wimpole Hall for £100,000.[63] In accordance with his belief in the importance of property, he once transported a man for seven years for stealing a 40–shilling cow.[64] In 1742 Batty Langley prefaced his *Ancient Architecture Restored and Improved* with a list of 'Encouragers to the Restoring of Saxon Architecture'. Heading the list was Lord Hardwicke.

So if a mansion is in some sense doing duty as a castle, the ring fence can be taken as representing the castle *enceinte* and, like it, had gates at strategic points guarded by gatekeepers, for whom gate lodges were built. Military symbolism appeared here too. Sanderson Miller again pioneered the castle form and presently castle gatehouses with stout towers, crenellations and machicolations stood ready, it seemed, to repel attackers, as at Croft Castle, Herefordshire, or Hillington Hall, Norfolk, while other mansions had a Roman triumphal arch proclaiming a victory already won, as at Stowe and Dyrham Park, Hertfordshire.[65]

The embattled boundaries of the park are a reminder that the century of landscaping coincided not only with Parliamentary enclosure, but also with the heyday of the game laws. From the late seventeenth to the early nineteenth century the complicated laws dealing with the illegal taking or killing of edible animals, birds or fish operated as a series of overlapping restrictions, which distinguished between the various species of animals, the places and times of the killing and the classes of people who were allowed or forbidden to hunt or shoot.[66] Deer, hare and rabbit were held not to be game as long as they were within a park, chase or warren, but were the property of the park owner. It followed that taking them constituted the common law offence of stealing, for which the penalties in the early eighteenth century were far more savage than for poaching game, especially where deer were concerned. According to whether the offence was charged under the deer stealing acts of 1719 and 1776 or under the Waltham Black Act of 1722/3, these could be either transportation for seven years or hanging without benefit of clergy.[67]

Game was dealt with under different laws. The creatures concerned – mainly birds – were deemed to be wild or free and so incapable of being private property. On the other hand, hunting or shooting them was a most jealously guarded privilege, reserved principally for owners of land worth £100 per annum or more. Qualified hunters could shoot over anyone else's land as well as their own: the unqualified could not legally shoot anywhere, even on their own land.[68] By the mid-eighteenth century, at the same time as the natural habitat of the waste was diminishing, game hunting became more gregarious and competitive, so that, for really good sport, it was necessary to preserve the game by providing pheasantries, feed and extra men to guard the birds at night. Rides were cut through dense thickets for easier access and the whole activity became more artificial and much more expensive. Consequently landowners grew reluctant for qualified gentlemen to come shooting – perfectly legally – over their preserves, yet they insisted on keeping the system of privileged qualification. So they kept the law of trespass in reserve, which meant that gentlemen could be sued for damages under the civil law, whereas ungentlemanly poachers could be prosecuted for crime for the identical action.[69]

As game hunting became more highly organised and the game more frequently concentrated into preserves, poaching grew worse, whereupon the penalties were stepped up, with both escalating in step until 1831, when the whole basis of the game laws was changed. The basic penalty for poaching was always a fine, but an aggravated offence, such as poaching at night, armed or in gangs, could lead to a whipping, imprisonment with hard labour or seven years transportation.[70] Yet no penalty provided an adequate deterrent and three years after an affray in which a gamekeeper was shot and the culprit subsequently hanged, the landowner, Lord Walpole (Horace's nephew), installed spring guns and man traps in his woods. His neighbours soon followed. These devices, which could easily break a thigh or even cause death, were not forbidden until 1831.[71]

According to Sir William Blackstone, the justification for game laws in general was that, besides encouraging agriculture and game preservation, they 'prevented idleness and dissipation in husbandmen, artificers and those of lower ranks'. But Blackstone was contemptuous of the existing game laws as being of feudal origin, 'a bastard slip of the Norman forest laws.'[72] And remarkably enough, Blackstone and Sir James Stephen after him, were extremely doubtful whether the qualified sportsman's privilege was in fact legally valid.[73] In addition, Blackstone questioned the legal status of many contemporary parks. He defined a park as 'an enclosed chase extending only over a man's own grounds', adding

but it is not every field or common, which a gentleman pleases
to surround with a wall or paling, and to stock with a herd
of deer, that is therefore constituted a legal park; for the king's
grant, or at least, immemorial prescription, is necessary to
make it so. Though now the difference between a real park
and such enclosed grounds is not very material.[74]

It was not very material, presumably, because those chiefly
affected, namely deer and rabbit stealers, could never challenge the
rights of the park-owning gentlemen, who, as it happened, were
also the Justices of the Peace, dealing summary justice or sitting at
Quarter Sessions.

So by Capability Brown's time, the essential feature of a park,
at least as far as the administration of justice went, was not the
king's grant but the wall or paling which defined its extent. Taking
or killing creatures within the park, not only deer or rabbit but
even semi-tame pheasants in a mew or fish in a pond, was a
common-law felony, but if any of them should 'escape and regain
their natural liberty' outside the park the owner's 'property
instantly ceases'[75] and therefore the penalties for taking them
outside the park were much milder.

Thus the park boundary was not merely marking the limit of
land ownership. It was also a physical barrier preventing the
animals escaping and so ceasing to be private property, while its
symbolism of castellations and spears served as a threat or warning.
'The care of a park consists, I apprehend, in an attention to the
sufficiency of its fences', wrote a land steward.[76] The importance
of the boundary is underlined by the fact that it was a specific
offence to 'pull down or destroy . . . the pale or pales or any part
of the walls of any forest, chace, purlieu, antient walk, park,
paddock, wood or other ground' where deer were habitually kept.
The penalty in 1718–19 was a £30 fine or, in default of that, one
year's imprisonment plus an hour in the pillory on market day. A
bill of 1776 re-enacted these penalties, though without the pillory.[77]

A general recorded two relevant incidents, from the gentlemanly
angle. In 1826

an uncomfortable incident had taken place by some incendiary
having set fire to the Park paling and woods at Four Oaks,
as it was supposed for some trifling species of arbitrary
proceeding . . . with regard to information under the wilful
trespass act against a man found in some enclosure near the
house

and in 1829,

Mr Dugdale, the Member of the County, has just suffered a most wanton piece of malevolence by some evil disposed person or persons having thrown poison into his dog-kennel and killed all his pointers [his hunting dogs]. Mr D has been the means of prosecuting and transporting a part of an audacious gang of poachers.[78]

Almost a century before, James Thomson, in a passage from his poem *Liberty*, had supposed that the problem was already disposed of:

> From the sure land is rooted ruffian force
> And the lewd nurse of villains, idle waste;
> Lo, raz'd their haunts . . .
> . . . beauteous order reigns!
> Manly submission, unimposing toil.[79]

It was wishful thinking, but it helps to complete the myth of the landscape park.

According to the myth, the park is a place expressive of English liberty, a natural landscape of freely-laid-out grass, water and trees. Ugly scenes of hard work and views of unsightly villages have been banished, though peasants may loll and cowherds rest. The animals are unconfined except by the invisible ha-ha, since the ancient palisade and lofty walls have been thrown down. Outside in the moral domain, the idle waste has been cleared of villains and poachers and instead the law-abiding husbandman toils in manly submission in the beauteous order of the rich, square fields.

Goldsmith understood the situation perfectly: 'Ask an Englishman what nation in the world enjoys most freedom, and he immediately answers, his own. Ask him in what that freedom principally consists, and he is instantly silent'.[80]

Notes

1 Nikolaus Pevsner, *Studies in Art, Architecture and Design*, 2 vols, 1968, vol. I, p. 82; Kenneth Clark, *Civilisation*, 1969, p. 271.
2 Cf. William Cowper, *The Task*, 1783–4, book V, pp. 331–490; Leon Radzinowicz, *A History of English Criminal Law*, 4 vols, 1948–68, vol. I, pp. 712–19.
3 Nikolaus Pevsner, *Studies in Art, Architecture and Design*, 2 vols, 1968, vol. I, pp. 82–9, quoting Shaftesbury, Addison, Pope; John Dixon Hunt and Peter Willis, *The Genius of the Place*, 1975, pp. 33–4, 40–1, quoting Addison.
4 Horace Walpole, 'The history of the modern taste in gardening' in *Anecdotes of Painting in England*, 4 vols, 1771, reprinted in James Dallaway (ed.), 5 vols, 1827–8, in vol. IV as 'On modern gardening'.

5 *An Essay on Liberty and Independency*, 1747, pp. 7–8; William Cobbett, *Parliamentary History of England*, 12 vols, 1806–12, vol. XV, p. 744, quoted in H. T. Dickinson, *Liberty and Property*, 1977, pp. 143, 128.

6 Horace Walpole, 'The history of the modern taste in gardening', in *Anecdotes of Painting in England*, 4 vols, 1771, reprinted in James Dallaway (ed.), 5 vols., 1827–8, in vol. IV, pp. 248–9.

7 Helen Darbishire, *The Early Lives of Milton*, 1932, pp. 83, 194, 211; George F. Sensabaugh, *The Grand Whig, Milton*, 1952, pp. 180, 190.

8 Horace Walpole, 'The history of the modern taste in gardening', in *Anecdotes of Painting in England*, 4 vols, 1771, reprinted in James Dallaway (ed.), 5 vols., 1827–8, pp. 263–4.

9 *Spectator*, no. 414, June, 1712.

10 *The Rise and Progress of the Present Taste in Planting*, 1767, reprinted 1970, p. 17.

11 William Mason, *The English Garden*, 1772–81, edn of 1777–8, book II, p. 92; Richard Payne Knight, 1794, second edn of 1795, reprinted 1972, book I, p. 143, book II p. 35.

12 Humphrey Repton, *An Enquiry into the Changes of Taste in Landscape Gardening*, 1806, reprinted 1969, p. 33; *Sketches and Hints on Landscape Gardening*, 1795, reprinted in J. C. Loudon (ed.), *The Landscape Gardening . . . of the late Humphry Repton esq*, 1840, p. 46.

13 Humphry Repton, *Observation of the Theory and Practice of Landscape Gardening*, 1803, reprinted in J. C. Loudon, *op. cit.*, p. 208.

14 R. B. Beckett (ed.), *John Constable's Correspondence*, 6 vols, 1982–8, vol. VI, p. 98.

15 J. R. Wordie, 'The chronology of English enclosure 1500–1914', *Economic History Review*, 2nd series, vol. XXXVI, no. 4, 1983, p. 500.

16 Cf. Joseph Heely, *Letters on the Beauties of Hagley, Envil and the Leasowes*, 2 vols, 1777 reprinted, 1982, vol. II, p. 24.

17 Sir William Blackstone, *Commentaries on the Laws of England*, 4 vols, 1765–9, 10th edn, 1787, vol. II, p. 33.

18 R. W. Malcolmson, *Life and Labour in England 1700–1780*, 1981, pp. 110–11.

19 John Harris, *The Artist and the Country House*, 1979, *passim*. Johannes Kip, *Britannia Illustrata*, vol. I, 1707; vol. II, 1715; *Nouveau Theatre de la Grande Bretagne*, vol. III, 1715; vol. IV, 1720. Dr John Harris, *The History of Kent*, 1719. Thomas Badeslade, *Thirtysix different Views of Seats in the County of Kent*, 1720.

20 Johannes Kip, *op. cit.*, vol. II, edn of 1740.

21 John Dixon Hunt and Peter Willis, *The Genius of the Place*, 1975, p. 15.

22 Isaac Ware, *A Complete Body of Architecture*, 1756, edn of 1767, p. 637.

23 Michael Turner, 'Cost, finance and Parliamentary enclosure', *Economic History Review*, 2nd series, vol. XXXIV, 1981, p. 237.

24 J. A. Yelling, *Common Field and Enclosure in England 1450–1850*, 1977, pp. 1, 15; Hugh Prince, *Parks in England*, 1967, pp. 35, 46.

25 Hugh Prince, *op. cit*, p. 14; T. W. Beastall, *A North Country Estate*, 1975, pp. 114–15; François de la Rochefoucauld, *A Frenchman in England*, trans. S. C. Roberts, 1933, p. 47.

26 Dorothy Stroud, *Capability Brown*, 1950, new edn 1975, pp. 129–32, 138, 238; Dorothy Stroud, *Humphry Repton*, 1962, p. 147; Michael Turner, 'Cost, finance and Parliamentary enclosure', *Economic History Review* 2nd series, vol. XXXIV, 1981, p. 247 (Stowe, Hartwell); T. W. Beastall, *A North Country Estate*, 1975, pp. 86–90 (Sandbeck); W. E. Tate, *A Domesday of English Enclosure Acts and Awards*, 1978, pp. 212–13 (Oxfordshire), 192–4 (Northants), 5–6 (Bedfordshire).

27 'Verses written at the garden of William Shenstone near Birmingham', 1756, in Alexander Chalmers, *Works of the English Poets*, 21 vols, 1810, vol. XIII, p. 334.

28 Richard Jago, *Edge-Hill; or the Rural Prospect Delineated and Moralized*, 1767, book I, in Chalmers, *op. cit.*, vol. XVII, p. 291; Joseph Heely, *Letters on the Beauties of Hagley, Envil and the Leasowes*, 2 vols, 1777, reprinted 1982, vol. I, p. 63; 'Travel journals of the 1st Duchess of Northumberland', *Country Life*, 1974, vol. CLV, p. 308.

29 William Gilpin, *Observations relative chiefly to picturesque beauty made in the year 1777*, 2 vols, 1786, vol. I, p. 7.

30 Paget Toynbee and L. Whibley (eds), *The Correspondence of Thomas Gray*, 3 vols, 1935, vol. II, p. 578 (1758), quoted in Michael Symes, 'New light on Oatland Park in the eighteenth century', *Garden History*, vol. IX, no. 2, 1981, p. 240.

31 Richard Payne Knight, *The Landscape*, 1794, second edn of 1795, reprinted 1972, book I, p. 41.

32 Humphrey Repton, *Observations on the Theory and Practice of Landscape Gardening*, 1803, reprinted in J. C. Loudon, *The Landscape Gardening . . . of the late Humphry Repton esq*, 1840, p. 210.

33 William Mason, *The English Garden*, 1772–81, edn of 1777–8, book I, p. 308; Joseph Heely, *Letters on the Beauties of Hagley, Envil and Leasowes*, 2 vols, 1777, reprinted in 1982, vol. I, p. 94.

34 William Marshall, *The Rural Economy of Yorkshire*, 1788, p. 94.

35 William Gilpin, *Observations relative chiefly to picturesque beauty made in the year 1777*, 2 vols, 1786, vol. II, p. 43.

36 William Cowper, *The Task*, 1783–4, book IV, lines 374, 407–9.

37 William Gilpin, *Observations relative chiefly to picturesque beauty made in the year 1777*, 2 vols, 1786, vol. II, p. 43.

38 'Harvest scene, haymakers' and 'Harvest scene, reapers', both dated 1785, Tate Gallery.

39 Architects, respectively, Henry Flitcroft (1748–9), Robert Adam (1769) Nicholas Revett (1778) Joseph Bonomi (1789–90); Howard Colvin, *A Biographical Dictionary of British Architects*, 1954, revised edn 1978, pp. 311, 50, 684, 125.

40 A selection is given by Mavis Batey in 'Oliver Goldsmith, an indictment of landscape gardening' in Peter Willis (ed.), *Furor Hortensis*, 1974, pp. 57–61.

41 Oliver Goldsmith, *The Deserted Village*, 1770, lines 304–5.

42 Kerry Downes, *Vanbrugh*, 1977, p. 109.

43 Pl. 8 of fifteen views of Stowe by Jacques Rigaud c.1733, reproduced in Peter Willis, *Charles Bridgeman*, 1977, pl. 144.

44 John Plaw, *Ferme Ornée or Rural Improvements*, 1795, pl. 2.

45 William Mason, *The English Garden*, 1772–81, edn of 1777–8, book II, pp. 294–5.

46 Geoffrey Webb (ed.), *Complete Works of Sir John Vanbrugh*, 4 vols, 1928, vol. IV, *The Letters*, p. 14 (c.1707).

47 Geoffrey Webb (ed.), *op. cit.*, pp. 173, 163.

48 David Green, *Blenheim Palace*, 1951, pp. 314, 198, pls 91, 92.

49 Cf. Isaac Ware, *A Complete Body of Architecture*, 1756, edn of 1767, pl. 12; Regents Park, Park Crescent.

50 [Gilbert West], *Stowe, the Gardens*, 1732, reprinted in *The Gardens at Stowe*, 1982, p. 24; George Bickham, *The Beauties of Stow*(sic), 1752, reprinted *op. cit.*, p. 30; Laurence Whistler *et al.*, *Stowe, a Guide to the Gardens*, 1965, revised edn 1968, p. 149.

51 Kenneth Woodbridge, *The Stourhead Landscape*, 1971, pp. 13, 22.

52 Dorothy Stroud, *Country Life*, 1965, vol. CXXXVIII, pp. 158–9; Rupert Gunnis, *Dictionary of British Sculptors*, 1953, revised edn 1968, p. 149.

53 H. T. Dickinson, *Liberty and Property*, 1977, pp. 63–4; John Brewer, *Party Ideology and Popular Politics at the Accession of George III*, 1976, pp. 260–1, quoting a letter of Dr John Davenant, 1761.

54 Batty and Thomas Langley, *Ancient Architecture restored and improved*, 1742, p. 1.

55 John Brewer, *Party Ideology and Popular Politics at the Accession of George III*, 1976, pp. 260–1; Reed Browning, *Political and Constitutional Ideas of the Court Whigs*, 1982, p. 125.

56 John Brewer, *ibid.* H. T. Dickinson, *Liberty and Property*, 1977, pp. 62–4, 73.

57 George Bickham, *The Beauties of Stow* (sic), 1752, reprinted in *The Gardens of Stowe*, 1982, p. 30.

58 David Watkin, *The English Vision, the Picturesque in Architecture, Landscape and Garden Design*, 1982, p. IX.

59 George Richardson, *New Vitruvius Britannicus*, 1802, p. 17.

60 *Ibid., passim*; John Woolfe and James Gandon, *Vitruvius Britannicus*, vol. IV, 1767, *passim*.

61 Peter Leach, *Country Life*, 1974, vol. CLVI, p. 836.

62 W. S. Lewis (ed.), *Horace Walpole's Correspondence*, 48 vols, 1937–80, vol. XXV, p. 148.

63 G. E. Cockayne, *Complete Peerage*, 14 vols, 1910–65, vol. VI, p. 305.

64 Philip C. Yorke, *Life and Correspondence of Philip Yorke Earl of Hardwicke*, 1913, p. 132.

65 Howard Colvin, *A Biographical Dictionary of British Architects*, 1954, revised edn 1978, p. 549; Timothy Mowl, 'The evolution of the park gate lodge as a building type', *Architectural History*, 1984, vol. XXVII, pp. 471–3, Nikolaus Pevsner, *The Buildings of England; Herefordshire*, 1963, p. 109; *North West and South Norfolk*, 1962, p. 196. B. Seeley, *Stowe, A Description*, 1777, reprinted in *The Gardens at Stowe*, 1982, p. 7. Pevsner, *Middlesex*, 1951, p. 39.

66 Sir William Blackstone, *Commentaries on the Laws of England*, 4 vols,

1765–9, 10th edn, 1787, vol. II, pp. 393–4, 411; Sir James Stephen, *A History of the Criminal Law of England*, 3 vols, 1883, vol. III, pp. 275–82; P. B. Munsche, *Gentlemen and Poachers, The English Game Laws 1671–1831*, 1981, pp. 8–27, 172–85.

67 5 George I c. 28; 16 George III c. 30; 9 George I c. 22: Leon Radzinowicz, *A History of the English Criminal Law*, 4 vols, 1948–68, vol. I pp. 49–79; E. P. Thompson, *Whigs and Hunters*, 1975, pp. 21–4, 245–8, 270–7.

68 Sir William Blackstone, *Commentaries on the Laws of England*, 4 vols, 1765–9, 10th edn, 1787, vol. II, p. 418; Sir James Stephen, *A History of the Criminal Law of England*, 3 vols, 1883, vol. III, pp. 275–82; P. B. Munsche, *Gentlemen and Poachers, The English Game Laws 1671–1831*, 1981, pp. 8–9.

69 P. B. Munsche, *op. cit.*, pp. 36–45, 111, 114; Sir William Blackstone, *op. cit.*, vol. II, p. 418; Douglas Hay, 'Poaching and the game laws on Cannock Chase', in Douglas Hay *et al.*, *Albion's Fatal Tree*, 1975, p. 213.

70 P. B. Munsche, *op. cit.*, pp. 169–86.

71 P. B. Munsche, *op. cit.*, pp. 69, 72–5.

72 Sir William Blackstone, *Commentaries on the Laws of England*, 4 vols, 1765–9, 10th edn, 1787, vol. II, pp. 411–13, 409.

73 Sir William Blackstone, *op. cit.*, p. 418; Sir James Stephen, *A History of the Criminal Law of England*, 3 vols, 1883, vol. III, p. 281.

74 Sir William Blackstone, *op. cit.*, vol. II, p. 38.

75 Sir William Blackstone, *op. cit.*, vol. II, pp. 392–3.

76 John Lawrence, *The Modern Land Steward*, 1801, p. 110.

77 5 George I c. 15; 16 George III c. 30.

78 R. W. Jeffery (ed.), *Dyott's Diary*, 2 vols, 1907, vol. I, p. 375; vol. II, p. 19.

79 James Thomson, *Liberty*, 1738, book V, lines 622–6.

80 Arthur Friedman (ed.), *Collected Works of Oliver Goldsmith*, 5 vols, 1966, vol. II, p. 210.

10
'Constable country'
between the wars

ALEX POTTS

I

A dwelling on the beauties of the English countryside is usually associated with social and political conservatism – a garden of England refuge from the tensions and ugliness of modern urban society. Here, among familiar lanes, meadows, hedgerows, copses, brooks and ponds, the embattled and weary upper-middle-class consciousness can briefly find peace and comfort, surrounded by images attuned to the movements of what it sees as its more melodious desires and aspirations: 'a Constable country of the mind' as J. G. Ballard called it.[1] This could be construed as a singularly English outlook, a defensive turning away from the realities and challenges of the present; but one that at the same time has been incorporated into a national mythology mobilised at times of political tension to figure some essence of true Englishness, an ideal for which it's worth killing foreigners and pulverising their less leisured and civilised landscapes.

Simply to pursue a hard-nosed metropolitican critique of such little-England ruralism, however, would be not just to miss some of the more significant ideological modulations you find associated with this kind of imagery as it has been deployed in British culture over the past hundred years or so. It would be to ignore the dichotomies that actually give these images their sustaining power and thus effectively to suppress any real examination of the cultural politics involved.[2] There are, for one thing, as many reactionary and backward-looking images of the city as there are of the countryside – the vogue for celebrating England and Englishness that reached a peak in the 1930s produced titles that ranged from *The Landscape of England* (1932) and *The Beauty of England* (1933) to *The Real East End*.[3] Conversely, there could be as much

13 'Wood on the Downs' by Paul Nash, 1929 (Aberdeen Art Gallery and Museums).

progressivism in discussions of the countryside as in those of urban and industrial life. Richard Jefferies, probably the most celebrated countryside writer of the late Victorian period, who entertained his urban middle-class readers with accounts of the purifying experience of corn fields, meadows, country skies and country bird songs, wrote not as someone seeking to evade change but as someone who stressed 'Now let us begin to roll back the tide of death and to set our faces steadily to a future of life . . . Erase the past from the mind – stand face to face with the real now – and work out all anew.'[4] A later book on the country scene, Robertson Scott's *England's Green and Pleasant Land* (1925), articulated the very kind of social criticism most often levelled at the genre: 'It is not everybody who can see through, who keenly wishes to see through the pleasing haze of the traditional, the ordered, and the picturesque, who has the stomach for radical change at the time it is needed.'[5]

This is not to deny the importance of the conservative side of the story, in particular the mobilisation of countryside images for promoting a little-England jingoism.[6] At times when the 'outside' world appeared particularly threatening, during the two world wars, and in the 1930s with the rise of Fascism, such images were often invoked to celebrate an English essence, enduring safe and beautiful, a home, a haven, and at the same time England's glory. But other countries had their similar national mythologies. Every bit as potent as the English meadow and the English village was the German forest (*Wald*) and German village (*Dorf*). Politically the phenomenon was not peculiarly British. Moreover, it could sometimes backfire as a propaganda exercise. If the troops in the trenches during the First World War were supposed to be fighting for an ideal England of unspoiled countryside, this image could also become a vivid reproach to the ugly inhuman landscapes of death and desolation that the war was creating. Materially such comparisons were reinforced by the fact that so many city-dwelling soldiers were billetted or hospitalised in the country during their spells in England away from the front. No modern industrial development had ever mangled 'nature' so dramatically before, produced an environment more alien to the landscapes of the pastoral ideal. As the painter Paul Nash put it, 'Sunset and sunrise are blasphemous, they are mockeries to man, only the black rain out of the bruised and swollen clouds all through the bitter black of the night is fit atmosphere in such a land.'[7]

In the Second World War, material circumstances were such that countryside images could be anchored more unambiguously in a celebratory nationalist ideology. The countryside was, quite literally for many people, a haven from the destruction being wreaked in the blitzed cities and could at the same time be seen as a vital part of fortress England threatened by alien forces of evil. The countryside could even serve as a sign of the beauty of the new order which might rise from the ashes of the battered cities, or as a symbol of the permanence of a heritage whose urban manifestations might not actually survive. As one of the most popular countryside writers of the period, S. P. B. Maïs, put it in *There will always be an England* (1940):

> They still stand, these Scottish [Englishness was a dominant ideal that generally suppressed the separate identity of Scottishness or Welshness] hills and English dales, unperturbed and unperturbable, reminders both of the beauty and indestructability of our precious heritage.[8]

The English ideal as promoted earlier this century, however, did not just exist as a public mythology invoked at times of national crisis. It also involved more pervasive myths of national and class identity, of 'what it meant to be English'. Images of the countryside enjoyed the success they did because they could accommodate a variety of different responses, not just celebratory notions of an ideal England purged of social and political tensions. The connotations of images of nature are always bound up with people's conceptions of the social order within which they live; and images of the countryside, as they occur in British fiction and poetry in this century, have invoked a range of associations for their largely urban audience, from ideas of a haven away from the threats and anxieties of the everyday, to an aestheticised invocation of those very feelings of alienation and insecurity which sustain the need for such uplifting and consoling images.

The diverse resonances of even the most stereotyped English countryside imagery included something that on the surface seems seriously at odds with the escapism and anti-progressivism with which it is unusually associated – the suggestions of an ideal modernity. A picture of the perfect countryside and village could act as the ideal image of what a modern Britain emerging from the unsightly ravages of Victorianism might become. The rural accent within a modernist utopia was not something peculiarly English, not even the implication that a new and better order would have more affinities with the values of pre-industrial society than with those of nineteenth-century urban society. A significant sector of the Russian architectural avant-garde, to take just one example, promoted the idea, in the late 1920s, that the only solution to the inherited problems of the modern city created by bourgeios capitalism was its liquidation and dispersion in the countryside.[9]

Urban involvement with countryside imagery in Britain has had quite distinct social resonances that cannot be accommodated at all easily within some amplification of a country house or *Country Life* aesthetic. In an attempt to secure notions of historical continuity, it is often suggested that the twentieth-century ideology of the beautiful countryside, promoting thatched cottages in picturesque farmland as the ideal home and refuge, is a modern democratic equivalent to the long-standing aristocratic mythology of a countryside of leisure and relaxed retirement. The urban middle-classes' countryside was not quite the parkland of the landed estates of yore; but they could lay claim to a holiday or weekend-outing 'garden of England', seemingly designed for their leisure and entertainment. But descriptions of the 'beautiful England' countryside experience were often produced by, and had their most committed devotees among, the large sectors of the middle classes who were not that well off and certainly had no cause at all to feel in a relation of ownership to the country. And it is important to remember that the standard images of country scenery projected by the countryside literature, and taken up by the media, though pervasive, were hardly representative of city-dwellers' notions of the ideal country outing; that is, they were hardly democratic, let alone populist. They excluded many people's notions of what was enjoyable, or desirable, about a visit to the country, most notably its sociable aspects. An East End Londoner's idea of an ideal outing to Epping Forest, say, would not necessarily be accommodated by the conventional countryside imagery.[10]

The middle-class cultural ideal of an intensely personal 'away from it all' immersion in the beauties of 'unspoiled' countryside was defined in opposition both to the vulgarity of those who frequented the popular seaside resorts, and the crass materialism and mindless socialising of the very wealthy country-house set. Rather than a countryside that existed as a natural adjunct to a life of privilege, this was one whose attractions lay precisely in its distance from immediate social and material interest. Discovering the beauties of the English countryside became a commitment and an obsession among a not-so-privileged middle class who on many counts felt marginal and who wished to possess a true inner identity more valuable than its external social persona.

It is not an ethos of confident ownership that underpins, for example, the country imagery of one of the best known of the so-called Georgian poets, the Welshman Edward Thomas. Take this passage from his essay 'This England' (1914):

Wildly dark clouds broke through the pallid sky above the elms, shadowy elms towering up ten times their diurnal height; and under the trees stood a thatched cottage, sending up a thin blue smoke against the foliage, and casting a faint light out from one square window and open door. It was cheeful and mysterious too. No man of any nation accustomed to houses but must have longed for his home at the sight, or have suffered for lacking one, or have dreamed that this was it.[11]

Of the earlier generation of writers who established countryside description as a distinct literary genre in the late Victorian period, the most celebrated, such as William Henry Hudson, an American, and Richard Jefferies, were neither of them of the wealthy established middle classes. Theirs was not a countryside of ownership and gracious living, but one they viewed largely as insecurely placed outsiders. They earned their keep writing for an urban audience.[12]

Rather than pinning down the unifying ideological assumptions of the ideal English landscape images fashioned in the interwar period and staking out connections with earlier modes of celebrating the countryside, the approach here will be to explore the more pervasive stereotypes by way of contrast – that is, highlighting how different both in form and content the countryside images active within modern British culture have been, how the more familiar stereotypes represent only one alternative among several. Particularly striking is the marked discontinuity between conceptions and images of the countryside prevalent in the interwar period, and those current earlier in late Victorian and Edwardian times. It would be quite possible to explore the cultural politics of countryside imagery by looking at its use in fiction, poetry and children's books, say; but discussion here will be confined to verbal and visual descriptions of the countryside that purport to be realistic representations, as well as having obvious aesthetic pretensions. Out of a tradition of describing the countryside in which discussion of the changing way of life of those living and labouring there was a major concern, where the state of country society was seen as a significant feature of the condition of British society as a whole, there eventually emerges a more purely aestheticising genre geared to presenting the country and its inhabitants as enjoyable objects of urban experience. Where social problems do feature, they are generally given a nostalgic aura and assimilated to a concern with conserving the beauty of the countryside.[13] There is still an ethical dimension but it is no longer explicitly social or political in character.

Of course, there is one very prominent political objective in this later countryside description – the definition of a lovely Englishness. As H. V. Morton put it with a characteristically precious but intense, and very masculine, self regard: 'as long as one English field lies against another, there is something left in the world for a man to love'.[14] For some time, it had been commonplace to view the country as the repository of the deep-lying values that had made England truly great. But where this idea began to play a prominent role in late nineteenth and early twentieth century nationalism – as much on the continent as it did in Britain – the notion of race and stock was paramount. Englishness was an essence residing in a race which was to be found in its purest form in the country, preserved by an honest and traditional way of life. The true English stock was sometimes characterised as being fostered by the English soil. But it was only in the interwar period that a nationalist ideology of pure landscape came into its own. Theories of racial identity were transferred to the inanimate landscape, a kind of reification in which the people still living and working in the countryside were assimilated, not just pictorially and aesthetically, but also ideologically, to the landscape.

It is significant that the wave of countryside books that followed H. V. Morton's trend-setting *In Search of England* (1927) were distinguished by the introduction of high-quality visual illustration – reproductions of the best modern photographs picturing the characteristic features of English country scenery. So the new techniques developed for disseminating attractive reproductions of photographs also played a role here. The clichéd stereotypes of chequer-board fields, hedgerows, copses and old buildings nestling in comforting hollows found today in calendars, advertisements, films of 'old England' and travel and guide books are in fact largely the creation of the period, and not, as is often imagined, the end product of a long tradition of English landscape depiction. In Morton's pioneering book, the new visual stereotypes have not as yet quite settled down. The title illustration of an English cottage on a slightly shabby English lane still looks rather like Victorian paintings of old cottages set in some indeterminate woodland. Even when the text, as in Burke's slightly later *The Beauty of England* (1933), makes great play of the distinctive visual aspect of the cultivated English countryside, traditional ideas of picturesqueness are still sometimes evident, in that the photographs are either architectural or tend to feature views of uninhabited beauty spots –

cliffs, moor and heaths, forests and deserted waterways and marshes – rather than farmland.

The image of a cultivated garden of England landscape that eventually takes over as the visual emblem of Englishness is of course far from being representative in any real sense. It is an ideal home-counties landscape. The picture of neatness and fertility, set off by small controlled pockets of picturesque shrub and tree, is one that, by excluding any implications of shabbiness or the unkempt, also runs against the common political perception of the countryside at the time as suffering from economic decline. Nevertheless, by the early 1940s the new stereotype had achieved such classic status that a government report commissioned in 1941, concerned with revitalising the rural economy, presented it without qualification as a true picture of the English countryside that could be set alongside hard facts and statistics.

> Our countryside is like a multi-covered chequer board. Its chief
> characteristic is its attractive patchwork appearance with an
> infinite variety of small, odd-shaped fields of brown
> ploughland or green pasture, bounded by twisting hedges,
> narrow winding lanes, small woodlands and copses and isolated
> trees and hedgerow timber; quiet streams and placid rivers;
> the whole giving place in remoter parts to open moorland and
> rolling downs.[15]

Yet virtually none of the more intensely cultivated farmland, even then, would have looked remotely like this.

If there has been a tradition in British art of depicting English landscape scenery going back at least to the eighteenth century, the conventions for rendering it and the type of scene given prominence have changed radically. Initially, Claudian parklands, Welsh mountains and Derbyshire dales were the favourites; and only in this century, after the First World War, did the now paradigmatic view of peaceful English farmland establish itself as the norm. If there are occasional explicit references in Victorian art to a typically English scene, as in Ford Maddox Brown's 'An English Autumn Afternoon' (1852–4), these remain isolated examples. They could not be said in any way to form a tradition. For the Victorians the most artistically favoured British landscapes were those most readily assimilable to a traditional old-master picturesque – river, harbour and coastal scenes that could be made to look like old Dutch paintings, dramatic hill and mountain views of a kind popularised by Turner, or views with obvious atmospheric or emotive overtones, such as the highlands in stormy weather, or desolate marshes and empty woods on cold winter afternoons.[16]

Victorian painting, like Victorian poetry, lingers most lovingly over grand scenes of gloom and dark, of melancholy wildness and isolation, intimations of some divine presence greater than man, or backdrops for tragic melodramas. There also existed an alternative, less ambitious, tradition of happy rural scenes, but these were designed to conjure up general ideas of contented pastoral life, not to describe some recognisably English landscape. Helen Allingham, Birket Foster and Kate Greenaway depicted sunny meadows, smiling cottages and playful children. Their landscape vignettes contain glimpses of countryside views, often inspired by the scenery of the North Downs where many of them lived, but pictorially and iconographically subordinated to the general evocation of an open-air joyfulness. These scenes form part of a recognisable tradition of countryside illustration that can be traced back to Bewick and the eighteenth century, where the rural setting is evoked by a visual shorthand of cottage doors, old church porches and towers, patches of meadow and bits of picturesque tree and shrub – a sort of landscape rococo.[17].

When critics and artists of the 1920s and 1930s decided to constitute a distinctive tradition of English countryside painting, they had to forget about the Victorian period, and forget too about the Frenchified and impressionist and realist landscapes recently in vogue, and conjure up a tradition that disappeared almost at the moment of its formation – an English watercolour and Constable tradition confined historically to the late eitheenth and early nineteenth centuries. While Constable had been much copied after his death, his work did not come to be seen as paradigmatic of the English landscape scene until this century.[18] Turner's dramatic seascapes and mountain views, if anything, set the precedents for conceptions of the picturesque English landscape during the nineteenth century, not 'the homely, lovely English scene that Constable had interpreted for all time on canvas', as the England's beauty books of the 1930s would have it. Constable had to be plucked up from the past, tidied up and tamed, and then reconstituted as the father of an English landscape vision no-one previously had thought to conjure into existence.[19] The 'Hay Wain' was first made into the visual cliché it has now become some hundred years after it was painted. For Constable what recommended the English landscape was not just its 'pastoral beauty', but its 'grandeur', as he made clear in his *Various Subjects of Landscape, Characteristic of English Scenery*, published in 1833.

It is important to distinguish between the idea of an English school of painting which particularly excelled in landscape, common in the early-to-mid-nineteenth century,[20] though less so afterwards, and the notion that the English landscape had a particular character which gave true English landscape painting a distinctive and immediately recognisable visual aspect. This required, among other things, a categorisation of country scenery where national character took precedence over long-standing typologies of landscape – hilly, flat, wild, cultivated, etc. In the early nineteenth century, landscape painting could be seen as distinctively English by virtue of the places depicted where they had patriotic or historical associations, and were appropriately distinguished by the painter's talent.[21] The closest you come to the idea of an English style of landscape painting is Constable's production *Various Subjects of Landscape, Characteristic of English Scenery* (1833); the point of the exercise, however, was not to demonstrate how English landscape scenery had a repertoire of characteristic shapes and thus demanded a particular style of painting, but rather to show how the art of painting, with all its devices, could be harnessed to do justice to various kinds of English landscape subjects, and above all the light and shade of atmosphere Constable had observed – 'the chiar'oscuro of nature'. No-one would have thought to suggest that these landscape depictions revealed systematically the distinctive traits of English scenery as compared, say, with French or Italian scenery, but at most would have been led to the conclusion that English beauty spots could do just as well as Italian ones for fine painting.

The idea of promoting a British school of high art (not just topography or portraiture) that would draw its inspiration from British subjects reached its peak during and in the immediate aftermath of the Napoleonic wars, but somewhat subsided afterwards.[22] Where national identity became an important issue in art in the Victorian period was for the depiction of national types in genre painting; that is, where it was tied up with the questions of racial identity, as were theories about the national character of language but not, by contrast, concepts of landscape or topography.

II

As the explicit intellectual and political pretensions of the later examples of the country book genre are generally so slight, so dominated by the job of providing an aestheticised travelogue, it is most fruitful to approach an understanding of their ideological horizons by exploring in some detail the options they closed off. The kinds of engagement with the country you find in earlier writers, particularly Richard Jefferies, whose successor many of the more popular countryside writers of the interwar period thought themselves to be, should help to remind us that there are powerful alternatives to the modern 'tradition' of little-England nationalism and nostalgia. A large part of what follows is then an essay in creating room for manoeuvre. It is a matter of ensuring that urban interest in and enjoyment of the countryside continues to be seen as a cultural phenomenon worth contesting – not left as the exclusive property of traditionalists and conservatives.

In the late Victorian and Edwardian period the more serious books describing the countryside pretty well took for granted that the experience of the countryside involved some understanding of the material conditions and way of life of those who lived and worked there. Richard Jefferies, who might easily be thought, on a superficial reading of a few anthology pieces, to be no more than a forerunner of the modern 'country diary' mode, celebrating the many little beauties of the countryside for the entertainment of a predominantly urban upper middle class, was at pains to make the reader reflect on how these remained tragically inaccessible, under present conditions, to the majority of people. Though surrounded by country beauty, the labourer was in little better position to enjoy it than the worker confined to a life in the city. To quote from Jefferies' *The Story of my Heart* (1883):

> At this hour, out of thirty-four millions who inhabit this
> country, two-thirds . . . lie within thirty years of that
> abominable institution the poorhouse. That any human being
> should dare apply to another the epithet 'pauper' is, to me,
> the greatest, the vilest, the most unpardonable crime that could
> be committed. Each human being, by mere birth, has a
> birthright in this earth and all its productions; and if they do
> not receive it, then it is they who are injured, and it is not
> the 'pauper' – oh, inexpressibly wicked word! It is the well-
> to-do, who are the criminal classes.

The intense individual experience of natural beauty and light at one level acted as a metaphor of the as-yet-unrealised possibilities of a major transformation of society: 'But the world is not mad, only ignorance, kept up by strenuous exertions, from which internal darkness it will, in course of time, emerge, marvelling at the past as a man wonders at and glories in the light who escaped from blindness.'

Jefferies's countryside was also pictured very differently from the trim and calm countryside of later years. Shifting from a foreground focus on odd isolated details – a bird, a tree, a leaf, a plant – his descriptions merge into a vitalist vision of burning light, vibrant growth, of the powerful movement of wind and waves.

The sun burned in the sky, the wheat was full ofa luxuriant sense of growth, the grass high, the earth giving its vigour to tree and leaf, the heaven blue. The vigour and growth, the warmth and light, the beauty and richness of it entered into me . . . I found the sea at last: I walked beside it in a trance away from the houses out into the wheat. The ripe corn stood up to the beach, the waves on one side of the shingle, and the yellow wheat on the other . . . The great sun shone above, the wide sea before me, the wind came sweet and strong from the waves. The life of the earth and the sea, the flow of the sun filled me.[23]

This nature could not be more different from the later home counties ideal England; but neither does it relate in any obvious way to predominant trends in late Victorian depiction of the English countryside – the cottage door vignettes of a Birket Foster or a Helen Allingham, or the dark and gloomy, usually water-logged, scenes of the landscape painters who attracted attention at the Royal Academy, such as Benjamin Leader and John MacWhirter. The equivalents that might now come to mind are the landscapes of vibrant light and colour being painted in France at the time – van Gogh perhaps. But this parallel was not made at the time, and the audience of Jefferies' landscape descriptions would neither have known, nor if it had would it have been likely to respond positively to, van Gogh's work.

There was little place in Jefferies' vitalist landscapes for the more obvious forms of pastoral nostalgia; for, say, the loving evocation of traditional forms of labour that had disappeared in the face of modern technology. Painters, he stressed, who banished modern machinery and modern dress from their work on the grounds that this would 'impair the pastoral scene intended to be conveyed', were making a serious mistake. Such painting lacked 'the force and truth of reality'; absent was

That something . . . the hard angular fact which at once makes the sky above it appear likewise a fact . . . somehow we feel as we gaze that these fields and these skies are not of our day. The actual fields, the actual machines, the actual men and women (how differently dressed to the conventional pictorial costumes!) would prepare the mind again to see and appreciate the colouring, the design, the beauty – what, for lack of a better expression, may be called the soul of the place – far more than forgotten, and nowadays even impossible accessories. For our sympathy is not with them, but with the things of our own time.[24]

Though Jefferies was popular among the late Victorian and Edwardian middle classes, at one level his writing was quite atypical. The more intense images of the countryside he projected were far from being current stereotypes even then. In books attempting serious social analysis of life in the countryside, such as those by Richard Heath and George Sturt,[25] for example, the standard image of the country invoked is the cottage door scene, the view of a picturesque, usually-thatched, cottage nestling among trees and shrubs and looking onto a meadow abundant with green grass and colourful flowers. These writers took this stereotype and measured it against the realities of material deprivation that were seen to be peculiarly acute in precisely the areas of heath and unreclaimed common land favoured by the painters of ideal pastoral scenes.[26] When the traditional country cottage, with its connotations of venerability and picturesqeness, was, in any of its actual manifestations, examined at all closely, it was found often to signify a neglect, decay and poverty only matched by the worst urban slums.

The guide-book characterisation of the English countryside as peculiarly intimate, fertile, garden-like and humane, has been so widely promoted that earlier echoes of it are usually taken to indicate its pervasiveness throughout much of the eighteenth and nineteenth centuries. But this was only one of a number of perceptions voiced by earlier descriptions of the English landscape. Travellers could just as easily be struck by the emptiness and bleakness of the less well-off areas of the country, or read the aspect of the richer countryside as a sign of the unusual power and wealth of the large landowner in Britain.[27] A mainstream publication such as Masterman's *Condition of England*, published in 1909, could still, without seeming at all controversial, characterise the British countryside as the exception to the garden-like quality of continental farmlands.[28] At a time when the countryside was still seen as an integral element in the social fabric of the country as a whole, the validity of the prevailing ideal image of the countryside was something that would necessarily be as contested as the different conceptions people had of the prevailing social order.

A tradition of countryside description as an engaged social analysis of country life continued well into this century, most notably in the writings of Robertson Scott, whose *England's Green and Pleasant Land* (1925) was particularly concerned with the economic problem of the decultivation of areas of the countryside during the serious agricultural slump of the immediate post war years. But by the 1930s countryside description had taken on an almost purely aesthetic function, as guide and travel book for the urban middle-class explorer of the beauties of the English landscape.[29]

Jefferies' writings, which on the surface seem to make the origin of tradition of countryside description which 'flourished' after the First World War, are revealing on yet another count as to the social and political disengagement of the latter. In Jefferies' descriptions, as in those of a number of other devotees of the countryside at the time, there is, alongside the insistence on the dying of the traditional rural way of life, a powerful suggestion that there existed the energy and initiative for a major positive transformation of society, or at least that there was a dramatic choice to be made, between disaster or collapse if things were left to go on as before, and the possibility of striking out anew. Morris was far from being alone on this. Images of the countryside then did not just work nostalgically, as intimations of a better order located in the past, but also as projections of the impulses which might help create a radically better order in the future. In Jefferies' case there is a quite explicit movement between his sense of the powerful yet misdirected dynamism of the city and his evocations of the vital forces of nature. The intimation of a new order was not something that simply emanated from a communion with 'nature', but also out of a fusion of this with a vision of London as 'the vortex, the whirlpool, the centre of human life today on earth . . . driving, pushing, carried on in a stress of feverish force that lifts the tides and sends the clouds away'. What he seeks in the intense experience of nature is 'something real now' that can 'endure the test and remain unmolten in this fierce focus of human life', 'something to shape this million-handed labour to an end and outcome that will leave more sunshine and more flowers to those who must succeed' (succeed, not in the Thatcherite sense, but come after).[30]

In part, what is involved here is a dramatically different conception of England than you get later when the myth of the English national countryside takes hold – England as an epicentre of dynamic change rather than England as a refuge from the more violent and thrusting tendencies of the modern world. Ironically, as the countryside became more and more marginal socially and economically, the ostensible peacefulness of its marginality came to stand more and more as an image of what was best about the character and identity of the country as a whole. The true England of Christopher Hussey's *The Fairy Land of England* (1924) was this beautiful 'legendary country', 'the dust we are made of, and to which we will return'.[31] The dominant note is one of nostalgia, of a sense of fragile unreality, of retreat from ideas of energy to ones of still and delicate beauty – a beauty which in much of the more interesting Georgian poetry of the time acted as the haunting image of alienation, the premonition of a decay and death from which there was no escape, and which permeated the most radiant refuges.

The sense of fragile nostalgia was widely cultivated by little-England countryside writers. The prolific J. H. Massingham, for example, concluded his rather later *The English Countryman* (1942) with the invocation:

> Does the English tradition survive? Does the English landscape? . . . Wordsworth could still lift his eyes to the everlasting hills and Blunden hear the same bluetit tootle as John Clare heard it enlivening eternity . . . There are quiet men in England to whom the lift of a hay-fork, an old book and the glistening coat of a shire-horse are like the evening sky, and there are men of zeal too whose Jerusalem is still full of primroses.

More significant than the precious tone is perhaps the carping defensiveness underlying the book's whole conception of an English tradition. Massingham seeks to define, through his picture of an 'old England' beautiful countryside, a national tradition – development from within growing up from an organic life as opposed to 'progress' breaking away from it' – that, though betrayed by modern capitalism, could still provide a bulwark against such horrid foreign modernities as Fascism and Stalinism.[32]

III

The country myth of Englishness propounded by J. B. Priestley was more robust than Hussey's or Massingham's and proved more pervasive, more in tune with the self-image of one-nation consensus politics in the 1930s. It received classic expression in Priestley's introduction to a book edited by him called *The Beauty of Britain* (1935). Here the English country, not the British, despite the title, was projected as an emblem of true Englishness, polite and reticent, a landscape without the dramatic contrasts of foreign scenery, one that pleased through its variety and moderate surprises: 'It looks like the result of those happy compromises that make our social and political plans so irrational and yet so successful. It has been born of a compromise between wildness and tameness, between nature and man.'

According to Priestley, the happy English compromise was now under threat because of the power of modern technology, or, should one say, the dynamic thrust of late capitalism. The central

ethical issue, then, posed by the present condition of the countryside was one of preservation, one of managing the countryside so as
to leave to posterity 'a country still happily compromising between
Nature and Man, blending what was best worth retaining from
the past with what best represents the spirit of our own age, a
country as rich in noble towns as it is in trees, birds, and wild
flowers'.[33] Alongside Priestley's landscape of happy compromise
you have another equally pervasive image, that of the English
landscape as one of restraint, without the blatant self-advertisement
of more striking foreign scenery – a polite landscape designed
to fit snugly with the self-image of 'the inarticulate and reticent
Englishman'.[34] This idea of Englishness as a beautiful reticence,
however, was far from being self-effacing. It was one that
nonchalantly arrogated to itself, among other things, the privileges
of England's imperial power. As Herbert Read put it so unselfcon-
sciously in his *The English Vision* (1933): 'England within the
meaning of this book "is not a tract of land," it is an ideal, a
dynamic vision with which many Irishmen, Welshmen and
Scotsmen have identified themselves.'[35] Herbert Read, who was
later to become a champion of surrealism, a member of the socialist
art group AIA, and a promoter of a radical progressivism in
education, is a good example of how such habits of mind were
common on the left, not just among the one-nation Conservatives.

The archetypal English countryside image of the inter-war
period visualised in quality photograpic pictures could be toned by
viewers to suit a variety of different, often seemingly contradictory, conceptions of British society. Bathed in a poignant poetic
glow, they could suggest nostalgically an eternal Englishness both
threatened by and standing apart from the forces shaping modern
society. Neat, calm and light, they could signify ideas of order
and health appropriate to a rationally modernised society emerging
from the gloom, disorder and dirt of Victorianism – both new and
organically related to the past at the same time. Central to this
mythology was the idea, still very active in progressive liberal
thought in the 1950s and 1960s, that the distinctive beauty of the
English countryside was 'man-made'. At times the characteristic
order and tidiness were seen as a comparatively recent development
– more a modernisation than something rooted in the mists of
time. *The Beauty of England* (1933), an illustrated survey of the
English countryside, whose title page carried the slogan 'England,
with all thy faults', invoked the idea of the traditional country
village in terms which were both poetic and slightly 'modern' at
the same time: 'the English village, in its tidiness, its casual but

effective grouping, its glowing tranquility, its snugness, and its youth-in-age, expresses a large part of the English spirit.[36]

But the more common notion of the making of the English landscape, and the one that later prevailed in little-England social democracy after the Second World War, was that the tidy humanised views were the accumulated work of centuries of Englishman's labour going back to prehistoric times.[37] In the words of one of the better known countryside writers of the 1930s, C.B. Ford, the typical English landscape, with 'the fine timbering of hedges spreading their chequer-work patterns up hill and down valley, the apparently haphazard yet delightful disposition of the trees, copses, and woodland masses, the scrupulous neatness of the husbandry, and absolute appropriateness of its old buildings to their surroundings', is landscape which, however much modified by local conditions, 'nearly always appears as green and carefully tended as a garden – a garden cleaned, tilled and tamed from primeval forest or swamp to its present rich productiveness by the persevering labour of centuries'.[38] Ideologically, this emphasis on long historical continuity had the advantage of backgrounding the impact on the countryside of the Victorian period which many progressives and conservatives alike looked upon as an ugly deformation of the English tradition.

The neat forming of the ideal English landscape, epitomised by the simple stone walls and buildings and rolling hills of the Cotswolds, could serve as the image of a rational and harmonious shaping of things appropriate to a modernist aesthetic of clear order and 'truth to materials'.[39] Indeed, the idea that traditional craft processes and forms of labour offered a model for a modern remaking of the environment, suggesting ways towards a clean and undestructive pattern of economic and social development that stood in contrast to the ugly industrialisation and urbanisation associated with the nineteenth century, was an important element in much high modernist theory. English versions of this ideology, though posed in a more cosy rhetoric, still posited a conjuncture between the traditional arts and crafts of unassuming country architecture and design, and the idea of a clean healthily-ordered modern design and manufacture. This is quite explicit in a promotional brochure produced in 1933 on the popular Cotswold village of Broadway by Noel Carrington, later the author of a number of influential books on modern British design. The image of the desirable contemporary environment projected here is that of the inn which easily combines tastefully restored ancient building in honest Cotswold stone with all the most sophisticated services provided by modern technology. The accompanying descriptions of the Cotswold countryside were well tuned to fit this aesthetic. Apparently the most compelling feature of the landscape was the broad sweep that would be spoiled by 'small plantations and coppices', normally the *sine qua non* of the cosier versions of the English countryside scene:

> There can be no smallness in the lines of a countryside that can contain the long woods and great fields and hold them as harmonious details in a serene whole . . . What a richly coloured pattern [the fields] make when the autumn ploughing is finished and there are great rectangles of red-brown earth forming a chequer with similar shapes of grassland showing a parched pale brown because of their hosts of dead stalks.[40]

It is important to stress how class-specific this seemingly progressivist conception of things was. Like the early Shell guides edited by John Betjeman in the 1930s, with contributions by 'modern' artists such as Paul Nash and John Piper, whose names would only have meant much to a fairly small upper-middle-class élite, this picture of the English countryside, far away from the resorts where the masses went for their holidays, was probably socially not too dissimilar from the scene invoked by Osbert Lancaster in his characterisation of the 'Culture Cottage' in *Homes Sweet Homes* (1939) – its inhabitants the 'writers, film stars, barristers, artists and BBC announcers' who favoured the clean look of 'hygienic distemper of an artistic pale shade' and signified their culture exclusivity with such possessions as 'a Shropshire Lad (hand-printed edition on rag paper, signed by the author and limited to 200 copies)' occupying 'an "accidentally" conspicuous position on an "artist designed" table of unstained oak'.

But if this ideology seems to lead confidently on to post-Second World War social democratic myths about the successful juxtaposition of the best of the old and modern, to visions of an ideal modernised Britain of simple concrete forms, honest ancient buildings and traditional lawns, which again only ever meant much to a small but perhaps differently constituted elite, it would be wrong to feel that here, in the 'modernist' countryside image, you could locate the outlines of a secure and expansive upper-middle-class cultural identity. What writers of almost all political persuasions, however progressive, stressed was that the ideal English scene was under threat, even where modern planning and rational redevelopment were being proposed as the way of preserving it and keeping it alive. Precisely those connotations of the beautiful countryside as something threatened by change – threatened either by a slow wasting away as it became more and more irrelevant to modern urban industrial society, or by its uprooting and destruction through modern technology and modern mass tourism – gave it its multiple resonances, made it the successful icon of a national identity no longer poised securely at the centre of things, or of the aspirations of large sectors of the middle classes that were not in a position to view change with much confidence; gave the country-side imagery its poetry, so to speak, and thus also suffused with poetry the ideal self-image of its admirers.

IV

The uncertainties implicit in the projection of a distinctively English countryside tradition are nowhere more apparent than in attempts made in the interwar period to define a stylistically distinctive picturing of the landscape in English art, the English landscape painting tradition. By far the most influential and sustained of these were initiated, not by the conservative anti-modernists, but by the artistic avant-garde, Herbert Read and his circle. In reaction to the Bloomsbury formalism of Roger Fry[41] and its championing of an internationalist French style against English parochialism, Read sought to rescue an English tradition in the visual arts that might point the way to a distinctively English modernism. But this projection of a supposed English tradition was deeply defensive in its whole conception. Firstly, while taking issue with the negative implications of Mathew Arnold's character-isation of English painting as lacking 'the highest form of compo-sition', 'architectonicé' and succeeding instead in areas not strictly relevant to the highest plastic art, 'in magic, in beauty, in grace, in expressing the inexpressible', Read actually ended up making this critique central to his whole conception of the distinctiveness of English art, and in particular of the English landscape tradition. Moreover, Read's was a tradition more notable for its gaps than for its continuities, the most striking separating the last 'flowering' during the Romantic period from the present. What happened since the heroic period of Turner and Constable, according to Read, was that British artists, unlike their French counterparts, 'shut their minds against the modern consciousness revealed in the work of Constable and Turner, and escaped into odd sanctuaries of pedantry and snobbery'. This, he argued, was only inevitable, given the stultifying atmosphere of England in the age of its 'indus-trial prosperity'. The sole option open to artists such as the Pre-Raphaelites was a shrinking away from the triumphant ugliness and vulgarity epitomised by the Great Exhibition – the inevitable expressions of the economic and moral ideals of the age.[42]

If the example of European modernism – of which Read was an energetic proponent – suggested an alternative, conditions were still not yet ripe for a major improvement, as Read himself explained in the introduction to the modernist manifesto *Unit I* (1934):

> The artist, in the present unsatisfactory organisation of society, has no definite status or responsible function, and until the structure of society is mended, the position of the artist must to some extent be anomalous, and his practice inconsistent. Meanwhile, all that he can do is to maintain his integrity.[43]

And what contemporary artist in the end best fitted the bill as the continuer of Read's somewhat tenuous English tradition? It was, almost by default, Paul Nash, a landscape painter who was open to the formal innovations of European modernism, yet 'as English a genius as anyone could find', painter of a nature which was 'so delicate and sensuous to British eyes'.[44] At an exhibition of his work held in 1938, Nash was celebrated for having 'discovered a new form of life' that he 'described with a precision of form and a harmony of colour which still remind us of those early masters, Girtin and Cotman, of the English tradition'.[45]

It was just at this point that the British art establishment was beginning to take to the idea of a reconstituted English yet modern landscape tradition. A neo-romantic movement was christened, embracing artists such as John Piper and Graham Sutherland; printmakers were busy producing modern equivalents of the visionary romantic landscapes of Samuel Palmer.[46] A recognisably modern, and at the same time English, taste was born, sanctioned as a recognised element in the English country scene by, for example, the early Shell guides to the English countryside. All this became grist to the mill for Pevsner's sensible social democratic characterisation of the *The Englishness of English Art* published in 1956. Here he defined Englishness in terms of a tendency to moderation, reasonableness and matter-of-fact observation, tinctured by an indulgence in phantasy – Priestly's happy English compromise combined with Read's English poetry. But the artist who more than any other had helped to fashion the idea of distinctively English modern art, Paul Nash, had envisaged the 'limitations' which set English art off from the more expansive continental avant-garde in terms that were sharper and rather more telling.

Nash's ideas on the Englishness of English art, elaborated in his contribution to *Unit I* (1934), are worth quoting in some detail.

Not only was Nash's statement in one form or other quickly taken up by any critics trying to define the national character of British art.[47] It also related interestingly to ideas of Englishness widely current in Britain at the time. In it you find a play upon a peculiar dialectic of unrealisable desire, a fixing of identity poised on the impossibility of its taking on definition in solid concrete form. Nash's sharp articulation of dualities, in place of the easy compromise or evasive reticence, results in a, for us, more telling indication of forms of cultural self-consciousness prevalent among the 'educated' middle classes in the 1930s than the obviously period-bound celebrations of the Englishness of the English landscape. There is the point, too, that Nash's painted landscapes of the 1920s and 1930s do not fit easily within the stereotypes of English picturesque landscape current at the time. His are deliberately emptied and highly formalised constructions of partly exposed yet bounded views, often disturbingly tightly tuned. At their more telling, they seem to refuse the easy expressiveness of the English neo-romantics, as they do surrealism's melodrama of strangeness and alienation – yet uneasily. To quote Paul Nash:

> English art has always shown particular tendencies which recur throughout its history. A pronounced linear method in design . . . A peculiar bright delicacy in choice of colours – somewhat cold but radiant and sharp in key. A concentration too on the practice of portraiture . . . But such characterisations will not help to explain what I have in mind. There seems to exist, behind the frank expression of portrait and scene. [Nash here is referring to landscape], an imprisoned spirit; yet this spirit is the source, the motive power which animates the art. These pictures are the vehicles of this spirit, but, somehow, they are inadequate, being only echoes and reflections of familiar images [in portrait and scene]. If I were to describe the spirit I would say it is of the land; *genius loci* is indeed almost its conception.

Hovering within the negations, there is the sense of some treasured unsullied aspiration – some ultimate haven for which a chosen de-socialised landscape[48] would act as beautiful emblem. This, of course, is to push the rhetoric to the point where it almost takes on the glow of easy romanticism which Nash's modernism – his sophisticated and spare self-denial – seeks to distance. All the same, the projection of landscape as the sign of a true highly charged English essence is not at all ironic. On the contrary, it is deeply involved in a mythology of Englishness widely current at the time.

After all this, it would certainly be satisfying to end with a fine

14   Cover illustration from 'The English Countryman. A Study of the English Tradition' by H. J. Massingham, 1942. The English tradition is here explicitly visualised as one based upon a once natural harmony between labourer and squire. Behind, country cottage (and church) and country house give a more muted social resonance to the beauties of the English countryside.

galvanising conclusion. But, as far as I am concerned, this is just not on the cards – however appealing the idea might be to exorcise once and for all the ghost of little-England nationalism and its appropriation of countryside imagery; or to conjure up the vision of a clear alternative socialist involvement with the country scene. Present political circumstances are such that neither option, in my view, appears at all credible. Trying to make sense of the efficacy and pervasiveness of the use of rural landscape in modern British culture, I found myself involved in situations where the most blatant myths of conservative and liberal ideology featured alongside tendencies that were undeniably intriguing and compelling. It appeared, for the moment, most fruitful to render these tensions more acute – not to seek some commanding explanation that would rationlise or abolish them.

Notes

1 *Guardian*, 29 November 1985, p. 14.
2 My analysis is inevitably deeply indebted to Raymond Williams' *The Country and the City* (1973), even if the perspective is rather more city-bound.

I am grateful to Alun Howkins for allowing me to read his article 'The discovery of rural England' prior to its publication in R. Colls and P. Dodds (eds), *England Nationalism*, to Graham Andrews for stimulating discussions on the subject, and particularly to Raphael Samuel, without whose stimulation and encouragement this study would never have been completed.

Two recent books that investigate in some detail the cultural aspects of the cult of the countryside in England are Jan Marsh's *Back to the Land; The Pastoral Impulse in England from 1880 to 1914* (1982) and Martin J. Wiener's *English Culture and the Decline of the Industrial Spirit* (1981). The latter is particularly illuminating though it assumes that an occurrence of a marked preoccupation with the country or country life, and the values these might represent, is the sign of some essential anti-industrialism and parochialism dominant in English culture since the late nineteenth century. This attitude Wiener seems particularly eager to identify with liberal and socialist thinkers, whose championing of a more or less radical progressivism on many issues is effectively ignored. Often, as in America and Germany in the same period, an obsession with values thought to be embodied by a traditional country way of life is prompted by a peculiarly sharp awareness of rapid and dynamic economic development. Both Marsh and Wiener neglect to point out the extent to which the back-to-the-land movement, and the tendency to identify a true national essence with the countryside, was a European-wide phenomenon, not just a peculiarly British one.
3 The first book is by the prolific countryside writer C. B. Ford, the

last two by Thomas Burke, an expert on subjects ranging from the English inn to Thomas de Quincey.

4 Richard Jefferies, *The Story of my Heart*, 1883, p. 146. It is no traditionalist who would write 'The truth is, we die through our ancestors; we are murdered by our ancestors. Their dead hands stretch forth from the tomb and drag us down to their mouldering bones' (*ibid.*, p. 145).

5 John William Robertson Scott, *England's Green and Pleasant Land*, 1925, postscript.

6 On this see Martin J. Wiener, *English Culture and the Decline of the Industrial Spirit*, 1981, pp. 50ff.

7 Quoted in Charles Harrison, *English Art and Modernism 1900–1939*, 1981, p. 139.

8 The patriotic message is driven home visually by the illustration opposite the title page, showing a photograph of a British soldier, standing (supposedly heroically) atop a large 'English' rock looking out . . . to eternity ? to sea ? The ground for this patriotism was well laid in Maïs's pre-war publications, as in *England's Character* (1936, p. 346), where he wrote: 'England's character is one of the few stable things left in a world of unreliability'.

9 See for example A. Kopp, *Town and Revolution. Soviet Architecture and City Planning 1917–1935*, 1970, pp. 168ff.

10 One of the most popular travel writers of the period, H. V. Morton, was able to record how a working-class image of the ideal country scene might be very different from his (Morton's) stereotype (Epping Forest as against his village with 'little red blinds shining in the dusk'). However Morton then appropriated the former as an instance of the latter without thinking to ask what the distinctions might mean (*In Search of England*, 1927, p. 2; see also his 'What is England' in J. B. Priestley (ed.), *Our Nations's Heritage*, 1939, pp. 157–8). The Woodcraft Folk, a progressive alternative to the Scouts and Guides, founded in 1925 ('The Movement for Worker's Children') used images of the forest to invoke the outdoor country experience.

11 Edward Thomas, *Selected Poems and Prose*, 1981, p. 164. Compare also the first stanza of the poem 'It was Upon' (*op. cit.*, p. 259)

> It was upon a July evening
> At a stile I stood, looking along a path
> Over the country by a second Spring
> Drenched perfect green again. 'The lattermath
> Will be a fine one'. So the *stranger* said,
> A wandering man. Albeit I stood at rest,
> *Flushed with desire* I was. The earth outspread
> *Like the meadows of the future, I possessed.*
>
> (my italics)

12 Neither, until very late in their careers, owned a desirable country residence of the kind becoming fashionable among well-off businessmen and artists, on which see Jan Marsh, *Back to the Land: The Pastoral Impulse in England from 1880 to 1914*, 1982, pp. 27ff.

13 Compare, for example, H. J. Massingham's *The English Countryman. A Study of the English Tradition*, 1942 (the book was based on material gathered during Massingham's time as a popular countryside writer in the 1930s), with George Sturt's earlier *Change in the Village* (1912). Among the many other countryside books of the 1930s, see for example Thomas Burke, *The Beauty of England*, 1933, and J. B. Priestley (ed.), *The Beauty of Britain*, 1935.

14 H. V. Morton, *In Search of England*, 1927, p. 280.

15 G. M. Young (ed.), *Country and Town. A Summary of the Scott and Uthwatt Reports*, 1943, p. 23.

16 The vogue for wild Highlands scenes was already in full swing in the mid-Victorian period. The animal painter Edwin Landseer is the best-known practitioner of the genre. The popular Victorian painter Atkinson Grimshaw specialised in dramatic night-lit city scenes, spooky old country houses set in dark winter woods, and views of the Lake District (see D. Bromford and A. Robertson, *Atkinson Grimshaw 1836–1893*, 1979; and Leeds City Art Gallery). There is a characteristic anthology of late Victorian landscape painting in Jeannie Chapel, *Victorian Taste. The Complete Catalogue of the Paintings at the Royal Holloway College*, 1982. See also Allen Staley, *The Pre-Raphaelite Landscape*, 1973. For the first half of the nineteenth century, see the invaluable *Landscape in Britain c. 1750–1850*, 1973, by Leslie Parris and Conal Shields, and A. Bermingham, *Landscape and Ideology*, 1987. The series of engraved views of British scenery published by John Tillotson in the 1860s provides an average, if hardly striking, survey of what the Victorians took to be picturesque scenery. The emergence of distinctive 'home counties' English landscape views in the visual arts during the 1920s and 1930s in the work of such artists as Stanley and Gilbert Spencer, Dora Carrington, John Nash, and the popular painter and illustrator E. B. White, is well illustrated in the exhibition catalogue *Landscape in Britain 1850–1950*, 1983, where there is also a good compendium of rarely illustrated Victorian landscape painting. See also Ian Jeffrey's *The British Landscape 1920–1950*, 1984.

17 Ian Reynolds, *Birket Foster*, 1984; Helen Allingham, *Happy England*, 1903.

18 On Constable's reputation and copies done after his work, see Leslie Parris and Ian Fleming-Williams, *The Discovery of Constable*, 1984. The book does not chart the emergence of Constable as the typically English landscape painter in this century, though it does briefly indicate how Constable gained favour at the end of the nineteenth century on the modern French ticket as a producer of supposedly unmediated and freely-worked sketches of nature.

19 In the 1930s descriptions of Suffolk would almost always make a point of stressing how Constable typified the English countryside, and *The Beauty of Britain. A Pictorial Survey* (edited by J. B. Priestley, 1935) gave particular pride of place to him. A colour reproduction of his 'Cottage in a Cornfield' (1833), an uncharacteristic work which fitted the 1930s countryside ideal, was the only painting reproduced in a

book entirely illustrated by photographs, and, what is more, it was placed at the very beginning, opposite the title page, an emblem of the English landscape.

20 See for example William Howitt, *The Rural Life of England*, 1844, pp. 326ff.

21 My attention was particularly drawn to this in a talk given by Andrew Hemmingway in spring 1985, 'Ideological needs and social functions: representations of agricultural landscape in English painting *c*. 1805–20'.

22 See A. Potts, 'Chantrey as the national sculptor of early nineteenth-century England', *Oxford Art Journal*, November, 1981.

23 Richard Jefferies, *The Story of My Heart*, 1883, pp. 160–1, 101–3.

24 Richard Jefferies, *The Life of the Fields*, 1884, pp. 144–5.

25 See for example Richard Heath, *The English Peasant*, 1893, and George Sturt, *Change in the Village*, 1912.

26 See notes 12 and 17.

27 Thomas Burke's *The Beauty of England* (1933, pp. 13–15) makes a case for a foreign recognition of a distinctively English beauty and senti- ment in English scenery going back to Washington Irving's impressions of his stay in Britain in the 1820s. However, a minor and somewhat impoverished German aristocrat who made his living as a travel writer, and who came to Britain in 1839 (Emeriten von Gauting, *Reise durch England*, 1841, particularly p. 10; his real name was Carl Theodor Baron von Hallberg-Broich) was struck by the extremity of the poverty he observed in rural England and by the large areas of land left uncultivated – his picturesque travels, of course, took him through a lot of moor and heath land. The parks of the aristocracy prompted him to the comment: 'An English garden is a landscape in miniature, created by the command of one man for his pleasure through the bitter work of thousands.'

28 C. F. G. Masterman, *The Condition of England*, 1909, p. 208.

29 See note 13. The combination of an interest in aesthetic description of country life and some serious social analysis to be found again in Noel Carrington's *Life in an English Village* (1949), a publication redolent of the sensible progressivism of the postwar period.

30 Richard Jefferies, *The Story of My Heart*, 1883, pp. 87–92.

31 Christopher Hussey, *The Fairy Land of England*, 1924, pp. 6, 80.

32 H. J. Massingham, *The English Countryman. A Study of the English Tradition*, 1942, p. 141.

33 J. B. Priestley (ed.), *The Beauty of Britain. A Pictorial Survey*, 1935, pp. 5–7. See also Ivor Brown, *The Heart of England*, 1931.

34 Thomas Burke, *The Beauty of England*, 1933, pp. 13–15. See also S. P. B. Mais, *England's Character*, 1936, p. 16 and C. B. Ford, *The Landscape of England*, 1933.

35 H. Read (ed.), *The English Vision*, 1933, p. x.

36 Thomas Burke, *The Beauty of England*, 1933, pp. 19–20. See also Ivor Brown, *The Heart of England*, 1931, p. 22.

37 See for example W. G. Hoskins, *The Making of the English Landscape*, 1960.
38 C. B. Ford, *The Landscape of Britain*, p. 1.
39 See for example W. B. Thomas, *The English Landscape*, 1938, p. xvi.
40 Noel Carrington (ed.), *Broadway and the Cotswolds*, 1933, pp. 57, 12. The brochure was published for the Russells, the family that owned the inn. The idea of the honest design of an old Cotswold village, here refined by a theory of its constant organic remaking and growth during its heyday, is even more explicitly linked with the idea of sensible modernism in Carrington's later *Life in an English Village* (1949), produced with colour illustrations of traditional activities and country types in a semi-modern style by the artist Edward Bawden.
41 See for example Roger Fry, *Reflections on British Painting*, 1934. There is an excellent account of the British art scene during the interwar period in Charles Harrison, *Modern Art and Modernism 1900–1939*, 1981.
42 Read's essay on English art (*Burlington Magazine*, 1933) is reprinted in *The Philosophy of Modern Art*, 1952, pp. 250–68. Mathew Arnold's comment on British art comes from 'On the study of Celtic literature', in *Lectures and Essays in Criticism*, 1866, pp. 353–5; see also p. 345.
43 Herbert Read (ed.), *Unit I. The Modern Movement in English painting, Architecture and Sculpture*, 1934, Introduction.
44 Herbert Read, *Paul Nash*, 1944, and Read's essay in Margot Eates (ed.), *Paul Nash*, 1948, pp. 9, 13. Both these essays represent views Read had already formulated in the late 1930s.
45 Quoted in Margot Eates (ed.), *op. cit.*, 1948.
46 On English neo-romanticism see David Mellor (ed.), *Paradise Lost*, 1987.
47 See for example Mary Chamont, *Modern Painting in Britain*, 1937, p. 16.
48 Nash is quoted as having written in a letter to a friend: 'I don't care for human nature except sublimated, or as puppets, monsters, masses formally related to Nature. My anathema is the human "close-up" ' (Paul Nash, *The Fertile Image*, edited by Margaret Nash, 1951).

Literature

11
Conrad and England

BENITA PARRY

If we were to suppose an improbable situation in which a reader knows of Conrad only through his essays, we would expect her or him to identify a turn-of-the-century English writer whose patriotic and imperial sentiments are familiar, even if the ornate idiom, surpassing the customary grandiloquence of similar pronouncements, does have a foreign intonation

> In the ceaseless rush of shadows and shades . . . we must turn to the national spirit . . . Like a subtle and mysterious elixir poured into the perishable clay of successive generations, it grows in truth, splendour and potency with the march of ages. In its incorruptible flow round the globe of the earth it preserves from decay and forgetfulness of death the greatness of our great men, and amongst them the passionate and gentle greatness of Nelson, the nature of whose genius was . . . such as to 'Exalt the glory of our nation.'[1]

What is not absurdly notional is that there are critics who, with benefit of a professional training and access to all of Conrad's work, have reached the same conclusion – an 'outright glorification of English history and its triumphant upward curve to 1900'[2] is how a recent exponent of this view categorises Conrad's notoriously heterogeneous and disjunctive writing. So resolutely literal a reading of the words on the page reduces polysemous texts to monologic tracts, and would use the equivocal utterances of a displaced emigré and Polish nationalist to position him as an acclimatised English patriot and propagandist.

The exile Konrad Korzeniowski who became a master mariner in the British merchant service, a British subject and the writer

Joseph Conrad, remained, despite his ardent public embrace of things English, an outsider in his adopted country, his urge to integrate arrested by affiliation to other and contrary traditions.[3] Because he continued to identify with the chivalric codes of the Polish gentry, Conrad was out of sympathy with British middle-class materialism and philistinism, contemptuous of bourgeois morality, and scornful of vulgar, self-congratulatory jingoism. Still it was England, with her long-established and stable nation-state that Conrad had chosen as a place of refuge from the political turbulence of his homeland and the disintegration of his family life this had caused.[4] 'It's all very well for Englishmen born to their inheritance to fling verse and prose from Italy to their native shores. I, in my state of honourable adoption, find that I need the moral support, the sustaining influence of English atmosphere even from day to day.'[5] Although distanced from the ways in which the circle amongst whom he had settled experienced the world, Conrad had been drawn to a social order which valorised his own prior allegiance to the work ethic and the principles of responsibility, duty and solidarity, all of which he perceived to be consummately realised in the rules of the British merchant service. Mistrustful of democracy, 'that very beautiful phantom', and fearful of revo-lutionary upheaval, Conrad sought and found in England's domi-nant culture a respect for order and tradition, a cohesive civil society and a widely-disseminated stance of self-assurance which the politically volatile continent lacked;[6] and when the expatriate patriot made it known that he found revolutionary ideas repugnant and dissociated himself from the 'subversion of any social or political scheme of existence',[7] he was using the ready-made language of the British ruling-class.

But this is not the whole story, and his expressions of support for preserving the 'national spirit' against the debilitating effect of 'international fraternity' were articulated in a mode distinct from the discourse of the British right. Paradoxically, one of Conrad's most intimate associates was Robert Cunninghame Graham, a maverick Scottish aristocrat whose political progress had taken him from a radical liberalism, when as an MP he had championed worker's rights in Parliament, to active membership of the Second International, and with whom Conrad felt at ease because of Cunninghame Graham's cosmopolitanism, his sympathy for oppressed nations and his anti-imperialism.[8] In February 1899 Conrad wrote to Cunninghame Graham declining his invitation to address a meeting of the Social Democratic Federation, although he did subsequently attend the gathering; and his refusal enunciates a conservatism wholly un-English, in that it dispenses with a formal deference to democracy, displays a nihilistic notion of 'human nature' and is committed to an abstract idea of the nation distinct from the British version of Queen/King and Country then current:

> As to the peace meeting. If you want me to come, I want still more to hear you. But – I am not a peace man, nor a democrat (I don't know what the word means really) and if I come I shall go into the body of the hall . . . I can not admit the idea of fraternity not so much because I believe it impracticable, but because its propaganda (the only thing really tangible about it) tends to weaken the national sentiment the preservation of which is my concern . . . International fraternity may be an object to strive for and, in sober truth, since it has Your support I will try to think it serious, but the illusion imposes by its size alone . . . What does Fraternity mean. Abnegation – self-sacrifice means something. Fraternity means nothing unless the Cain-Abel business. That's your true fraternity . . . No. It is necessary to have a definite principle. Even if the national idea brings suffering and serving it results in death, this is still better than serving the shadows of an eloquence that is dead precisely because it has no body . . . I look at the future from the depth of a very black past and I find that nothing is left for me except fidelity to a lost cause, to an idea without future.[9]

Conrad's identification with the English and his ability to camouflage his foreignness was never more than incomplete, always inhibited by uncertainties and sensibilities which did not oppress his peers. For Conrad, the 'English spirit' he so admired was inseparable from Britain's long naval history, and his fictions articulate patriotic tributes to an imperial nation where the island itself is transfigured in nautical imagery: 'a great ship! . . . A ship mother of fleets and nation! The great flagship of the race; stronger than the storms! and anchored in the open sea' (*The Nigger of the Narcissus*, 1897, p. 163). Yet it was this very interpenetration of England's domestic stability with her maritime tradition and colonial power which presented an insuperable dilemma for Conrad and led his writings to produce tortuous apologetics and self-contradictory discourses. When his first books appeared, there had been a proliferation of expository and fictional writing vaunting the prodigious qualities and spectacular achievements of the British as empire-builders. His own original readers were subscribers to the pro-imperialist magazines *Blackwood's* and *New Review*, a constituency secure in the conviction that they were members of a superior race, an invincible imperial dominion and a chosen nation called by destiny to fulfil a mission to backward peoples; and his contemporary audience remained those to whom overseas possessions appeared a natural extension of their own national boundaries. By registering the beliefs of inviolable racial identity, ethnic solidarity and national prowess, Conrad's fictions can appear to endorse the official prejudices and conceits of the English at their moment of imperialist triumph and public confidence. But while the narrative material, with its themes of adventure and heroism in the dark places of the earth, and its ideological constructions of the colonial world, did meet audience expectation, the multiple modes of narrative presentation acted to undermine authorised perceptions, precepts and values, so that every manifest affirmation of British culture is countermanded by a cryptic critique, every declaration of acclaim written in a code concealing an impugnment.

II

Conrad's life will not explain his writings, but his writing, to which he brought dispersed perceptions, a divided sensibility and incompatible loyalties, is an indispensable source for understanding the historical, social and ideological circumstances within which his textual practices were formed and constrained. A writer of self-interrogating texts who supports an extensive critical industry proposing diverse interpretations of his multiple vision, and about whom numerous biographies exploring his discordant make-up have been written, raises in an acute form the problem of how to use writing in order to draw a map of an author's ideas, moral convictions, social postures and sense of identity. With advances in textual analysis centring on language's performative function in originating meaning, and the governance of individual utterances by the socially constructed, regulated and impersonal discursive formation, the innocent assumption that a writer's intentions issue as reproductions of pre-existing concepts and experiences, is no longer available. In the present climate where discourse analysis has attained an intellectual pre-eminence, anyone undertaking to discuss a writer as the socially construed and ideologically bounded author of his or her statements, must be aware that a formidable criticism will dismiss the project as worthless. How then to account for the exorbitant discontinuities in Conrad's writing, where 'nothing is uncontradicted', in which the textual practices instigate dialogues between political doctrines, cultural forms, modes of thought, moral standards and social goals, and the use of incommensurable narrative forms and rhetorics engender internal inconsistencies?

A critical practice concerned with Conrad's singular idiom (his parole if you like), as this is ruled by *and* transgresses the existing system of discourse, would analyse how writings which are immersed in the discursive practices of imperialism, that do elaborate the language of European ascendency and act to consolidate the power of western culture, *also* generate a counter-discourse against the grain of the premises, values and aspirations of that same culture. It could then be argued that the textual representations are the labour of Conrad's agency, of an authorial authority formed from diverse social practices and experiences, and producing through writing a construct of English society that partakes of and infringes the hegemonic discourse. It was Conrad's situation on the borderlines of various civilisations that made for a disenchanted perspective on the very society with which he sought to integrate, an estrangement which distanced him from the dominant ideology and drove his writings to produce Aesopian language where ostensibly unctuous professions of obeisance and loyalty to English norms are negated by radical criticisms of England's imperialist culture. If Conrad did not see imperialism steadily (and he did not, since his writings develop colonial discourse by representing the colonial world as the negative form of a universal, i.e. western, standard, in being immobile, immutable, timeless, unreconstructed and without a past), he did see it whole – as the culture of western capitalism in its expansionist moment.[10] In writing of the American millionaire Holroyd that he joined 'the temperament of a Puritan with an insatiable imagination of conquest', and in disparaging the 'misty idealism of the Northerners, who at the smallest encouragement dream of nothing less then the conquest of the earth' (*Nostromo*, 1904, pp. 76 and 333), Conrad bequeathed a laconic analysis of imperialism's triumphalist rhetoric, where a mystical zeal for power and a utilitarian zest for expansion and exploitation is articulated. Whereas the liberal and Fabian 'enemies of empire' deplored colonialism's excesses while energetically or apologetically endorsing the undertaking as both materially and morally beneficial to low-type and unprogressive races, and essential to world wide efficiency, and only small groups of socialists spoke out against imperialism as a threat to international social democracy, Conrad's writings interrogated the dominative tendencies, the drive for global mastery and the exorbitation of 'material interests' in the culture of imperialism.

III

It has been repeatedly alleged in critical commentary that Conrad's writings issued a special dispensation to English colonialism, and the two instances usually cited are a letter to a Polish relative where he wrote that liberty 'can only be found under the English flag all over the world',[11] and his correspondence with his pro-imperialist publisher scorning 'the criminality of inefficiency and pure selfishness when tackling the civilising work in Africa',[12] a reference to Belgian rapacity in the Congo and by implication an affirmation of Britain's positive colonial role. Perhaps such were his opinions, in the one case written down during a felt moment, in the other as a useful strategy; but it is worth noting that those fictions which do formally propose that good work is being done in the red places of the map also negate the exemption, and that, when repeated in the texts, the very notion of 'civilising work' is derided as colonialist cant. As a young man Conrad had been exposed to the experience of being both a colonial and a colonialist, since the Polish gentry who were politically and culturally oppressed by Russia and Prussia in turn exercised domination over the Ukranian serfs on their estates. His years with the British merchant navy and a short period of service with a Belgian company operating in the Congo had taken him into the belly of colonialism and developed his perspective on colonialism as an enterprise in which the whole of Europe was implicated: 'The original Kurtz had been educated partly in England, and – as he was good enough to say himself – his sympathies were in the right place. His mother was half-English, his father half-French. All Europe contributed to the making of Kurtz' (*Heart of Darkness*, 1899, p. 117). It is difficult to ignore the sardonic implications of these words, but another passage in the same fiction, which is as barbed and as productive of ironies, is frequently quoted to establish that Conrad's writings do celebrate Britain's great imperial history:

> And indeed nothing is easier for a man who has . . . 'followed the sea' with reverence and affection, than to evoke the great spirit of the past upon the lower reaches of the Thames . . . It had known and served all the men of whom the nation is proud, from Sir Francis Drake to Sir John Franklin, knights all, titled and untitled – the great knights-errant of the sea. It had borne all the ships whose names are like jewels flashing in the night of time, from the *Golden Hind* returning with her round flanks full of treasure . . . to the *Erebus* and *Terror*, bound on other conquests – and that never returned. It had known

the ships and the men . . . the adventurers and the settlers . . .
captains, admirals, the dark 'interlopers' of the Eastern trade,
and the commissioned 'generals' of East India fleets. Hunters
for gold or pursuers of fame, they had all gone out on that
stream, bearing the sword and often the torch, messengers of
the might within the land, bearers of a spark from the sacred
fire. What greatness had not floated on the ebb of that river
into the mystery of an unknown earth . . . The dreams of men,
the seed of commonwealths, the germs of empires. (*Heart of
Darkness*, p. 47)

A casual reading could indeed suggest that this is a glorification of
British colonialism. However the imagist mode of address acts to
defy the conventions of triumphal oratory, since the dualistic
motifs offset praise for idealist impulses by intimations of sordid
motives, juxtapose agents of order and enlightenment to sinister
and lawless buccaneers, and metonyms of glorious achievement
are nullified by those of menace, so that the very words which
purport to utter a eulogy carry the seeds of their own subversion,
and are ultimately annulled in the novella's closing pages where
the great spirit of the past haunting the Thames takes shape as a
power of darkness.

At every point then in Conrad's writings, the declaration of
patriotic sentiment comes up against England's colonial history
and her culture of imperialism, an obstacle the texts negotiate in
devious ways. In proffering saving ideas, moral purpose and spiritual value as a means of redeeming conquest, exploitation and
the pursuit of material interest, the fiction contradicts its own
representation of imperialism's inspiration and aspiration.
Although always disproved, this way of atonement returns in
different guises, and its effect is to rewrite the narrative of imperialism so that not only are the agents of imperialism exonerated
from blame but they are endowed with virtue. On its own this
strategem will not 'save' England from its imperialist history and
practice, and it is underpinned by the commendation of duty and
fidelity to 'the nation' – which may or may not be England – as
a moral imperative overriding consideration of the values uniting
the community or the ends to which it is committed. But where
Kipling's prose and verse hymned law, order, duty and restraint,
obedience, discipline as a creed which would satisfy the souls of
the servitors while fulfilling their obligation to serve national needs,
the positing in Conrad's writings of 'glorious and obscure toil',
'austere servitude', compliant service and adherence to established
custom, is subverted by assertions of heterodox canons enjoining

other standards of conduct, other goals. In *The Nigger of the Narcissus*, which ostensibly urges the claims of action and social conformity, the authoritarian rhetoric of the narrative discourse is countermanded by the fiction's mythopoeic mode advancing an antagonistic tradition validating quiescence, inertia and indifference to the pragmatic requirements of the established social order. With *Lord Jim* the rules and beliefs of the dominant culture – deeds and duty, defence of the *status quo*, adherence to the laws of order and progress - are registered and subjected to withering scorn:

> Jim's father [a clergyman] possessed such certain knowledge of the Unknowable as made for the righteousness of people in cottages without disturbing the ease of mind of those whom an unerring Providence enables to live in mansions . . . The old chap goes on equably trusting Providence and the established order of the universe . . . Virtue is one all over the world, and there is only one faith, one conceivable conduct of life, one manner of dying. (*Lord Jim* 1900, pp. 5 and 341)

Because Conrad's writings dismantle the intellectual and moral precepts of Britain's dominant culture, the demand for fidelity to that particular nation cannot be sustained, and in using Marlow, the thinking person's man of action, as narrative voice and the protagonist who always suffers crises of faith, the official ethos is both intelligently enunciated and as intelligently torn apart. It is true that Conrad's fictions do affirm patriotism as the noblest sentiment, racial solidarity as the ultimate loyalty, and a sense of national identity as essential to right conduct, but these are not injunctions to submit to the historically constituted British nation. Thus the panegyrics to Home are not to England but to a mysti-cally conceived ideal, to the idea of a national culture as a spiritual realm, a moral republic: 'the land itself . . . its disembodied, eternal and unchanging spirit . . . its severity, its saving power, the grace of its secular right to our fidelity, to our obedience' (*Lord Jim*, pp. 221–2). This is not the language of patriotism attesting to the traditions and practices of a specific nation-state, but an enunciation of an exile's hope which because history offers no ratification, is deferred to the future; and in redeploying an older text, Conrad's writing articulates this utopian desire as the 'quest for the Ever-undiscovered Country' (*Lord Jim*, p. 338).

Notes

1 'The Heroic age', in *The Mirror of the Sea*, 1906, p. 194. All references are to the Dent Uniform/Collected edition of The Works of Joseph Conrad.

2 Martin Green, *The English Novel in the Twentieth Century: The Doom of Empire*, 1984, p. 38.

3 See Zdzislaw Najder, *Joseph Conrad: A Chronicle*, 1984:

> Conrad wanted to belong to English literature and to England. The choice was unambiguous and explicit. But he did not want to, or did not know how to . . . be fully immersed in the English environment. Even had he wanted to, it would have been made impossible by the English tendency to keep foreigners at arm's length – there are many allusions to this fact in Conrad's own books. He had his reservations about even a purely psychological immersion. Family memories rankled in his mind; he had a lively sense of Polish and continental cultural continuity. In short, he was aware of his own dissimilarity and strangeness – yet he strove for the comforting sense of belonging. How many stories and reminiscences there are about Conrad's efforts to become a real English gentleman! They are always a bit comic or ironic; something would always give away his foreignness. (p. 231)

4 Members of his immediate family had been associated with both the moderate and the militant wings of the Polish nationalist movement fighting Prussian and Russian domination. His father was imprisoned and later exiled with his wife and only child to northern Russia, where Conrad's mother died of TB in 1865 when Conrad was eight.

5 Joseph Conrad, letter to Edmund Gosse, 11 April 1905, in *Notes on Life and Letters*, vol. II, p. 15.

6 Cf. Perry Anderson, 'Components of the national culture', *New Left Review*, May–June, 1968, writing of the 'white emigration' of a later period: 'The wave of emigrants who came to England in this century were by and large fleeing the permanent instability of their own societies – that is their proneness to violent, fundamental change. England epitomised the opposite of all this: tradition, community and orderly empire. Its culture was consonant with its special history.'

7 Joseph Conrad, Author's Note to *A Personal Record*, 1912, pp. ix–x.

8 See Zdzislaw Najder, *Joseph Conrad: A Chronicle*, 1984. Conrad was also able to form a close friendship with another eccentric, Bertrand Russell.

9 Joseph Conrad, *Joseph Conrad's Letters to R. B. Cunninghame Graham*, edited by C. T. Watts, 1969, pp. 116–18. Part of this letter is written in French, and the translation given in Najder is used (Zdzislaw Najder, *Joseph Conrad: A Chronicle*, 1984, p. 252).

10 The term 'imperialism' is marked by ambiguities and fluctuations in usage: see Roger Owen and Bob Sutcliffe (ed.), *Studies in the Theory of Imperialism*,

Marxists since Lenin have fluctuated in their use of the term
imperialism. Very often it is used to describe the whole capitalist
system; just as often it refers to relations between advanced and
backward countries within the system. Sometimes it is used in
both senses simultaneously, either with, or more often without,
an acknowledgement of the ambiguity involved. (p. 314)

11 Letter to Aniela Zagorska, dated 25 December 1899, quoted by
Zdzislaw Najder, *Conrad's Polish Background*, 1964, p. 232.

12 Letter to William Blackwood dated 31 December 1898 in *Joseph Conrad:
Letters to William Blackwood and David S. Meldrun*, 1959, pp. 36–7.

Selected bibliography.

Fredric Jameson, chapter on Conrad in *The Political Unconscious*, 1981.

Frederick Karl, *Joseph Conrad: The Three Lives*, 1979.

Zdzislaw Najder, *Joseph Conrad: A Chronicle*, 1984.

Edward Said, *Joseph Conrad and the Fiction of Autobiography*, 1966.

Edward Said, 'Conrad: the presentation of narrative', in *The World, the
Text, and the Critic*, 1984.

Ian Watt, *Conrad and the Nineteenth Century*, 1980.

12
Time space and unity: the symbolic discourse of The Faerie Queene

PETER STALLYBRASS

In 1660, after Charles II's address to the House of Lords, the Lord Chancellor said to the House:[1]

> You are now returning to your Countries, to receive the Thanks and Acknowledgements of your Friends and Neighbours for the great Things you have done, and to make the Burdens you have laid upon them easy, by convincing them of the inevitable Necessity of their submitting to them . . . Your Lordships will easily recover their Estimation and Reverence that is due to your high Condition . . . you will cause your Piety, your Justice, your Affability and your Charity, to shine as bright as is possible before [the people] . . . [W]e are no more than just, when we say that England is an Inclosure of the best People in the World, when they are well informed and instructed . . . And this Exercise of your Justice and Kindness towards them will make them the more abhor and abominate that Parity upon which a Commonwealth must be founded, because it would extirpate, or suppress, or deprive them of their beloved Nobility, which are such a Support and Security to their full Happiness.

The speech is striking for its juxtaposition of internal contradictions. The aristocracy will receive 'thanks' from their neighbours, but the neighbours will at the same time have to be convinced of the 'inevitable Necessity' of submitting to the 'Burdens' laid upon them by the aristocracy. Or again, England is an enclosure 'of the best People in the World', but the people include those who signed the death warrant of a king and those who do not believe in the inevitability of aristocratic rule. So there follows the crucial qualifying clause: these are only the best people 'when they are well informed and instructed'. The Lord Chancellor, then, attempts to combine a rhetoric of happy reciprocity with a rhetoric of social control. The speech reveals the oscillation between a language of consent and a language of correction as the governing elite attempted to efface social divisions through the myth of a nation of obedient subjects and 'their beloved Nobility'.

In analysing the formation of the national enclosure in the late sixteenth century, we shall concentrate on the manipulation and reorganisation of space and time. A nationalist ideology was developed which collapsed social division and cultural heterogeneity into the geography of England and the body of the monarch whilst it established a 'national past'. Ernst Gellner is surely right in arguing that 'nationalism is not the awakening of nations to self-consciousness: it *invents* nations where they do not exist'.[2] But it is equally true that nations 'always loom out of an immemorial past, and . . . glide into a limitless future'.[3] What, then, is the relation between the 'presentness' of the nation and its inscription upon ancient tablets? An answer is perhaps to be found in the conditions of the nation's emergence from what Benedict Anderson calls the 'religious community' (with its sacred language and texts) and the 'dynastic realm' (with its emphasis upon divine centres).[4] The sacred language and the dynastic centre aspire to transcend any existing time or place and are in principle indefinitely extensible. The nation, on the other hand, is by definition limited, pressed in upon by all that it is not. But while the nation is inscribed within geographical boundaries which separate inlaws from outlaws, brothers from others, it is not only a spatial entity. The nation has to be invented or written; and written, what is more, in the crucial and troubling knowledge that it could be written otherwise. It is *because* the nation could be written otherwise that the act of writing must be forgotten, transformed instead into the act of reading a pre-given past.

Reading the past

In his defence of the theatre, Thomas Heywood claimed that the representation of English monarchs, and above all of Henry V, would 'new mould the hearts of the spectators and fashion them to the shape of any noble and valiant attempt'.[5] Such 'fashioning' of the audience is implicit in Shakespeare's *Henry V* (1598–9). The 'festival' of the play itself refers back to the festival of St Crispins Day – the celebration of Agincourt: 'God for Harry, England and Saint George' (III.i.34).[6] But the play, like the Lord Chancellor's speech in 1660, reveals contradictory notions of England. On the one hand, Harry is supported by a 'band of brothers'; on the other, he rules through 'awe and fear' (IV.i.245; IV.iii.60). If true Englishmen are indeed a 'band of brothers', there can be no recalcitrant Other except for a foreign enemy. Thus, the 'community' of England (including Fluellen, Jamy and MacMorris, the 'loyal' officers of Wales, Scotland and Ireland) effaces political and social domination.

But the play constructs a contradictory perspective in which 'awe and fear' are the necessary supports of rule. For the French are not the only demonised Other. In the course of *Henry V*, Bardolph and Nym are hung as thieves; Pistol returns to England to pursue a new career as cutpurse and beggar; Falstaff's old companions must be forced into battle as 'dogs' and 'cullions'. In fact, the very existence of a unified nation is at stake. Is Henry V no more than a powerful baron who, inheriting his father's usurped power, attempts to fashion subjects through subjection? Or is he the legitimate sovereign whose rule is supported by God and popular will alike?

Henry V thus raises some of the problems that trouble the construction of 'the national past'. But the play attempts to contain those problems within the chronology of a patriotic calendar which celebrates St Crispin's Day and the victory at Agincourt, but not the Peasant's Revolt. Elias Canetti suggests that 'the regulation of time is the primary attribute of all government' and that 'a new power which wants to assert itself must also enforce a new chronology'.[7] The England of Elizabeth I and James I, stripped of much of the Catholic calendar, witnessed the creation of new festivals: 17 November, the accession day of Elizabeth; 5 November, the deliverance of James from a Catholic plot. Elizabeth's accession day was transformed into a major state festival, celebrated throughout the country: 'Bells rang, bonfires blazed, guns were fired, open house was kept, festival mirth reigned'.[8] But new regimes must also legitimate the 'time' of their rule by relating it to the past. Consequently, historians and propagandists constructed new genealogies: the Tudors were traced back to King Arthur and the Trojan, Brutus; Elizabeth was proclaimed as heir to Constantine's imperial rule, or as the fulfillment of Virgil's 'prophecy' of the return of the golden age – 'iam redit, et virgo'.[9] Past and present are woven into a narrative of national destiny.

In *Henry V*, for instance, when Henry returns from France victorious, Shakespeare condenses three separate historical conjunctures in a vision of imperial triumph:

> But now behold,
> In the quick forge and working-house of thought,
> How London doth pour out her citizens!
> The mayor and all his brethren, in best sort, –
> Like to the senators of the antique Rome,
> With the plebeians swarming at their heels, –
> Go forth, and fetch their conquering Caesar in:
> As, by a lower but by loving likelihood,
> Were now the general of our gracious emperess, –
> As in good time he may, – from Ireland coming,
> Bringing rebellion broached on his sword,
> How many would the peaceful city quit
> To welcome him. (V.i.22–34)

The general was Essex, and when he returned unsuccessfully from Ireland, he ordered a performance of Shakespeare's *Richard II*, a play about the deposition of a monarch, and the following day rebelled. But in the fictional scenario of *Henry V*, Henry's victory at Agincourt is a repetition of triumphant Roman imperialism and an affirmation of the present 'destiny' of England – the conquest of Ireland. Time is collapsed into a series of mutually reinforcing homologies; as Caesar and Henry V, so Elizabeth I.

Spenser's *Faerie Queene* also celebrates a past whose fulfillment is inscribed as the present moment of Tudor rule. In Book II, Arthur and Guyon enter a library, where they see:[10]

> Old records from ancient time deriv'd,
> Some made in books, some in long parchment scrolles . . .
>
> (II.ix.57)

While Guyon reads *Antiquitie of Faerie land*, Arthur picks up a book called *Briton moniments* and is 'quite ravisht with delight' at the genealogy which traces Britain's imperial rule from the Trojan Brute, who 'spred his empire to the utmost shore', to Constantine and his successors. This 'remembraunce' is the 'perpetuall band' which attaches Arthur to his 'Deare countrey'. What Spenser himself creates is just such a 'remembraunce', a repetition of the already known. Yet Spenser's book, unlike Arthur's, is full of twisting paths that lead to Error's den. The one, true narrative has to be discerned amongst the endless multiplications of false narratives. The problem which Spenser works upon is the reconciliation of a sacred text which lies outside or above history with the specific formation of a national history and a national geography. Innovation has to be reinscribed as the paring away of false narratives from the religious community which is now elided with England. Spenser, of course, did not have to start from scratch: indeed, *The Faerie Queene*, at once national epic, national romance, and national apocalypse, can be read as an encyclopedia of all the previous attempts to conflate sacred text and national destiny.

The most important of these conflations was Foxe's *Acts and Monuments*.[11] The first English edition of 1563 is dedicated to Elizabeth I and the dedication opens with the word 'Constantine', the first Christian emperor whom Arthur was to read in Book II of *The Faerie Queene*. The capital C of Constantine contains a picture of Elizabeth I; she is the inheritor of imperial rule and, like him, she heals the division between church and state. Beneath her feet lies the pope with broken keys, entangled with serpents; above her head is a cornucopia, the bounty which her rule has brought. And in the cornucopia are three Tudor roses, emblematising the unification of the houses of York and Lancaster. The woodcut is, then, a specific articulation of Tudor imperialism, drawing together disparate narratives through a process of analogy and antithesis. Analogically, Elizabeth *is* Constantine, the unity of church and state, just as she *is* the Tudor rose, the unity of warring aristocratic factions. And she is set in antithesis to the pope, who is responsible for the divisions of church and state and who is analogous to the serpent through whom the sacred enclosure of paradise was destroyed. From this perspective, Protestantism and empire are but two names for the same thing; the restoration of godly enclosure through the process of one-ing.

That one-ing is the burden of Foxe's account of church history, which is depicted as a continual battle between godly emperor and antichristian pope. The 'flourishing time' of Constantine will only return when the pope is broken under the feet of the ruler, and oneness is restored. In the seventeenth-century, the Puritan Richard Baxter reiterated this point; the 'cause of all our church confusions', he claimed, was the obscuring of 'the true dignity of Christian Princes and Magistrates' by papists.[12] To overcome 'Church confusions', it was necessary to restore Moses above Aaron, the ruler above the priest, and to insist upon the sacred person of the prince as a master text, within which all the narratives of godliness were condensed. Hence, Nicholas Breton's obsessive reiteration of the unity of the Queen in his 'character of Elizabeth I'.[13]

was she not as she wrote herself *semper eadem* alwaies one? zealous in one religion, believinge in one god, constant in one truth, absolute under god in her self, one Queene, and but one Queene; for in her dayes was no such Queene, one Phoenix

for her spiritt, one Angell for her person, and one Goddesse
for her wisdome, one alwayes in her word, one alwayes of
her word, and one alwaies, in one word ELIZABETHA
Basilthea a princelie goddesse, Elizabeth – deliverer of godes
people from their spirituall thraldome and a provider for their
rest: one chosen by one god to be the one and onlie Queene
of this one kingdom, of one Isle . . . Oh heavens, if there was
a paradise on the earth, where was it, but heere?

One god, one ruler, one kingdom, one isle – it is this imaginary
unity which structures Book I of *The Faerie Queene*, the Book
of Holiness. Holiness, Spenser implies, is but another name for
wholeness or for Una (the book's 'heroine'), a unity whose
geographical location is symbolically secured by the betrothal of
Una to St George. The Book of Holiness is, indeed, a reworking
of Foxe's version of history – the freeing of Una and St George
from the toils of Duessa and Archimago, of godly rule from papal
duplicity.

Nationalism and enclosure

Foxe located the nation temporally in the prolonged history of
Una's struggle against Duessa, but it was also necessary to locate
the nation spatially. The Tudor state was reformulated within
nationalist ideology as a *hortus conclusus*, an enclosed garden walled
off from its enemies. In the Ditchley portrait, Elizabeth I is
portrayed standing upon a map of England. As the virgin who
ushers in the golden age, she symbolises at the same time as she
is symbolised by an island which resists all 'foreign bodies'. And
in a Dutch engraving of 1598, Elizabeth's body encloses Europe;
her breasts are France and the Low Countries, her left arm is
England and Scotland, her right arm is Italy. Under her left arm,
an island is enclosed by a fence against the Catholic navies. What
these two pictures share is the conjuncture of imperial virgin and
cartographic image which together constitute the terrain of Elizabethan nationalism.[14]

The mapping of space was of crucial significance both literally
and symbolically in the formation of the nation. The map on which
Elizabeth stands in the Ditchley portrait is Saxton's map of 1583.
There were major advances in English map-making during the
1570s and 1580s, shaped both by foreign policy and internal colonisation: for the former, maps were required to chart the coast and
to prepare defensive fortifications against invasion; for the latter,
they were needed in the expropriation and 'redistribution' of Irish

land, in depicting the locations of JPs, and in the formation of 'a more detailed knowledge of the internal topography and resources . . . of provincial society'.[15] At the same time, maps were used symbolically in the 'discovery of England': they accompanied the production of histories of England, they were made into tapestries to adorn the walls of the gentry's houses, they were reproduced on playing cards. Mapping was thus an instrument in the charting of ideological as well as geographical boundaries.

But if the nation was articulated as the area incorporated 'within the pale', it was also fashioned by its exclusions. Una, the unity of church and state, the pure virgin who had abandoned 'the cuppe of spirituall abhominations',[16] was set in opposition to Duessa, the false church, a whore who, in *The Faerie Queene*, has a fox's tail 'with dong all fowly dight' (I,viii.48). The enclosed body is valorised by opposition to the demonised grotesque. Duessa's dirt is, as Mary Douglas says of all dirt, 'the by-product of a systematic ordering and classification of matter, in so far as ordering involves rejecting inappropriate elements'. Dirt is necessary to construct the concept of order or, as James I put it in *Daemonologie*, 'there can be no better way to know God than by the contrarie'.[17]

This ideological configuration had real effects. The 'contraries' or 'inappropriate elements' were concepts applied to specific groups, constituting them as sinners and criminals to be purified or exterminated. The yeoman was contrasted to the rogue, the vagabond and the gypsy (St Nicholas, Durham, 8 August 1592: 'Simson, Arington, Fetherstone, and Lancaster, hanged for being Egyptians'); the godly mother was contrasted to the witch and the infanticide ('infanticide . . . may have resulted in more executions than the famous witch craze'); the loyal subject was contrasted to the rebel and the traitor.[18] Ireland provided perhaps the richest repository of 'contraries', pointing by antithesis to the emergent notion of 'Englishness'.

If the English were 'an Inclosure of the best People', the Irish were represented as a nation of vagabonds who refused to cultivate the earth. Spenser, like many other Elizabethans, compared the Irish to the nomadic tribes and Sir John Davies was scandalised by the mobility of the 'wild Irish' who lived 'by the Milke of the Cowe, without Husbandry or Tillage'.[19] How could those who did not cultivate the earth have a culture? And how could nomads claim the geographical settlement that was a prerequisite of nationhood? Thus Irish nomads became a crucial justification for conquest. In 1610, Davies wrote to Robert Cecil that if the Irish[20]

were suffered to possess the whole country as their septs have done for many hundreds of years past, they would never (to the end of the world) build houses, make townships or villages or manure or improve the land as it ought to be; therefore it stands neither with Christian policy nor conscience to suffer so good and fruitful a country to lie waste like a wilderness.

For Davies, the very mark of civilisation was the containment of 'Mountaines, Bogges, and woods within the limits of Forrests, Chases and Parkes'. Living in the absence of such enclosures, the Irish were more 'hurtfull and wilde' than 'wilde Beastes' (pp. 162–3).

Failing to enclose wild land, the Irish also failed to contain the 'wildness' of women and children within the bounds of 'civility'. 'Matrimonie emongs them is no more regarded in effect than the conjunction betweene unreasonable beastes', Sir Henry Sidney wrote to Elizabeth in 1567,[21] and Davies complained of 'their promiscuous generation of Children; their neglect of lawfull matrimony' (p. 181). Spenser recorded the *Monashut* or wandering women who, he claimed, did nothing but 'light services' and lay in the sun, refusing to work (p. 53). According to Smyth, the wandering women were 'great blasphemers of God, and they run from country to country, sowing sedition amongst the people'.[22] At the same time, the Irish were accused of 'uncleannesse in Apparrell, Diet and Lodging' (Davies, p. 181). Their mantles were said to disguise outlaws, rebels, thieves, and pregnant women and to act as a form of lodging, protecting the wearer 'from the wrath of heaven, from the offence of the earth, and from the sight of man' (Spenser, pp. 50–3). The glibs or locks of hair which hung down over their foreheads were also said to be a form of disguise as well as a 'loathly filthiness' (Davies, p. 273; Spenser, p. 53). Similarly filthy, according to Fynes Moryson, was their preparation of food: 'They scum the seething pot with an handful of straw, and strain their milk taken from the cow through a like handful of straw, none of the cleanest, and so cleanse, or rather more defile, the pot and milk.' Worse still, they sometimes did not prepare their food at all, but 'as they run and are chased to and fro, they snatch [shamrock] like beasts out of ditches'.[23] As for their lodgings, Spenser portrayed them as 'swinesteads' where the Irish lay with their animals in a 'foul dunghill' (pp. 82–3).

Finally, the Irish were accused either of irreligion or of papism. In Sir Henry Sidney's view, the Irish were simply without religion: 'I cannot finde that they make any conscience of synne and doubtless I doubt whether they christen there children or no'.[24] Spenser similarly believed in their resistance to any religious belief, but he also argued that they had drunk 'the cup of fornication with which the purple harlot had then made all nations drunken' (p. 85). And Barnaby Rich claimed that 'it is popery that hath alienated the hearts of that people from that faith, fidelity, obedience, love, and loyalty that is required in subjects towards their sovereigns'.[25] Thus, in agriculture, family structure, sexual habits, diet, clothing, hygiene, housing and religion, 'Ireland' – ie that form of discourse which the Elizabethan élite misrecognised as originating 'over there' – defined all that England was not.[26]

But, of course, the 'English' were in reality no more homogeneous than the Irish. Indeed, one of the arguments used to support the colonisation of Ireland was that 'poor and seditious' people in London would be drawn forth, 'whereby the matter of sedition is moved out of the city'.[27] In other words, Ireland could be made into a dumping ground for the 'unEnglish' English. This latter category elided poverty, vagabondage and sedition into a symbolic form which bore strong similarities to the Elizabethan élite's concept of the Irish. John Norden, for instance, stated that in the 'great and spacious wastes, mountains and heaths' of England the people are given to 'little or no kind of labour . . . dwelling far from any church or chapel, and are as ignorant of God or of any civil course of life as the very savages amongst the infidels'.[28] English 'vagabonds' were, like the Irish, accused of nomadism, sexual incontinence, robbery, filth and irreligion. Indeed, one of the most important features of emergent nationalism was its construction of the Other as a cultural/racial type which categorised the English poor as much as the Irish and the Indians. The significance of this construction is worth emphasising, given its persistence and elaboration. Mayhew, for instance begins *London Labour and the London Poor* not with a project of social reform but with a chapter 'Of wandering tribes in general', in which he contrasts 'two distinct and broadly marked races, viz the wanderers and the settlers – the vagabond and the citizen – the nomadic and the civilised tribes'. And he defines the 'nomadic' (including the street people of whom he writes) in terms which differ little from Elizabethan accounts of the vagabonds:[29]

> The nomad then is distinguished from the civilized man by his repugnance to regular and continuous labour – by his want of providence in laying up store for the future . . . by the looseness of his notion as to property – by the absence of chastity among his women, and his disregard of female honour – and lastly, by his vague sense of religion.

From such lists, Mayhew, like Spenser and Davies, constructs by antithesis the 'civilised': regular and continuous labour, providence, property, chastity, religion.

But whilst noting the persistence of this discourse, we also need to examine how it is articulated in a specific historical conjuncture. If in Mayhew the nomadic is constructed largely in opposition to bourgeois domestic life, Spenser and Davies depict nomadism as a rejection of the practice and symbolic value of enclosure. Thus Davies can demonstrate the wildness of the Irish by noting that 'at this day, there is but one Parke stored with Deere in al this kingdom' (p. 163). The deer park is taken as emblematising the extension of the monarch's rule into the darkest reaches of the land. With the deer parks would come the 'Forest Law, and the Law *de Malefactoribus in parcis*' and consequently, Davies believed, the Irish forest dwellers would be forced out into the plains where they could be kept under the 'eye and observation' of the magistrates (pp. 161–2).

But forest-dwelling 'barbarism' and 'sedition' were not, of course, uniquely Irish. If Spenser compares Ireland to ancient Britain, 'every corner having in it a Robin Hood that kept the woods' (p. 144), the forests of sixteenth and seventeenth-century England were equally the site of economic and ideological conflict. A report of 1609 complained of the 'lewd poore' who destroyed the king's woods and deer, and enclosures were pulled down and deer killed in Gillingham Forest (1628), Leicester Forest (1628), Braydon Forest (1631), and Waltham Forest (1642–3).[30] And at the symbolic level, the Robin Hood whom Spenser denounces as a bogey of the past was the hero of ballads such as 'Robin Hoods Progresse to Nottingham', in which he kills fifteen foresters, and 'Robin Hood's Birth, Breeding, Valor and Marriage' in which, after feeding on venison, the outlaw carries his poached deer into Titbury. The ballads, then, are not restricted to a romantic celebration of sylvan life. In 'Robin Hood and the Ranger', forest law becomes a topic of debate, the ranger asserting that 'these are his majesty's deer' whereas Robin Hood claims that the forest is 'my own' where 'freely I range'; and in 'Robin Hood Rescuing Three Squires', when the outlaw hears that the squires are condemned to die only 'for slaying the king's fallow deer', he disguises himself as a beggar and, after offering his services as a hangman, rescues the squires and hangs the sheriff.[31] The monarch's enclosures, then, did not go unchallenged.

Indeed, to the extent that the Elizabethan élite succeeded in establishing analogies between the enclosure of property, the enclosure of 'true religion' and the enclosure of the nation, it was possible to associate the evils of rural enclosures with the evils of state and church. Whilst England was presented as the enclosed isle protected against the wolf-like Spanish, popular hatred of enclosures could lead to an attack upon the ideological enclosure which is a necessary constituent of the nation-state. By the mid 1590s at least some of the non-Catholic poor were declaring their support for Philip of Spain. In 1596, a Canterbury artisan claimed that 'if the Spaniards did inhabit here it would be better for us . . . for we could not live worse unless we were starved'. In Oxfordshire during the same period, Bartholomew Stere, a carpenter, was accused of pulling down enclosures as an 'outward pretence'. His real intention, it was claimed, was 'to kill the gentlemen of that countrie and to take the spoile of them, affirming that the commons long sithens in Spaine did rise and kill all the gentlemen in Spaine and sithens that time have lyved merrily there'.[32] The development of state hegemony created wider possibilities for political resistance when the government's idealised version of the national enclosure was clearly not protecting God's elect from 'the curse of brambles and briars'.[33] The very elisions which, within the dominant discourse, naturalised, spiritualised and legitimated enclosure could become the means by which the rejection of agricultural enclosure was linked to the subversion of ideological enclosure. The manufacture of the nation as a pregiven unity, 'a band of brothers', could be tied back to the 'awe and fear' which underpinned the state.

At the same time, the notion of any pregiven unity was constantly under attack in Ireland. Spenser dedicated *The Faerie Queene* to the 'Most High Mightie and Magnificent Empresse renowned for Pietie, Vertue, and all Gratious Government, Elizabeth, by the Grace of God Queene of England, Fraunce and Ireland, and of Virginia, Defender of the Faith'. The list of titles ascribed to Elizabeth has the effect of erasing difference, as if Elizabeth's claim to be Defender of the Faith gave her equal rights in France, Ireland and Virginia as in England. But Spenser knew otherwise: much of *The Faerie Queene* was written in Ireland and although, as we have already suggested, the construction of Ireland as demonised Other was a powerful strategy in the formation of English nationalism, at the same time it threatened the unity of imperial rule.

That threat troubles the analogical structure of Spenser's thought, for how can Ireland be part of Gloriana's kingdom when it is, simultaneously, its antithesis? One strategy for conceptualising the problematic status of Ireland is developed in Book V, the Book of Justice. There, Ireland is allegorised as 'Irena', a name derived both from the Greek *eirene*, meaning 'peace', and from the

Gaelic *Ierna*, the ancient name of Ireland. This concept of Ireland as intrinsically 'peaceful' (i.e. well fitted to become an English subject) is recapitulated in Spenser's *A View of the Present State of Ireland* where it is described as 'a most beautiful and sweet country as any is under heaven' with its 'ports and havens opening upon England and Scotland, as inviting as to come to them, to see what excellent commodities that country can afford'.[34] Ireland, like Virginia, is imagined as virgin land, opening itself alluringly to its master. Why, then, is Ireland in arms? The answer of Book V is that it has been attacked by Grantorto, the oppressive powers of Catholicism, under the pope and Philip of Spain. Spain, then, has forced Ireland to seek justice from England, or in the symbolic discourse of *The Faerie Queene*, the defenceless woman (Irena) is in need of protection by the virtuous male, Artegall.

By emphasising Ireland as subject to Grantorto, Spenser can retain the view that it was in the immemorial past, 'pure' land. But this is contradicted by a myth of conquest, according to which even England was originally 'a salvage wildernesse,/Unpeopled, unmanurd, unprov'd, unpraysd' (II.x.5). Indeed, Spenser suggests that Albion was originally peopled with giants who polluted the soil with 'their filthinesse' until they were dispossessed by Brute. The name of England's patron saint, George, is derived from the Greek *georgos* – 'one who tills the earth' – and it is the unrighteousness of those who do not cultivate the land which gives St George the right of conquest.

But the myth of conquest subverts the stable equation of 'one God, one ruler, one kingdom' since, however, far back in time, it suggests that nations are historical and that their destiny is formed, not simply given. The formation of nations thus raises troubling questions: who forms them, and by what right? The nation appears, at that moment, as scripted. In the apocalyptic version of the nation, the scriptor is God and, in the first book of *The Faerie Queene*, all the proliferating narratives are folded back into the 'Holiness' of the script which unites St George and Una. But in Ireland, that unity broke down into competing, incompatible scripts. In Ireland, it became clear that the nation could be written otherwise.

It was, of course, this possibility of rewriting which made colonisation possible. Sir John Davies believed that Ireland 'must first be broken by a warre' (p. 5), but then its legal system, its customs, its agriculture and its language must be eliminated 'so as we may conceive a hope, that the next generation, will in tongue and heart, and every way else, become English' (p. 272). But on the other hand, Ireland presented disturbing evidence of how the English could themslves be 'rewritten', for it was the Anglo-Irish who had settled in Ireland since the Norman Conquest as well as the 'wild Irish' who were in arms against the Elizabethan colonisers. And the Anglo-Irish were a striking example of a group which had deliberately rejected 'the Civil and Honorable Lawes and Customes of England', scorned the English language, were 'ashamed of their very English Names, though they were Noble and of great Antiquity', and 'tooke such pleasure in their beastly manner of life, as they would not returne to their shape of men againe' (p. 182). Ireland then, might be the space of transgression, of the seeping away of 'Englishness', rather than the site of national enclosure. This possibility was the greater, given that many of the colonists both in Ireland and the New World were the poor and unemployed of England who were 'not only poorly motivated but were ideologically opposed to colonisation'.[35] English troops frequently sold their weapons or deserted to the Irish, and the armies of Shane O'Neill, Turlough Luineach O'Neill were substantially reinforced by English deserters.

Similarly, the New World offered a release from nationalism as well as new terrain for colonisation. Nicholas Canny describes 'a regular haemorrhage to the Indians' in Virginia until the massacre of 1622.[36] And the fugitives often adopted Indian customs and dressed as Indians. The Portuguese Bernal Diaz records a common seaman, Gonzalo Guerrero, who had written: 'I am married and have three children, and they look on me as a *Cacique* here, and a captain in time of war . . . My face is tattooed and my ears are pierced. What would the Spaniards say if they saw me like this? And look how handsome these children of mine are!'[37] Even those who saw the Indians as 'cruell salvages' might see their customs as comparable, not antithetical, to English customs. Jane Dickenson, who had been captured by the Indians in 1622, complained of her slavery but argued that it was no worse than being an indentured servant.[38] And the myth of the new 'golden land' contained the subversive possibility of comparisons unfavourable to the colonising nations. In *Complainte contre Fortune* (1559), Ronsard wrote of the Brazilians as free from malice, as ignorant of kings and senates as of good and evil, and living happily without any fear of the law.[39] And if the supposed liberty of the Indians could be used as a critique of hierarchy, the sensual pleasures of their lands conjured up visions of escape from the bonds of 'civility'. In *A Relation of the Commodities of Nova Hispania* (1572), Henry Hawkes writes that 'you shall have such sweete smels, with such great content and pleasure, that you shall remember nothing, neither wife, nor children . . . the oderferous smells will be so sweet', whilst Peter Martyr moralistically states that 'smooth and pleasing words might be spoken of the sweet odors, and perfumes of those countries, which we purposly omit because they make rather for the effeminating of men's minds, than for the maintenance of good behaviour'.[40] But it was the very definition of 'good behaviour' which was put in question at the margins of godly rule.

It is, perhaps, Spenser's recognition and fear of the subversion of godliness at the margins which leads him in Book V of *The Faerie Queene*, the book which deals most explicitly with Ireland, to replace the golden world of Gloriana with the iron world of Talus, the agency of Justice which is 'made of yron mould/Immoveable, resistlesse, without end' (V.i.12). It is also in Book V that the Blatant Beast first appears and, with it, the collapse of any unitary script. The Blatant Beast represents slander, and it is slander which has the final word in Spenser's last completed book:

> Ne may this homely verse, of many meanest,
> Hope to escape his venemous despite.
>
> (VI.xii.41)

In Book I, all discourse led back to Una; but in the iron world of Book V, unity is the vicious act of enforcement by Talus who cuts off hands and feet, and put nails through the poet's tongue. There is no doubt that Spenser believed in this enforcement (as he believed that the Irish bards should be suppressed), but the excluded Other returns to haunt the very process of reading. Both within and at the boundaries of the 'Inclosure of the best People in the World', the invented nation was forced to contemplate its own dissolution.

Notes

I am particularly indebted to Paul Brown, whose article 'This thing of darkness I acknowledge mine': Shakespeare's *The Tempest* and the discourse of colonialism' is in Jonathan Dollimore and Alan Sinfield (eds), *Political Shakespeare*.

1 *Journals of the House of Lords*, 1660–6, vol. XI, p. 238. I am indebted to Linda Merricks for this reference.
2 Ernst Gellner, *Thought and Change*, p. 169, quoted in Benedict Anderson, *Imagined Communities: Reflections on the Origin and Spread of Nationalism*, London, 1983, p. 15.
3 Benedict Anderson, *op. cit.*, p. 19.
4 Benedict Anderson, *op. cit.*, pp. 20–8.
5 T. Heywood, *Apology for Actors*, 1612, quoted in P. Edwards, *Threshold of a Nation*, Cambridge, 1979, p. 69.

6 All references to *Henry V* are to J. R. Brown's edition, New York, 1965.

7 E. Canetti, *Crowds and Power*, trans. C. Stewart, Harmondsworth, p. 462.

8 Roy Strong, *The Cult of Elizabeth: Elizabethan Portraiture and Pageantry*, London, p. 114.

9 See Frances A. Yates, *Astraea: The Imperial Theme in the Sixteenth Century*, Harmondsworth, 1977, pp. 29–87.

10 All references to *The Faerie Queene* are to the edition of J. C. Smith and E. de Selincourt, Oxford, 1912.

11 On the importance of Foxe, see William Haller, *Foxe's Book of Martyrs and the Elect Nation*, London, 1963. My discussion of the woodcut in Foxe is indebted to Frances Yates, *Astraea: The Imperial Theme in the Sixteenth Century*, Harmondsworth, 1977, pp. 42–3.

12 See William Lamont, *Richard Baxter and the Millennium: Protestant Imperialism and the English Revolution*, London, 1979.

13 Nicholas Breton, 'Elogy of Queen Elizabeth', in V. Kentish-Wright (ed.), *A Mad World My Masters*, vol. II, London, 1929, p. 5.

14 See Roy Strong, *Portraits of Queen Elizabeth I*, Oxford, 1963, pp. 75–6, plate XV and plate E32.

15 Victor Morgan, 'The cartographic image of "the country" in early modern England', *Transactions of the Royal Historical Society*, 5th Series, 29, 1979, pp. 134, 136–7.

16 'An Order for Prayer and Thanksgiving (necessary to be used in these dangerous times)', London, 1594, sig. A 4.

17 Mary Douglas, *Purity and Danger*, London, 1969, p. 35; James I is quoted in Stuart Clark, 'Inversion, misrule and the meaning of witchcraft', *Past and Present*, 87, 1980, p. 107.

18 R. E. C. Waters, *Parish Registers in England*, London, 1883, p. 57; J. A. Sharpe, 'The history of crime in late medieval and early modern England: a review of the field', *Social History*, 7, 1982, p. 200.

19 Sir John Davies, *Discovery of the True Causes why Ireland was never Entirely Subdued*, London, 1612, p. 160. References to Spenser's *A View of the Present State of Ireland* are to the edition of W. L. Renwick, Oxford, 1970. All further page references to the *Discovery* and *A View* are included in the text.

20 Quoted in Nicholas P. Canny, *The Elizabethan Conquest of Ireland: The Pattern Established 1565–76*, Hassocks, 1976, p. 119.

21 Quoted in Nicholas P. Canny, *op. cit.*, p. 124.

22 Quoted in David Beers Quinn, *The Elizabethans and the Irish*, Ithaca, p. 82.

23 Fynes Moryson, *An Itinerary*, London, 1617, vol. III, pp. 162, 163.

24 Quoted in Nicholas P. Canny, *The Elizabethan Conquest of Ireland: The Pattern Established 1565–76*, Hassocks, 1976, p. 124.

25 Barnaby Rich, *A New Description of Ireland*, London, 1617, p. 90.

26 For similar misrecognitions of the Indians, see Bernard W. Sheehan, *Savagism and Civility: Indians and Englishmen in Colonial Virginia*, Cambridge, 1980, pp. 37–88; for a brilliant account of Spenser which

touches on his relations to Ireland, see Stephen Greenblatt, *Renaissance Self-Fashioning*, Chicago, 1980, pp. 157–92.

27 Quoted in David Beers Quinn, *The Elizabethans and the Irish*, Ithaca, p. 157.

28 John Norden, *The Surveyor's Dialogue*, quoted in Keith Thomas, *Religion and the Decline of Magic: Studies in Popular Beliefs in Sixteenth and Seventeenth-Century England*, Harmondsworth, 1971, p. 195.

29 Henry Mayhew, *London Labour and the London Poor*, London, 1967, vol. I, pp. 1–2.

30 Buchanan Sharp, *In Contempt of All Authority: Rural Artisans and Riot in the West of England, 1586–1660*, Berkeley, 1980, pp. 172, 88, 90, 108, 223.

31 Francis James Child, *The English and Scottish Popular Ballads*, vol. III, New York, 1965, pp. 152–3, 180. See also Peter Stallybrass, ' "Drunk with the cup of liberty": Robin Hood, the carnivalesque and the rhetoric of violence', in Nancy Armstrong (ed.), *The Rhetoric of Violence*, special issue of *Semiotica*, 54, 1/2, 1985, pp. 113–45.

32 Peter Clark, *English Provincial Society from the Reformation to the Revolution: Religion, Politics and Society in Kent, 1500–1640*, Hassocks, 1977, pp. 249–50; Buchanan Sharp, *In Contempt of All Authority: Rural Artisans and Riot in the West Of England, 1586–1660*, Berkeley, 1980, pp. 39, 20.

13
Kipling and masculinity

PREBEN KAARSHOLM

Kipling, the poet laureate of British imperialism, was no admirer of British national institutions or British national character. His heroes, typically, are those who transcend the limits of time and place and class; they are born in a nether-world of dark imaginings. Given these ambiguities – the subject of this essay – it is surprising how Kipling's imperialism is taken for granted, as though it were of a piece with the official propaganda of the day. Indeed, rather little has been written about the impact of Kipling's imperialism on the thought and imagination of his time.[1] The reason may paradoxicaly be the unique extent of Kipling's popularity – particularly in the 1890s – and the fact that he attained his popularity for expounding an authoritarian world-view and style which later versions of nationalist ideology have attempted to excrete as essentially 'foreign'. Many of the mental structures and emotional energies that give Kipling's writings their peculiar form and power are difficult to distinguish from those that helped to constitute the mass influence and ideological domination of fascism (particularly in its German version), i.e. of a cultural construct which modern British nationalism has fought to pose as its own opposite.[2] Therefore Kipling's immense influence and the fact that it was a popular rather than a 'high' cultural influence has a certain embarrassment attached to it.

Kipling's reception and influence

Kipling's relations with the London literary establishment were complex. In 1889–90, shortly after he had arrived from India, he became the craze of the season and a critics' favourite when *Departmental Ditties*, *Plain Tales from the Hills*, *Soldiers Three* and *Wee Willie Winkie* came out in English editions – a burst of original and effective poems and short stories dealing with British colonial life in India and first published when the author was still a journalist in Lahore and Allahabad.

But already within a year, after the publication of his novel *The Light that Failed* in late1890, Kipling's star among the literary élite was on the wane – or at least among the part of the élite that was considered most trendy. Through the 1890s he continually drew the fire of critics like J. K. Stephen, Francis Adams, Richard le Gallienne and Max Beerbohm and aroused the scepticism of literary 'lions' like Oscar Wilde and Henry James.[3] The literary establishment, however, was divided, and Kipling became the paragon of the group of writers and critics surrounding W. E. Henley who through the *Scots (National) Observer* and later the *New Review* fought for a masculine, activist 'realism' as an alternative to the 'sickly' aestheticism of the decadents.[4] At the same time, Kipling's popularity with what was really a mass audience continued to grow, no matter how the debates of the literary élite might fluctuate.[5]

Even the unappealing *The Light that Failed* was brought out in three editions in its first year and was subsequently dramatised and filmed several times over.[6] *Barrack-Room Ballads*, the first instalments of which had been printed in Henley's *Scots Observer* in February 1890, came out in book form in 1892 and made a sensational and lasting impact.[7] One of the things that Henley and his group of alternative modernists fought for was a counter-decadent populism, and Kipling was quite good at ridiculing abnormal *littérateurs*, as in his poem 'In partibus' from 1889:

> But I consort with long-haired things
>   In velvet collar-rolls,
> Who talk about the Aims of Art,
>   And 'theories' and 'goals',
> And moo and coo with womenfolk
>   About their blessed souls.
>
> But what they call 'psychology'
>   Is lack of liver-pill,
> And all that blights their tender souls
>   Is eating till they are ill,
> And their chief way of winning goals
>   Consists of sitting still.
>
> It's Oh to meet an Army man,
>   Set up, and trimmed and taut,

> Who does not sport hashed libraries
> Or think the next man's thought,
> And walks as though he owned himself,
> And hogs his bristles short.

Kipling wrote in 'the vernacular' of 'ordinary people' – or something that posed as such. His rhythms and vocabulary were learned from street jargon and from music-halls, which then in turn put Kipling songs on the programme – most successfully at the beginning of the South African War in November 1899, when singing of 'The absent-minded beggar' helped to stimulate jingoism.

The 'punch' and economy of his prose originated in journalistic practice, and in turn Kipling provided an example for the star reporters of the *Daily Mail* and the 'new journalism', for writers like George Steevens and Edgar Wallace. Wallace – a typical example of the 'ordinary man' who would fall for Kipling[8] – tried to imitate the success of *Barrack-Room Ballads* in his book of Boer War poetry, *Writ in Barracks*, and later, in his Sanders novels and stories, like A. E. W. Mason and many others, produced a brand of imperialist popular literature whose clue was unmistakably taken from Kipling.

Through channels like these Kipling's influence moved beyond the narrow limits of 'high' literary culture and became a powerful ideological force.

Imperialism and male neurosis

If the reception that Kipling met with was divided, the world-view that he communicated and his attitudes towards Britain and his readership were hardly less so. 'England is a stuffy little place mentally morally and physically', he wrote to Cecil Rhodes from Cape Town in October 1901.[9] In many ways his arrogance seems to have made him operate with a set of double optics that provided different visions for different parts of the public – those who 'knew' and those who didn't. This may explain, for example, the mystery of the two versions of *The Light that Failed* that came out in 1890–1, one with a sentimental hero-gets-heroine ending, another concluding with a deeply pessimistic study in aggressive male self-destruction.

In any case Kipling's imperialism was not just an instance of flatly optimistic pro-British chauvinism: on the contrary his tales from the outposts of Empire imply a criticism of contemporary over-civilised and 'degenerate' British society for which imperialism and the military life might provide a necessary cure of revitalisation.

A good example of this is 'The head of the district' from *Life's Handicap* (1891) which contrasts the idiocy of Liberal colonial administration with the practicalities of life on the frontier. In the story the balance of colonial society is threatened from two sides – on the one hand by the unbridled fanaticism of the 'natives' represented by the Blind Mullah, on the other hand by the humanitarian attempts at democratic reform that are introduced by the Viceroy who has appointed a Bengali to the post of Deputy Commissioner. A revolt of the mountain tribes is the result, and the balance is restored through a series of particularly *in*humanitarian pragmatic measures by the unassuming and hardworking soldier Tallantire and the faithful chief Khoda Dad Khan.

The threat to the balance of organic society is provided by those who don't 'know' – the theoretically minded and over-civilised whites and the breeds without the Law – and is restored by those who do – the pragmatic white administrator and his unquestioning 'native' assistant who both recognise, and do not want to challenge their positions within, the given hierarchy, and whose qualities in a 'natural' way complement each other.

The authoritarian view of social and racial relations brought out in this story pervades all of Kipling's writing and at times attains an almost hysterical character, which has its roots – as Eric Stokes has argued – in a certain type of psychology and is reflected even in the style of writing:

> The nervous breakdown [Kipling] suffered as a foster child . . . and the partial breakdowns he suffered from overwork when alone in Lahore and later in 1890 in London left him a prey to 'the sensation of nameless terror', he described in his early tale 'The strange ride of Morrowbie Jukes' . . . Hence his psychological need to grasp the certitude of outward reality with 'violent precision'; hence the importance of work, the tribal group, and the ordered authority structure. In these he was safe.[10]

Importantly, however, we are dealing here not merely with the peculiarities of an individual psychology, but with elements of the collective mentality of a whole period. This is what gives Kipling's output its centrality and helps to explain his exceptional influence – as well as that of imperialist ideology more generally. Kipling's world-view is a deeply depressed and neurotic one – of a life whose sense is dissolving and only held together by desperate effort and of a society where the trend towards *anomie* and total alienation can only be countered by an authoritarian traditionalism whose most topical form is imperialism.

The destructive influences in Kipling's universe are represented by a variety of phenomena – by Liberal degeneration, by the miseries of metropolitan life, by proletarianisation and poverty, and later also by socialism. In his story 'My son's wife', from the year of the Russian revolution, he describes an uprooted intellectual, Midmore, who is being destroyed by left-wing company in the big city and is only healed by his return to the organic simplicity of the traditional English countryside and the bosom of the gentry.

However, the neurotic and authoritarian aspects of Kipling's writing come out most clearly when he deals with women and with sexuality, and probably nowhere more clearly than in the two novels *The Light that Failed* (1890) and *The Naulahka* (1892) – texts that in the critical tradition are normally considered too 'weak' in literary terms to be worth investigating in depth.

In his book *Männerphantasien* from 1977–8 about the pre-fascist Freikorps that were used to annihilate attempts at socialist revolution in Germany between 1919 and 1923, Klaus Theweleit has tried to explain the exceptional brutality of the white terror against socialist women. Not only were such women massacred in great numbers; their torture and killing was indulged in again repeatedly in scores of autobiographical novels and memoirs by Freikorps members, a genre that became popular in the late 1920s and was given state promotion after the Nazi takeover in 1933.

According to Theweleit, the anti-socialist and anti-proletarian elements in the world-view of the Freikorps male fraternities were inseparable from their deeply ambiguous attitudes towards women and sexuality. In the novels and memoirs women fall into two categories – 'red whores' and 'white sisters or mothers'. The first category is extinguished by means of 'orgiastic killings' (shot through the mouth, blown up by hand grenade, etc.); the second category often seems to contain the incarnation of a *Krankenschwester* who nurses the wounded soldier, then turns out to be the sister of some beloved soldier comrade, and can thereafter be proposed to and married by the patient (after which she is not normally heard of again).[11]

The common pattern behind these woman figures, Theweleit argues, is partly a fear of proletarian sexual habits, which were often more liberal than those of the German middle classes, but more particularly a fear of active women, women who work, fight and are capable of initiatives, and who by the 'white' soldiers are identified with a threat of castration. Thus it is not – as Freud would have it – the female lack of a penis that arouses the fear of castration, but the vision of a self-reliant and liberated womanhood that activates subconscious anxieties. The 'white' women on the contrary – mothers, sisters, nurses – never move beyond their roles in the allegories of the male phantasy. They can be worshipped (usually in a strictly stereotyped fashion) and then safely forgotten about.

It may seem bad taste to bring such a Germanic digression into the discussion of a quintessentially British writer like Rudyard Kipling, but there are striking similarities. Kipling, though, did not go as far as the Freikorps members who actually killed off the 'red' women: he stuck within the inhibitions of a neurotic imagination, which he wrote out most consistently in *The Light that Failed* and *The Naulahka*.

The Light that Failed is a bad novel with 'a singularly unpleasant hero'.[12] It deals with the career of a painter, discusses aesthetic principles, journalism and metropolitan life, contains some famous descriptions of battles in the Sudan, but more than anything else it is about men and their relations with women. In a letter to Olive Schreiner, who had asked about the background to the book, Kipling explained:

> If all the girls in the world sat quiet and still, at the right moment, by all the men in the world, when those were in trouble, we should all be perfectly happy instead of being hurt and worried. I'll show you about this time next year [in *The Naulahka*?] why Maisie was made as she was.[13]

The hero, Dick Heldar, is a painter, whose art is highly topical. Among his *sujets* are 'Somali muleteer flogged', 'Star shell bursting over camp at Berbera', and 'Soldier lying dead in the moonlight outside Suakin – throat cut by Fuzzies' – pictures that go well with war correspondence. These are the roots of his success. Dick has an unhappy childhood and an evil fostermother behind him and is not satisfied merely with artistic achievement and recognition. He wants a wife as well and goes for Maisie, who unfortunately wants to be a painter herself and not a wife as Dick understands. Even worse, she prefers travelling abroad with an impressionist red-haired girl friend to staying at home with Dick.

Dick suffers from an old head wound received in the Sudan on the very day in 1885 when Khartoum fell and Gordon was killed. He goes blind gradually, but before manages to finish a master-piece, 'Melancholia', using the proletarian servant girl Bessie as a model. Bessie is the second woman in Dick's life, but no good either. Spiteful and without sense of art, she ruins 'Melancholia'

('Great heavens! to think that a little piece of dirt like you could throw me out of my stride! . . . What an enormous amount of mischief one little woman can do!') At the end of his tether the blind man follows his fraternity of war correspondents back to the Sudan and seeks death in the arms of a male friend: 'His luck had held to the last, even to the crowning mercy of a kindly bullet through his head.'

The background to Dick's tragedy is a world of decadence and dissolution, represented partly by the Binat establishment in Port Said that Dick paints realistically, a sinful drinking place where 'to the tinpot music of a Western waltz the naked Zanzibari girls danced furiously by the light of kerosene lamps', partly by the grey wilderness of metropolitan London, where fog is eternal and poverty drives people to abominable degradations. But first and foremost the decadence of modernity is represented by the women – by the vulgarity and greed of proletarian Bessie, who is one with the worst sides of London, and most importantly by Maisie, who keeps the man from his life's fulfilment by insisting on unnatural ideas of equality and independence. Fortunately, there is an imperialist war on which allows even the blind Dick his place in the masculine formation of the 'square', in which to face an honourable death.

In its first version *The Light that Failed* was published without its last third and ended idylliclly with Maisie submitting herself to Dick in marriage. A similar happy ending is found in Kipling's second novel. *The Naulahka* from 1892, written in collaboration with another man, Wolcott Balestier. The plot of this work is so silly that it is almost painful to paraphrase, but its main thrust runs parallel to that of *The Light that Failed*. A very aggressive and enterprising young American from 'Topaz, Colorado', Nicholas Tarvin, has two aims in life. Firstly, he wants to bring the railroad to Topaz before it gets to the competing neighbouring town: secondly, he wants to marry Kate Sheriff, who, however, has decided that she must go out on her own as a nurse to India and help Indian women in their unbearable plight. To attain the objects of both his desires, Tarvin follows after his beloved to the East, partly in order to bring back a priceless necklace, the Naulahka, for the wife of the tycoon who decides which way the railway runs, partly to prevent Kate from doing anything sensible and bombard her with propaganda about the true role of woman in life.

Thus, like the earlier novel, *The Naulahka* is primarily about men and women, but also, as the subtitle runs, 'A Story of West and East' – in that order. Like Dick Heldar, Tarvin is confronted with the challenge of a woman who insists on a life of her own:

> I can't think of you throwing yourself into the dangers and horrors of that life alone, unprotected, a girl. I can't think of it and sleep nights. I daren't think of it. The thing's monstrous. It's hideous. It's absurd. You won't do it! . . . Great Scot, Kate, if you are looking for some misery to set right, you needn't go off the road. Begin on me.

What is new in *The Naulahka* is the way in which the contradictions and dangers of womanhood are linked up and identified with an elaborate ideological imagery of India and 'the East'. The Indian society that Kate is attracted to is one of ultimate decadence and static hopelessness. As represented by the opium-crazy Maharajah and the women of his palace, India is a conglomerate of obscenity, infection, maliciousness, lack of willpower, sensuous seduction, engulfment and dissolution.

As the Maharajah has lost his will, his court is dominated by the women and predominantly by the 'Gipsy Queen', a murderous creature who has already killed off one husband, attempts to assassinate the boy-child of a slightly more sympathetic fellow-wife, tries to seduce Tarvin, and controls the mysterious and repulsive 'interior' of the palace, where hundreds of unseen women gaze and murmur 'like the hiss of a hidden snake'. India as a whole is a hot and malignant nightmare, 'a vast sleeping land' of 'white poppy-fields' and 'insolent nakedness', where 'monstrous and obscene gods' stare at you from all quarters.

The dangers and corruption of India and its identification with womanhood are worked out most thoroughly in Chapter 12, where the country itself assumes the form of a female body. In his search for the precious necklace, Tarvin is forced to descend into a cave that is probably the most impressive *vagina dentata* in English literature. The cave is called 'the Cow's Mouth' – 'There were mouths of all kinds in India, from the Burning Mouth in the north to the Devil's Mouth . . . in the furthest southern corner of Madras' – and is situated in a 'city of the dead'. A ghastly laugh comes up from the cave, and 'the man of the West' slips and slides into it:

> All sight of what lay below him was blocked by the thick foliage of trees that leaned forward, bowing their heads together as night-watchers huddle over a corpse . . . Before he had realised it, he was out of reach of the sun, and neck deep in tall grass. Still there was a sort of pathway under his feet,

down the almost perpendicular side. He gripped the grass and went on. The earth beneath his elbows grew moist, and the rock where it cropped out showed rotten with moisture and coated with moss. The air grew cold and damp. Another plunge downward revealed to him what the trees were guarding, as he drew breath on a narrow stone ledge. They sprang from the masonry round the sides of a square tank of water so stagnant that it had corrupted past corruption, and lay dull blue under the blackness of the trees.

Tarvin tastes 'all the agonies of pure physical terror', but is led on, 'his revolver in his hand', by 'his racial instinct of curiosity'. The 'ground beneath him [is] strewn with bones', his heel crashes 'through a skull', but on and downwards he penetrates until he hears 'a howl that might have been bestial or human' and realises that something really terrible lies at the bottom of the 'the Cow's Mouth': 'It floated slowly across the tank, a long welt of filth and slime. Nothing came out of the hole between the fig-tree roots, but the mud-bank grounded under the ledge almost at Tarvin's feet, and opened horny eyelids, heavy with green slime.' The bottom of the cave is the hide-out of a 'sacred crocodile . . . waiting for his morning meal', and Tarvin only desperately, and without being able to explain how, escapes 'the darkness and the horror below'.

Here the fears and images of castration that were found in *The Light that Failed* (Dick's going blind after Maisie has turned him down, Bessie's destruction of his masterpiece) are elevated to a new and more intense level. The real danger to Tarvin's masculinity, however, is not represented by 'the Cow's Mouth' and 'this infernal land' – after all, he soon without many scruples gives up his quest for the Naulahka, making rubbish of the already weak plot – but by Kate and her attempts at independence. Luckily, the hopeless degeneration of the Orient soon brings Kate's civilising mission to a halt, as a 'holy man' persuades the patients to leave her hospital. Kate must recognise defeat and what it means to be a woman:

'It was a mistake,' she said.
'What?'
'Everything. My coming. My thinking I could do it. It's not a girl's work. It's my work, perhaps; but it's not for me. I have given it up, Nick. Take me home.'

In this manner Tarvin gets 'the crisis of his life' behind him.

Within the conceptual framework of *The Naulahka* womanhood presents a dualism: on the one side evil and destructive gipsy queens that must be fought off; on the other side white nurses, sister and mother figures that require male strength to protect them and keep them on the right path, but without the care of whom, on the other hand, 'the man of the West' is unable to keep up his good work of bringing railways to virgin spaces and controlling 'infernal lands'.

The happy ending has the effect of something superimposed, if not unexpected. It would have been most unconvincing for any heroine to be able to resist Tarvin and the narrator's joint endeavours to force her into submission. But the novel operates with such powerful antagonisms between masculinity and images of womanhood that a reconciliation seems out of this world. In this sense, the brutal, death-seeking solution to *The Light that Failed* appears more 'realistic' and appropriate.

Kipling's universe in both texts is one without peace, where the man is haunted by fears, depressions and phantasies of terrible punishment and revenge, and where meaning and order can only be established compulsively and through authoritarian measures – hard work, the laws of the male fraternity and ultimately war and death. Meaning is no longer inherent in life: it must be forced upon it in the form of the imperialist allegory, an ideological filter through which the world can be approached, but which also prevents access.

Is there no light at all, then, in Kipling's universe of male neurosis? Perhaps flashes of light can be seen in the passages of his work where he attempts to represent nature in its own right – in some of the *Jungle Book* stories for instance – or when he deals with children, i.e. with something in relation to which the laws and rules that govern the life of men and society do not make sense. The Maharajah's son in *The Naulahka* seems to stand for some utopian vision of an existence that is not torn apart by grown-up tensions. The protagonist of *Kim* (1901), who moves around as naturally and adroitly as an animal, shares the same quality. The most radical utopian vision, however, is found in Kipling's adoration of machines, of a form of order, regularity and discipline that is totally perfect.[14]

Kipling's utopia does not bring much dialectical tension into his world-view. It is a flat dream of a state of innocence and smooth functioning that lies beyond any social or historical influence. It is the other side of his pessimism. The influence of human beings and of society on the world is a corruption. His imperialism is a sort of cultural crisis-management directed against the most mischievous modern versions of this corruption.

No figure epitomises the impact of imperialism on British culture like Rudyard Kipling. And no writer was probably ever more the prisoner and victim of his period than he.

Notes

1 Imperialism was a theme in some of the contemporary discussion about Kipling, most famously in Robert Buchanan's 'The voice of the hooligan', *Contemporary Review*, LXXVI, Dec. 1899, pp. 774–89. Among more recent critcal works, cf. C. A. Bodelsen, *Kipling*, Copenhagen, 1964; in the English edition of Bodelsen's work on Kipling, *Aspects of Kipling's Art*, Manchester, 1964, however, imperialism is hardly mentioned; Eric Stokes, ' "The voice of the hooligan": Kipling and the Commonwealth experience', in N. McKendrick (ed.), *Historical Perspectives. Studies in English Thought and Society in honour of J. H. Plumb*, London, 1974; J. A. McClure, *Kipling and Conrad. The Colonial Fiction*, Cambridge, Mass., 1981; Alan Sandison, *The Wheel of Empire. A Study of the Imperial Idea in Some Late Nineteenth and Early Twentieth Century Fiction*, London, 1967; and Angus Wilson, *The Strange Ride of Rudyard Kipling. His Life and Works*, London, 1977. Kipling is placed in an interesting international perspective of imperialist fiction in Hugh Ridley, *Images of Imperial Rule*, London, 1983. Wilson's account of Kipling's imperialism as a 'right-wing radicalism' is quite good, cf. Angus Wilson, *op. cit.*, pp. 171ff.

2 Especially after 1940. Cf. the way in which during the Falklands War in 1982 ideological discourse would compare Galtieri to Hitler and justify the British war effort as the battle of 'democracy' against 'dictatorship'.

3 Cf. Charles Carrington, *Rudyard Kipling. His Life and Work*, 1955; Harmondsworth, 1970, Chapter 14 and Roger Lancelyn Green (ed.), *Kipling. The Critical Heritage*, London, 1971.

4 Cf. Jerome Hamilton Buckley, *William Ernest Henley, A Study in the 'Counter-Decadence' of the 'Nineties*, Princeton, 1945 and André Guillaume, *William Ernest Henley (1849–1903) et son groupe*, Lille, 1972. Henley's poetry praises imperialism and war as anti-decadent antidotes and is full of phallic and anti-feminist energy. Cf. 'The song of the sword' from 1892, which Henley dedicated to Kipling:

> Sifting the nations,
> The slag from the metal,
> The waste and the weak
> From the fit and the strong;
> Fighting the brute,
> The abysmal Fecundity; . . .
> Clear singing, clean slicing;
> Sweet spoken, soft finishing;

Making death beautiful . . .
Arch-anarch, chief builder,
Prince and evangelist,
I am the Will of God:
I am the Sword.

In his Boer War poetry (*For England's Sake, Verses and Songs in Time of War*, London, 1900) Henley becomes almost delirious as he paints a Britain that 'Goes fattening, mellowing, dozing, rotting down/Into a rich deliquium of decay', but which will now, thanks to the war, become 'Another than it was . . ./New-pithed, new-souled, new-visioned'.

5 Cf. Angus Wilson, *The Strange Ride of Rudyard Kipling. His Life and Works*, London, 1977, Chapter 3 and M. van Wyk Smith, *Drummer Hodge. The Poetry of the Anglo-Boer War 1899–1902*, Oxford, 1978, Chapter 4.

6 Cf. Charles Carrington, *Rudyard Kipling. His Life and Work*, 1955; Harmondsworth, 1970, p. 217. The book was also quite successful abroad, e.g. in France and in Denmark where it was championed by the prominent novelist and Kitchener-fan Johs, V. Jensen in his book on *Rudyard Kipling* (1912). Cf. Bodelsen, *Kipling*, Copenhagen, 1964, p. 87 and B. Haugaard Jeppesen, *Johannes V. Jensen og den hvide mands byrde. Eksotisme og imperialisme*, Copenhagen, 1984.

7 Not a few senior citizens in both Britain and the old colonies can still recite *Barrack-Room Ballads* by heart.

8 About the appeal of imperialist ideology to Edgar Wallace as a young 'Lumpen-proletar' in South London, cf. Margaret Lane, *Edgar Wallace. The Biography of a Phenomenon*, London, 1939.

9 Rhodes House, MSS Afr, s 228, C 28, 121.

10 Eric Stokes, ' "The voice of the hooligan": Kipling and the Commonwealth experience', in N. McKendrick (ed.), *Historical Perspectives. Studies in English Thought and Society in Honour of J. H. Plumb*, London, 1974, p. 293.

11 Klaus Theweleit, *Männerphantasien*, vol. I, *Frauen, Fluten, Körper, Geschichte*, Frankfurt am Main, 1977, chapter 1.

12 Charles Carrington, *Rudyard Kipling. His Life and Work*, 1955; Harmondsworth, 1970, p. 216.

13 Charles Carrington, *op. cit.*, p. 234.

14 Cf. C. A. Bodelsen's discussion of Kipling's poem 'McAndrew's hymn', *Kipling*, Copenhagen, 1964, pp. 106f.

14
Orwell revisited

BEATRIX CAMPBELL

It's an odd thought that Britain's best selling modern writer, and, according to recent polls, the most highly esteemed, was a socialist who was best known for his anti-socialism. Orwell articulates Left paranoia about the use of power and about popular discontent with the state, for still few on the Left can conceive of a socialism which isn't about state power. Thus Orwell utters a scepticism about the popularity of socialism which the Left itself cannot own to. In this decade of Thatcherism, of populism grounded in the commonsense of decency, domesticity and anti-democracy, Orwell has gained a new meaning.

What then does Orwell's present-day 'meaning' tell us about the state of England? He is popular because he is conservative, because he is a pessimist who doesn't much like women and who knows little about the working class. That fits with the spirit of our times. If there is anything that the Right and the Left share it is a pessimism about the people and their political proclivities. Perhaps Orwell is also popular because you don't have to have read him to know what he is on about. I spent a year or so living with *The Road to Wigan Pier*. I couldn't remember having read it when Virago publishers suggested that I make the return journey up the road. But I thought I must have. Throughout the journey I would ask if people had read *Wigan Pier* and most who said 'yes' also said 'but I can't remember when – it must have been at school'. (Only a few remembered what it said and most of them had the original Left Book Club edition on their shelves. Typically they remembered the first half of the book, the documentary account of his travel through the unemployed North, and ignored the second half – a rash rant about socialism. I imagine many of his re-visitors are going to enjoy the second half and forget the first.)

When I did get round to reading Orwell – and today you can't admit to not having read his work – it was a disturbing experience. That is mainly because he wasn't talking to me, the daughter of working-class parents in the North, though a journalist now; or to people like me. Although much of his work is about 'the masses', we, the masses, are the objects in his narrative. He is the subject. That's the case in *Wigan Pier* and again in *1984*. Some of the best material in *Wigan Pier* is his personal–political stream of consciousness about being an upper-class gent finding himself on the same side as the lower orders. It is a good record of his outrage, not of what life felt like for the working-class people he appears to describe. Yet part of Orwell's outrage is that he sees the working class as a class without a voice, without an idea, without resources. It's a class without consciousness; it's a degenerate class.

There might seem little in this view of the working class that a compassionate, upper-class Tory would not share; and indeed both Right and Left do share the myth, most clearly articulated in Orwell's critique of modern socialism, of the working class as both corrupt and unconscious. Raymond Williams, in his unsurpassed little book *Orwell*, traces the depiction of the working class in *Animal Farm* and *1984* as 'powerful but stupid' and an 'apathetic mass', people who 'have never learned to think'. Those expressions come from the pens of Orwell's apostles and from the mouth of every pious activist complaining that people don't come to meetings these days because they are too busy watching videos; that, unlike the middle class, they are corrupted by consumer goods.

Orwell's understanding of power – the actual theme of most of his works – depends on his view of the masses. And in *1984* our first meeting with the 'proles' demonstrates his view. Three men are standing reading a newspaper, two others are studying it over their shoulders. 'Winston could see absorption in every line of their bodies. It was obviously some serious bit of news they were reading.' But what was it? The lottery! The proles are a rabble of *Daily Star* readers and Rangers supporters (all men, of course).

If these men are socialist at all, their vision is merely of a 'society with the worst abuses left out'. Orwell warns us in *Wigan Pier* that socialism can't be reduced to economic justice and reform, but he never 'imagines' what a non-reductionist socialism would look like. He has a problem there because the interest groups which have challenged modern economic reductionism are precisely those for whom Orwell reserves his vintage vitriol: 'that dreary tribe of high-minded women and sandal-wearers and bearded fruit juice drinkers'.

In the end Orwell abandons socialist politics for a kind of southern suburban consensus in which many of his characters face a hopeless future because the only political processes that Orwell can imagine (outside war) can neither touch the exercise of power nor can they change 'consensus man' himself. This politics about what is good and valuable in life depends on nostalgia, in which the past is always better than the future. It is thus a politics of pessimism. Orwell's writing in fact, as Williams shows, creates 'the conditions for defeat and despair'.

It is odd that Orwell should see so little about how people can change, since he himself was transformed by his own contact with the oppressed. Yet there remains a gap between his feeling for the people and his thought about political action by the people. This is all the more ironic since in *Wigan Pier* and, later, in *The Lion and the Unicorn*, Orwell is prescient enough to put 'everyday life' on to the political agenda and to demand a cultural revolution. He does not see how, if changing everyday life and pursuing a cultural revolution do become prime political objectives, this in itself will expand the parameters of politics in ways that will necessarily disturb the eternal verities of his common sense.

For what, in his common sense, would Orwell have made of the Greenham Common women, the kind he loved to hate, who have maintained a majority against nuclear missiles despite the state machine, the blunders of the Labour Party at the last election and the 'normal' lapse into apathy of the masses? It took all those bearded and bright ecologists to alert the nation to the pollution of the planet – when Orwell just thought, like much of the macho Left, that such types were naive and silly.

As for women generally, Orwell either sees them as disturbing sexual magnets with whom pleasure promises peace but produces punishment; or they are crazy woolly, ugly old crackpots whose radicalism takes them to the edge of society. He must, of course, reject feminism, for in his time too it offered a critique of all those 'decent' suburban values he holds dear. Feminism is Orwell's Achilles' heel, and he pays dearly for it. For he is left without those ingredients which do transform limited economic objectives into radical aspirations precisely for the reasons that he has rejected them (they are nakedly emotional and vulgarly unsophisticated). What Orwell offers instead is a radical repossession of key words in consensus politics – patriotism, decency and justice.

In Orwell's future, there is no opposition that succeeds, there is only surrender. After all, Winston Smith embraces his own defeat. His 'completion' as a character comes with his embrace of Big Brother. His self-hatred has no resolution in the present, nor in politics or in protest; it only finds peace in the past.

Throughout his work, Orwell mobilises nostalgia for an

Edwardian England when a pint was a full pint and vehicles went on four legs and domestic life was decent. It's a forgetful kind of memory which is constantly recruited to serve conservatism. Childhood memories are falsified memories which bury the pain of the past, but they make up so much of the substance of Orwell's critique, his bad temper about the present and his panic about the future.

In *1984* and in *Wigan Pier*, Orwell's polemic is less about history than about accommodating flight from modern life. We find it again in *Coming Up for Air*. It's a commonplace and popular theme in English culture; Englishness is the rustic village where every season is summer, everybody's mum makes jam, everybody's dad does the pools and neighbours look after the old folks. Typically, both Right and Left are susceptible to this myth. The Right draws on Victorian truths and the Left on a do-it-yourself ideology of community and craft. Not surprisingly, Orwell's commonsense Englishness finds force with both. But the trouble I have with these traditions is that they are conservative and that they lie about the condition of most people then – an exhausted, insanitary and subordinate condition – by turning it into a romantic myth.

What's in that way of life for a woman like me? What was ever in it for working-class women? Come to think of it, there wasn't much to it for working-class men either. Modern life may feature all those things Orwell doesn't like – electronics, state surveillance, mass media, birth control. But it is also about greater mass participation in politics than ever before. Women of my age and class – mid-thirties – have skills to sell, sexual pleasure to seek and satisfy and a vote. As like as not we have a trade union card as well, children, our own name on the rent book. We haven't had that before, not all at the same time. That's a function of politics of course. It's also an expression of a new form of resolution of the historic settlement between men and women. It is less and less at women's expense while more and more it demands not only the transformation of the female condition but of the masculine way of life too.

Just as Orwell's future ascribes an unchanged role to the sexes, so it is for the different classes. He imagines a prole class forever sad and subordinate, doomed to drink and gambling, gossip and superstition. The working class is, of course, in the image of its men, its apparently degenerate sex. In Orwell, the future is always worse, and always brings the consummation of coercive power. And his new vocabulary of absolute state power is his great contribution to the torture. There is in Orwell's projection no future for democracy, for all his artful celebrations of our democratic way of life. In foreseeing the future of power he only saw negative force, not power mediated or modified by a countervailing popular force. In foreseeing the future, he didn't see us.

Orwell's appeal to decency represents an appeal to a culture which has women at its centre; the rendering of women, in fact, as polite and private and poor. Undoubtedly the culture of respectability and decency is affirmed in Orwell not so much because it belongs to the working class, but to the middle class which, in the end, is his hope for the future.

And what does the appeal to patriotism mean to a woman, to a feminist? The most recent echoes of mass patriotism occurred during the Falklands war when the position of women in relation to that war appeared at its most contradictory. We had on the one hand the warrior Margaret Thatcher wishing she'd been flying those bombers, and on the other hand a war conducted between men. Women, it seemed were cast in their proper position, prone - waiting and weeping for their loved ones sent off to war. Thinking about patriotism in the context of Orwell is more problematic though, because his thesis depends upon the representation of England as a nation hegemonised by a sense of a shared, essentially domestic, culture defined by the family. Nation and family are one in Orwell. White and English. What does that mean to the black families, all those citizens of the Commonwealth family who can't get in? I think of myself certainly as white, but I never think of myself as English. Not because I'm against the idea, just because it's not a word I'd use to describe myself. Why not? My father is English, so aren't I? My father's family were from the isolated fells of Cumbria, they'd been shepherds in the Scottish lowlands, rural artisans around the Cumbrian coalfield, women who'd gone into service for the local gentry, illiterate Irish peasantry and Scottish orphans. My father ran away to the second 'Great War' of the world against Fascism, or was it against the Germans? And once the war was over, his allies became our enemies. There were no heroes' homes or jobs for him. That war and the peaceful reconstruction should have been the last great testament to something patriotic in England, but who remembers whose side we were on. And whose side is England on now? My mother came from Holland, where her people were devout Christians; descended from the itinerant Huguenots, they were tailors. My parents met when my father's regiment liberated my mother's village. Some of her family were in the Resistance, some were sent off to camps in Germany. They had to walk home when the war ended. Are their jailors on our side now? When my brother and sister and I were little, my mother started her job in the local psychiatric 'asylum', caring for – in every sense of those words – the senile old mothers of the town, and she remembers hearing whispered protests in our street about foreigners taking 'our' jobs.

Now, I'm the only person in my family with a full-time job.

A propos patriotism, what do I make with all this family history? It doesn't make me a patriot. How could it? Even with a leap of my communist or feminist imagination, where is patriotism's place? If this picture seems confused, that's because it is. I understand notions of democracy, collectivism, equality, but I don't understand what patriotism can mean to me, my class or my sex. I don't want not to be English, but neither do I want to be English. I don't like England very much. Why should I? I was only born here. All my allegiances oppose what England means in the world. I want us to stop being that kind of England. And here there is an interesting problem for revolutionaries. We who are white western revolutionaries carry our own international mission – that's the strength of it, its internationalism. But inscribed into that mission is an image of ourselves, us white westerners, as the missionaries.

But our black sisters and brothers have had enough of missionaries.

And so, I think, have I.

15

George Smiley and post-imperial nostalgia

GEOFFREY HEMPSTED

When John Le Carré has a book published the reviewers stampede to be quoted in the blurbs. The competition is stiff. 'At least a masterpiece.' 'One of the most interesting writers alive.' The post-imperialist condition is a grave matter, 'a sombre and tragic theme', and Le Carré has been numbered off as having the qualities to do it justice – 'romantic and despairing', 'ironic, mournful and introspective'. The BBC gave two of the books 'classic serial' treatment: *Tinker, Tailor, Soldier, Spy*, a sort of Philby/Hollis story (who is the mole in the SIS?): and *Smiley's People*, about a cunning plot to force a Russian spymaster to defect. The *Radio Times* cover, 'Alec Guinness is George Smiley', was deeply reassuring – Guinness is good for you, and Smiley is fresh from *Star Wars*. The viewer could sit back and enjoy the style, forget about the politics, write funny letters to the *Guardian* about the impenetrable plot, and let George work it out.

No wonder we need George Smiley. Le Carré reminds us that great Britain has lost its Empire, and is a founder member of the club of second-class nations. Worse, its most secret servants have been for fifty years moling away at the foundations, blindly enslaved by what Andrew Boyle (*The Climate of Treason*) has called the 'inhuman philosophy' of Karl Marx. Smiley is of the old school and, even though he thinks too much, he plays the game through to the end. We need him to sort out friend from enemy in a world where it is increasingly hard to tell them apart, where 'half angels fight half devils'. We may well have failed to follow the plot, because the power struggles behind the scenes are beyond us these days, but George has understood everything and in the last episode the mole is smoked out, or Karla is in the hands of skilled interrogators. George is congratulated – by his senior prefect Guillam (irreproachable tweeds), by the foreign but endearing Esterhaze (one of us, so we will forgive the fur hat), and by Strickland, wearing 'the awful green suit, the shoes of brushed pigskin got up as suede leather'. We know Karla is evil because he is Russian, and we have seen the well-tortured corpse of his victim Otto in episode four. His henchmen sweat a good deal and, the text would confirm, exhibit their 'incurable mediocrity' in their dedication to 'the new but ill-chosen striped suit'.

We can leave the philosophy to Smiley, who knows that 'political generality is meaningless'. The signs of tailoring and body-odour will tell us that there are goodies and baddies. George is above these coarse discriminations ('his tailor robs him') but he would agree with the underlying proposition, that the style proclaims the man. When he reads the confessional creed of the traitor Heydon in *Tinker, Tailor* we are told 'With much of it Smiley might in other circumstances have agreed; it was the tone, rather than the music, which alienated him'. Yes, it is a pity about Strickland's Hush Puppies.

That the style is the man is important, because the books invite the reader to join particularly male freemasonries. Smiley's acolytes speak in a Kiplingesque public-school code in which only outsiders would be so gross as actually to name things. Here is a passage from *The Honourable Schoolboy*, hailed in *The Times* by Michael Ratcliffe as 'simply one of the finest English novels of the seventies'. Jerry Westerby is summoned to the Circus (the secret service offices in Cambridge Circus) after long absence.

> As he approached the gabled and familiar turrets – the moment never failed him – a sort of muddled saintliness came over him: 'this is what service is all about' . . .
> 'Gosh, super, George, hello.'
> 'And don't ask him about his wife,' Guillam warned . . .
> Father and son? That kind of relationship? Brawn to brain? More exact, perhaps, would be a son to his adopted father, which in the trade is to be held the strongest tie of all.
> 'Sport,' Jerry muttered, and gave a husky laugh.
> English friends have no real way of greeting each other . . .
> For a fraction of a second Jerry laid his cricketer's fist alongside Smiley's soft, hesitant palm, then lumbered after him at a distance to the fireside, where two armchairs awaited them: old leather, cracked, and much sat in. Once again, in this erratic season, a fire burned in the Victorian grate, but very small by comparison with the fire in the rumpus room.

The readers of *The Times* book page have not been misled. This kind of stuff has kept generations of Englishmen happy. They know that in 'the trade' actual generative fatherhood is not allowed. (More of this later.) The Le Carré fan dates an event by the cancellation of the Sarratt cricket match, and knows Ann Smiley, for what she is when she calls her more serviceable lovers her first eleven. The cracked leather armchair and the Victorian grate are preferred to CIA high tech. We are amateurs at heart. The Circus, with its turrets, is the old school, and this is the housemaster's study. We call the operations room 'the rumpus room' because we are part of an inner group. Remember the private language? Reptile fund, bearleaders, honeytraps, goldseam and the rest? Like thieves' cant this talk is designed to confuse the overhearer, but more, by developing arcane practices, Le Carré gives the impression that there is something of substance to conceal and protect. It is too fascinating to be empty ritual. Surely, 'this is what service is all about'.

In *The Honourable Schoolboy* Le Carré skilfully burlesques Kipling in the talk of the journalist-spy Craw and his drinking companions, who engage in 'a tireless pursuit of legends about one another', covering feeling in a language of manic pastiche. They spend a lot of time playing a game they call 'Shanghai bowling', which involves throwing a napkin at a wine rack. These rites of game and myth-making are instructive. The Smiley books are frequently validated by the suggestion that the stories they tell have already become legend, the folklore of the initiated. 'George went five times round the moon to our one'. On the other hand this is made to sound spurious, rather as the convoluted conversations of the drinking brotherhood suggest a desire not to grow up. But the reader is still encouraged to feel that the myth-making celebrates values (generally unnamed), which are sadly lacking in a world where 'everything is grey'. Shanghai bowling shares with Smiley's way of espionage, the way Kipling called The Great Game, a fine attention to rules, to tone rather than music. At the margins of power, it is the more necessary to maintain the forms. By ritualising the idea of service it is possible to suspend the question 'In the service of what?'

Le Carré is careful to hold at arm's length familiar sentiments of 'there was an England once', for example as they are spoken by Connie Sachs, the crippled and discarded Moscow-watcher who is of Smiley's inner circle. Her manner incorporates infantilism, jingo, and self-parody, with a witty echo of Philby. 'It was a good time, do you hear! A real time. Englishmen could be proud then . . . poor loves, poor loves. Trained to Empire. trained to rule the waves. All gone. All taken away. Bye-bye world'. Smiley, the weary relativist, 'longed to be free of her'. This slightly shifty ambivalence is pervasive. First, we get the bleak record of decline. Hong Kong is a fit setting for imperialist afterthought – the lease-hold version. London is Graham Greene territory, in a formula put together by a *Daily Mail* leader writer to break into literature. At an inner-city school 'on the other side of the wire boys stood in silent groups, like pickets at a factory gate, blacks and whites separated'. Westerby sees Hong Kong as 'the empty city waiting like a carcass for the hordes. For a moment it was all one vanishing world – here, Phnom Penh, Saigon, London, a world on loan, with the creditors standing at the door, and Jerry himself, in some unfashionable way, a part of the debt that was owed'. If the Chinese will have Hong Kong, it is not quite clear who the hordes will be in London's case. It is unclear whether Le Carré wishes to disown or exploit the schmaltz and mystification. Jerry is moved at this point to question Smiley's priestlike affirmation of the ideal of service ('I've always been grateful to the service that it gave me a chance to pay'), but the message survives. Our world is falling apart. Let us at least act without self-interest. The inevitability of our defeat is a virtue. Westerby is, 'in some unfathomable way, part of the debt that is owed' because his redundancy must be reconstructed as sacrifice. We are not like the Americans, on the make, and we do not, like them, speak our faith in the marketplace of politics ('Ask not what your country can do for you . . .') At least when George speaks of 'a chance to pay' he does not say 'pay whom' or 'for what'. That too is unfathomable. Forget the music. The tone distinguishes us.

   This mystification of 'service' is not new, and nor is the contra-diction which demands it. It is the contradiction Conrad identified in *Heart of Darkness*, when Marlow, urged to wean the African millions from their ignorant ways, 'ventured to suggest that the enterprise [of empire] was run for profit'. In his turn Kipling seeks to show a disinterested face of imperialism. At the heart of his sodality of service. in *Kim*, he locates those who play the Great Game in brotherhood where there is no oppressor or oppressed, only the common interest of keeping the Russians out of the north. Instructively, he recorded in his autobiography *Something of Myself* that he could find interracial intimacy only in his masonic lodge – all the boys together. Le Carré, at the later stage, has a less profit-able enterprise on his hands, and, perhaps, less to be embarrassed about. The schoolchildren stand like pickets at the factory gate. The firm is 'begging for a place at the top table' or, in *A Small Town in Germany*, at the EEC trough. The Great Game is increas-ingly like Shanghai bowling, and it is important to keep the rules intact. As Craw says, 'don't change anything. You won't stop the wheel . . . you're a bunch of suicidal tits to try.'

Has Le Carré, then, diagnosed a collective sickness, a delusion that leads us to behave as though we still had a role to play? May we seek a fuller account of this post-imperial neurosis in his construction of George Smiley? If the reviewers have been right, if we are treated to a serious ('sombre and tragic', 'mournful and introspective') vision of disorder, we may be comforted to find that the plots still unravel in the end and Smiley is still a sort of great detective. Better, he is the focus of a historical condition, and the equipment by which we know him is not merely decorative, like Sherlock Holmes's pipe and deerstalker, or Poirot's moustache. It includes all this: a scholarly and priestlike propensity: a sense of going backwards; a preoccupation with death; an implied incapacity to father children; and a wife who has sexual relations with lots of men but uncertainly with George.

In *Smiley's People* we find him 'toiling obliviously, with whatever conviction he could muster . . . in the Parnassian fields of German baroque poetry . . . trying loyally to distinguish true passion from the tiresome literary conventions of the period'. The mustering of conviction often gives him trouble, but this is codebreaking of a kind, so George is plainly keeping his hand in. His scholarship takes him backwards to a Europe undefiled by the horrors of modern history. In *A Small Town in Germany*, Le Carré, in knockabout mood, shows the dreamy disenfranchisement of the British ruling class in the new Europe. The more sensitive of them withdraw into a fey inactivity. 'Bonn is a very *metaphysical* spot. We live somewhere between the recent future and the not-so-recent past.' Smiley is an advanced case of this malaise. He gets attacks of *déjà vu* when brought out of retirement. Here he is (*Tinker, Tailor*) in Lacon's – you guessed it – rose garden. 'Perhaps I never left this place, he thought . . . perhaps we're still here from last time.' He seems to find himself in a kind of ante-room from which he will emerge, as a seeker-after-truth, into the real world of power and betrayal. Then he pursues his quest as a nightscholar, alone among dog-eared files, and here his case passes from the chronic to the acute. 'As Smiley retraced path after path into his own past, there was no longer any difference between the two: forwards or backwards, it was the same journey, and its destination lay ahead of him.' He is at it again in *Smiley's People*, reading all night and wondering if he's Karla. The quest is set as at the moment before death, but he is roused from torpor by the sensation (authenticated by cricketing metaphor) that he has 'a chance to return to the rained off contests of his life'. Success leaves him 'subdued' and 'glum'.

Ostensibly the stories are grounded in a realist tradition; east is east and west is west and so forth. But frequently that kind of specific historical reference is dissolved in favour of a mystifying and ideal treatment of Smiley as dying sage and seeker, with its vague and suitably religious resonance. 'He had the delusion that he kept visiting the same high place over and over again . . . a single proving ground for virtues not yet stated.' Westerby was right. There is something of the failed priest in old George. Playing the Great Game, he is more the Lama than he is Kim.

These motifs combine to produce (and to camouflage) a familiar reactionary appeal. Le Carré is careful to protect his credentials as the liberal analyst of corrupt imperialism, of the caste-ridden impotence of the British, of the CIA's gun-barrel ethics. He does not absolve Smiley from the collective guilt of his trade; 'these people terrify me, but I am one of them'. He canvasses a blunt thesis of historical determinism. Smiley cannot imagine himself as Karla because his childhood 'has not been fired in the same kiln of revolutionary upheaval', and he is fascinated by 'the sheer scale of Russian suffering, its careless savagery, its flights of heroism'. (In what sense 'careless'?) But through all this the conventions of thriller and spy story come unscathed. It is hard to see in Le Carré's typologising of the 'enemy', with his 'incurable mediocrity', any sophisticated advance on Ian Fleming's. There is not a lot going for humanism behind the Iron Curtain. If 'half angels fight half devils' they remain fractions in a recoverable equation. The fancy writing about Smiley as scholar-priest, if taken seriously, enables loss of empire to be recuperated in the blurbs as a 'sombre and tragic theme'. 'The chance to serve' can still echo 'white man's burden'. George, limbering up in his philosophical gymnasium, lends dignity to the stale posturings of the Cold War.

By an odd displacement, Smiley's status as cuckold-celibate functions as a further qualification for him to read the burial-service for imperialism. We should note to begin with a disturbing incidence of impotence or woman-trouble among officials of the British foreign service. In *A Small Town in Germany* we find the apologetic Crabbe ('Can't make it old boy. Not for years'), and Turner, the SIS hard man who confuses his sense of being betrayed by allies and colleagues with memories of his wife's infidelity. In *Tinker, Taior* Guillam falls for a music student (does she, we ask ourselves, care for the music but not the tone?) who turns out to be sleeping with, perhaps married to, her tutor who is called Sand. (Karla is codenamed the Sandman.) The experience focuses

Guillam's tendency, learned from Smiley, to see all life in terms of conspiracy. 'Whole vistas of deceit opened before him. His friends, his loves, even the Circus itself, joined and rejoined in endless patterns of intrigue.' In *Smiley's People* the adulteress Elvira is undoubtedly a daughter of Eve. 'In motion, she was insinuating, with fluid haunches and a sullen hint of challenge.' *The Little Drummer Girl* is valued as a recruit for her beliefs, 'the more confused they are, the more irrational, the more *frustrated*,' and is reliably motivated only by sexual desire.

Le Carré strikes a rich vein, and a raw nerve, by equipping Smiley with a wife whose sex life is indiscriminate and 'insecure'. She is niftily patrician, cousin to cabinet ministers and to the arch-mole Haydon, whom she takes as a lover. The literary type to which Smiley contributes is scattered. Its catalogue would have to include Ford Maddox Ford's Tietjens, last of the Tories, selfless public servant, and cuckold; Castle, in Greene's *The Human Factor*, sterile, but pretending to the fatherhood of his wife's child; and Thackeray's Esmond, the epitome of service, Tory become Whig, woman-betrayed (he marries his adoptive mother, who gives birth to daughters).

Consider some equations. How do you write the history of imperialism as something other than exploitation? You construct it not as 'an enterprise run for profit' but as 'a chance to serve'. You wash your hands of the profit, and, bold-faced, devise codes of reward and privilege which proclaim your disinterestedness. The British Raj, accordingly, spent generations perfecting tribal snobberies to cover its origins in trade. In the ideology of high imperialism, as 'white men's burden' memories, racialism, patriarchy and the concept of service are inseparable. White carries the burden of black, and for black. 'Service' is ritualised in institutions of male sodality, only ambiguously superstructural (school, army, foreign service, government service), and the truth, that blacks carry burdens for white profit, can be invisibly inscribed in sexual double standards. The production of profit requires that 'black' remains commodity labour, the other, one of 'the lesser breeds beyond the law'. Maternity cannot be denied, and the white woman in this equation must only bear white children. The white man may carry the burden, but he draws the line at having a commodity in the family. The woman's sexuality imperils the order.

What then of Smiley's marriage? To symbolise disinterestedness and closure, there will be no dynasty. George, fittingly for 'an old man at a country railway station', is at the end of the line. In our post-imperial phase, America and international capitalism are getting the profits, and we are left with the ritual, the remembering faith. As Craw says, 'Never despise it. We've precious little else to offer these days.' And since we have lost access to the wealth we never admitted enjoying anyway, we are freer to indulge a sense that the old values are being lost, that it is 'all one vanishing world'. The enemy is all around us, at the gates, and the Le Carré reader, taught by Kipling tricks to be one of the initiated, knows he can only trust the man who speaks the password. But there is worse to come. The enemy is standing at our very shoulder. When Connie Sachs bemoans the loss of 'our time', the time when Englishmen could be proud, she says 'You're the last of them George. You and Bill.' George Smiley does not tell her that Bill, who sleeps with George's wife, not only knows the password but betrays it to the enemy. In the spy story the traitor is 'the other' of a faded imperialism.

Le Carré has Smiley journey into the past to find the source of this corruption. First you cleanse the stable, then you close ranks and wait for the end. The fable you construct to celebrate this moment does not require women, because there will be no succession and the masonic rites have always been best kept by men. As the reviewers have recognised, at this late stage of our imperial history Le Carré has a lot to offer, especially to those readers who cling to the imperialist neurosis. Generations of them have learned to fear the woman as the betrayer, who by her indiscriminate and self-pleasuring sexuality would admit to their company a child who is dubiously their own. The cuckoo in the nest. The enemy within the gates indeed.

Theatre

16
Inverted emblems for Albion: Wellington and Napoleon on stage

LOUIS JAMES

Looking for the emblems of patriotism in the nineteenth century, one can find few more vivid sources than melodrama and music hall. Nowhere were the patriotic songs more plangent, the Union Jacks waved more vigorously, the Jack Tars and Standfasts more valiant for Britannia. But on closer look, this fervour has undercurrents, the icons are less simple than they appear. For the purpose of this short paper I will consider in particular two plays staged by theatres associated specifically with patriotic sentiments: Sadler's Wells, which Dibdin made into the first home of nautical drama and the paragon of British valour, the sailor; and Astley's Amphitheatre, run by the ex-soldier Philip Astley to display the greatness of British military prowess. To sharpen the focus I have taken the plays from the period immediately following the Napoleonic wars, when Britain could be expected to be celebrating its triumph over Bonaparte and his armies.

It is useful to preface this with some remarks on theatrical conventions of the period – conventions we may usefully, if somewhat loosely, associate with 'melodrama'. Melodrama, Wylie Sypher has asserted,[1] is the 'Marxist aesthetic'. Presenting in naked terms the dialectic between social and moral forces, the form put in theatrical terms the infrastructure of the socialist vision. Recently Franco Moretti has extended this to the themes of melodrama,[2] showing how the monsters of the Gothic quest not only reflect the polarisation of class conflict – a point made as early as 1848 by Mrs Gaskell[3] – but the psychic energies mobilised by this schism. Approaching the subject from a different angle, George Levine[4] has argued that Frankenstein's monster is more 'real' than the characters of the 'realistic' novel, for it embodies the inner crisis

of nineteenth-century society more directly than naturalistic presentation can do. Melodrama was instinctively expressed in terms
of social consciousness, from the opposition between the seductive
upper-class villain and the 'poor but honest' heroine, to the figures
of Gothic fantasy; Frankenstein on the stage immediately became
an aristocrat,[5] and as for Vampires, working-class Ruthven,
Varney or Dracula would be unthinkable.

Yet, one could argue, the genre undermines its own framework.
The presentation of dialectic is compromised by the simplistic
closure of the triumph of 'good'; the energies of confrontation are
dissipated in the sentimental emotion of the happy ending. In terms
of our subject here, the patriotic sentiments of melodrama lend
themselves too readily to jingoism. If melodrama celebrates the
courage of the common seaman and soldier, this embodiment is
simplistic, emotive, and lacking in critical insight. How should we
approach the genre? I would suggest both points of view can be
true. Melodrama is clearcut with the directness of parable. Yet, as
Brecht knew well, the clarity of parable can be the context for
complexity, both the 'given' and the starting point for revaluation
of conventional truths.

The first play I wish to examine is *Napoleon; or the Emperor and
the Soldier* by John Walker, first performed at Sadler's Wells theatre
on 15 December 1828. Walker will be known to socialist historians
of the theatre as the author of the finest surviving industrial play
of the English Victorian theatre, *The Factory Lad* (1832). Written
within the conventions of melodrama, complete with villainous
mill-owner and virtuous, downtrodden workers, the play nevertheless achieves an extraordinary strength of both theme and
expression. In particular the workers, thrown out of employment
with the coming of mechanisation, are economically presented as
human and unsentimentalised, and the violence that leads to riot
and factory-burning, incited by the half-crazed poacher Rushton,
opens up, if it does not solve, the implications of insurrection. The
play ends with Rushton shooting the corrupt magistrate, Bias, and
the curtain comes down to his wild, defiant laughter. Although
the achievement of the play has been recognised for some time, it
has been assumed that Walker wrote nothing else of interest, and
his *Napoleon* is a minor discovery.

Napoleon is recognisably less mature than *The Factory Lad*, yet
it possesses the same ability to orchestrate melodramatic conventions in a complex way. The play opens with a pastoral scene,
cottage, running stream with bridge, cornfields and a village in
perspective. A young man Guillaume appears in the window of
one cottage with a guitar and speaks of his love Mary and dancing

on the green all night; his sweetheart emerges in the cottage opposite; there is a song, and comic business between the respective fathers of the two lovers, Pendulum and Bonneau. It is only towards the end of the scene that the audience begins to realise that the scene is set in France during the Napoleonic wars, the English Pendulum having been made a French prisoner of war, and settling down in his adopted country. When Pendulum wishes to visit 'Happy England . . . the soil that gave me birth', he remembers a 'delightful spot – in the parish of Clerkenwell, near the House of Correction'. There was 'a churchyard in the front, a carpenters shop at the back, Bridewell on the left, the workhouse on the right, with the liberty of walking into either if you pleased. Ah, there's nothing like old England after all! That's the place for liberty.' Where in England the poor are ground down, in post-revolutionary France even the labourers have food to eat. 'Not much trouble in providing – provisions here are as plentiful as blackberries are in England', says Pendulum, 'we sow and grow what we eat'.[6]

Having established one position, Walker confronts it with another. The scene moves from the idyllic countryside into the gloom of a wood, where Regniere moves in terror. It is still France, but Regniere, an old soldier, is starving, and turns to robbery to give his wife and child food. He exits to be followed by no-one less than Napoleon, concealed in his military cloak. Regniere the impoverished ex-soldier is succeeded by the general who directed the war, and Walker emphasises the point: 'some men like to be, and some men must be, like it or not, the stepping-stone to another's fortune', declares Napoleon. In a short-hand impossible in naturalistic drama, Walker has presented three issues: a country freed from class tyranny; a victim of revolutionary war; and, opposed to him, the ambivalent figure of reestablished order. Napoleon muses that society is ordered by destiny, but when Regniere appears with a pistol and demands money, we see that fate involves choice. Napoleon wrests the pistol from Regniere but refuses retaliation, instead helping him escape justice, taking with him his watch. He recognises that in taking a decision, even to rob, Regniere, like Napoleon himself, is refusing to accept the *status quo*.

At this point Bonneau puts the alternate case. He, too is poor, but he has found happiness in acceptance. 'There is a providence above who tells us in our afflictions not to repine, but to bear with content our lot here.' Napoleon is wrong to accept necessity as the basis for action. 'If the baneful laws of necessity were true, vice and virtue, justice and injustice, have no meaning, and good and

evil are the same.' And, as proof of his point that poverty with
acceptance brings happiness, Bonneau invites Napoleon to the
simple wedding celebrations of Mary and Guillaume. The scene
shifts back to the idyllic cottage, and the country celebrations. But
not only does Regniere steal the scanty provisions; at the high
point of the wedding dance Baton and recruiting officers move in
to take the bridegroom away for active service. The whole group
follow in the hope of reclaiming him, Napoleon, not unkindly,
reminding Bonneau of his professed acceptance of suffering.
'Remember your own words – "not to repine in our afflictions,
but bear with content our present evils".'[7]

The final scene reflects the darkening mood of the play. It shows
Regniere's hut, partly destroyed by fire, a child covered by straw
and wife and daughter anxiously awaiting the return of the father.
Thunder rolls in the distance, presaging a storm. Regniere returns
with food just in time to save his child, but no sooner are the
couple expressing their joy than the door is beaten in by the soldiers
accompanied by Pendulum, Guillaume, Bonneau and Napoleon,
seeking refuge from the storm. Regniere is recognised as a robber,
and is about to be seized when Napoleon interposes. Unabashed,
Regniere launches a comprehensive attack on the Emperor. 'Is not
his ambition as insatiate as a miser's avarice? Has he not for years
deluged the world with bloodshed?' Napoleon insists on him
having his say, and declares 'I like the lofty spirit that dares to
speak the truth.' Napoleon releases Regniere, and returns Bonneau
and his son to their village.[8]

In the end then, the potential tragedy is resolved by a melodramatic *deus ex machina*. But by making this benevolent force Napoleon, Walker has not left the matter simple. Napoleon is the instigator of the social action that creates the injustice suffered by
Regniere; at the same time he embodies the humanity that can
resolve injustice at a personal level. As he recognises, in certain
ways he is the *alter ego* to Regniere; both instigate action against
circumstances, and action may hold ambivalent consequences.
Both are in oppostion to the Englishman Pendulum, whose name
suggests easy accommodation. If he escapes bigoted patriotism,
his easy swing to another country's way of life points to the
weakness challenged by Napoleon. When Pendulum tries to kneel
to him, Napoleon tells him 'rise and imitate [Regniere]'. At this
point it is hard not to hear Walker addressing his countrymen in
the years immediately prior to the Reform Act agitation. Above
all, in Napoleon, Walker presents a head of state who can both
create order and intervene with humanity and justice, a figure of
particular importance to England in the last years of the Regency.

Napoleon indeed offered an inverted image of patriotism to a range of English opinion. On one hand the popular ballad 'The grand conversation on Napoleon arose' celebrated his democratic generosity:

> Ah! England, he cried, did you persecute that hero bold,
> Much better had you slain him on the field of Waterloo,
>
> Napoleon he was friend to heroes both young and old,
> He caused the money to fly wherever he did go.[9]

On the other hand he offered an image of royalty and power portrayed in the anonymous *Napoleon Buonaparte: General, Consul and Emperor* (c. 1822).[10] Here there is a plot on Napoleon's life, at first reminiscent of Shakespeare's *Julius Caesar*. But the conspirators are shadowed by Napoleon himself, who appears a cloaked figure to save the brave St Victor who opposed them, and the play ends with a chorus surprising to be published in an England who a few years previously had been facing Napoleon across the channel:

> Kneel to Napoleon the Great,
> Our Preserver, sent hither by fate
>   Long live the might Napoleon;
> Let the trumpet's shrill sound
> Make the heavens resound,
>   While we kneel to the might Napoleon.[11]

Walker's *Napoleon*, if performed at Sadler's Wells, was not a typical play: we may turn therefore to J. H. Amherst's *The Battle of Waterloo*, probably the most enduringly popular play performed at that central Victorian institution, Astley's Amphitheatre. First performed in 1824, it was being revived into the second half of the century, when, it was reported, the shortage of horses led to Napoleon and Wellington sharing the same charger, prompting the player acting Napoleon to improvise to his troops 'you have rescued from the the hated thraldom of the bloodthirsty British soldiery my favourite charger'[12] Much of the initial effect, however, came from the dramatic creation, in three acts, of the battle itself, with a huge equestrian cast and a careful representation of the scenes as they first occurred. The play opens with the tragic figure of the Prussian Phedora, who speaks for wartorn Europe. All but one of her sons have been murdered, and her daughters raped, by Napoleon's troops at Jena. 'You know – you must have heard! – myself and husband bound together, were compelled to *see* these fiendish deeds. Bredowski, my husband wept, but I became a statue, and my heart was turned to stone; I shed not a drop of

moisture; I shall never weep again'.[13] Now she follows the war
with her remaining son, bent on claiming whatever revenge she
can. Yet this scene is followed by a scene in which Napoleon
reviews his troops before the battle, making a speech about patriotism and national liberty without evident irony. Later he learns
the lie of the land by befriending Jean, a peasant – sharing with
him his snuff box – and, when Jean expresses fear of the French
troops if they win, reassures him 'it is never the policy of a good
general to destroy needlessly'.[14] If this may be seen as a devious
manipulation of the peasantry, there is a long scene between Napoleon and Jean, as the battle moves into its final phase, in which
they discuss the respective lots of national leader and peasant. Jean
expressed his horror of the responsibilty for others' deaths. 'I
would rather play at blind buff with my little boys and girls, than
strew all Waterloo with dead bodies.' When Napoleon begins to
explain the role of a leader, Jean says, *with simplicity and affection*,
'I humbly hope I have not hurt your heart.' The conversation ends
with Napoleon expressing his concern for Jean's crops in the battle,
giving him gold Napoleon coins, and a personal ring to ensure his
safe conduct in the battle. In his dealing with the captured British
officer Standfast, Napoleon likewise shows respect and honour.

This curious piece of melodrama, interposed in the ferocity of
Astley's military exercises, is all the more pointed when compared
with the presentation of Wellington, who only comes on the scene
when Napoleon has established his and the French army's stature.
Where Napoleon presents his troops with the issues behind the
battle – France's liberty, the sufferings he and his men have shared
together – Wellington's address is positively curt.

> Gentlemen, the world has fixed its eyes upon us, England
> expects much; no-one is here, I trust, who would not rather
> die than disappoint his country's hope. I have just received
> advices that must *march us on to Ligny*. Be our password –
> England's king, and England's honour. March![15]

Later, at Quatre Bras, he makes a longer speech, revealing his
efficiency, and even a note of concern for the wounded, though
this is immediately related, not to compassion, but to duty: 'Are
the best arrangements made for the wounded that circumstances
will permit? Right, for that is a duty never to be neglected.'[16]
Napoleon's long conversation with Jean about the relative sufferings of leader and governed is set against the scene at 'Duke of
Wellington's tree',[17] where Wellington wilfully exposes himself to
the French fire while their bullets chip away the tree beside him.
This block-headed bravura – 'Good practice, gentlemen, I think

they fire better in Spain' – has tragic consequences when Sir Alexander Gordon begs him to 'be more careful of our person' and is
immediately himself shot dead. Wellington makes a brief aside,
'heaven receive the faithful servant', and comments 'to win such
a battle as this of Waterloo, at the expense of so many gallant
friends, could only be esteemed a heavy misfortune, were it not
for its important results to the public benefits'. It might have been
a Tory apologist for a later battle fought at St Peter's Fields,
Manchester, under the Duke's more remote control. Napoleon
remarks, 'it is said I wear a coat of steel; no ruler chosen by the
people need wear such breastwork',[18] a comment that could not
have been made by Wellington.

Patriotic attitudes are not confined to Wellington and Napoleon.
Through the battle, attitudes change. Phedora, at first the spokes-
woman against the rapacity of the French troops, is about to
dispatch a wounded soldier when she discovers he once was
wounded defending her against his compatriots and rescuing her
husband; she now saves him, taking him up in her arms, and
placing him on a hospital waggon. 'Thine eyes shall see thy native
land, and bless thy wife and little ones. Lean upon me. Alas, he
has a heart; and it shall be preserved.'[19] The predatory French
villain Antoine is set against Maladroit, originally played by the
author Amherst himself. French in name and appearance,
Maladroit is in fact a mixture of European nations: 'my modere
was a Frenchman, my two or three fathers in French, Dutch,
English, and a great deal more countries besides!' A volatile
precursor of the Good soldier Schweik, he accomodates himself to
whatever army he finds himself in. Molley Maloney an Irishwoman allegedly based on 'an extraordinary woman (who)
followed the regiment from England, and was found dead on the
field the morning after the action of the 18th',[20] looks forward to
Brecht's Mother Courage, for she wanders the battle selling
whiskey to the troops, although she does show a drunken patriotism for the allies and wields a brace of pistols to good effect.

She, too, changes. At first a mainly comic character, towards
the end she meets her old 'husband' (one of many), Robert
Thompson, only to discover that he has been blinded in battle.[21]
Deflecting this horror with a coarse joke, 'Och, the cratur's short
o' daylight', she fumbles a sovereign from her bosom and presses
it into his hand with a still crueller comment, 'Put it out of *sight*'.
At this point Robert makes a patriotic speech in praise of his
country that provides 'good Chelsea quarters for every disabled
soldier, and snug Greenwich moorings for weather-beaten tars –
God bless the king and country that upholds such regulations',

Molly remarks 'the man Bob drives me to drink (*she fills*) Well, here's may Georgy love his people and may his people love him; my compliments to his majesty (*curtsies and drinks*)'.

How do we take this scene? It would be missing the spirit of melodrama to see it as directly ironic. The battle is moving into its final stages, and Phedora, who has spoken of the desolation of battle – 'the oppressed and the oppressors now lie mingled on their beds of death and silence' – finally exits giving a rose to Molly and Bob: ''tis an emblematic flower of England. Bright in colour – say such is Phedora's gratitude; and though its colours soon may fade, its scent will last even as the recollection of the generous Briton's valour. Farewell, farewell.' There is no doubt that the grand military tableau that concluded the play loudly celebrated the victory of the British and the allies over the French. Yet within the play itself, as we have seen, other points have been put; Napoleon depicted with sympathy and in some depth, and Wellington portrayed as an efficient machine with a certain ambivalent delight in the business of war – 'sharp shooting this, gentlemen' he enthuses when a volley of bullets fly. Bob and Molly provide a tableau of patriotic sentiments. yet, even within the ceremonial presentation of melodrama, it is not insignificant that the one patriotic toast is made by a comic, drunk Irishwoman (played by a man), and a soldier with his eyes shot out.

Notes

1 Wylie Sypher, 'Aesthetic of revolution: the Marxist melodrama', *Kenyon Review*, 10, summer, 1948, pp. 431–44.
2 Franco Moretti, *Signs Taken as Wonders*, 1983.
3 Mrs Elizabeth Gaskell, *Mary Barton*, 1848, Chapter 15.
4 George Levine, *The Realistic Imagination*, 1981.
5 H. M. Milner, *Frankenstein*, 1825.
6 John Walker, *Napoleon; or the Emperor and the Soldier*, a Dramatic Anecdote in one Act. No. 961, *Dick's Standard Plays*, nd, scene I. Plays on Napoleon were a major feature of French popular theatre – Louis-Henri Lecomte claims 596 Napoleonic plays were produced in France between 1797–1899. See Louis-Henri Lecomte, *Napoleon et l'Empire raconte par le theatre 1797–1899*, Paris, 1900, and Arthur H. Saxon, *Enter Foot and Horse*, New Haven, 1968. For the spate of Napoleonic plays in England following the 1830 French revolution, see Martin Meisel, *Realizations*, Princeton, 1983, Chapter 11. Here Napoleon is again given sympathetic and heroic treatment.
7 *Ibid.*, scene III.
8 *Ibid.*, scene V.
9 Anon., 'The grand conversation on Napoleon arose', undated broad-

sheet, *c.* 1819. See also the teller's 'Napoleon's farewell to Paris', 'Dream of Napoleon'.

10 Printed, adapted for Juvenile drama presentation, Hodgson and Co., 10 Newgate Street, nd [1822–4].

11 *Ibid.*, p. 22.

12 Anthony D. Hippesley-Coxe, in David Bradby, Louis James and Bernard Sharratt (eds), *Performance and Politics in Popular Drama*, 1980, p. 114.

13 J. H. Amherst, *The Battle of Waterloo*, act I, scene I.

14 *Ibid.*, act II, scene III.

15 *Ibid.*, act II, scene II.

16 *Ibid.*, act III, scene II.

17 *Ibid.*, act III, scene VI.

18 *Ibid.*, act III, scene III.

19 *Ibid.*, act III, scene III.

20 *Ibid.*, *Dramatis Personae.*

21 *Ibid.*, act III, scene VI.

17
Penny plain,
tuppence coloured

NICOLA JOHNSON

Amongst the more immediately attractive items in the Museum of London's extensive holdings of printed ephemera is a large collection of sheets of characters and scenes – 'penny plain, tuppence coloured' – intended for use with the so-called toy theatres which provided entertainment and occupation for countless children during the mid-nineteenth century. Even the most cursory examination suggests that they are not only, as is generally acknowledged, excellent sources of information about popular London stage productions of the time, but that they are also reflective of much wider social and even political concerns than those normally associated with them. As I gained familiarity with other items in the collections it became apparent that the images used in connection with a wide range of items of cheap 'ephemeral' juvenilia could well be equally revealing. Furthermore, whilst the literature, home and working life, clothing, education and more durable playthings of children growing up during that period of patriotic fervour which followed the Battle of Waterloo and continued, with varying degrees of intensity until the outbreak of the 1914–18 war, have aroused a considerable and growing interest, relatively little attention has so far been paid to the cheap printed paper items which were accessible to, and I suggest a surprisingly formative influence upon, young people.

The following short paper, then, represents a tentative and necessarily selective exploration of a field which I hope later to examine in far greater depth – that of the ephemera of a nineteenth and early twentieth century childhood. Essentially, I feel that the examples described or illustrated will speak for themselves. I propose to draw no formal conclusions; merely to offer observations which will doubtless be open to criticisms of anything from subjectivity to myopia. The value of presenting such material within the context of a group of volumes on patriotism is perhaps twofold. Firstly, the fact that they rarely exhibit a clear verbally-stated ideology serves to highlight a major problem in the wider discussion of patriotism; that is, how often is it possible to make a clear and honestly derived assessment of patriotism as distinct from nationalism, jingoism, feudalism, heroism, imperialism, commercialism, capitalism or even Anglicanism? Secondly, whereas other primary sources largely provide evidence of the workings of patriotic feeling in a world of adults, these items throw a little more light upon the childhood world in which those patriotic adults were formed.

Any line drawn between formal education and play is bound to become blurred. Toys, even for tiny children, can after all be educational tools in the sense that they encourage recognition, coordination, matching and other vital physical and spatial skills. They can, too, be specifically instructional even when apparently recreational. 'Historical' board games offer interesting examples both of this type of toy and of shifting emphases during the century. In such games produced during the last years of the eighteenth century and the first of the nineteenth, there is a definite tendency towards the depiction of monarchs or famous people as 'markers' of chronology and historical events, whilst the depiction of battles, conquests and acts of both individual and collective patriotic heroism is characteristic of such games produced in the post-Napoleonic period. Indeed, card and paper board games, generally, are richly informative of predominating ideology, both implicit and explicit. In their different ways, a 'New game of emulation', produced by Harris in *c.* 1804, which rewards correct and virtuous conduct in a gently moralising context, and 'Every man to his station', published by Wallis as early as 1825 and popular for some considerable time thereafter, where the fabric of the nation is shown through delicately coloured illustrations as consisting of a society in which everyone knows their place and has a sense of the necessity of accepting it as preordained, might be seen primarily as encouraging the maintenance of the *status quo* rather than anything else. However, it was probably precisely such reinforcement which strengthened and increased that moral conviction which underlay so much nineteenth-century national sentiment. The generation whose childhood recreation was informed by such toys and whose education was shaped by a growing sense of nationalism and patriotism was the generation which, as manufacturers, teachers and parents, was providing the young people of the mid-century with such delights as the 'Game of the Overland Route to India', in which the superior virtues of the British are emphasised by drawing attention to the unfortunate shortcomings of other races. (The Beduin, we are told in the explanatory rule book, is an apparently friendly person who, through the misfortune of having an unenlightened background, will entertain you lavishly but will not hesitate to rob you or even knife you in the back once you have passed beyond the geographical limits obligatory of hospitality!) A 'Tour through British Colonies and Foreign Dominions', on the other hand, emphasises the philanthropic and civilising nature of colonialism, and although it is both tempting and dangerous always to equate colonial with commercial expansion, in this case it is, I feel, not unreasonable; 'stops' are made *en route*, illustrated by representations of material and moral superiority over exploited peoples, and the flag is omnipresent.

Acquisition even of relatively cheaply-produced board games, however, generally depended upon the benevolence of adults, So too did the careful accumulation of an army of lead soldiers with their horses, tents, guns and other appropriate accessories, and although they cannot strictly be regarded as ephemeral, such models did generate their own cheap paper and card counterparts.

It is probable that the flat lead models of soldiers discovered in various parts of the Roman empire were intended as playthings, and there can be little doubt that by the fifteenth century figures of jousting knights, archers and so on were designed for a juvenile rather than an adult market. Such toys, however, were possibly intended less as vehicles for aggressively 'patriotic' play than as counterparts to the elaborate dolls houses given to young girls; that is, as a matter-of-fact way of preparing for adulthood. Seen in this light, I feel it important that connotations of force and nationalism be under- rather than over-played. Boys of relatively wealthy families who were not intended for the church were frequently destined for the army, and just as girls whose lot was likely to be the administration of a household had models of that adult world, so boys had of theirs. In both cases it is surely social conditioning which is the principal issue. There is even a sense in which model soldiers – possibly excluding those whose limbs can be moved independently – remain curiously apart from the rising tide of nineteenth-century patriotic fervour which to a greater or lesser degree informed cheaper ephemeral playthings. Talk to model soldier fanatics today, and for every one who fights a war there will surely be several whose chief delight is in the minute and detailed accuracy of each figure.

More specifically relevant is the growth, from the mid-eighteenth century and principally in France and Germany, of a trade in paper and cardboard soldiers which must surely have influenced the production of engraved 'military sheets' in early nineteenth-century England. The quality of the engraving is variable, particularly in the English examples; there is a general tendency to have separate sheets for individual soldiers, cavalry groups, rows of figures, etc. Such popular printed sheets probably originated in Strasbourg, where a printer named Seyfried, inspired by the triumphal entry into the city of Louis XV – and no doubt with a shrewd eye to business – produced engraved and coloured sheets depicting the entire royal guard of honour. By 1791 another printer, Striedbeck, was producing a 'complete collection of troops of the line and the national guard for the amusement and instruction of young people'. The subsequent development of lithographic techniques meant that such items could be increasingly easily and cheaply produced, although in England the military figures published by theatrical print-sellers tended to be engraved even towards the end of the century.

As I suggested earlier, the whole question of an inherent patriotism/nationalism in relation to toy soldiers, whether cast or printed, needs to be treated with a degree of caution. The paper cut-out models do seem to carry a stronger patriotic emphasis, perhaps because the engraver was at liberty to exploit a wider range of imagery than the metal caster, but in both instances the models were often produced as part of a range which might well include domesticated and wild animals, buildings, farm workers, dolls-house furniture and figures and equipment for toy shops and other models of the adult world. To isolate them from this broader context would perhaps be as misguided as to suggest that because of that context they could not, and did not, serve as excellent vehicles for a pervading patriotism.

Publication in England of printed 'military sheets' was, however, very much of secondary importance to the business of printing and selling sheets for the juvenile drama, or toy theatre. It is probable that the juvenile drama was a development from the popular engraved theatrical portrait sheets first produced during the last decades of the eighteenth century and sold through stationers and print warehouses as mementoes of personalities and productions of the contemporary stage. From the publication of a sheet with a single portrait of 'Mrs X as Portia in the Merchant of Venice as performed at the Theatre Royal, Drury Lane' to one illustrating a number of characters from a particular play was a relatively small step. From this followed in turn sheets with each of those characters in a number of different poses, designed to evoke quite specific moments in the stage action and, eventually, sheets of scenery, wings and even of pantomime 'tricks', so that the spirit of the whole performance might be recaptured. The manufacture and marketing of a toy theatre to house all these delights was almost invevitable. Boys up to the age of about fourteen were the principle enthusiasts, with the greatest enjoyment tending to be centred on the purchasing, colouring and cutting out of the sheets rather than on the performance of a complete 'piece', although suitably edited copies of many plays were available for the more adventurous enthusiast who was prepared to risk his cut-out figures and his dignity on a full-scale production. (Quite apart from the sheer physical difficulty of manipulating a large number of scene changes and small figures on wooden or metal rods and stands across the stage, the dramatically essential proximity of candles to such quantities of paper and card . . . Sheets making up a particular play were normally issued separately at intervals, though there was frequently demand from the young customers for the next sheet almost as soon as the preceding one came off the press. Accurate documentation of many plays can prove difficult, since although they do often bear both a publisher/printer's name and a date, the engraved plates tended to change hands as individual printers went out of business and to become palimpsests bearing the figures of one printing and the lettering and trading details of one or more subsequent owners of the plate. What is clear is that well before 1820, sheets had appeared containing figures suitable, if not specifically designed for, cutting out.

The years which saw the emergence of the juvenile drama also witnessed the massive flame of national pride which followed Wellington's success at Waterloo and which was fanned not only by political and literary activists but by theatrical spectacles which pandered to popular patriotic tastes. The juvenile drama productions exploited this state of affairs to the full, although it would be difficult to prove that they ever initiated patriotic feeling in isolation from other influences. As fast as the *Battle of Waterloo* was staged at Astley's or Davis's ampitheatre, it was transformed into paper in the print seller's window and thus found its way into the homes of thousands of adolescent boys, where its exuberant patriotism no doubt worked to great effect.

Battle scenes and deeds of heroism abounded in the juvenile drama, and as British militarism ventured into Alma, Balaclava and Inkermann, so too did its paper counterpart, with panoramas of thunder but little evident blood, and acts of stupendous heroism without attendant suffering. Neither was patriotism confined to the battlefield; juvenile editions of all the major stage successes were issued, often within days of the first performance, and they included such splendid vehicles for national sentiment as *Robin Hood, Guy Fawkes, Richard I* or *Couer de Lion, Union Jack, The Rifle Volunteers, King Arthur* and *Edward the Black Prince*, or the *Glories of England in 1359*. A less blatant but perhaps more powerful form of patriotism is evident in the 'tricks' or 'transformations' which came with pantomimes and burlesques and were designed to emulate the mechanical wizardry of the stage performance. Thus, after much careful folding of paper and manipulation of cotton threads, Britannia could be made to rise from a barrel of British spirits, plentiful and mouthwatering old English fare is hidden behind a tableau of the Elizabethan age and, rather more alarmingly, a box of 'pills for the Chinese' is transformed into the mouth of a cannon and two cannon balls! In the heyday of the juvenile drama, from around 1830–50, there can scarcely have been a child, certainly in any of the major urban centres, who had not at least stared at the sheets of characters in the printsellers' windows, and thus absorbed some of the flavour of their imagery and content, even if ownership was an impossibilty.

By the last quarter of the century interest in the juvenile drama, which had so successfully fed two or three generations of youthfully optimistic patriots, had all but died out. Not only had almost all of the printers and publishers gone out of business, but the consolidation of imperialism had led to less flamboyant, although arguably more intense, expressions of national feeling than those represented by the theatrical extravaganzas of the middle years of the century. Board games with a patriotic flavour continued to be produced, and it was possible to buy such card games as 'Staff', which centred around the accumulation of cards illustrating the various ranks composing a regiment. (Interestingly, the lower ranks sometimes seem to have been drawn to a smaller scale than the officers.) Smaller children were provided with appropriately decorated cardboard or tin drums, printed jigsaw puzzles and rattles, or perhaps a cardboard flip-over toy with pictures of variously uniformed soldiers, and even a rag book illustrating the peculiarities of various colonised races. With the advent of a British alternative to the predominantly German toy soldiers of earlier in the century, the popularity of military toys continued to thrive, partly perhaps as a result of the apparent success of the army in maintaining an ordered empire. State-funded education, by now increasingly widely available, reinforced as always the established values, and there was an element of national self-congratulation at the apparently improved status of the children which does not seem to have been substantially shaken even by the revelations of

Mayhew and Dickens, and later Barnardo and Booth. On the whole, though, as continued expansion became almost commonplace, national energies were partially directed toward that pursuit of dominance in the field of the manufacturing industries which is characterised by the various trade fairs which followed the 1851 exhibition.

For all their apparent patriotic fervour, however, the images presented in even the most overtly nationalistic scenes and tableaux for the juvenile drama and military sheets were in the tradition of the popular print; they lack both in form and content that exclusive virulence which is characteristic of political cartoon and prints and which is so immediately apparent in the specific 'anti-otherness' of Boer and Great War ephemera. That is, the patriotism of the toy theatre is largely of a confirmatory kind, dwelling as it does on success already achieved, and even though many of the pantomime tricks are aimed at making other societies appear ridiculous, the general lack of physical aggression involved in their manipulation seems somehow to defuse them. Toys and games which rely for their full effect, and presumably entertainment value, upon a more precisely aggressive physical activity than the simple movement of items from one place to another are, I suggest, of a rather different kind, a kind revealing seduction of and by designers and manufacturers in the face of increasingly systematised jingoistic propaganda. For a penny it was possible to purchase a variation on the hand-held 'get the ball into the socket' game in reverse, in which one knocked out Kruger's teeth with a flick of the wrist. A similar sum bought a cut-out figure of Kruger with his trousers rolled up above the knees, which involved the insertion of a forefinger and middle finger to form 'live' legs dangling in a bowl of hot water. Again for a penny, it was possible to knock the eye out of a remarkably high-quality head-and-shoulders portrait of Kruger with a glass bead on a length of elastic, and tuppence secured a jigsaw map of Africa with Boer defeats graphically, if somewhat inaccurately, depicted.

By the outbreak of war in 1914 the range of 'patriotic novelties' had been considerably extended and was already feeding the growing national hunger for things anti-German. The toy manufacturers had a particularly sharp axe to grind, in that the industry had been dominated throughout the nineteenth century by German imports, generally of an undeniably higher quality than those produced at home. Particularly rich sources of information on the production of patriotic toys are trade papers. *Games and Toys*, which considered itself 'the leading trade journal', carried an editorial in September 1914 urging manufacturers to rise to the challenge of replacing banned German imports with well-made domestic substitutes and thus capturing both the German nation and its trade. It contained advertisements for various, no doubt hastily-produced, ephemeral items, such as Faudels Patriotic Favours – flags for the buttonhole and buttons, badges and rosettes in red, white and blue, billed not surprisingly as 'the selling lines of the moment'. There was, too, a full-page spread offering 'Compocastles'; toy forts, castles, etc., that are 'British Made by British Labour with British Materials – indeed, British Throughout'. The October 'Christmas bazaar number' carried advertisements for a far wider range of cheap patriotic items. There was a variation on the previously mentioned 'Kruger in hot water' theme, in which it was the Kaiser's finger-legs which dangled in the steaming bowl and a splendidly inventive novelty was on sale which carried instructions, beneath a portrait of the Kaiser, to 'lower his moustache or raise his helmet'. When this was done the raised helmet revealed horns, and the pulled moustache became a pair of fangs. Items of this kind were plentiful, cheap and popular. You could throw cardboard quoits over stand-up cut-out figures of the Kaiser and Tirpitz, conquer Berlin in 'an entirely New War Game' which came (mysteriously) with 'paper cards, putter, glider and seven citadels' and could be played 'without disarranging rooms'! 'Europe in Arms' was a board game enacting a race between the allies to reach Berlin, and there were dozens of different patriotic rag books and dolls to chose from for younger children. Truly patriotic parents might even be tempted to buy a 'Dean's Patriotic Pinafore' for their children. An enormously popular 'penny line' was a toy which consisted of:

> a figure of the Kaiser, cut out on cardboard, nicely lithographed
> in attractive colours. At the neck there is a long piece of
> elastic. The elastic is pulled and an aim is taken for the face of
> the Kaiser. The force of the elastic knocks the Kaiser's head
> off, and in its place there springs up the head of Lord Kitchener.
> The toy then takes the form of a cut-out of our War Minister.
> On the breast appears the words 'Got 'im'.

As is probably clear from the examples given above, the emphasis of the juvenile ephemera produced during the Great War was as much anti-German as patriotically pro-British. There were less blatantly jingoistic souvenirs of particular victories and military displays, in the form of delicately printed paper napkins, and there were many kinds of paper flags and patriotic mottoes with which to decorate sandcastles and mud trenches. Generally speaking, however, children were exposed to a fiercely aggressive nationalism in their pocket-money toys which would have been largely unfamiliar to their grandparents, reared on the battles of the toy theatre and peep-shows of the British and colonial galleries in the Great Exhibition. It is virtually impossible to determine the extent to which they were experiencing the cumulative effects of a century of patriotic play and education as opposed to the results of a vastly increased awareness, on the part of manufacturers, of the selling power of the topical novelty. Similarly, although it would be comfortable to conclude that it was as a result of education combined with exposure to such items, as expressions of pervasive national sentiment that young men were prepared to sacrifice themselves in numbers that would have been unthinkable fifty years previously, it is quite clear that to begin with at least, as many were motivated to enlist by the monotony or insecurity of their daily lives as by any nobly patriotic feeling.

It is arguable that the real patriots – in the sense of giving selflessly for the good of the country – have always been women. The degree to which many middle- and upper-class women during the nineteenth century were encouraged by upbringing and conditioning to see their homes as divinely ordained power-houses for the nation is easily understated, if not underestimated. However, although it is possible to identify toys and games which encouraged boys to see themselves as potential heroes and can thus be loosely termed patriotic, equivalent toys designed specifically for girls are far less easily distinguished. Before the Crimean War, of course, scope for girls to go out and demonstrate patriotism in any really active sense was fairly limited, but that alone surely cannot explain the absence of such items? No doubt the domestic and social virtues to which girls were historically encouraged, through play as well as education, to aspire were excellently adapted to their potential roles not only as daughters, wives and mothers but as the daughters, wives, mothers and nurses of (and ultimately substitutes for) the heroes of the British empire. An arena of play beyond the dolls house, with all its implications, was hardly deemed necessary. On the other hand, it is difficult to believe that girls did not play with their brothers' model soldiers, that they were not as captivated as were boys by the juvenile drama, or that they did not spend at least some of their pocket-money pennies on anti-Boer or German novelties. Many of them, too, would probably have been willing to follow other male contemporaries to war. A picture postcard, postmarked April 1915, carries a transparently romanticised reproduction of a painting showing a group of foot soldiers crossing a bridge over a sparkling stream, through which their officers are wading on horseback. The men are apparently happy and it is quite clearly springtime. The picture is entitled 'Off to the Front'. On the reverse is the following handwritten message: 'Harry: to wish you all the very best in your new adventure. How I do envy you. It is wonderful to take up that position for which your education, family and country have raised you. I wish sometimes that I were a man! S.'

This paper is a preliminary sketch. A fuller enquiry would need a far more detailed survey of trade catalogues and museum and private collections. An even richer source of information on precisely how and by whom such items were bought and used would no doubt be personal reminiscences. A great deal more research will be necessary before childhood ephemera can be restored to the postion they occupied in the nineteenth century as the imaginative world in which ideas of nationality were theatrically rehearsed.

18
Doing the
Lambeth Walk

ALISON LIGHT *and*
RAPHAEL SAMUEL

When mass Observation, those pioneer ethnographers of the 'beliefs and behaviour of the British Islanders'[1] produced their book on *Britain* (a Penguin Special published in January 1939), they devoted a whole chapter to the phenomenon of 'The Lambeth Walk', monitoring its impact as a song hit (41 per cent of those they questioned had first heard it on the wireless), charting its progress as a dance craze and recording memories and opinions in Lambeth, the old London borough from which the 'Walk' allegedly derived. *Me and My Girl*, the musical which launched the Walk on its career, had opened at the Victoria Theatre, Westminster, at Christmas 1937 and was to play for the following four years. The Walk was introduced later as a 'novelty dance' at the Locarno, Streatham, and popularised by instructors at the great public dance-halls. Tom Harrison and Charles Madge, the founders of Mass Observation, would have liked to believe, as socialists, that it was the working class who had taken up the Lambeth Walk, yet they were bound to admit that its popularity was a cross-class phenomenon: 'You . . . can . . . find them doing the Lambeth Walk in Mayfair ball-rooms, suburban dance-halls, cockney parties and village hops.' The Lambeth Walk became an international success. As in England, its popularity transcended political and social divides. The Nazis, relieved apparently that the dance did not come from the blacks nor its libretto from a Jew, permitted it to be broadcast on German radio, whilst in Italy, Mussolini took instruction in its steps. It was no less popular in Czechoslovakia, hitting Prague about the time of the Munich crisis in September 1938. As the war clouds gathered, it offered a magical escape from care: 'The first contemporary dance from this country that has put the world on its feet.'[2]

The success of the recent production of *Me and My Girl* ('Musical

15   Bill (Lupino Lane) and Sally (Teddie St Dennis) are reunited, in the
original 'Me and My Girl', as Lord and Lady Misrule.

of the Year' for 1985) hardly reached these proportions, although it played to packed houses at the Adelphi in the Strand and on Broadway.[3] Any play which can get an audience stomping and clapping in the rigid hierarchical seating of a West End theatre is worthy of respect, but *Me and My Girl* invites something more than that. Like other revivals, this one tells us as much about the present as the past and its reworkings provide some interesting clues about conservative appropriations of 'tradition'. It also tells us something about the tricks memory plays on itself.[4]

Me and My Girl, with the exception of one Lambeth scene and one village pub, takes place in a minor stately home, Hareford Hall, Hampshire. The sets in the recent production are unashamedly flimsy: the luxury motor which opens the show – to our untutored eyes a Rolls or a Daimler – turns out to be made of collapsible panels and is transformed into the weekend guests' luggage; the props are jokey (ancestral busts come alive and join in the song and dance routines). In short, there is little of the mellow dignity normally evoked by Loamshire settings, nor yet of the mystifications of class and birth in *Brideshead Revisited*. The aristocracy in the musical, though wealthy, are absurd, neither power-brokers nor landed gentry, but a completely idle rich (whisky-drinking Sir John, a Colonel Chinstrap figure, is a sentimental old buffer; young cousin Gerald a flannelled fool). The real force of the humour and the dramatic energy of the performance lie in Bill and Sally, the London cock-sparrow and his Lambeth pal, and in their own ways of living and loving. Against the starched tones of the upper-class characters, they are at once vulnerable and open, their speech and movements flamboyantly expressive, theatrical and selfassured. Left alone for the first time in the lofty vestibule of Hareford Hall, Sally looks forward to making the place more cheerful and less like 'the bleedin' Odeon', whilst Bill (the improbable heir to an ancient title) starts giving away the objects he now owns in a mad rush of generosity.

Me and My Girl conforms to the traditional conventions of the pastoral, in which the 'natural' behaviour of plain folk is contrasted with the artificial glitter of the salons, the warmth and vitality of the plebs with the lifelessness of the patricians. The basic appeal of the original 1937 production, to judge by the rehearsal script – the only 'book' which survives - was that of the 'world turned upside down'. It re-enacts, albeit in the theatre rather than in the market-place or on the village green, the enthronement of the Lord of Misrule. In the folk festivals and fetes (in Garret Town, Wandsworth, a gypsified London suburb, they survived down to the 1860s), the meanest of beggars would be dressed in regalia, and treated for the day as king. Here it is the low comic, Bill, the Lambeth wide boy and coster, who inherits a country estate. The comedy offers us a reverse-image of the social order; instead of shop-girls imitating debutantes, it is the high-born who are revitalised from below.

For the role reversal of *Me and My Girl* is more than just that of social position; it is expressed too in the speech and gait, the whole demeanour of the people from Lambeth. It is not the rich but the poor who comport themselves as aristocrats. They dominate the play with their songs, dances and humour, and nowhere more so than in the highly individualised hero and heroine. Bill and Sally are representatives of a working-class great estate – the world of costers and pearlies which produced the Lambeth Walk. The plot may be in the hands of the aristocracy but the moving force of the action is theirs. Their love of display is not the conspicuous consumption of the moneyed classes but a making accessible and public the pleasures of being human. The sensuality and intelligent affection of Bill and Sally's love affair is contrasted – both in the duet which gives the show its name and in Sally and Bill's solos – with the mercenary onslaughts of his gold-digging cousin Jacqueline and her miserable follower, an archetypal chinless wonder who finds the idea of a day's work 'disgusting'.

It is *excess* which gives Bill such powerful subversive force. He defies his would-be tutors and relentlessly transgresses good taste. Larking about on stage – somersaulting, clowning, miming – reverting to comic patter or calling on old-time puns, the very idea of his gentrification is absurd. And the subversion seems complete when, in the carnivalesque scene which brings the show to a stop, Lambeth takes over the stage *en masse* – the ladies in their bank holiday finery, the pearlies in their regalia. Footmen, major domo, maids, and finally the aristocracy themselves, are drawn into doing the Lambeth Walk as in a series of reprises everyone succumbs to cockney vitality and, 'shouts oi and the duchess goes in to dinner wearing Bill's bowler on her head'. At such a moment in the theatre (and in the original production it was repeated fully at the end of act II) the generosity and the self-confidence of the performers is irresistible, as indeed is the tune. 'Do as you damn well pleasey' – a favourite line from the song – is hardly a revolutionary injunction, but contrasted in *Me and My Girl* to the anxious strategems and repressive dictates of the upper class it certainly seems liberatory.

Me and My Girl was based on both real-life and stage originals. The 1937 star, Lupino Lane, 'an alert little cockney, on his toes the whole time like a boxer', had already created the stage character

of Bill Snibson in the previous year when he had appeared in
Arthur Rose's *Twenty to One* at the Coliseum. It was then too that
he invented (or reinvented) the Lambeth Walk which was to serve
him for many years as a classic piece of comic stage 'business'. An
earlier lineage which suggests itself is of course back to Lambeth's
most famous comic son, Charlie Chaplin, though Chaplin denied
the connection. Lupino Lane's 'cocky grey bowler' is second cousin
to Charlie Chaplin's still more famous hat, and his rolling gait,
'half lilting, half swaggering', has obvious affinities to Chaplin's
crab like walk. Indeed, as early as 1915, in *Watch Your Step*, he
had sung a number called 'That Charlie Chaplin Walk' (Chaplin
himself, in a 1938 letter to Mass observation, attributed his walk
not to 'Lambeth' but to 'the necessity of wearing ill-fitting shoes').[5]
The song was even more antique. Under the same name, though
with a different tune, it had been a smash hit of 1903. (Mass
Observation suggests that it may have been based on the 'Cake
Walk', 'a coon dance' that came to England from the United States
in a minstrel show.)

There were also, as the admirably comprehensive inquiry of
Mass observation documents, real-life originals. Lupino Lane, 'a
cockney born and bred', attributed the Walk – aggressive, hips
swaying, arms out at the side – to one he had known all his life,
'just an exaggerated view of how the cockney struts'. Douglas
Furber, the Cambridge-educated composer of the song, claimed
to have drawn his inspiration from the singing of the factory lasses
of his Yorkshire boyhood. A spontaneous talent for dancing and
song, Mass Observation argues, was Lambeth tradition, surviving
at Saturday night parties if not in the streets; a tradition which
interestingly crossed genders:

> For the men it is a swagger, arms out from the sides, like a
> boxer playing for position; for the women it is more of a lilt,
> with hips swaying. The two get mixed, though, when the men
> dress as women and behave like them . . . which is part of
> the tradition. Also, men dance with men and women with
> women quite freely.

There was a real life place called Lambeth Walk, still a street
market, as it was in the days when it was described by Mayhew
(*London Labour and the London Poor*, 1851), though surrounded in
1938 by what appeared as 'huge blocks' of London County Council
flats, Mass observation did not find it difficult to discover residents
of Lambeth who claimed to have been familiar with the original
song and the walk, and it may be that it continued to linger on
even though by 1938, it was almost certainly archaic (even after

an August bank holiday booze-up). As the old-timers did not fail to inform Mass observation, things weren't what they used to be. The term 'free and easy', which runs through the song and dance, also stems from the pre-music hall pub, although it was one which still lived on in late Victorian times. Above all – the one point on which Mass Observation have surprisingly little to say – there was the tradition of street dancing, a mass phenomenon of the later nineteenth century, associated on the one hand with children's play – that of girls especially – and on the other with the ubiquitous presence of the barrel-organ.

The 'Lambeth' of *Me and My Girl* thus drew on venerable tradition, and was already, in 1937, a throw-back to Edwardian and even late Victorian times. Yet, for all its archaism, *Me and My Girl* was evidently in tune with the times. The dance adapted by Adel England to the needs of the Locarnos, offered an antidote to shyness, saving young people the embarrassment of making initial overtures to each other. And if the dance cut across sexual conventions, the comedy as a whole offered a fantastic easing of class differences in which the claims of common humanity ruled supreme. *Me and My Girl's* popularity may have owed something to this reassurance: the working class, however rough their ways, are basically harmless; the aristocracy, however stuck-up, benovolent; the English a race of lovable eccentrics. If, as the play suggests, the working class are the 'coming class', it was neither because of their spending power, nor on account of their industrial might, still less because of their politics, but because they were pleasure-loving – in the words of Mass Observation, 'the class who knew how to have a good time'.

Me and My Girl perhaps captured, or anticipated, something of the mood with which working-class England entered the second World War – not the clenched fist of their more politicised counterparts in occupied Europe, but the downbeat stoicism of 'smiling through'. 'Knees up Mother Brown', an old Cockney favourite, appeared in sheet music for the first time in 1939, and by 1940, when Mass Observation produced *Britain at War*, it had outrivalled the Lambeth Walk as a song and dance number. *Me and My Girl* rehearses what was to be a major theme of war-time propaganda – cross-class fraternisation, 'all in it together' – and the pleasing illusion that 'ordinary people' had come into their own. It could also be said to prefigure the terms of Labour's 1945 victory: on the one hand it appeals to a democratic sense of being English, a patriotism which is dependent upon a dream of classlessness; whilst on the other hand, deriving its specific force and passion from a version of distinctly working-class community – an informing belief that it was the working-class who were really the heart of the nation. In the 1985 production both the optimism and the confidence of this appeal to working-class vitality have shifted quite dramatically.

This recent production of *Me and My Girl* at the Adelphi, though claiming to be a faithful rendering of the original, is a self-conscious play with nostalgia, and a whole pastiche of 'period' effects. A new scene in the servants' basement clearly owes more to *Upstairs Downstairs* than to the original, though an Electrolux fridge is offered as a gauge of authenticity. Memories of the silver screen are insistently invoked. Sally, played in this production by cockney actress Lorraine Chase (she of the Campari ads and *Blankety Blank* (fame)) is given a number to herself, its force and poignancy, however, owe more to a Brecht – Weill Jenny than to any Jollier London Prototype.

More tellingly, though, the whole social balance of the show has been tilted in favour of gentrification. In the original production, the cockney hegemony was uncontested; it was not only Bill who spoke rhyming slang but also – because it was so catching – the aristocrats. The Lambeth Walk not only brought the first act to a climax; it also served as the opening of the second act, and at the end brought the play to a grand finale.

In the original production, the opening scene of the second act has Bill instructing his aristocratic listeners on how to play the mouth-organ and learn the notes of the Lambeth Walk. The newer production scraps this scene and replaces it with a kind of celebration of the bright young things. Instead of the Lambeth Walk we have 'The Sun has Got His Hat On' – a number imported from a very different musical and it becomes the occasion for the aristocratic house-guests to disport themselves and in some sort to match the vitality of Lambeth with their own. Instead of being stuffed shirts, they blossom out in leisure wear, toting tennis rackets and croquet mallets, all blazers and charming frocks. If there are Labour supporters in the audience with tears in their eyes at the Lambeth Walk with all its memories of the days when ordinary people (at least in make-believe) could be kings, there must be quite as many old time Tories fondly remembering *Salad Days*.

The second half of the current production seems to be a class revenge in which it is the working class rather than the aristocracy who are consistently out-witted. Sally, in her loyalty to Bill is persuaded by Sir John to undergo a transformation, Pygmalion-like, into a 'real' lady in order to be a fit consort for the new earl. This twist features in both versions but in the 1985 version the change is for real. And the second addition to the show's song sheet marks a further shift. George Formby's 'Leaning on the Lamp Post' is crooned mildly and elegiacally by Bill – its original quirky edginess and rough and ready humour transposed into a kind of misty 'lyricism'. This is followed by a dream sequence in which Bill and Sally become Fred Astaire and Ginger Rogers gliding over the stage suitably swathed in silk and dry ice.

Running parallel to this shift is a scene in the Hareford library

16 The music sheet for 'Lambeth Walk', published by Cinephonic Music Co. Ltd, 1937.

in which Bill's own specific class of masculinity is threatened and absorbed by an appeal to Englishness, to a universal heritage – his 'lineage' not just as the new earl, but, it is implied, as a 'freeborn Englishman'. In the 1937 production, at least in the eyes of Mass Observation, this scene was a kind of send-up of the Coronation, but here the comic business is firmly subordinated to a reassertion of tradition. His statesmen and warrior ancestors descend from their portraits in pageant-like procession and the absurdity of this is forgotten in the solemnity of the music and ritualistic splendour. No doubt meant as a moving reassertion of Englishness, the anthem of *noblesse oblige* is shown to have the superior claims.

The aristocratic counterpoint is even more insistent in the last scene, when Bill is reunited with his Sally – no longer a Lambeth girl, but, at least in outward appearances, carrying herself like a duchess. This magical moment is crucial to both productions but it is handled very differently, and the differences are revealing. In the original production, her transformation is only skin-deep; reunited in the semblance of Lord and Lady, Bill and Sally revert to cockney, mocking the lah-dee-dah:

Bill: Ger cher! Oi-oi, Sal!
Sally: Wot cher; Bill!
Bill: Ssh, Don't let the ancestors hear us. I think we'll return.
Sally: Well, we'll nevah forget old Lambeth, Bill:
No, not the Lambeth Walk.

They do the Walk together and the curtain descends on the whole cast joining in; the coming class, whatever assaults are made upon it, seems here to stay.

The newer production runs otherwise. The above dialogue is absent and the dignity and pathos of Sally's earlier characterisation is replaced by the smooth elegance of a mannequin. Bill still speaks cockney – 'Where the bloody 'll 'ave you bin?' he asks. But Sally takes the change seriously. She speaks with the voice of a queen, and the crowd of aristocratic bystanders cheer her on, with grey toppers waving and morning coats bobbing, in anticipation of a society wedding. Against this background, the Lambeth Walk, though sounding again from the orchestra pit, sounds more like a dying fall.

Me and My Girl is a pantomime of class, which by exaggerating social differences robs them of their pain. It offers an anti-heroic view of national character, in which the men, of whatever class, are philanderers, and it is the women who keep them up to the mark. But in the recent revival it has been given a conservative twist. The workers are no longer the coming class; the cockneys no longer know how to be true to themselves. Energy may be with the masses, but it is no match for the guile of their betters and even when it comes to having a good time it seems the upper classes can teach them a thing or two.

What has perhaps shifted in the forty years since the first production, along with the terrain upon which working people might find some sense of collective self-regard and enthusiastic purpose, is also the confidence with which transgressing class boundaries can be seen as a brave and correct impulse, one which might be politically productive or even generate some happiness.

Part of the effect of this shift is to suggest that romance within the working class life is a contradiction in terms – it has to take place elsewhere; partly it signals a much more thorough move in the later production whereby the power of traditional heterosexual romance is used to take over and subsume the claims of class solidarity. As ever (and as the ending reveals) it is the woman who comes to bear the brunt, at least symbolically, for the man's gentrification.

Doing the Lambeth Walk – or rather watching it done in the West End theatre – like any other trip down memory lane, is certainly not a short cut to some unmediated and untarnished haven of authentic working-class culture. But it does encompass some of the compassionate collectivity which is the basis for a solidarity across social difference. *Me and My Girl* might seem a bit of a meagre celebration, even if you remember shouting 'oi' with the best of them, but it is still heartening to hear that finale when you consider the odds now militating against any form of collective engagement. If the point of celebration of popular working-class culture appears so often at the point also of its disintegration (a comment which might be made about the fantastic community of the contemporary television *EastEnders*), then this makes the recognition of the positive potential of those class forms more, not less, urgent. The last line in *Me and My Girl* remains a Lambeth line – if only Lambeth could continue to have the last laugh.

Notes

1 Mass-Observation, *First Year's Work, 1937–8*, London, 1938, p. 8.
2 *Ibid.*, p. 184.
3 It was still playing in Spring 1988, and in 1985 was voted 'Musical of the Year' by theatre critics.
4 The original script is in the Lord Chancellor's papers which have now been deposited at the British Museum.
5 David Robinson, *Charlie Chaplin, His Life and Art*, London, 1985, pp. 152–3.

Cinema

19

Docklands Dickens

RAPHAEL SAMUEL

Dickens's work was never far distant from the idea of performance. He was a lifelong amateur actor and, as is well known, in his later years a great public reader. His earliest writings were for the stage. He conceived novels themselves as a species of performance art in which the characters were actors. As he put it in a well-known passage, 'every good actor plays direct to every good author, and every writer of fiction, though he may not adopt the dramatic form, writes in effect for the stage'. In the early novels in particular the stage analogies are inescapable. Pickwick was modelled on the comic monologues of Charles Mathews, the leading comedian of his youth. The capering, grimacing Quilp, (Dickens's anarchic ego, some critic suggest) was a figure taken from pantomime; Ralph Nickleby, the wicked uncle, corresponds to the villains of melodrama. *Little Dorrit*, the most restrained and complex of Dickens's novels, is not less melodramatic than its predecesors, whether in the play of mystery, the build-up of guilt, or the dialectic of good and evil.[1]

Dickens's cinematic qualities have been less frequently discussed, though they were handsomely acknowledged by D.W. Griffith, the father of the American cinema, who proclaimed Dickens as his master, while the structural similarities between Dickens's narrative and avant-garde film-making is the subject of a brilliant essay by Sergei Eistenstein. Both declared that Dickens was the pioneer of montage, as also of that animistic view of the universe in which landscape and setting were living protagonists of the drama: 'settings that reflect the characters' states of mind'.[2] *Little Dorrit* – the novel but not alas the film provides plenty of examples, where London itself becomes a metaphor for imprisonment. 'Nothing to see but the streets, streets, streets. Nothing to breathe but the streets, streets, streets.'

This 'optical' quality of Dickens' (as Eisenstein called it) is very much to the fore in David Lean's *Great Expectations* (1946) and his *Oliver Twist* (1948). Each is a visual translation of the plot, making an expressionist use of the background to secure stunning dramatic effects, most memorably in the desolate scene on the marsh which provides the shock opening of *Great Expectations*. Lean's films were important not only as landmarks of British *film noir*, but also for fixing a notion of the Victorian as a time of oppression and fear. They represented a social-democratic as well as a Gothic imagination, the summit of some three decades of modernist revolt. In Miss Havisham, a death-in-life figure, festooned in cobwebs was a very emblem of nineteenth century claustrophobia, while the settings of *Oliver Twist* helped to fasten the epithet 'Dickensian' to slum housing. *Oliver Twist* is played for the most part in Dead of Night; *Great Expectations* is showed by marshland mists. Mental states, in either case, are projected by visual terrors. Both films end in the most basic of melodrama's forms, the chase. Coming at a time when cinema attendances were at an all time high, these films were hugely influential in identifying the Victorian era as a time of darkness.

Imaginatively as well as cinematically, Christine Edzard's *Little Dorrit.* (1987) which opened to critical acclaim, belongs to a different world, one in which 'Victorian', so far from being a term of opprobrium as it was in the 1940s, has been assimilated to notions of 'heritage' and serves as a *signifier* for *objects d'art*. Where David Lean, a practitioner of the Gothic, set out to astonish and shock, pivoting his film on sensation scenes and underlining disturbing effects, *Little Dorrit* soothes. The lighting is flat rather than, as in David Lean's Dickens, theatrical; the frames are regular; the camera perspective is fixed, a succession of eye-level shots which never disturb the viewer's gaze. Where Lean worked in the shadows, using black and white photography to create a landscape of fear, *Little Dorrit* bathes its scenes in colour. The musical score – orchestral selections from Verdi – amplifies these effects. It does not evoke the ghostly presences which haunt the Dickens plot, nor create a tense expectancy. It is used, rather, to underline the film's lyric moments – such as the sunny afternoons in Twickenham – or to sound a positive note.

London in the intervening years (even, it seems, the malodorous London of *Little Dorrit*) has been spring-cleaned. The Thames is no longer a 'deadly sewer' running through the heart of the city, but rather a quiet retreat; not an industrial highway but the resort of sailing boats and seagulls. The air is no longer polluted, but fresh. The 'penitential garb of soot' has been stripped from the buildings; when they appear in the film the 'old blastened and blackened forests of chimneys' (painted in as backdrops) miraculously emit no smoke. The 'poor mean shops' of Borough High Street in this film now look quietly prosperous: the brickwork has been newly pointed and sand-blasted, it seems, to give a honeyed glow. Bleeding Heart Yard, the slum court off Gray's Inn Lane, is rendered here as quaint, a kind of *rus in urbe* with old-time pantiles. Industry, too, has been given a face-lift. At Doyce and Clenam's workshop the machinery positively glistens, with not so much as a speck of oil or a trace of iron filings. The brass wheels are spotless, the engine no longer frantically throbs. The inscription on the door-posts has become an artistically lettered facia, 'DOYCE AND CLENNAM. PRESSURE GAUGES'. (The treatment of Chivery's the tobacconists is even more Heritage, with Egyptian Gothick lettering and a door-bell which tinkles to the customer's touch).

The weather too has improved out of all recognition and there are none of those atmospherics which we are accustomed to think of as Dickensian. The fog has lifted, the skies have cleared; in all the six hours of the film there is hardly a drop of rain. In most of the scenes the sun (or its studio lighting equivalent) is shining, its rays penetrating to what in the novel are lightless depths. At night 'equinoctial gales' no longer sweep in on the metropolis, plunging down chimneys and blackening the walls with rain; nor are there 'wild clouds' chasing across the skies: when Little Dorrit and Maggie are forced to walk the streets, the sky deepens to a midnight blue. Not until some five hours into the film is there a serious break in the weather, but after a premonitory roll of thunder, the storm dies away.

The *dramatic personae* of the film have also been spruced up. All of the cast are tastefully dressed; cottons have been hand-sewn for the production; linens have been well laundered. Pancks, the rent collector, sports a brilliant show of cuff, and his 'dirty broken hands' and 'dirty broken fingernails' have apparently been manicured. Amy Dorrit's 'old worn dress' has become a powder-blue gown; Maggie, the idiot girl she befriends, is no longer in rags: she appears to be dressed in a Laura Ashley print; her bonnet – 'monstrous' and 'black' in the Dickens original – is now a gaily coloured primrose. The poor of Bleeding Heart Yard are no longer the Great Unwashed but look for the most part in the pink of condition, well fed, with ruddy countenances, good complexions and colourful clothes. Mrs Plornish alone looks pinched, (but her children are rosy-cheeked) while the urchins of the yard, acting as look-outs for the rent man, look more like little Lord Fauntleroys than street arabs: there is not a smudge to be seen on their faces, nor a rent or patch on their clothes.

If the poor have been sanitised, with well-scrubbed faces and no trace of physical deformity, the rich have been glamourised, an Upper Ten Thousand not imprisoned by their wealth, as in Dickens' glittering. They are pictured as living in palaces – literally so in the Italian scenes, metaphorically so in London. The Merdle establishment in Harley Street is a court; the Circumlocution Office, with its marble halls, Palladian. Lord Decimus Barnacle is no longer an aristocratic nincompoop – the windbag of the Meagles wedding – but a genuinely imposing authority figure, radiating patrician charisma. The parasitic Henry Gowan is invested with a handsome figure and good looks. Mrs Merdle, the bosom of Dickens's satire, is played by Eleanor Bron as a dazzling society lady, an object of envy and admiration rather than scorn. If lowlife glows in this film. High Society glitters.

The shabby-genteel, too, have been up-graded, their threadbare clothes forgotten, their tattered dignity repaired. At the Marshalsea they are by no means down at heel. The needlework teacher, with her RADA voice and brilliant dress, though notionally a seamstress, is every inch a lady. The dancing master looks like a fashion plate. Tip, Little Dorrit's brother, dresses like a dandy and looks like Dorian Gray. William Dorrit, the Father of the Marshalsea, is a figure of dignity rather than pathos. In the novel he is a 'shabby old debtor' weak and self-deluded with trembling lips and irresolute hands, feebly bursting into tears when his pretensions are ignored. In the film, played by Alec Guinness, he looks positively majestic, moving about the set with stately grace, gesturing regally and dressed in silks and satins. His talk, fragmentary and disjointed in the original, taking refuge in circumlocution and periphrasis, is serene rather than agitated, and always clear as to where it is going. Translated into the world of High Society his dignity is unimpaired. Even his breakdown – the great scene where his mind gives way and he addresses a Society banquet as though the guests were fellow prisoners – is played as a kind of triumph. In the novel he looks confusedly about him and makes a rambling speech, punctuated by pauses and collapsing in self-pity. In the film he is grandiloquent.

Visually, *Little Dorrit* in this film has been robbed of its potential terrors. The streets, photographed by day rather than by night, are neither menacing nor claustrophobic but picturesque. They are represented not by high, imprisoning walls, as in Phiz's original illustrations to the novel, but by make-believe 'period' shop-fronts, remarkably similar to those in Covent Garden. Domestic interiors too, so far from being prison-like, are emblems of sweetness and light: one admiring critic has likened them to the genre paintings of Vermeer. In the novel the Marshalsea prison is an 'oblong pile of barrack building, partitioned into squalid houses standing back to back'. In the film it is a loose assemblage of period cottages (one of them weather-boarded); the windows are leaded lights and the panes are dust-free; in the courtyard – improbably for a scene supposedly set in the 1820s – there is a brand new Victorian street-lamp.

The 'dark horrors' of Mrs. Clennam's house have also been eliminated. In the novel it is a 'debilitated old house . . . wrapped in its mantle of soot, and leaning heavily . . . on crutches'. In the film it is a splendid Georgian mansion. The 'ugly old chairs without any seats' have been upholstered; the 'threadbare pattern-less carpet' to has been replaced by Persian rugs; the 'maimed table' has given way to a Chippendale piece; even the copperware in the kitchen has been polished. The dark airless room where Mrs Clennam imprisons herself – a kind of prototype for Miss Havisham and her cobwebs – has become a handsome morning room, with sunlight playing on the window seats. The ceilings, with their ornate mouldings, are spotless. It comes then as some-thing of a surprise when in what should have been one of the dramatic climaxes of the film (as it is in the Dickens original) the house collapses.[3]

It is not only the photography which has been purged of its Gothic element but also the narrative. The story no longer opens with a Dantesque vision of hell: a Marseilles dungeon. It begins in the altogether more reassuring setting of a coffee house on Ludgate hill. Rigauld, the satanic figure who haunts the novel – there is a terrifying engraving of him by Phiz – has been eliminated from the plot. So has the 'enigmatic and perhaps lesbian Miss Wade', a truly subversive feminine figure. The surviving figures of evil have also lost their terror. Mrs Clennam is no longer a vengeful fury but, as played with 'dangerous refinement' by Joan Greenwood, she is more of a queen than a witch. The more melodramatic passages in the narrative have disappeared. Merdle the millionaire financier suicides off-stage. Flintwich's 'dreadful end' (he is buried alive in the house-fall) is hardly less invisible, without so much as a glimpse of his mutilated body or the sound of his dying groans. Acoustically too the film dispenses with shock effects. No heavy footfalls echo on the staircases, as they would do in *film noir* versions of Dickens; doors do not creak on their hinges, even when they are being opened by sinister characters; nor does the musical score become agitated. The most that is attempted in the way of extraneous sound is an occasional background buzz.

The rationale for these transformations is an aesthetic of ordinariness. The film-makers have wanted, it seems, to make *Little Dorrit* more believable to moderns. Where Dickens caricatures, the film tries to make its characters lifelike, eliminating their more extravagant dimensions and returning them to the world of everyday appearances. Thus Mr Merdle, the millionaire swindler, is no longer at sixes and sevens with his body (in the novel his hands and feet are perpetually disappearing) but plods impeturably about the set. At the other end of the social scale Mrs Plornish, the fantasist of Bleeding Heart Yard with her make believe Arcadia becomes a hard-pressed mother. Above all, everything is done to diminish Little Dorrit's otherness. Her speech is invested with a faint London twang, as if to offer assurances that she is made of the common clay. She busies herself with domestic chores even when offering love. She is also in some sort despiritualised, no longer the subject of a drama of suffering and redemption but rather – in the film's reworking of the narrative – the woman who gets her man. The 'strong passivity' which Dickens saw as the noblest aspect of the truly womanly disappears; so does the theme of the Martyr – daughter. Where Dickens's plot thickens, building up suspense, here it is simplified to the symmetries of romance, one to be understood in contemporary terms. *Little Dorrit*, the film's editors have decided, is a love story.

The romance is not that of Arthur Clennam and Little Dorrit, whose encounters lack any of the tensions or electricity of desire, but of the camera and Derek Jacobi, the actor who takes Arthur's part. He plays it in a way that seems to be deeply appealing to women. In the opening scene of the film he is a Little Boy Lost, a child-adult with neither mother or home; and he is pictured throughout the film in 'becoming' settings: seated majestically at his desk in one moment; ostensibly locked up in the Marshalsea with romantically dishevelled hair in another (whereas Little Dorrit is distanced throughout the film by her bonnet, Jacobi is generally hatless). He does not say much; he does not do anything. *He looks*, and the camera plays about his face lasciviously. (People who have wanted to highlight the fact that the film has a woman director have speculated on some possibly feminist reading of Amy Dorrit. It would be more rewarding to consider the way in which the script has elevated Clennam from a narrative cipher into a romantic lead, and the ways in which the camera transforms him into an object of filmic desire.)

The film-makers' approach to *Little Dorrit* is reverently conservationist. Truth to the original rather than dramatic invention has been their guiding star. The lines of the original dialogue have been faithfully reproduced, foreshortened but without embellishment. Incidents and events have been transcribed literally and re-enacted as though in answer to stage directions. Significant moments are paused upon to allow them to have their weight. In one aspect the film resembles nothing so much as a series of cameos in which the chapters of the book are replayed as scenes. Speech mannerism and posture too have been imitated, as, for example, Flintwick's 'crab-like' walk or Flora Finching's flounces.

Closely related to, but consorting uneasily with this, is the concern for historical verisimilitude. Verdi's music, for instance, was chosen for 'period' reasons, 'an almost obvious accompaniment to Dickens's work' (the programme notes tell us) because he was born within a year of Dickens and shared (the film makers believe) Dickens's 'romantic quality'. The sets have been lovingly antiqued: hand-grained panels, for instance, in the Clennam household: designer-craftsmen chairs at Mr Merdle's; both of them on show, along with the film's costumes, at the exhibition in the Museum of London. The film-makers have lavished a vast amount of attention on the costume, and it says something of the production values of the company that Olivier Stockman, the co-scriptwriter and film editor, also designed the hats. Coats and gowns have been copied down to the last buttonhole, individually handmade to guarantee an absolute authenticity, and following the pattern books of the 1830s and 1840s. A host of talents were mobilised for the task – some twenty-five designer craftsmen working for a period of two years – and the costumes have now received the ultimate accolade of exhibition space at the Museum of London. Here the constumes and artefacts of the film have been reverently labelled, as though they were real-life antiques, with a set of colour plates by Lord Snowdon to serve as mementoes. The self-presentation is untroubled by blood on the needles or *The Song of the Shirt*. It celebrates the seamstress' art as one of England's glories:

> The three hundred or so costumes for the film were entirely made by hand, as they would have been at the time, with the greatest attention to the shape and cut of the period, and to every possible detail. For over two years, dresses and coats were cut and fitted and sewn, waistcoats were embroidered, buttons were made, straw bonnets were plaited, petticoats, shirts, corsets were stitched up, gentlemen's hats, ladies shawls

and even jewels were made in the workshops of Sands Films, the work of some twenty-five people.

The historicity of the film, and the fetishisation of period effects is inseparable from the claim that it is 'intensely real'. As the film-makers put it: 'A very large amount of work and affection and care have gone into making every part of it . . . as richly detailed and authentic as possible.'

The film's preoccupation with period effects is singularly at variance with Dickens himself, who was notoriously cavalier in his treatment of history and contemptuous of notions of heritage.[4] In his autobiographical novels, *David Copperfield* and *Great Expectations*, the past – the remembered past of his childhood – is a prison-house, a time of cruelty and oppression; in his historical novels, *A Tale of Two Cities* and *Barnaby Rudge* it is a theatre where his phobias have free play. In *Little Dorrit* it is a nightmare weight on the living which the protagonists desperately try to escape. Dickens had a radical contempt for the past and his *Child's History of England* is the very reverse of reverential: James I is 'his Sowship', Henry VIII a 'Pig', George III 'that swine-headed annointed of the Lord'. In the battle of Ancients and Moderns he was uninhibitedly on the side of the latter. Among the false book-backs with which he decorated his study at Gad's Hill, Humphry House tells us (*The Dickens World*, p. 35) was a set called: 'The Wisdom of our Ancestors – I Ignorance. II Superstition. III The Block. IV The Stake. V The Rack. VI Dirt. VII Disease.' When antiquarianism makes a brief appearance in *Little Dorrit*, it is an object of scorn, 'scratching up the driest little bones [he writes of Mrs General in Rome] . . . and bolting them down whole'; and he is no more respectful of Mr Meagles' picturesque souvenirs.

Dickens was not a period novelist in the way in which, say, Thackeray was in *Henry Esmond* or *Vanity Fair*. Even when a story seems to be taking place at one moment, the characters may be drawn from another. In *Little Dorrit* itself he cheerfully conflates entirely different epochs – the Marshalsea of his 1820s childhood, where his father briefly served a term of imprisonment and the administrative scandals and financial swindles of the 1850s. The story is set, like many of his novels, 'thirty years ago', but the Circumlocution Office and the Tite Barnacles were the campaigning targets of the day. The film-makers have compounded this difficulty by drawing their costume from originals which belong to neither time: to judge by the credits at the Museum of London, the *Journal des Desmoiselles* (1839) was a leading model. The period effects in this film are not only pedantic;

in relation to *Little Dorrit*, a novel which belongs chronologically speaking – nowhere, they are by definition misplaced.

For better or for worse. Dickens was not a realist in the way in which the film-makers want him to be. His Victorian England has only the most accidental relation to that of the historians who, by and large, have found it prudent to ignore him. Alienation, the great theme of his 'dark' novels, has very little or no place in accounts of the Age of Equipoise, nor do the shabby-genteel (one of his basic points of social reference and the very subject of *Little Dorrit*) have even a walk-on part in the Age of Improvement. Dickens's realism was a grotesque realism; his genius was in caricture; he made a fantasy of Victorian England and peopled it with creatures of his own imaginings. The attempt then, to make the characters of the novel lifelike, whether by playing down evil or, as in the treatment of Amy Dorrit, by eliminating the symbolic, seems self-defeating. The film is in fact most successful when it breaks from the reality frame and allows the actors to be theatrical, as in the wonderful performances by Miriam Margoyles as Flora and Amelda Brown as Fanny.

Film requires a different aesthetic from conservation, and *Little Dorrit* illustrates some of the difficulties of attempting to marry the two. The sets, so lovingly reconstructed, take on a life of their own. The period costume, with its high arm-holes, turns the actors and actresses into clothes-hangers. Hats depersonalise; disastrously so in the case of Little Dorrit who for much of the time is invisible by reasons of her enormous poke-bonnet. The beautiful copper-ware makes even the Clennam kitchen cosy; the simple table in the Dorrit garret, even if intended to signify poverty, takes on a vernacular charm.

The authenticities of this film undermine the narrative. The dialogue, though faithfully drawn on the original, sounds stilted, with long silences which underline the laboured effect ('Time for your oysters' Flintwich at one point improbably asks his mistress). The 'period' music, however chronologically apt, is totally at variance with the murky world which Dickens is describing, one which, if the musical score were to be taken from a composer of the time, might more fittingly have used Wagner rather than Verdi. The Marshalsea here may be truer to the historical original than the phantasmagoria conjured up by Dickens and by Phiz, but as depicted in the film it is not so much a closed world as a theatre of comings and goings. The look of this film, in short, continually belies the words. A house can hardly function symbolically as a morgue when it looks like the *World of Interiors*; nor the city as a prison – a guiding metaphor of Dickens's novel – when it is full of inviting shops.

The past can never be transcribed, but has always to be re-invented. In the case of Dickens, it seems, this necessarily involves an attitude to Victorian values. The discovery of the 'dark' Dickens, as much a phenomenon of the 1940s in literary criticism, with the new attention to the later novels, as in the films of David Lean, was intimately bound up with the revolt against Victorianism in politics and the arts. *Little Dorrit* might speculatively be explained by the rehabilitation of Victorian values which has been such a feature of recent years. In one aspect it reflects that urban pastoral which emerged in the 1960s as an antiphon to modernisation and slum clearances; in another the aestheticisation of dying industries. One could note here the representation of the slum as an Arcadia and of machinery as pretty – no longer the monstrous engines of *Hard Times* but, as in the industrial museums, historical monuments. In another aspect the film reproduces the enthusiasms of conservation, in which the past is not a dead weight to be thrown off but a heritage to preserve, and here it seems no accident that Sands films should be located - and the film should have been made – in that temple of conservation-led redevelopment, London docklands.[5]

Little Dorrit, though making an occasional gesture in the direction of social criticism, celebrates Victoriana, discovering a new dignity in both high and low estates. In its own way it endorses 'old-fashioned' family values, displacing images of patriarchal oppression with those of connubial love and transforming a novel of alienation into a commonplace romance, *Little Dorrit* reflects, too, the 'heritage' industry. In the manner of a contemporary theme park, it invites us to take a Victorian Day Out, in the words of an admiring critic, to 'luxuriate' in the recreation of a past world'.[6] As a spectacle, it resembles nothing so much as a succesion of 'Athena' block prints. As documentary it resembles a gallery of Hill Adamson photographs. It sets out neither to shock nor disturb but to please, purging the novel of evil and fear, and doing nothing to offend the canons of good taste. It is a *Little Dorrit* of our time, one in which London is not a prison-house but a playground, and poverty – provided it is safely period, – picturesque.

Notes

1 For a biographical account see J. B. Van Amerongen, *The Actor in Dickens. A Study of the Histrionic and Dramatic Elements in the Novelist's Life and Work*, London, 1926. Among later works, William F. Axton,

Circle of Fire: Dickens' Vision and Style and the Popular Victorian Theatre, Lexington, 1966. For melodrama, see Peter Brooks, *The Melodramatic Image*, New Haven, 1976.

2 Sergi Eisenstein, 'Dickens, Griffith and the Film To-day' in *Film Form*, London, 1951. A. L. Zambrano, *Dickens and Film*, New York, 1977 is a critical account which includes detailed discussion of Dickens adaptations on both stage and screen.

3 The rationale for this astonishing transformation, argued by John Carey the Oxford literary critic in the films brochure, is that we are seeing the house in the second part of the film through Little Dorrit's eyes. In fact the house is quite as elegant in the first part, where the narrative is supposedly Arthur Clennam's. Carey, in any event, celebrates the transformation. 'It is, we realise, a stately and beautiful house, with its polished woods and ornate moulded ceiling.'

4 For an excellent early discussion of Dickens and history, see G. K. Chesterton's introduction to the Everyman edition of *A Child's History of England*, London, 1912. Later discussion takes its cue from the splendid chapter on 'History', Humphry House, *The Dickens World*, Oxford, 1950. There is a chapter on the historical novels in Michael Hollington, *Dickens and the Grotesque*, London, 1984, and Andrew Sanders, *The Victorian Historical Novel, 1840–1880*, London, 1978 discusses the transformations in the genre.

5 For an admiring account of the making of the film 'amidst the yuppification of London's docklands', see *Films and Filming*, December 1987.

6 *Time Out*, 12 December 1987.

Name index

Ford, C. B. 176
Ford, Ford Maddox 239
Ford, John 137
Formby, George 269
Fortuna 28
Foster, Birket 168, 171
Fox, Charles James 4, 8–9, 13, 150
Foxe, John 203–4
Franklin, Sir John 194
Freud, Sigmund 82
Froude, James Anthony 90
Fry, Roger 178
Furber, Douglas 266

Garvey, Marcus 110, 114, 119
Gaskell, Mrs 243
Gayle, Carl 100–1, 121
Gellner, Ernest 200
George III, King 11, 12, 15, 78
George IV (as Prince of Wales) 15
George IV (as Prince Regent) 21
George V, King 83
Gibbs, James 150
Gillett, Charlie 135
Gillray, James 4, 8, 9, 11, 12, 17, 20
Gilpin, William 145, 146
Girtin, Thomas 179
Gleig, G. R. 52, 55
Goldsmith, Oliver 147, 155
Gomes, Albert 106–7
Grafton, Augustus Henry Fitzroy, 3rd Duke of 19
Graves, Robert 28
Greenaway, Kate 168
Greene, Graham 236, 239
Greenwood, Joan 279
Grieg, Edvard 89
Griffith, D. W. 275
Guerrero, Gonzalo 211
Guinness, Alec 233, 278
Gurney, Ivor 91–2
Gwynn, Nell 52

Haile Selassie, Emperor 73, 114
Haley, Bill 135
Hall, Stuart 136, 137
Hamilton, William 76

Hampden, John 150
Hardwicke, Philip Yorke, 1st Earl of 141, 152
Hardy, Thomas 92, 131
Harman, Dawn 71
Harriott, Joe 118
Harris, Dennis 119–20
Harris (publisher) 253
Harrison, J. F. C. 38
Harrison, Tom 262
Harvey, Will 92
Hawkes, Henry 211
Heath, Richard 172
Hengist 31
Henley, W. E. 216
Henry VIII, King 93, 94
Herkomer, Hubert von 55–8, 60
Herriot, James 135
Herth 28
Heywood, Thomas 200
Hill, Draper 20
Hitchin, George 70
Hobsbawm, Eric 77, 85, 90
Hogarth, William 7–8, 145
Holbrook, David 134, 136, 137
Holl, Frank 57, 60
Holland, Henry 150
Hood, Robin 208, 257
Hourd, Marjorie 136
Hudson, William Henry 165
Humphrey, G. 39
Hunter, Evan 135
Hussey, Christopher 173, 174

Jack English 8, 11
Jack-in-the-Green 65, 68
Jack Tar 11, 243
Jackson, Brian 134
Jacob, Margaret 35
Jacobi, Derek 280
James, C. L. R. 106
James, Henry 216
James I, King 30, 31, 201, 205
Jefferies, Richard 162, 165, 169–73
Johnson, Dr Samuel 78
Johnson, Linton Kwesi 121
Johnson, Richard 133
Jonson, Ben 31

Subject index